GEORGE ROGERS CLARK

George Rogers Clark, attributed to Matthew Harris Jouett. Courtesy The Filson Historical Society, Louisville, Kentucky.

GEORGE ROGERS CLARK

"I Glory in War"

By William R. Nester

UNIVERSITY OF OKLAHOMA PRESS : NORMAN

ALSO BY WILLIAM R. NESTER

"Haughty Conquerors": Amherst and the Great Indian Uprising of 1763
    (Westport, Conn., 2000)
The Frontier War for American Independence (Mechanicsburg, Penn., 2004)
The Epic Battles for Ticonderoga, 1758 (Albany, 2008)
Globalization, War, and Peace in the Twenty-First Century (New York, 2010)
Haunted Victory: The American Crusade to Destroy Saddam and Impose Democracy on
    Iraq (Washington, D.C., 2012)

Library of Congress Cataloging-in-Publication Data

Nester, William R., 1956–
    George Rogers Clark : "I glory in war" / by William R. Nester.
        p. cm.
    Includes bibliographical references and index.
    ISBN 978-0-8061-4294-4 (cloth)
    ISBN 978-0-8061-6042-9 (paper)
1. Clark, George Rogers, 1752–1818.   2. Generals—United States—
Biography.   3. United States. Continental Army—Biography.   4. Frontier
and pioneer life—Northwest, Old.   5. Northwest, Old—History—Revolution,
1775–1783.   6. United States—History—Revolution, 1775–1783.   I. Title.
    E207.C5N47 2012
    973.3'3092—dc23
    [B]

                                                                    2012017570

The paper in this book meets the guidelines for permanence and durability
of the Committee on Production Guidelines for Book Longevity of the
Council on Library Resources, Inc. ∞

Contents

Illustrations

Figures

Map

Acknowledgments

Of all the many people I would like to thank for their help in publishing my biography of George Rogers Clark, none deserves my deeper appreciation than Kelly Parker for her meticulous editing. I also want to thank Emily Jerman for her wonderful work as the production editor. Tony Roberts designed the beautiful jacket and Jason Petho the excellent map. I was honored to have such a trio of distinguished historians as William Heath, Jim Holmberg, and William Foley recommend that my manuscript be published and for the suggestions they made for its improvement. Finally, I want to thank acquisitions editor Bob Clark for his willingness to publish my work and for his strategic guidance at each stage of the process.

The American Frontier of George Rogers Clark

0　25　50　75　100 miles

0　50　100　150 kilometers

Illinois

ILLINOIS

Ouiatenon

White

Vincennes　Fort Sackville
　　　　　　　Warrior's Island
Upper Mammelle　Sugar Camp
　　　　　　Lower Mammelle

Cahokia

St. Louis

Missouri

Wabash

Prairie du Rocher

Kaskaskia

Ste. Genevieve

Mississippi

Ohio

MISSOURI

Fort Massac

Cumberland

Fort Jefferson

New Madrid

TENNESSEE

Petho Cartography 2018

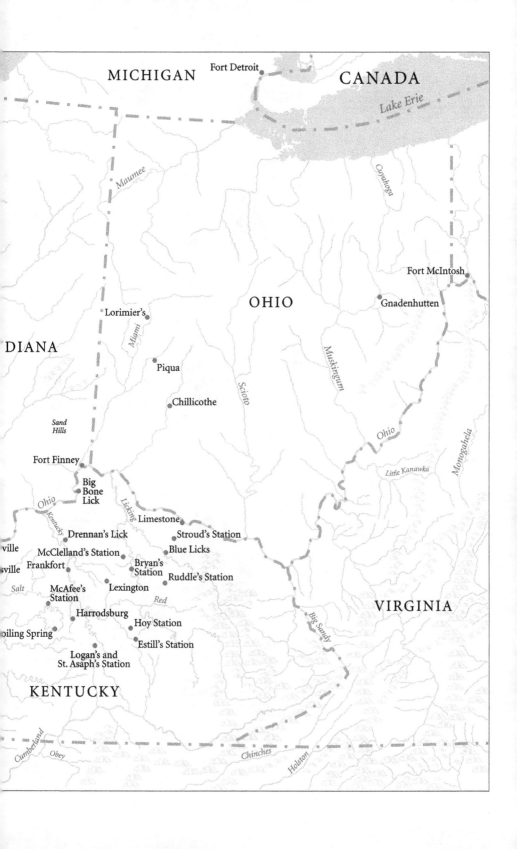

GEORGE ROGERS CLARK

Introduction

I Glory in War and want enemies to fight us, as the English cant fight
us any longer, and are become like Young Children. . . . This is the
last Speech you can ever expect from the Big Knives; the next thing
will be the Tomahawk. And you may expect in four Moons to see Your
Women & Children given to the Dogs to eat, while those Nations that
have kept their words with me will Flourish under the care and nour-
ishment of their father the Big Knives.

George Rogers Clark

Great things have been affected by a few Men well Conducted.

George Rogers Clark

H istory reveals no more than a handful of individuals who at once lived
in and beyond their time. In American history, Benjamin Franklin,
Abraham Lincoln, and Franklin Delano Roosevelt come to mind for their
power to transcend the prevailing prejudices, fears, and ignorances of their
respective eras, and eventually to change their worlds for the better.

George Rogers Clark was not among such rare individuals. Like virtually everyone, he was born into and remained a prisoner of his time and place

and was a product of the late-eighteenth-century American frontier. His extraordinary efforts advanced but did not transform that frontier.

Clark had many talents and interests, but foremost he was a warrior, unsurpassed in relentless courage and ferocity. During the war for independence, he led four victorious campaigns against the Indians and British in the Ohio River valley and ambushed an enemy column in Virginia. His most astonishing coup was to spearhead some 130 men on a midwinter, 180-mile, eighteen-day wilderness trek in which they mostly splashed through frigid waters during the light and shivered away the long bone-chilling nights. Their target was Fort Sackville, commanded by Lieutenant Colonel Henry Hamilton, the notorious "Hair-buyer" of American scalps. Through a deft mix of guile and violence, Clark intimidated Hamilton into capitulating.

For such triumphs, George Rogers Clark is ranked among the American Revolution's greatest commanders. In a letter pleading for more troops and supplies from Virginia governor Patrick Henry, Clark penned a line that would sum up his own brilliant war record: "Great things have been affected by a few Men well Conducted."

Implacable drive and daring, along with ample doses of luck, only partly explain Clark's astonishing feats. A keen intellect and curiosity shine through Clark's erratic spelling in hundreds of pages of his surviving letters, speeches, proclamations, and memoir. The natural world fascinated him; his interpretations of such phenomena as Indian mounds and mammoth bones inspired Thomas Jefferson and nurtured their enduring friendship. Clark wielded his acute understanding of human nature like a weapon, most notably as a diplomat. Time after time Clark was able to bend the wills of defiant officials, politicians, merchants, Indian chiefs, British officers, and even his own malnourished, and at times near mutinous, troops to his own. He did so by skillfully manipulating their emotions and reason. Clark's charisma was as powerful as his mind. From a young age, he learned how to orchestrate his booming voice, looming six-foot bulk, fierce expressions, and piercing eyes either to inspire or subdue others, depending on circumstances.

Yet, no matter how extraordinary his feats, none could satisfy Clark's greatest ambition. Throughout the war his attempts to win what to him was the ultimate prize would be repeatedly frustrated. The capture of Detroit was Clark's obsession, his Moby Dick. To that end he launched three campaigns. Despite his incessant efforts to scrape up enough men, munitions, provisions, and transport, he and his troops never set foot within three hundred miles of Detroit. Each failure had its own unique set of reasons, but common to all was that, through no fault of his own, Clark always lacked a critical ingredient or so. His grueling labors were Herculean by any measure, but above all resembled those of Sisyphus.

Detroit was not Clark's only mirage of a campaign. For a half dozen years from 1787, he dabbled in a series of conspiracies either against or for the Spanish empire, none of which came close to fruition. At one point he offered to become a Spanish subject in return for founding a colony in that empire. Then, during the 1790s, he pledged allegiance to France in its war against Spain. Clark's plan was to muster and lead an army that conquered Spain's Louisiana province down the Mississippi valley from Saint Louis to New Orleans. To that end, he was commissioned a French major general and went deeply into debt to mass supplies for an army that would never exist. Yet that phantom campaign and Clark's rants against the federal government worried President John Adams enough that he ordered Clark's arrest under the Sedition Act. Clark fled to Saint Louis, where he stayed until his backers assured him that he could safely slip back from exile.

The turncoat phase of Clark's life jars the popular image of the fierce, dauntless American patriot. That apparent paradox, however, masks a rational explanation, at least in Clark's seething mind. He was embittered at what he felt was the lack of public acclaim and financial support for all his sacrifices during the war. He insisted that he did not turn his back on the government and people; they turned their back on him.

Ironically, Clark made a crucial decision in 1784 that kept him from being forever immortalized in the pantheon of American history's greatest leaders. He turned down Thomas Jefferson's offer to lead an expedition across the continent to the Pacific Ocean and back. Jefferson's vision would gestate for another two decades before the Lewis and Clark expedition set forth. Had George Rogers embraced Jefferson's vision from its conception, then he rather than his youngest brother William might well have been Meriwether Lewis's partner two decades later.

Then again, by 1803, George Rogers Clark may not have been fit to command anything, let alone such an epic venture. His life had all the elements of a Shakespearean or Greek tragedy. His character was as flawed as it was heroic. Clark not only failed to transcend the era in which he lived; he

failed to transcend his own tormented self. He was plagued by inner demons that filled him with rage and drove him to excessive drink. Throughout his life, he lunged between volatile bursts of energy, drive, and ambition,
and prolonged wallows in sloth, drunkenness, and self-loathing. He never
married, and his only known romantic liaison with Teresa, allegedly the
sister of upper Louisiana's Spanish governor, may have been outright fabri-
cated. One of his officers reported that as early as 1781, Clark "has lost the
confidence of the people and it is said become a sot; perhaps something
worse."[1] Clark eventually died bitter, crippled, and alcoholic.

Given all that, George Rogers Clark has not lacked biographers. The
trouble is that, of the three best, one was written more than half a century
ago and the other two three decades before that.[2] Since then scholars have
greatly advanced their understanding of both Clark and the revolutionary
era in which he lived.[3] *George Rogers Clark: "I Glory in War"* offers a fresh rein-
terpretation of one of America's most fascinating yet flawed heroes.

CHAPTER 1

Nature and Nurture

There are many people in this world; but there are only two families—
the Clarks and Rogers.

George Rogers Clark

George's mind was like the fruit which was long ripening—the better
when it did ripen.

Clark's uncle Donald Robertson

George Rogers Clark was not the sole warrior in his family, only the most famous one. The mingled forces of nature and nurture had a uniform effect on him and his brothers—all would serve in the army, four during the war for independence and the youngest, William, during the 1790s and as Meriwether Lewis's partner in leading the Corps of Discovery across the continent to the Pacific and back from 1804 to 1806.

Whatever martial genes the Clark boys inherited more likely came from their maternal than paternal side. John Clark, the father of George Rogers, was described as a hardworking and taciturn farmer, "not apt to say much in company." He was twenty-four when he married his second cousin, Ann Rogers, then only fifteen, in 1749. Ann made up for her husband's reticence. She was a commanding presence of outspoken mind and apparently stunning body, impressing at least one admirer as "the grandest, most majestic woman he ever saw." Ann's strengths ran in her family, causing Clark to take great pride in being counted among her progeny, although he was inordinately proud of both of his lineages. He once boasted to his brother Edmund that "there are many people in this world; but there are only two families—the Clarks and Rogers."[1]

There was certainly nothing novel in that wedding between second cousins. The Clark and Rogers families had been farming and intermarrying in the Virginia tidewater region since the late seventeenth century. John Clark's grandfather, also named John, arrived sometime early that century. Ann Rogers's grandfather set foot in the New World in 1680. Eventually, the families became neighbors in Drysdale Parish of Caroline County.

After marrying, John and Ann Clark emigrated to Albemarle County and carved a 410-acre farm from the wilderness in the shadow of the Blue Ridge Mountains. Their land spread across rich bottomland along the Rivanna River, just two miles east of the future town of Charlottesville, which would not be founded until 1762. All their reasons for relocating have been lost, but at least two were certain. Like countless other pioneers, they left behind an increasingly overcrowded land whose soil was exhausted from rapacious farming methods. The Clarks headed west to lands where virgin timber and soil were still abundant and inexpensive, while neighbors were scarce.

The Clark family's most distinguished neighbors were the Jeffersons. After settling in the region in 1734, Peter Jefferson had expanded a farm into a plantation that he proudly named Shadwell. Farming was only one of his skills. He was more renowned as a land speculator, surveyor, and cartographer. In 1749, Jefferson and a group of investors formed the Loyal Land Company and eventually claimed 800,000 acres across parts of present-day Virginia, West Virginia, and Kentucky. In 1751, he and Joshua Fry published their map of Virginia, based on their surveying journeys of previous years. That map was the first to render a relatively accurate image of the trans-Allegheny frontier and include the Great Wagon Road, by which tens of thousands of pioneers, including a young Daniel Boone, would journey in an arc from eastern Pennsylvania through valleys of western Maryland, Virginia, and the Carolinas. Those were noteworthy accomplishments, but one of Jefferson's sons would far surpass him in fame. Thomas Jefferson was born at Shadwell in 1743. The life of Thomas Jefferson would mesh with two of John Clark's sons, George Rogers during and after the War of Independence, and William for the most epic expedition in American history.

Two and a half miles from Shadwell, George Rogers Clark was born on November 19, 1752. He entered the world with an auspicious sign—family legend insisted that Clarks with red hair were destined for notable achievements.[2] He was the second son; his older brother Jonathan had been born two years earlier.

Clark's time in his first frontier home was fleeting. Not long after staking a claim and clearing land, his parents discovered two drawbacks to living in the region. Their farm was a score of miles from the nearest stretch of navigable river below the fall line, which made getting crops to market expensive. That was serious enough, but an even more potentially catastrophic problem loomed over them.

Two years after Clark was born, the French and Indian War erupted when Major George Washington ordered his men to creep up to and open fire on French troops encamped in disputed territory in the upper Ohio River valley. The outbreak of war posed a dilemma for the Clark family. They could make good money selling their surplus harvest to troops moving along the nearby Three Notch'd Road, which linked distant Richmond to the Shenandoah Valley. Yet with each year of war, Indian raiders struck farther eastward, murdering, looting, kidnapping, and burning. John and Ann debated whether whatever profit they reaped from that trade was worth the worsening risk.

A chance to escape that dilemma appeared in 1757. The Clarks got word that John Clark's namesake and bachelor uncle had died and left him his 170-acre farm on the Rappahannock River in Caroline County. The Clark family sold their homestead and moved to their inheritance. There they stayed put until 1784, when they pulled up stakes and journeyed to a farm outside of Louisville.

Caroline County had been designated in 1728, when it was formed from parts of Essex, King and Queen, and King William Counties. Yet even after three decades there was still plenty of elbow room as settlers remained scattered and few. The county was named for Caroline of Ansbach, the wife of King George II. Eventually, it would be renowned as the birthplace of the American Thoroughbred horse.

More siblings joined George Rogers and Jonathan, with Ann born in

1754, John in 1757, Richard in 1760, Edmund in 1762, Lucy in 1765, Eliza-beth in 1768, William in 1770, and, finally, Frances in 1773. Like most Virgin-ians, the Clarks attended the Church of England, a denomination that after the revolution would be known in America as the Episcopal Church. Al-though the Clark family owned slaves, their wealth was never great enough to allow them to live solely off that labor; John and his sons worked the fields beside their chattel. American history celebrates one of those slaves. York was born around the same time as William, served as his childhood playmate, and eventually accompanied his master all the way to the Pacific and back.

Of all his siblings, Clark was the closest to Jonathan for the first few de-cades of his life. The natural tendency of a younger brother to look up to his elder was reinforced by Jonathan's intelligence and calm, reflective person-ality. He provided a counterweight to Clark's volatility and impetuousness. When George Rogers was eleven, he and Jonathan were sent to live with their maternal grandfather, John Rogers. Their father had high hopes for the boys' future, and knew that education was essential. Not far from the Rog-ers home was a renowned school taught by Donald Robertson, their mater-nal Aunt Rachel's husband. Tuition for the courses in geography, history, and mathematics was thirteen pounds sterling. James Madison was among the Clark boys' classmates.[3]

Clark's time there was fleeting, probably only eight months. Like most boys, he preferred high jinks to lessons. Although he was bright, his restless energy demanded vigorous activities. By one account, Clark avidly joined in such "whimsical and comical diversions" as "twelve boys of twelve years of age do" such as "run one hundred twelve yards, for a Hat at the cost of twelve shillings" or "that a pair of silver Buckles be wrestled for by a num-ber of brisk young men."[4] Robertson soon reluctantly concluded that Clark was "not very apt at learning" and had no clear "marks of talent." Despair-ing over whether he would ever bend his unruly charge to his books, Rob-ertson returned him to his parents with the advice that they were better off investing their money elsewhere. A family friend, Richard Higgins, may have provided Clark a few more months of learning. Though Clark rebelled against the dull rote of schooling, once he learned to read he avidly devoured books of history and geography. Robertson later explained that "George's mind was like the fruit which was long ripening—the better when it did ripen."[5]

CHAPTER 2

The Surveyor

The ... Americans ... acquire no attachment to place; But wandering about Seems engrafted in their Nature; and ... they Should forever imagine the Lands further off are still better than those upon which they have already settled.

John Murray, Lord Dunmore

I left Fort Pitt on Tuesday June 9, 1772, in company with George Rogers Clark, a young gentleman from Virginia, who with several others inclined to make a tour in this new world.

Rev. David Jones

A s his teenage years unrolled, Clark faced an increasingly vital question—what path in life should he follow? Farming was no more suitable to such a rambunctious lad than schooling. However, surveying did offer an appeal. Although the profession demanded precision and method, it kept the adept on the move through diverse landscapes.

Surveying also potentially led to wealth and power. Westward beyond the Appalachian Mountains were rich river-bottom lands to be claimed and developed or sold to eager settlers. The more land one took, the richer one became. Then, by carefully investing one's wealth, an ambitious and skilled man could amass political power and social prestige that in turn begat yet more riches.

Shortly before Clark's birth, three groups of investors sought to master that virtuous cycle of wealth and power by founding the Ohio Company and Loyal Land Company in 1749, and the Greenbrier Company in 1751. The initial burst of enthusiasm that led to those enterprises soon wore off. The first step was to lobby the crown for vast swaths of western lands. The investors soon learned to their chagrin that just getting a royal patent for distant blank spots on a map was time-consuming, frustrating, and expensive enough given all the red tape and bribery that entangled their agents in London. That done, exploring, surveying, and, finally, selling their claims to speculators or settlers at times seemed near impossible. An implacable obstacle stood between those investors and their ambitions. Indians either inhabited or hunted and trapped that territory, and did all they could to turn back intruders, including robbing and killing them.

With dreams of exploring and taking new lands, Clark eagerly learned the craft of surveying from his grandfather John Rogers. His studies ended in April 1772, when he was nineteen. His father's account book records the transfer to Clark of seven pounds sterling worth of surveying equipment and the book Euclid's *Elements*. With that along with a rifle, a blanket roll, and a few other essentials, Clark headed west to seek fortune and adventure.[1]

That rifle would prove more useful than his surveying equipment, and not just for hunting. The frontier that Clark entered was still dangerous despite the victories of British and American troops, first over the French and then the Indians. The French and Indian War, known in Europe as the Seven Years' War, was history's first genuine global war, with the fighting that broke out in North America in 1754 spreading to Europe in 1756, and then to parts of the Caribbean, West Africa, India, Argentina, the Philippines, and the seas linking those far-flung lands.[2] After seven years of fighting, Canada was conquered in 1760, but the French and their allies held out for another three years until the belligerents signed the Treaty of Paris in 1763. By that treaty, France ceded Canada and its lands east of the Mississippi River to Britain, and all lands west of the Mississippi River along with New Orleans to its ally Spain. Those cessions ended a century-and-a-half rivalry between Paris and London, bloodied by five wars for the eastern third of North America. Alas, the war's end did not end violence on the frontier. The ink was no sooner dry on the treaty when most Indians across the Great Lakes region rebelled against the arrogance, greed, and stinginess of their new would-be landlords. The Indians captured nine frontier forts and killed over 2,500 soldiers and settlers before finally being defeated by overwhelming numbers of British and American troops in 1764.[3]

King George III and his ministers recognized that their own policies had provoked that Indian uprising, commonly known as Pontiac's Rebellion after its most prominent leader. General Jeffrey Amherst, who commanded His Majesty's forces in North America, had enraged the tribes by denying them the munitions and other essential supplies that they had grown dependent upon from their French "Great Father." Meanwhile, a growing number of American traders, hunters, and settlers were invading and exploiting their lands. To partly alleviate the Indian grievances that provoked their rebellion, on October 7, 1763, the king issued a proclamation that forbade any American settlements west of the Appalachian Mountain divide. Yet those greedy for profits or land ignored those restrictions.

By the time Clark was ready to cut loose and explore the world, no western region was more legendary than Kentucky. The handful of whites who had penetrated that wilderness extolled it as a paradise of unsurpassed richness of game for hunting and soil for farming. Two known routes led to Kentucky, one via the Cumberland Gap in southwestern Virginia and the other via the Ohio River. Thomas Walker led the first expedition through the Gap in 1750. More than a decade would pass before the next explorations of that region as first the French and Indian War and then Pontiac's War rendered it too dangerous for even the most daring of frontiersmen to set foot there. But in 1761, even before the fighting ended, the first party of what became known as the Long Hunters crossed the Appalachians and ranged across eastern Kentucky and Tennessee in search of deerskins, beaver pelts, and other furs.

The eagerness of Long Hunters, along with land companies, to exploit Kentucky soared in 1768, after two treaties were signed with powerful Indian tribes with a stake in the region. With the Treaty of Hard Labour, the Cherokees ceded their rights to Kentucky down to the mouth of the Kanawha River. With the Treaty of Fort Stanwix, the Six Nations or Iroquois, who lived in central New York yet claimed suzerain rights over the Ohio valley tribes, ceded to the British crown all lands south of the Ohio River down to the mouth of the Tennessee River. Both the Iroquois and Cherokee chiefs signed their respective treaties after receiving piles of gifts. And both did so without the permission of the Shawnee, Mingo, and Delaware tribes that lived just north of the Ohio River and hunted in Kentucky. The treaties violated the 1763 Royal Proclamation that reserved all lands west of the Appalachian Mountains for the Indians living there.

No Long Hunter was more famed for his exploits than Daniel Boone.[4] He made his first foray into Kentucky in 1767, lingered there from 1769 through 1771, and returned again in 1772. His attempt to settle there with his family and several others in 1773 died when Indians killed his son and another youth on the trail.

The tragic end to Boone's first effort to settle in Kentucky was not an isolated event. Tensions and outbursts of violence rose steadily as ever more Americans infiltrated Indian lands. Virginia governor John Murray, Lord Dunmore, explained the problem: "The established Authority of any government in America and the policy of Government at home, are both insufficient to restrain the American. . . . They acquire no attachment to place; But wandering about Seems engrafted in their Nature; and . . . they Should forever imagine the Lands further off are Still better than those upon which they have already settled."[5]

Yet Dunmore fed that land hunger—shared by Clark—in several crucial ways. In 1772, he got Virginia's House of Burgesses to designate Fincastle County to encompass all of Virginia's claims from the Appalachian Mountains to the Mississippi River. He then dispatched surveying parties to map that land and prepare it for settlement. In 1773, Thomas Bullitt led an expedition down the Ohio River to survey parts of northern Kentucky. The following year, two other surveying parties penetrated Kentucky—William Preston's down the New and Kanawha Rivers to the Ohio River, and James Harrod's down the Ohio River and up the Kentucky River. Harrod and his men came to stay—they founded Kentucky's first settlement, named Harrod's Town, on June 16, 1774.

The chiefs of the Ohio valley tribes vainly protested all these intrusions. By common consent, the northern and southern tribes did not inhabit that land, but reserved it for hunting and occasionally war. That the Americans would carve out settlements in Kentucky threatened, to varying degrees, the livelihoods and security of all those tribes.

Exacerbating the tensions with the Indians was the rivalry between Pennsylvania and Virginia for the upper Ohio valley. Pittsburgh was the epicenter of that struggle as land company agents, surveyors, hunters, and settlers from both colonies overran the village and surrounding region. Virginians and Pennsylvanians accused each other of inciting Indian attacks. Their respective governors, Dunmore and John Penn, issued dueling proclamations forbidding the other's colonists from that disputed territory. George Croghan, the crown's deputy Indian agent for the Ohio valley, tried to keep the peace by discouraging further inroads from either colony and thus provoked the wrath and incendiary charges from both. In 1774, Dunmore tried to trump Croghan's authority by commissioning his friend and business partner John Connolly a captain and ordering him to lead a militia company to rebuild Fort Pitt, which the army had abandoned in 1772. The fort was renamed Fort Dunmore.[6]

It was amid these frontier tensions that George Rogers Clark reached Pittsburgh in early June 1772. He did not linger long in the crude settlement at the forks of the Ohio River. He hooked up with frontiersman David Owens, Reverend David Jones, and several others eager to head farther west. With Owens as his interpreter, Jones intended to proselytize at the cluster of Shawnee villages midway up the Scioto River. But before they embarked on that mission, Owens wanted to break in the greenhorn with a hunting trip down the Ohio River. Jones wrote, "I left Fort Pitt on Tuesday June 9, 1772, in company with George Rogers Clark, a young gentleman from Virginia, who with several others inclined to make a tour in this new world."[7]

Clark's first wilderness expedition lasted about six weeks. Clark and the others descended as far as the Kanawha River mouth, three hundred river miles below Pittsburgh, where they set up camp and ranged the surrounding forest for several days before slowly making their way back upstream. Most of that time must have been quietly exhilarating for Clark and his comrades as they canoed, fished, hunted, explored, swapped ideas and tales around campfires, and at night rolled up in blankets beneath the star-strewn black sky. Undoubtedly, there were fleeting moments of fatigue and fear along with pangs of homesickness for the twenty-year-old. Like most youths far from his loved ones for the first time, Clark was likely at times Janus-faced on his journey. Those feelings would undoubtedly have been even more disturbing if Clark had learned of the interpreter's past—a spasm of insanity had overwhelmed Owens in 1764, when he murdered a group of seven Delaware Indians, including his own Indian wife and two children, scalped all the adults, and sold the scalps for the bounty offered by Pennsylvania.[8]

Although their encounters with Indians along the way were friendly, Clark and the other explorers could be forgiven if they were a bit nervous. As they shook hands or traded trinkets, nightmarish stories of Indian massacres or prolonged fiendish tortures must have echoed through their minds. For greenhorns, the appearance of Indians alone was startling and intimidating: "They are tall, manly, well shaped men of a Copper Colour with Black Hair Quick pierceing [sic] Eyes and Good features. They have rings of Silver in their nose and bobs to them which hangs over the upper lip. Their ears are cut from the tip two thirds of the way round and the piece extended with Brass wire till it touches their Shoulders in this part they hang a thin Silver plate . . . with plates of Silver round their arms and in the Hair which is all cut of except a Long Lock on top of their head. They are in whitemen's dress except Breeches . . . they have a girdle around them with a piece of Cloath drawn through their legs and turned over the girdle and appear like a short apron before and behind. All the Hair is pulled from their eye brows and eye lashes and their Face painted."[9]

While the Ohio valley Indians shared similar dress and customs, they were divided politically and linguistically. Most tribes like the Shawnees, Delawares, and Miamis spoke dialects of Algonquin; some like the Mingos (originally Senecas) or Wyandots (originally Hurons) spoke Iroquois dialects. As for politics, each village was autonomous. A council of elders presided over each village and sought to reach consensus on crucial questions of war or peace, staying or moving. Among that council the most important voices were those of the war and peace chiefs, who attained that status by their prowess in either of those fields. Once a decision was reached, the appropriate chief explained it to the rest of the village and asked the people to support it. A village might remain politically divided even after the elders hammered out a decision among themselves. The reason for this division was that each village was a polyglot, dynamic mixture of clans, cults, and clubs, and often included migrants from villages or tribes along with white captives and their descendants. Gaining a consensus among the members of a loose knit "tribe" of many villages like the Shawnees or Miamis was even more time consuming. Over the years, Clark would gain a better understanding of the complexities of Indian politics and use that to his advantage in war and diplomacy.

The hunting party ground ashore at Pittsburgh's crowded riverfront on July 22. There, Clark bid his comrades farewell and headed home. Clark's adventure tales beguiled his father into joining him when he trekked back to the Ohio valley in early autumn.[10] The father, son, Clark's friend James Higgins, and three others reached the confluence of Fish Creek with the Ohio River, 130 miles below Pittsburgh and forty miles below Wheeling, the nearest settlement. Fish Creek was a beautiful setting with the stream flowing through a valley filled with meadows and edged by steep mountains. The rich bottomland inspired thoughts of transforming that patch of wilderness into a settlement.

While the others struggled back to civilization to file a claim, Clark and Higgins got to work. First they made a "tomahawk claim" by slashing tree trunks around an expanse of desirable land. That was the easy part. Then came the backbreaking labor of clearing the thick forest. They sawed or chopped down the smaller trees and girdled or hacked deep into the behemoths for a slow death. They cut, trimmed, and fitted logs into a crude cabin; gaps were chinked with mud. Day by day they expanded their stump-filled clearing. They alleviated that tedium by taking turns hunting game up the valley. They stretched and scraped buckskins, beaver pelts, and other furs, imagining what they could gain in trade. By January 1773, Clark could write with contentment that "I am settled on my land with . . . plenty of provisions and drive on pretty well as to clearing hoping by spring" to sow "a full Crop."[11]

Occasionally, a holler startled them, and they eagerly greeted other explorers and hopeful settlers ambling up. They swapped information and stories; a buckskin or so may have changed hands to bolster dwindling stores of flour or gunpowder. Most visitors were heading much farther downstream. But a few were so impressed by what they saw that they offered to buy out Clark. Though Clark had "an offer of a very considerable sum for my place," he then had no intention of selling. Instead, he got "a good deal of cash" by surveying adjoining tracts of land for would-be settlers.[12]

In early spring, after the men finished sowing their cornfield, Clark headed back alone to Caroline County to fetch more supplies and, ideally, hands. He reached his older brother Jonathan's home at Woodstock on July 24, 1773.

Clark faced west once again on September 24, 1773, accompanied by William Higgins, James's brother, and Colonel George Muse. This time his father not only did not join him, but watched his son leave with "some onease [*sic*] apprehensions."[13] Clark most likely confirmed rumors that the frontier was primed and ready to explode again with violence between the original inhabitants and the intruders. A war would indeed erupt, and George Rogers Clark would find himself in the thick of it.

CHAPTER 3

Lord Dunmore's War

The Virginians are haughty, Violent and bloody, the savages have a
high opinion of them as Warriors, but are jealous of their encroachments, and very suspicious of their faith in treaties.

Henry Hamilton

T he upper Ohio valley was locked into an increasingly vicious cycle of
hatred, robbery, murder, and vengeance between the Indians and the
intruders. Henry Hamilton, then a British army captain who would soon
be reviled by Americans as the "Hair-buyer," captured that dynamic: "The
Virginians are haughty, Violent and bloody, the savages have a high opinion of them as Warriors, but are jealous of their encroachments, and very
suspicious of their faith in treaties."[1] Clark would participate in some of the
skirmishes that ignited a new frontier conflagration, this one known as "Dunmore's War," named after Virginia's governor.[2]

Tension and fear swelled steadily among Clark and several score other
men who had gathered at the mouth of the Little Kanawha River in April
1774. Although the men had not suffered attack, each group of travelers passing by on the Ohio River shared news of the latest depredations. Whether
the local Indians participated or not, nearly all naturally saw any attacks on
whites as perfectly justified. They were enraged that ever more Americans

were decimating game and carving homesteads along that stretch of the Ohio valley. The more whites who lost their belongings or even lives, the greater the possibility that they and countless others might be deterred from further trespasses.

Though the sporadic Indian attacks did scare off some of the intruders, the violence hardened the resolve of the rest of the newcomers. Many of the raiding parties were reckoned to have originated at the Shawnee village of Horsehead Bottom on Pine Creek, a tributary of the Little Scioto River, not far from the Little Kanawha River mouth. The frontiersmen debated whether to wipe out that village.

Clark recalled that "eighty or ninety men" reached "the appointed rendezvous where we lay some days. A small party of hunters that lay about ten miles below us, were fired upon by the Indians, whom the hunters beat back and returned to camp. This and many other circumstances led us to believe that the Indians were determined for war." Rather than passively sit tight and await an attack, Clark and his companions resolved to strike first: "The whole party was enrolled and determined to . . . cross the country" and destroy Horsehead Bottom.[3]

One crucial element was missing: "There were but few among us that had experience in Indian warfare and they were such as we did not choose to be commanded by." One of the men remarked that Captain Michael Cresap, the region's most notorious Indian fighter, was at a settlement about fifteen miles upstream. Cresap was among the more hair-triggered and violent settlers in the upper Ohio valley. He hated Indians and sought any opportunity to vent that hatred. His immediate target was Killbuck, a Delaware chief, who was rumored to have tried to murder Cresap's father, Thomas.

The frontiersmen "unanimously agreed to send for him to command the party. Messengers were dispatched," and, undoubtedly to the astonishment of the eagerly awaiting would-be raiders, "in half an hour [they] returned with Cresap. He had heard of our resolution from some of his hunters that had fallen in with ours, and had set out to come to us. We now thought our army, as we called it, complete, and the destruction of the Indians sure."[4]

Then a stunning thing happened to Clark and the other hotheads who were eager for war: "A council was called and to our astonishment, our intended commander-in-chief was the person that dissuaded us from the enterprise. He said that appearances were very suspicious, but there was no certainty of a war. That if we made the attempt proposed, he had no doubt of our success but a war would at any rate be the result, and that we should be blamed for it, and perhaps justly. But if we were determined to proceed, he would lay aside all considerations, send to his camp for his people and share our fortunes."[5]

Somewhat bewildered, the frontiersmen asked Cresap what to do. He urged them to head upstream to Wheeling and along the way simply to ask each group of Indians and whites they encountered if a war had broken out. A consensus to do so was swiftly reached "and in two hours the whole were under way." Of all the potential encounters they might have made as they ascended the river, the frontiersmen ran into Killbuck, himself, and a small party on the north shore. Clark and the others "had a long conference with him, but received but little satisfaction as to the disposition of the Indians. . . . Cresap . . . kept on the opposite side of the river. He said he was afraid . . . that . . . his fortitude might fail him and he might put Killbuck to death."[6]

After the party reached Wheeling, the dispute persisted over whether a state of war existed and, if so, what to do about it. Word of that debate reached Captain John Connolly, the region's commander headquartered at Fort Pitt. He sent instructions for the frontiersmen to wait until he had consulted with the chiefs of villages throughout the region.

Connolly soon learned that most Indians believed "that war was inevitable." On April 25, he issued a proclamation calling on the militia to turn out and protect the settlements. For Clark, that message marked the beginning of "the epoch of open hostilities with the Indians." As he wrote, "War was declared in the most solemn manner, and the same evening two scalps were brought into camp. The next day some canoes of Indians were discovered on the river. . . . They were chased fifteen miles down the river and driven ashore. A battle ensued, a few men were wounded on both sides. . . . On our return to camp, a resolution was adopted to march the next day and attack Logan's camp on the Ohio about thirty miles above us."[7]

Neither the surviving accounts of Clark or of other participants reveal what role Clark played in those debates and skirmishes. Was he among those who demanded that the frontiersmen strike first and hard? Was he in the thick of the fighting? Given Clark's hotheaded passions and energy, the answer is most likely yes to both those questions. What is certain is that

Clark was not involved in the mass murder that transformed a blood feud into an all-out war.

Talgayeeta, or John Logan as he was better known, was the chief of a small village of Mingos, the name for a group of people of mostly Iroquois heritage but mixed with members from other tribes and races in the Ohio valley. Logan's father was the Cayuga chief Shikellimus, who moved from Lake Cayuga to the town of Shamokin, on the Susquehanna River, to be near the whites whom he had grown to love. Logan was born at Shamokin and received his white name in honor of his father's best friend. But the whites eventually betrayed that trust by squeezing the Mingos from their land. In 1772, Logan moved with his family and followers to Yellow Creek, fifty miles below Pittsburgh. Somehow Logan's name was implicated in attacks on whites, although he was then innocent of those charges.

Learning of Logan and his people's presence, Cresap, Clark, and the others resolved to kill them. However, on April 28, 1774, as the frontiersmen paddled upstream, their consciences overcame their bloodlust. Clark recalled, "[We] halted to take some refreshment. Here the impropriety of executing the projected enterprise was argued. The conversation was brought forward by Cresap himself. It was generally agreed that those Indians had no hostile intentions as they were hunting, and their party was composed of men, women and children. . . . In short every person seemed to detest the resolution we had set out with."[8] So they turned back.

That change of plans only briefly lifted the shadow of death from Logan and his people. On April 30, five of his men, along with his sister and her baby, crossed the Ohio River to trade at the camp of Jacob Greathouse; Logan remained behind. As Greathouse and his men watched the Mingos approach, they quickly concocted an evil plot. They pretended to welcome the visitors, plied them with alcohol, then suggested a shooting contest. After the Mingos had emptied their muskets at the targets, Greathouse and his men turned their rifles on them and pulled the triggers. They murdered not just all the men, but also Logan's sister. They did spare her baby, the son of John Gibson, a prominent trader who would rise to command the Thirteenth Virginia Continental regiment, be stationed at Fort Pitt, and at times assist Clark's campaigns.[9]

Vowing vengeance, Logan and his surviving followers fled to Wakatomica, a Shawnee and Mingo village midway up the Muskingum River valley. There, at a war council, he reported the massacre and called on all warriors to drive the whites from their lands. Runners were sent with the same message to other villages throughout the region. Logan gathered his own war party and headed toward the settlements. For months, he and his men terrorized isolated homesteads, killing, looting, and burning, before disappearing back into the wilderness.

Meanwhile, Clark received his first formal military command. On May 2, 1774, Lieutenant Colonel Charles Lewis commissioned him a captain in Virginia's militia. The commission was pre-signed by Governor Dunmore, one of scores that he had handed to militia officers to issue to promising leaders. Clark's duties included "exercising the Officers and Soldiers under your Command, taking particular Care that they be provided with Arms and Ammunition . . . and you are to observe and follow such Orders . . . from me, or any other superior Officers, according to the Rules and Discipline of War."[10]

Word of Connolly's proclamation and the series of atrocities propelled Governor Dunmore into a flurry of actions. On June 10, he issued a circular letter to the county lieutenants, each county's top official, to muster the militia. He began planning expeditions to crush the Indians in the upper Ohio region and seize their lands. He ordered forts built at the Ohio River mouths of Wheeling Creek and the Kanawha River. He dispatched scouts to spot any approaching war parties. The governor sent Daniel Boone and Michael Stoner into Kentucky to warn the groups of surveyors, hunters, and the settlers at Harrod's Town and elsewhere that an Indian war had erupted and that he needed their aid. Upon hearing that message, the Kentuckians abandoned their activities and hurried either to join Dunmore or to seek safety in the eastern settlements.[11]

During the war for independence, Daniel Boone would be the only man who rivaled George Rogers Clark as an American hero on the Kentucky frontier, while his overall fame would endure through the centuries as Clark's faded. While Boone's heroism and feats were genuine, they would be immortalized in John Filson's 1784 book, *The Discovery, Settlement, and Present State of Kentucke*. By contrast, Clark's exploits would not be celebrated by a writer in his lifetime. Boone also enjoyed an eighteen-year head start to make history, having been born in 1734. By Dunmore's War, Boone was already a frontier legend, highly esteemed by both his officers and fellow frontiersmen. Captain

John Floyd lauded Boone for his extraordinary feat of hurrying to warn those in Kentucky of the pending Indian war then dashing back to join the ranks: "You know what Boone has done for me by your kind directions, for which reason I love the man." In recommending that Boone receive a captain's commission, Captain Daniel Smith described him as "an excellent woodsman. If that only would qualify him for no man would be more proper. I do not know of any Objection that would be made to his character which would make you think him an improper person for that office."[12] Boone's long career as a frontier leader, however, would not escape criticism, most notably for surrendering his twenty-six man camp of salt makers without a fight in February 1778. But that aside, Boone remains an American icon for many good reasons, including the fact that, unlike George Rogers Clark, he did not suffer any deep, festering flaws in his character.[13]

Dunmore ordered Major William Crawford to take a company of men and build Fort Fincastle where Wheeling Creek joins the Ohio River. He then had Major Angus MacDonald gather eight companies, or a total of four hundred men, at Fort Fincastle, then march against the cluster of Indian villages on the Muskingum River. Clark's company was among those that filled their powder horns and shot bags and stuffed seven days' rations in their blanket rolls before crossing the Ohio River on July 26.

The company reached the first village, called Wakatomica, on August 2. Learning of the approaching enemy, most Shawnees abandoned their village and hid in the forest. A handful of warriors tarried to snipe at the invaders. Soon the frontiersmen and Indians were blazing away at each other. The whites suffered two killed and six wounded and took three scalps and a prisoner. After looting and burning the village and crops, the Virginians headed up the trail to Snakes' Town. Along the way, they heard "a kind of noise, like a cough . . . they saw an Indian coming up towards them on the road, at whom they fired but missed." That fleeing Indian led them into an ambush: "After proceeding a little further they were fired upon by a party of Indians by which five white men were wounded and two killed; and an Indian supposed to be a Delaware was also killed; but how many Indians were wounded is unknown . . . Leaving 25 men to guard the wounded, they pursued the Indians to the ford leading to Snakes' town." Shots were exchanged; one wounded an Indian. MacDonald shouted across a demand that the Shawnees release two white women they held captive. When the

Shawnees refused, MacDonald and his men charged across. The Indians fired, wounding a frontiersman, and then fled. The Virginians returned fire, killing an Indian, then burned the houses and crops. MacDonald then hurried his men back to Fort Fincastle. Once again, just what feats Clark performed along the way have been lost to history.[14]

MacDonald's raid was designed as a spoiling attack to put the Indians on the defensive. Dunmore meanwhile was organizing a two-pronged offensive designed to crush the tribes. Colonel Andrew Lewis was to mobilize 1,100 militiamen at Camp Union on the Greenbrier River, march down the valley to the Kanawha River, then down to it to the Ohio. Dunmore commanded the other army that would mass at Fort Pitt before heading down the Ohio River to the Hockhocking River mouth, and then up it. Eventually, those armies would converge on the cluster of mostly Shawnee Indian villages midway up the Scioto River.[15]

Dunmore split his 1,200 men, one of which was Clark, in two, with 700 descending the river in boats and the other 500 marching along the south bank. They reached Fort Fincastle on September 30. After resting a few days, they crossed to the Ohio River's north bank, and then west up the Hockhocking River.

Major MacDonald's men led the advance. Along the way, they "were boldly attacked by about 30 Indians. His men were marched in 3 Columns, himself at the head of the middle one, which was attacked and . . . 4 men killed & 6 wounded. He ordered the right & left Columns to File of[f] & try to Surround the enemy which could not be effected but they killed 3 or four Indians & took one. MacDonald afterwards marched into a little Town and found his mens scalps hung up like Colours but the town evacuated."[16]

Meanwhile, on September 6, Lewis and his 1,000-man militia began the long march toward the Ohio River and the Shawnee heartland far beyond. On October 6, they reached the confluence of the Kanawha and Ohio Rivers. Their campsite was known as Point Pleasant. It would not live up to its name. On the night of October 9, nearly 1,000 Indians, mostly Shawnees led by Cornstalk, but joined by Mingos, Wyandots, Ottawas, and Delawares, crossed the Ohio River on rafts. They attacked at dawn the next morning of October 10, 1774.[17]

It was a chaotic battle, fought through thick forest, with the ever-shifting fronts revealed by gunshots, war whoops, catcalls, and screams of pain and terror. The Indians fought fiercely to drive the invaders from their home-land: "The Enemy behaved with inconceivable Bravery. The Head men walked about in the Time of Action Exhorting their Men 'To lie close, shoot well, be strong, & fight.'"[18] The behavior of the raw militia, enlisted and officers alike, was much more mixed. Captain John Floyd noted with disgust that "there were never more than three or four hundred of our men in action at once, but the trees & logs the whole way from the camp to where the line of battle . . . served as shelters for those who could not be prevailed on to advance to where the fire was . . . many of the officers fought with a great deal of courage and behaved like heroes, while others lurked behind and could by no means be induced to advance to the front."[19]

The Indians finally withdrew after they ran out of ammunition. The Virginians retained the field, but at a terrible cost. Fifty-three were killed, and ninety-two were wounded, of whom fifteen later died. The spoils of "victory" were slender: "The Scalps of the Enemy were collected & found to be 17 they were dressed & hung upon a pole near the river Bank & the plunder was collected & found to be 23 guns 80 Blankets 27 Tomahawks with Match coast Shot pounches powderhorns Warclubs &c." Colonel Lewis was among those killed. Three musket balls hit Colonel William Fleming, the second in command; one shattered his left arm.[20]

The two armies converged on the Indian villages in the middle Scioto valley, Dunmore's from the east and Lewis's from the south. Cornstalk, the principal Shawnee chief, and other chiefs recognized that they could not defeat that onslaught. They sent a runner to Dunmore with word that they wanted to talk. Dunmore halted his advance and invited in the chiefs. Negotiations opened on October 17, 1774. Within days a deal was cut.

What is known as the Treaty of Camp Charlotte was merely a tenuous unwritten deal. A truce was declared. The chiefs agreed to cede their rights to all land south of the Ohio River down to the Kanawha River mouth, return all prisoners, and provide hostages to ensure that they lived up to their promises. But Dunmore also made a concession on behalf of the whites. He agreed that whites were forbidden from Kentucky west of the Kanawha River. Finally, they promised to meet and negotiate a formal treaty the following spring at Fort Dunmore.[21]

An inescapable problem underlay virtually any agreement between Indians and whites. Each was nearly always merely a prelude to the next war.

The deal was usually no sooner done when whites resumed trespassing, exploiting, and outright stealing Indian lands. Meanwhile, those chiefs who signed usually only represented the immediate concerns of themselves and their followers. The defiant chiefs spurned any settlement unless they had suffered complete defeat. So any treaty bitterly split tribes between those who gave in and those who were determined to fight on. The peace chiefs and a lack of ammunition generally upheld the truce for a while. But the hatreds and thirst for vengeance smoldered until the next round of American aggression provoked another war.[22]

Cornstalk would remain committed to the peace he had promised at Camp Charlotte. Over the three years until the Americans murdered him, he worked incessantly to restrain his people from the war path. Those efforts were in vain. But he had no illusions over who was ultimately responsible for the bloodshed. To American Indian agent George Morgan, Cornstalk offered a powerful appeal: "I open my hand & pour into your heart the cause of our discontent that you take pity on us your younger Brethren." He then explained, "All our Lands are covered by the white people, & we are jealous that you still intend to make larger strides—We never sold you our Lands which you now possess on the Ohio between the Great Kanawha & the Cherokee, & which you are settling without ever asking our leave, or obtaining our consent."[23]

Dunmore's War had many causes, including American land hunger and Indian hating, but none was greater than its namesake. War was all but inevitable after Dunmore granted land to the companies and unleashed that influx of surveyors and settlers into Indian territory. Yet he got off lightly for that crime. William Legge, Earl Dartmouth, the colonial secretary, rapped his knuckles for granting lands to companies in territory forbidden by the 1763 Proclamation. Though King George himself was highly displeased, he forgave the Virginian governor. Dunmore expressed his gratitude for the king's "tenderness and lenity," but denied any wrongdoing. He insisted that the government's inability to suppress the footloose Americans had caused the war: "In this Colony Proclamations have been published from time to time to restrain them: But impressed from their earliest infancy with Sentiments and habits, very different from those acquired by persons of a Similar condition in England, they do not conceive that Government has any right to forbid their taking possession of a Vast tract of

Country, either uninhabited, or which Serves only a shelter to a few Scattered Tribes of Indians. Nor can they be easily brought to entertain any belief of the permanent obligation of Treaties made with those People, whom they consider, as but little removed from brute creation."[24]

George Rogers Clark epitomized that aggressive, indomitable, rapacious American spirit articulated by Lord Dunmore. With the war over, the question for Clark was what came next. He could return to his Fish Creek farm. But that choice appears to have lost its appeal. Perhaps that lonely, vulnerable site near such recent scenes of carnage troubled him. More likely that restless man was happy to sell out and head farther west. One thing was certain. He was eager to winter with his family and could not get home fast enough. He must have fumed helplessly as illness delayed his return. He dashed off an explanation to Jonathan that he "would have calld to see you but was so unwell that I was afraid of making any stay. By the way I would write more but I expect to see you so soon that I need not be particular in writing."[25]

By spring, Clark was once again brimming with energy and wanderlust. On April 1, 1775, he eagerly grabbed an offer by Hancock Lee, the Ohio Company's surveyor, to serve as his deputy in Kentucky for a yearly salary of eighty pounds sterling "and the privilege of Taking what Lands I want." Clark asked Jonathan to "spare me no Money nor pains to that patent . . . for my Land before June if you possibly Can as delays is dangerus."[26] Presumably he meant title for his Fish Creek holdings. With Jonathan's reassurance and a heartfelt farewell to his family, he set off from home on the long trek to the Ohio valley.

CHAPTER 4

The Dark and Bloody Ground

I have had nothing but a series of Misfortunes this four Month past too tedious to mention, but I hope to get the Better of them yet.

George Rogers Clark

L ike any frontiersman, Clark traveled lightly with his rifle in his hand, bullet pouch and powder horn strapped within easy reach, hatchet in his belt, and probably dried meat and other necessities in his blanket roll. He made good time, a score or more miles a day on the roads and trails leading to the upper Ohio valley. In early May, he strode into Fort Fincastle at Wheeling on the Ohio River.

There he joined a party that included Nicholas Cresswell, an Englishman in search of adventure. In his fascinating journal, Cresswell noted on May 4, 1775, that "we took into our Co a Captn George Clark." In later entries, he would describe Clark as "an intelligent man" who "always behaved well while he stayed with us."[1]

The party descended the Ohio River in two dugouts, dubbed the Charming Polly and Charming Sally. By common consent, Clark served as the group's guide because of his previous journey down the Ohio to the Kanawha River mouth, farther than any of his comrades had gone. Along the way, he led them ashore to reveal such curiosities as the Indian mounds at Grave

Creek and patches of bloodroot plants. Of the latter, he explained that snakebite could be cured with a poultice from the plant's mashed roots and a tea boiled from its leaves; the smashed roots also emitted a red dye with which the Indians painted themselves.

A Huck Finn–like lyricism animated most of their river trip as the carefree young men paddled with the powerful current, and fished, hunted, and explored ashore. Most evenings they would beach their canoes before a grassy meadow and set up camp. Other times they "lashed [their] canoes together and drifted all night."

Yet tension undercut their idyllic journey. The deal Dunmore had struck with the Shawnees at Camp Charlotte the previous October was merely an armed truce, one that many a vengeful warrior or frontiersman would be happy to break. One day Clark's party "met with some people who gave us very bad encouragement, say that the Indians are broke out again and killed four men on the Kentucky River. My courageous companions spirits begin to droop." Then there was the political tension between the Englishman Cresswell and the outspoken American patriots in the group. Cresswell recorded a close call: "This morning very wet—after breakfast Mr Edmund Taylor and I entered into discourse on politics which ended in high words. Taylor threatnd to Tar & Feather me. Obliged to pocket the affront."

Clark split off from the company at the Kentucky River mouth on May 24 and made his way alone on foot up the valley to Harrod's Town, which had been resettled after Dunmore's War. His announcement that he was the Ohio Company surveyor stirred eager requests for his services. His first job was to survey a tract known as Leesburg, near the future settlement of Frankfort: "I am Ingrosin all the land I possibly Can expecting him. We have laid out a Town seventy Miles up the Kentucke [River] and I dont doubt but there will be fifty familys living in it by Christmas." Yet surviving—let alone flourishing in the promised land—was a constant challenge. In July, Clark admitted in a letter home that "I have had nothing but a series of Misfortunes this four Month past too tedious to mention, but I hope to get the Better of them yet."[2]

It was easy for Clark to be philosophical about his trials. All he needed to do was lift his head and gaze at Kentucky's horizons: "A richer and more Beautifull Cuntry than this I believe has never been seen in America yet." That inspired in Clark visions of vast holdings not just for himself but for his family, with his father foremost in his mind: "I shall not advise him whether to come or not but I am convinced that if he once see the Cuntry he never will rest until he gets in it to live."[3]

For decades that vision of Clark and countless other Kentucky settlers would be blurred by two powerful forces beyond their control. One was the conflicting claims of the Transylvania Company, Ohio Company, and smaller companies for divvying up Kentucky. And those were just the initial contenders. In the years and decades to come, Kentucky's heartland would be crisscrossed with ever more overlapping claims and crowded with a greater number of farms and towns. The best legal claims rested on who was the first to file rather than the first to settle. That legal, political, and social Gordian knot would swell for decades, entangling Clark and thousands of others.

Then there were the Indians. For decades the region's tribes had upheld an understanding that Kentucky was a place in which not to live but to hunt, a privilege the Indians confined to themselves. As game diminished in their own lands, the surrounding tribes recognized that Kentucky could supply all of them with dried meat and hides in perpetuity. That under-standing unraveled after the French and Indian War. The faraway Iroquois League that sprawled across central New York had its own dubious claim to the region rooted in previous wars that forced the tribes of the region to acknowledge Iroquois suzerainty. With the 1768 Treaty of Fort Stanwix, the Iroquois, without even informing let alone consulting the peoples who actually lived there, signed away that "right" over Kentucky all the way to the Tennessee River; they did so in return for huge piles of goods that they did not share with the Ohio valley peoples who hunted in Kentucky. The Cher-okees had a much better claim since their four clusters of villages began a hundred or so miles southeast of Kentucky. The Fort Stanwix Treaty forced the Cherokees to make a tough choice. They could protect their stake in Ken-tucky with war or sell it for desperately needed goods. Having been devas-tated during a frontier war against Virginia, North Carolina, and South Carolina from 1761 to 1762, the Cherokees had neither the munitions nor will to fight. With the 1768 Treaty of Hard Labour, they sold off their stake in Kentucky all the way down the Ohio River to the Kanawha River mouth. The other Ohio valley tribes adamantly rejected both treaties and insisted on their right to hunt in a Kentucky void of any settlements.

Over the next half a dozen years, white settlers crowded the Caroline piedmont just east of Cherokee country and slipped through the Cumberland Gap into Kentucky to explore and hunt. Then in late 1774, word came of two disastrous events—the founding of a settlement in Kentucky and the defeat of the Shawnees and their allies in Dunmore's War. The Treaty of Camp Charlotte contradictorily confirmed both the Treaty of Fort Stanwix, by which the Iroquois had yielded the right to land down to the Tennessee River, and the Treaty of Hard Labour, by which the Cherokees ceded their land right east and retained their land rights of the Kanawha River. A consensus slowly emerged among the Cherokee elders that reselling their rights to some or all of Kentucky might divert some of the relentless current of trespassers from their homeland.

Richard Henderson was well aware of that swelling Cherokee belief that they had better sell Kentucky before the whites stole it, and sought to capitalize on that sentiment. Henderson was a renowned lawyer and judge who sought to fatten his wealth through land speculation. On August 27, 1774, he founded Richard Henderson and Company, briefly renamed it the Louisa Company, and finally, on January 6, 1775, named it the Transylvania Company. In early January, he dispatched runners to the Cherokee bands to meet in two moons at Sycamore Shoals on the Watauga River to discuss the purchase of Kentucky. In mid-March, Henderson and his partners met with 1,200 Cherokees led by Attacullaculla, or Little Carpenter, Oconostota, and Raven. After a week of at times heated haggling, Henderson and the three chiefs signed the Treaty of Sycamore Shoals (or Watauga). In return for £2,000 worth of trade goods, the Transylvania Company received 20 million acres between the Kentucky and Cumberland Rivers from their confluence with the Ohio River all the way to their headwaters and beyond to the westernmost white settlements![4]

Henderson and his investors were ecstatic, but the judge, of all people, should have known better. Three formidable obstructions separated the investors from their dream. First, that purchase was completely illegal as it violated numerous royal laws and edicts that forbade private investors from buying Indian lands without official authorization. Henderson had not troubled himself to seek official permission. He would spend much of his next couple of years lobbying for approval from first the crown and later from the North Carolina and Virginia state governments.

Then there was the problem that a settlement already existed on a patch of that vast territory ceded by the Cherokees. The Transylvania Company had bought the land from beneath James Harrod and his company. Henderson sent word to Harrod's Town that the settlers there were trespassing on Transylvania Company land and must either pay up or move on. Presented with the Transylvania Company's "legal" title to the land, those settlers would acquiesce at first. After all, they were squatters who had no permission from either Indian or colonial authorities to be there. But later, led by George Rogers Clark, the Kentuckians would lobby Virginia's government for freedom from their would-be and increasingly rapacious landlord.

Finally and worst of all, some Cherokee leaders condemned the sale. The most outraged was Dragging Canoe, Attacullaculla's son and the leading war chief. He and his followers would break with the Cherokees and form their own towns along Chickamauga Creek, which flows north into the Tennessee River near present-day Chattanooga. At Sycamore Shoals, Dragging Canoe angrily warned Henderson that Kentucky "was the bloody ground, and would be dark and difficult to settle" for him and all other trespassers.[5] His words were prescient. For the next two decades, Kentucky would indeed be ominously known as "the dark and bloody ground."

Nonplussed, Henderson dispatched Daniel Boone to blaze a trail, soon to be known as the Wilderness Road, through the Cumberland Gap to the Kentucky River, and on its bank found the capital of Henderson's land empire. Boone and a dozen men set off on March 10 and reached the Kentucky River on April 1; an Indian ambush along the way on March 27 killed one man and wounded three. Soon after arriving with fifty men on April 20, Henderson drew up and distributed lots for the new settlement of Boonesborough. Boone promptly headed back to the Yadkin valley of western North Carolina, gathered his family and several others, and returned to Boonesborough later that year.

In early autumn of 1775, Clark headed the opposite direction, probably passing Boone's party along the way. Like Boone, Clark returned to his distant home to round up more supplies and settlers. He lingered with his family that winter, recruiting a party and pondering all the possible threats and opportunities that had arisen with the American rebellion against Britain.

CHAPTER 5

Rebellion

We hold these truths to be self-evident; that all men are created equal;
that they are endowed by their Creator with certain inalienable rights;
that among these are life, liberty, and the pursuit of Happiness.

Declaration of Independence

If a country was not worth protecting it was not worth claiming.

George Rogers Clark

Clark would be among those who carried back to Kentucky the electrifying news that war had erupted between the thirteen colonies and
Britain in the early spring of 1775. The first shots were fired on April 19,
at Lexington, Massachusetts. There a militia company blocked the road to
Concord, where a British column of nine hundred troops was marching to
seize war supplies and the colony's dissident political assembly. Although
the redcoats routed that militia company, the British were repulsed by patriot
troops at Concord and harried all the way back to Boston, losing a couple of
hundred men along the way. Militia regiments from across the northeastern
colonies converged on Boston and besieged the British army. The redcoats
suffered a thousand casualties in a Pyrrhic victory that took Bunker Hill

overlooking Boston on June 17. That deterred British general Thomas Gage from another attempt to break the siege.

The rebellion soon spread far beyond Boston. In the Lake Champlain valley, Colonels Benedict Arnold and Ethan Allen led forces that captured Fort Ticonderoga on May 10, and Fort Crown Point the next day. Meanwhile, the Second Continental Congress opened at Philadelphia on May 10. Its most decisive acts that summer were to create the Continental army with George Washington as its commander on June 14, and to send the Olive Branch Petition to King George on July 8, urging him to resolve in its favor the colonial conflicts with Parliament.

The revolution's causes had been fermenting for at least a dozen years. Britain's leaders had trapped themselves in the dilemma of a vicious political cycle or a battle for hearts and minds. They sought to realize two contradictory goals, reaping taxes and keeping legitimacy. They could have either but not both. The more British leaders tried, the worse they failed and the more Americans they radicalized. Trying to enforce His Majesty's laws with bayonets embittered rather than inspired the loyalty of His Majesty's subjects. The result was worsening violence and extremism on both sides that made reconciliation impossible. Thus did a succession of illy conceived and illy enacted policies alienate and eventually drive the Americans to revolt.

Specifically, Britain's king, cabinet, and parliament collaborated to impose a series of taxes and regulations on the colonies, including the Proclamation of 1763, the American Duties Act of 1764, the Stamp Act and Quartering Acts of 1765, the Townsend Act of 1767, the Tea Act of 1773, and the four Intolerable (or Coercive) Acts and the Quebec Act of 1774. Two rationales, one asserted and the other muted, lay behind those policies. The victory over France and its allies in the Seven Years' War had not come cheap—Britain's national debt soared from £73 million in 1754 to £146 million in 1763. Whitehall, the government's palace in London, reasoned that the colonists should help pay off some of that debt since the war had eliminated France's North American empire. Behind that was an unspoken but even more powerful reason. A growing number of British political and commercial leaders feared that without a French threat to bind the colonists' dependence on Britain, the Americans would become economically and politically autonomous until they were able to seek outright independence. So the taxes and other regulations were partly intended to weaken the Americans. And to back that the British kept thousands of troops in the colonies.

That logic proved to be severely flawed. The result was a self-fulfilling prophecy. The measures that the British took to smother American nationalism enflamed it instead, provoking a rebellion that eventually led to American independence. That resistance began in 1765 when delegates from eight colonies convened a congress at New York City, condemned the Stamp Act, and organized a boycott of British goods until it was lifted. In all thirteen colonies, the political elite formed committees of correspondence to coordinate their resistance while radicals formed Sons of Liberty groups to harass crown officials. Whitehall soon gave in and rescinded the Stamp Act, only to impose the Townsend Act a year later to assert its power. Each new British tax and restriction backfired as it inspired rather than quelled greater American patriotism and unity.

The First Continental Congress met from September to October 1774 in response to the Intolerable Acts targeted against Massachusetts earlier that year. Three of those laws were designed to make an example of Massachusetts by dismissing its assembly, imposing martial law, and closing the port of Boston until full damages had been paid for all the tea destroyed by the Boston Tea Party of December 1773. Two other acts had a broader impact on the colonies. The Quartering Act empowered the crown to billet troops in public buildings. The Quebec Act extended Canada south to the Ohio River, thus trumping the conflicting claims of several American colonies for those lands. In response to that array of offensive and burdensome measures, Congress resolved to strengthen its boycott of British goods.

That dozen years of a worsening vicious cycle of British repression and colonial resistance accelerated the development of American nationalism that had begun almost from the arrival of the first colonists a century and a half earlier. The settlers in the New World increasingly saw themselves as a distinct people from the lands their ancestors left behind. Relative geographic isolation, political autonomy, and war nurtured American identity. Three thousand miles of ocean separated the nearest colonies from the mother country. Although nearly all colonies had governors appointed by the king, each had an assembly elected by white male taxpayers. War was perhaps the most powerful bond of all. Each of the five wars against the

French and Indians boosted American nationalism, especially the last one. During the French and Indian War (1754–60), American and British troops fought together in virtually all the campaigns. Yet that familiarity and common purpose bred British contempt and American resentment rather than affection for each other. George Washington and hundreds of other American officers bristled at the incessant snubs from their British counterparts.

By the spring of 1775, war between the Americans and British was virtually certain. Nicolas Cresswell, that adventurous Englishman who briefly accompanied Clark and traveled through Virginia, the Ohio valley, and other colonies from May 1774 to July 1777, was a keen observer of the conflict's early years. In May 1774, a year before the fighting erupted, he noted, "Nothing talked of but the Blockade of Boston Harbor the people seem much exasperated at the proceedings of the Ministry and talk as if they were determined to dispute the matter with the sword." By October, he observed, "Independent Companies are raising in every County on the Continent appointed adjutants and train their men as if they was on the eve of war." Loyalists suffered being "tarred and feathered [and] their property Burned and destroyed."[1] That brutal treatment usually at once intimidated them into silence while reinforcing their allegiance to the crown. Each colony and, from July 1776, state, was split among American nationalists, British loyalties, and fence-sitters, with the proportions varying with the fortunes of war and how individuals and groups defined their interests and identities.

Virginia was a microcosm of the American rebellion. Since becoming governor in 1772, John Murray, Lord Dunmore had behaved like a petty despot. In doing so, like the British crown and his counterparts in other colonies, Dunmore had unwittingly trapped himself in a dilemma whereby he diminished his authority the more he tried to assert it. He dismissed the House of Burgesses on May 26, 1774, after it declared a day of prayer in solidarity with Massachusetts, which bore the brunt of the Intolerable Acts. Although most of Virginia's 116 delegates dutifully headed for home, 39 defied the governor and stayed put. On May 30, they passed the five Virginia Resolves, which asserted the people's rights and liberties. Then, on June 1, 1774, that rump House of Burgesses adjourned. It would never meet again.

Instead, two months later, a new government began to coalesce when the Convention of Delegates met at the Raleigh Tavern in Williamsburg on August 1, 1774. The members issued a letter to all the colonial assemblies, calling on them to send delegates to what would be known as the First Continental Congress at Philadelphia. The Second Convention, held from March 20 to 27, 1775, was best expressed by Patrick Henry's immortal cry, "Give me liberty or give me death."

While Virginia's patriots fervently supported American colonial unity against the crown's rapacious policies, they did not lose sight of their conflicts with other colonies, especially Pennsylvania, with which Virginia had overlapping claims to the upper Ohio valley. To assert that claim, Virginia organized West Augusta County, with its seat at Pittsburgh, on May 16, 1775. That same day Pennsylvania organized Westmoreland County with its seat at Hannastown. That conflict would hobble the ability of either Virginia or Pennsylvania as well as Congress to fight the Ohio valley Indians after war broke out.

His Majesty's government in Virginia effectively disappeared on June 8, 1775, when Dunmore and his family fled Williamsburg for refuge on a British warship in the James River. The Third Convention opened at Richmond on June 17, 1775, the same day as the Battle of Bunker Hill. The members declared a Committee of Safety that would govern the colony in Dunmore's absence. They made two other crucial decisions. They would send troops to Boston and peace commissioners to Pittsburgh.

The last thing the Virginians wanted was to fight both the British and Indians. A truce rather than a peace had ended Dunmore's War. Part of the understanding reached at Camp Charlotte was that peace delegations from Virginia and the upper Ohio valley tribes would meet in 1775 and negotiate a lasting peace treaty. To that end on June 17, the convention appointed five Indian commissioners—Thomas and John Walker, Andrew Lewis, James Wood, and Adam Stephens.

Congress also recognized the importance of keeping peace with the Indians while fighting the British. The Indian policy devised by Congress complemented that of Virginia. On July 12, 1775, Congress designated Northern, Middle, and Southern Indian Departments, each led by commissioners with broad supervisory powers. The Northern Department included the New York and New England tribes, the Middle Department included the Ohio valley tribes, and the Southern Department included those of the Carolinas and Georgia. The Northern and Middle Departments each had three commissioners while the Southern Department had five. They in turn would employ agents as troubleshooters to deal with specific tribes or issues. For the Middle Department, Congress tapped James Wilson, Lewis Morris, and Thomas Walker.

Armed with £2,000 worth of trade goods, Virginia's commissioners opened a peace council on September 12. The negotiations continued until a treaty was signed on October 21.[2] Between those days, the conference lurched along in a start-and-stop fashion, shaped by tribal protocol, the arrival of new contingents, and the occasional drunken binge among the Indians that left them seemingly senseless and hungover. Among the more prominent chiefs were the Delawares' White Eyes and Killbuck; the Mingos' White Mingo and Kyashuta; the Shawnees' Cornstalk, Nimwha, Wry Neck, and Silver Heels; the Wyandots' Half King; and the Ottawas' Shaganaba, Pontiac's son.

The commissioners repeatedly explained why they had rebelled against the English king and argued that peace with the Americans was crucial to the well-being of the tribes. The commissioners knew well that Indians respected strength and disdained weakness. Thus an essential element of Indian diplomacy was to exude confidence. The commissioners boasted, "We are not Afraid these People will conquer us, they Cant fight in our Country, and you Know we Can; we fear not them, nor any Power on Earth." They darkly warned the Indians of their fate should they ally with the redcoats: "Your Interest is Involved with ours so far as this, that in Case those People with whom we are contending shou'd Subdue us, your Lands, your Trade, your Liberty and all that is dear to you must fall with us, for if they wou'd Distroy our flesh and Spill our Blood which is the same with theirs, what can you who are no way related to or Connected with them Expect?" They emphasized the unity of the thirteen colonies and their determination collectively to crush their enemies. Finally, the commissioners reassured the tribes that "we have not the most Distant thought of Possessing any part of your Lands."[3]

While the Indian delegations were no doubt impressed by the eloquence of such speeches, most remained skeptical of the arguments. It was the Americans who were pushing farther west, killing off the game, and stealing the land. It was the English Great Father who had tried to limit that relentless American advance. With time, that stark contrast would push ever more Indians into the arms of the British.

Although Governor Dunmore's authority in Virginia was confined to his cramped quarters aboard a British warship, that did not stop him from doing all that he could to crush the rebellion. He and now Major John Connolly, his friend and business partner, concocted a brutal plan for first retaking the Ohio valley and then Virginia. But before they could act they had to get General Gage's approval. Connolly sailed to Boston, conferred with Gage, and then returned with his authorization. Dunmore dispatched Connolly with the mission of journeying to Detroit, rallying the Indians, and descending on the upper Ohio region "to destroy Fort Pitt and Fort Fincastle if the Americans should make any resistance." Connolly would then lead his forces eastward to help Dunmore retake the rest of Virginia. Fortunately for the American cause, alert patriots arrested Connolly and three companions near Hagerstown, Maryland, on November 20, 1776. Foolishly, Connolly carried damning documents with him and verbally revealed the details. The publication of Dunmore's incendiary instructions and Connolly's confession was a great propaganda coup for the American cause and a clear warning to frontier settlers of a looming danger, especially in Kentucky.[4]

Kentucky then had four settlements. James Harrod founded two of them, Harrod's Town, increasingly known as Harrodsburg, and Boiling Spring. Then there was Saint Asaph's (or Logan's Fort) founded by Benjamin Logan and John Floyd, and Boonesborough, founded by Daniel Boone. Relations among those settlements were tense as the claims of each conflicted with the others. That was not the only division. Although most Kentuckians favored the patriot cause, many were Loyalists or fence-sitters. They would soon unite with Clark and other leaders against a common enemy, the Indians and British, with the patriots doing so passionately, the fence-sitters reluctantly, and the Loyalists bitterly.

By the spring of 1776, patriots in Kentucky and elsewhere across the thirteen colonies had good reason to be optimistic about their cause. So far the rebels had trounced the redcoats in nearly every clash of arms—the battles of Concord, Bunker Hill, and Great Bridge; the captures of Forts Ticonderoga and Crown Point; and the conquest of much of Canada's Saint Lawrence valley except for Quebec—and had witnessed the flight of all the royal governors and their entourages and finally of the British army from Boston when it sailed away after March 17, 1776. That last astonishing event was a bloodless victory. Cannons captured at Fort Ticonderoga were dragged to the Boston siege lines and emplaced on Dorchester Heights overlooking the bay crammed with hundreds of British warships and transports. An understanding was reached between the enemy commanders—Generals George Washington and William Howe—that the British could sail away unmolested if they did not leave Boston in ruins behind them.

Not a single redcoat remained in the thirteen colonies. But sooner or later the British army would be back, perhaps in overwhelming force. King George had replied to Congress's Olive Petition by declaring the colonies in a state of rebellion that would be crushed. Spies brought word that General Howe was massing a vast army at Halifax, Nova Scotia, that would descend on the colonies in the summer. If the British did succeed in vanquishing the Americans, the retribution could be horrendous. Rebellion was a hanging offense. The British might well send the top leaders to the scaffold while imprisoning and confiscating the wealth of subordinates.

As a fervent American patriot, George Rogers Clark was undaunted by that possible fate. If anything, it stoked the fire in that hotheaded young man to do everything he could for the cause. He returned with a party to Kentucky in late February 1776. His ostensible reason for going was for the family patriarch. To his brother Jonathan, he explained, "I left my father's last Saturday. All was well. He is determined to go to . . . Kentucky, but hearing of some disturbances there with ye Indians, he sent me . . . to learn the truth."[5] But Clark intended to do much more in Kentucky than merely assess the Indian threat. He was nurturing a plan that could be a major step in fulfilling his patriotic duties as well as his dreams of amassing wealth and power.

By chance, a crucial event in Kentucky would enable Clark to advance his ambitions. As Clark and his followers plodded west, a delegation from each of the four settlements met at Boonesborough for six days of often rancorous debate from May 23 to 29. The delegates finally agreed to recognize the Transylvania Company as "Sovereigns of the Country as well as Lords of the Soil." That endorsement granted the Transylvania Company the power to own, sell, or settle all land claims as well as govern the settlers.[6] George Rogers Clark would soon dramatically upset that arrangement.

Clark knew that any allegiance to the Transylvania Company was a matter of convenience rather than conviction. The settlers had simply bowed to the prevailing power. Henderson and his cronies soon discredited themselves by abusing that power. Clark explained that the "proprietors at first took great pains to win the favor of the settlers, but too soon for their own self-interest they began to raise the prices on their lands, which gave rise to much complaint . . . I saw clearly that the proprietors were working their own ruin, that . . . their conduct would shortly exasperate the people and afford the opportunity to overthrow them."[7]

Upon reaching Harrodsburg, Clark called for an assembly to convene on June 6, 1776. After the settlers gathered, he first explained all the extraordinary events that had taken place along the Eastern Seaboard since those Kentucky settlers had left their distant homes. He then called for an election of two delegates to Virginia's assembly. Clark was among those nominated and, along with an attorney named John Gabriel Jones, was elected to be Kentucky's first representatives to what had become the sovereign state of Virginia. That was not the only election. A Committee of Twenty-One was chosen to govern Kentucky's affairs. Along with their credentials, Clark and Jones would convey to Williamsburg two petitions written by that committee. One was a request for Virginia's recognition of the county of Kentucky with all the rights, privileges, and duties that would entail. The other was to supply a list of items vital for Kentucky's defense, with five hundred pounds of gunpowder foremost.

The county-hood petition was a well argued and styled expression of the same spirit of natural law and rights that would animate America's Declaration of Independence. The signatories challenged the validity of Henderson's land purchase, "being well informed that the Cherokee never extended their claims north of Cumberland River, nor wou'd warrant any lands on the other side." If true, that charge mooted any of Henderson's claims to Kentucky lands. They castigated him and his Transylvania Company for selling lands "at an exorbitant price." They declared his policies at odds "with that lately adopted by the United Colonies" and would "afford a safe asylum to those whose principles are inimical to American Freedom." In stark contrast to Henderson's Loyalist leanings, the Kentuckians asserted themselves firmly committed to the American cause against the British government. They requested that "our infant settlements become the object of your deliberations, and be taken under your protection and direction." To do so would accord with general principles of humanity and natural rights. But there were good strategic and economic motivations for the government to recognize the settlements as a county—Kentucky would serve Virginia as a growing market, source of products, and bulwark against hostile Indians.[8]

Convening an assembly and winning an election to serve as one of Kentucky's delegates were extraordinary feats for a twenty-three-year-old who had spent little time in the region. How did Clark pull it off?

Clark's powerful mind and appearance partly explain his coup. He rose an imposing six feet in height, and had a stocky build and moon face with piercing blue eyes and thinning strawberry blond hair. That "appearance, well calculated to attract attention," as one anonymous settler observed, "was rendered agreeable by the manliness of his deportment and the intelligence of his conversation."[9]

Even more crucial was Clark's mastery of psychology. His deliberately vague reply to those who asked why he was calling for an assembly is the first recorded instance of that power. All he would say was that "something would be proposed to them which much concerned their interest." In his memoir, he explained, "My reason for withholding information as to what I wished to be done was in part to prevent the settlers from dividing into parties on the subject, in part to insure a more general attendance, as everyone would wish to know what was to be done."[10] Clark's ability to understand and manipulate human nature, combined with his hard-driving charisma, courage, and conviction, reveals how he could repeatedly inspire followers and prevail against often overwhelming odds.

Misery and terror stalked the journey of Kentucky's two delegates back east. Clark recalled that they "set out without waiting for other company. We soon had cause to repent our rashness, however, for on the second day we discovered alarming signs of Indians."[11] Then on the third day, Jones's horse went lame, so they had to pile all their belongings on Clark's horse. It rained for four straight days and nights, but they dared not light a fire for fear of attracting a passing war party. The skin of their feet rotted from being incessantly soaked, an affliction known as scalded feet because, as Clark explained, the "skin seems too hot on every part of our feet." They slowly hobbled along the trail in "greater torment than I ever before or since experienced."[12]

After crossing the Cumberland Gap, the men stumbled into Powell's valley near the frontier between Virginia and North Carolina, eagerly looking forward to recovering among the settlers there. To their crushing disappointment, the cabins were abandoned. Clark noted, "We sat still for a few moments looking at each other, and I found myself reduced to a state of perfect despair."[13]

Clark swiftly regained his composure. He reckoned that the settlers had forted up at nearby Martin's Station because the Cherokees were on the warpath. But they found Martin's Station deserted as well. Despite the danger, the men decided to rest up until their feet healed and their strength was restored by feasting off the abandoned livestock. They did not risk a shot; instead, Jones ran through a hog with his hanger, a short sword. The men winced in fear at the hog's dying squeals, but no Indians appeared. Clark climbed with pain every inch of the way up to the roof of the most fortified cabin then down the chimney, before crawling over to unlock the door. They kindled a fire and eagerly devoured barely cooked slices of meat that Jones cut from the hog. They found corn meal, a cask of water, and a container of grease in another cabin and carried them over to their own. They greased their feet to ease the pain and start the healing. They then readied themselves for defense. The men cut gun-loops in the walls. They carefully cleaned, reloaded, and laid out their rifle and two pistols. They found a pole with which to knock off any shingles that the Indians might set afire, a relatively easy task since for just such a danger each shingle was attached to the beam with a single peg. Clark recalled that "Our agreement was that in case of an attack, Mr Jones should continue to load the pieces as I discharged them, without paying any attention to the enemy unless they stormed the house."[14]

A horse bell jingled not far off. Clark and Jones hobbled to the loopholes and tried to spy the source. An Indian trick was to ring a horse bell or cowbell to lure victims to what they thought was a stray. Men with rifles were indeed creeping toward the cabin, but, to the immense relief of Clark and Jones, they were whites. Clark called out to them. With their own relief, the men rose and strode toward the cabin. A few of the homesteaders had returned to retrieve some of their possessions.

After resting for the night, Clark and Jones set out eastward early the next morning. Upon reaching Botetourt County, they learned that Virginia's assembly had adjourned until early autumn. They decided to split up. Jones headed for a brief visit with his family in the upper Holston River valley. Clark headed on to Williamsburg in hopes of procuring gunpowder for Kentucky.

In returning to Virginia, Clark walked into a political world stunningly different than the one he had left. On May 15, 1776, Virginia's Convention of Delegates declared independence for the state. On June 12, the convention approved the Virginia Declaration of Rights, penned by George Mason, that guaranteed life; liberty; property; the pursuit of happiness; equality before the law; freedom of the speech, press, assembly, petition, and trial by a jury of one's peers; and, finally, to the freedom to "reform, alter, or abolish" any government that violated those rights. Using the Declaration of Rights as the core, the convention then crafted a constitution. Under the final draft approved on June 29, Virginia would be governed with a bicameral legislature composed of a Senate and House of Delegations, and a governor annually elected by that assembly. That same day the delegates elected Patrick Henry as Virginia's first governor as a sovereign state. Then, perhaps exhausted from the emotional weight of those revolutionary changes, the assembly went into recess, and an ill Governor Henry withdrew to his home at Hanover. Only the state's three-man executive council remained at Williamsburg to oversee most affairs of state.

Inspired by these revolutionary events in Virginia and elsewhere, American independence soon followed. On May 10, Congress called on the other colonies to transform themselves into states with liberal constitutions. On June 7, Virginia delegate Richard Henry Lee presented a resolution to Congress that it declare independence. On June 11, after several days of debate, Congress formed a committee composed of Thomas Jefferson, John Adams, Benjamin Franklin, Robert Livingston, and John Sherman to compose a declaration. Jefferson wrote a draft, and the committee edited it. On July 2, Congress voted overwhelmingly to approve Lee's resolution, with twelve states in favor and the New York delegation abstaining until it got specific instructions from the state government. Congress then went over the declaration line by line, making minor corrections. On July 4, Congress approved and President John Hancock signed the Declaration of Independence for the United States of America.

It was amid these revolutionary events that George Rogers Clark lobbied Virginia's new government. His first step was to present the petitions to Virginia's executive council. The three councilors explained that they could not approve such extraordinary measures without the governor's consent. Clark trekked to the governor's home to meet with Patrick Henry, then hurried back to Williamsburg with a letter from the governor advising the councilors to consider the gunpowder petition for now and set aside the county-hood petition for when the assembly reconvened.

That was the easy part of Clark's mission. With the war with Britain now more than a year old, gunpowder, lead, and other crucial tools of war were all in short supply. As if that were not a big enough obstacle, there was the controversial legal status of the Kentucky settlements. On August 23, after a prolonged and heated debate, the executive council "agreed to furnish the powder; but as we were a detached people not yet united to the state of Virginia, and until the session of the Assembly it was uncertain whether we would become united, they could only lend us the ammunition as to friends in distress, and I must become responsible in case the Assembly should not receive us as citizens of the state."[15] As for the question of Kentucky's status, that would be up to the governor, executive council, and assembly to decide when those institutions reunited at Williamsburg in the autumn.

Should the government not recognize the Kentucky settlements, Clark was authorized to declare independence. That possibility did not faze Clark, who observed, "I was sorry that we would have to seek protection elsewhere, which I did not doubt of getting; and that if a country was not worth protecting it was not worth claiming."[16] What did worry him was that he would be liable for the gunpowder and other supplies since he was not authorized to purchase them.

Virginia's equivocation over what to Clark was a clear-cut convergence of the state's interests and moral duty enraged him. Clark stormed out of the capital and headed for home. That did the trick. A courier caught up with him with a message from the council. To Clark's relief, the councilors promised to forward twenty-eight kegs, or five hundred pounds, of gunpowder to Fort Pitt, where the Kentuckians could take possession. They urged him to return to Williamsburg to resolve other vital matters.[17]

There Jones joined him. Together they squared off with two formidable opponents to Kentucky becoming a county—Richard Henderson, who wanted Kentucky to be his separate colony, and Col. Arthur Campbell, who represented Fincastle County, which officially extended westward over most of Kentucky to the Mississippi River. The debate would not be decided until after Clark and Jones departed for Pittsburgh on their gunpowder mission.

They left their petition in the hands of a formidable proponent. On October 23, Thomas Jefferson introduced a bill to designate Kentucky a county and gradually built a consensus behind it. The governor and council approved that bill on November 23, and the assembly on December 6. As of December 31, 1776, Fincastle County would be eliminated and split among three new counties named Kentucky, Montgomery, and Washington. Kentucky's lands would stretch west from the Big Sandy River to the Mississippi River. Harrodsburg, which Harrod's Town was thereafter called, was designated the county seat.

Henderson was the big loser. His hopes to rule his own colony and enrich himself with land sales were dead. Virginia now held legal title to that territory and promised that army volunteers would lead the line when it was distributed. Eventually, Virginia's government would preempt all other land company claims to Kentucky. That development, however, would not begin to resolve the myriad of conflicting titles sold to settlers by the various companies and individuals.

By November, Clark and Jones were at Fort Pitt, trying to round up enough men to safely convey the procured gunpowder to the Kentucky settlements. Floating it down the Ohio River was obviously the fastest way to do so, but that route was now more dangerous than at any time since the end of Dunmore's War. British agents were presenting war belts to village councils north of the river and urging the young men to attack the rebels along the long frontier, including the Kentucky settlements. Spies among Indians living near Fort Pitt passed the word down the Ohio valley of the huge pending gunpowder shipment.

Given the odds against their mission, Clark and Jones were lucky to talk seven men into joining them.[18] They packed the gunpowder and other supplies aboard a barge and shoved off. Paddling steadily, they made good time in the rain-swelled current. They got as far as a day's hard row from the mouth of Limestone Creek when they spotted Indians pursuing them. Redoubling their efforts, the frontiersmen widened their lead and the Indians disappeared from sight. When the men thought they were far enough ahead, they grounded their boat on the Kentucky shore and hid the kegs in several places. They then resumed their journey only to disembark after a few miles at Limestone Creek. There they set their boat adrift with hopes that the Indians would follow it. Then the frontiersmen strode down the long trail to Harrodsburg where they could gather horses and volunteers to pick up the supplies. En route, they reached a cabin inhabited by four men. To their relief, they learned that a surveying party led by John Todd was nearby. Clark hurried on to Todd to request his help in getting the gunpowder safely to the settlements. Somehow they missed each other, and Clark strode on toward McClelland's Station, the nearest settlement.

Todd reached the cabin and, after resting briefly, united his party with Clark's men and the settlers, and together they headed with seven horses to the caches. On Christmas morning, they blundered into a Shawnee ambush near the Lower Blue Licks. The first volley of musket balls dropped three Kentuckians, while the rest scattered to take cover and fire back; Jones was among the dead. Screaming war cries, the Shawnees dodged through the trees to encircle the frontiersmen. Todd and a few others fled. The warriors captured James Callaway, Josiah Dickson, and Joseph Rogers, Clark's cousin.

Meanwhile, Clark reached McClelland's Station, where he dispatched a messenger to Harrodsburg, explaining all that had happened and asking for the gunpowder to be retrieved. Whatever rest he may have been enjoying after his long arduous journey was shattered when a Mingo war party led by Pluggy attacked the settlement. The Mingos killed a defender and wounded three others, while rifled balls shot down Pluggy and another warrior, and scattered the rest. Although McClelland's Station's defenders were safe for now, they agreed that they were too exposed, undermanned, and ill-equipped to resist another attack, so they packed up and withdrew to Harrodsburg. Now that post, along with Boonesborough and Logan's Fort, were the last three settlements in Kentucky.

James Harrod, thirty men, and as many horses left Harrodsburg for the gunpowder cache on January 2, 1777. To their astonishment and relief, the gunpowder was safe. They packed the kegs on the horses and safely brought it back to Harrodsburg. The use the Kentuckians would make of that gunpowder would save most of the settlers from extinction in that very bloody year of 1777.

Clark and Jones were not the only patriots who had embarked on a gunpowder mission the previous year. That crucial ingredient for modern war was scarce throughout the newborn United States. American manufacturers could not keep up with the soaring demand. However, what could not be made at home could be purchased abroad. By December 1776, a trio of diplomats, Silas Deane, Arthur Lee, and Benjamin Franklin, were in Paris trying to secure French munitions along with other vital supplies, and, ideally recognition and an alliance. Virginian captain George Gibson conceived another possible foreign source of all those needs. He lobbied Williamsburg for authorization to lead an expedition that would journey all the way to New Orleans, purchase gunpowder, and then haul it back. Governor Patrick Henry and his executive council approved the plan.

That mission would benefit America's cause in two crucial ways. In the short term, that gunpowder helped alleviate the shortage. Indeed, without that gunpowder Clark's ambitious operations in the Ohio and, eventually, upper Mississippi valleys would have been all but impossible. Even more importantly, that mission opened a backdoor relationship with the Spanish empire that would be of incalculable value to America's cause in the years ahead. Here too Clark would directly benefit.

Spain would be a crucial if unofficial ally of the United States by secretly supplying munitions to the rebels and turning a blind eye to their not-so-covert operations throughout the Mississippi valley and Gulf coast. Two men served successively as Louisiana's governors during the war for independence, and both greatly aided America's cause. Luis de Unzaga did so reluctantly, and Bernardo de Galvez enthusiastically. Galvez, who replaced Unzaga on January 1, 1777, is probably the war's least known outstanding military leader. In three years from 1779 to 1781, he systematically conquered West Florida from the British.

Both governors were a giant diplomatic stride or two ahead of their own government. Unlike France, Spain would not ally with the United States even after it declared war on Britain on June 16, 1779. That policy made perfect sense. Madrid ruled the world's largest and most far-flung empire, an empire filled with restless peoples. The Spanish certainly did not want to encourage potential rebels against themselves by openly aiding the liberal and nationalist American struggle against the British monarch. Yet Charles III did act on the request of his cousin Louis XVI that he send secret military aid and loans to the United States. Here again logic lay behind the seeming contradiction. Wielding that classic maxim of statecraft, "the enemy of my enemy is my friend," Madrid naturally hoped that the United States would break free of the British empire and thus inflict a powerful blow to Spain's mightiest foe.

One man was responsible for wringing that aid first from Unzaga then from Galvez. Oliver Pollock is perhaps the American Revolution's least known hero. He was as brilliant a diplomat as he was a businessman, and eventually sacrificed his vast fortune in selflessly aiding the cause. He got rich after winning an extraordinary business advantage at New Orleans in 1768. Pollock generously opened his warehouse to Governor Alejandro O'Reilly as he prepared an expedition at Havana to crush a revolt in New Orleans. O'Reilly, in gratitude, granted Pollock free trade privileges at New Orleans. With that edge over his rivals, Pollock grew ever wealthier. When word arrived that fighting had erupted between the Americans and British, he offered his services to Congress. Though Congress would officially name Pollock its envoy to Louisiana on June 12, 1777, he had been serving that role for well over a year. His first act was in April 1776, when he got Governor Unzaga to ignore the operations of American merchant and privateer vessels on the Mississippi River. But his first major coup was procuring twelve thousand pounds of gunpowder for the United States.

Captain Gibson, Lieutenant William Linn, and forty-six troops, all disguised as traders, set off from the Pittsburgh landing on July 19, 1776. After three months of hard rowing, they reached New Orleans in September. Pollock talked a reluctant Unzaga into donating four tons of gunpowder from the government warehouse. To keep up appearances of neutrality, Gibson was arrested and held until the expedition was well under way. On September 22, 1777, Linn and forty-three men began the grueling journey upstream, rowing and poling barges piled high with ninety-eight barrels or more than nine thousand pounds of gunpowder. Gibson, meanwhile, was released and sailed back to Philadelphia aboard a ship packed with the other three thousand pounds of gunpowder; he arrived on November 2. Linn and his men reached Arkansas Post near the mouth of the Arkansas River on November. After wintering there, they resumed their journey and reached the relative safety of Wheeling on May 2, 1777. Along the way, they conducted another secret mission at the mouth of the Ohio River that would be essential for Clark's future Illinois campaign.

Governor Henry expressed his deep appreciation to Governor Unzaga for that gunpowder and tried to reassure him that he "must be too acquainted with the nature of our States to entertain any jealousy of their becoming your Rivals in trade, or overstocked as they are with vast tracts of land, that they should ever think of extending their territory."[19] If the governor was at all acquainted with the history of the Americans, he would have felt nothing but alarm for the future of Spain's empire in North America. Regardless, Clark and his men would make good use of their portion of that gunpowder.

CHAPTER 6

Promotion

This led me to a long train of thinking, the result of which was to lay aside every private view and engage seriously in the war, having the interest and the welfare of the public my only concern until the fate of the continent could be known; divesting myself of prejudice and partiality in favor of any particular parts of the country, I determined to pursue what I considered to be the interest of the whole.

George Rogers Clark

Kentucky's hard-pressed settlers received encouraging news early in 1777. Virginia's assembly had designated Kentucky a county as of December 31, 1776. That allowed the inhabitants to abandon their makeshift efforts at governance for something more efficient and durable. In the face of worsening attacks by the Shawnees and other tribes, the Kentuckians' priority was to organize the militia. It was decided that Kentucky would field a regiment, with a company mustered from each settlement. Elections for officers were held on March 5, 1777, at Harrodsburg. John Bowman was elected colonel; Anthony Bledsoe, lieutenant colonel; George Rogers Clark, major; and William and James Harrod, Benjamin Logan, and John Todd, captains. A later election would name John Todd as the county attorney and Richard Callaway as the county representative to the Virginia assembly.

Clark swiftly emerged as the militia's acting commander. Bowman returned east to manage his affairs while Bledsoe declined his post. Clark had little time to celebrate his promotion. Kentucky's defense rested in relatively few but highly determined and skilled hands. That spring there were only about 150 frontiersmen and perhaps another 100 women, children, slaves, and those not fit for service scattered across the settlements.

That year's first attack came in March when a Shawnee war party led by Blackfish ambushed brothers William and James Ray and William Coomes at their maple sugar camp not far from Harrodsburg. William Ray was wounded and captured; James Ray dashed off through the woods and made it back to the fort. Coomes hid in a hollow log and struggled to keep silent as the Shawnees dragged Ray nearby and tortured him to a horrific death. Blackfish and his warriors appeared around Harrodsburg the following evening. They ran down and butchered a man just beyond rifle shot of the fort as his horrified family and others helplessly watched. They burned outlying cabins and slaughtered stray livestock. But they did not dare to attack Harrodsburg even though the stockade and blockhouses were not finished. Instead, Blackfish and his men set off to terrorize Boonesborough. Their attack on April 24 killed one man and wounded four others, including Daniel Boone. Blackfish and his men raided Boonesborough and Saint Asaph's again in late May, killed one man, wounded several, and slaughtered any cattle and hogs that they found. Blackfish's raids were only a harbinger of the horrors that lay ahead that year.

Those Indian raids against the Kentucky frontier were mere pinpricks compared to what the British government planned and unleashed in 1777. Lord George Germain, the colonial secretary, and General John Burgoyne devised a grand strategy that they were confident would crush the rebellion once and for all. Three armies would converge on Albany, destroy any American forces in their way, and split the New England colonies from the rest. And then there was the fourth and longest front of all—the American frontier straddled the Appalachian Mountains from northern New England to the Carolinas before arching around to southern Georgia.

Of Whitehall's counterrevolutionary policies, none was more morally reprehensible and ultimately self-defeating than unleashing the "savages" against the frontier. General Thomas Gage, the commander of His Majesty's forces in North America, first suggested that policy in a letter to General Guy Carleton, Canada's governor, on April 21, 1775, two days after fighting erupted at Lexington and Concord, noting that "a number of Canadians and Indians would be of great service on the Frontiers . . . under the command of a Judicious person."[1]

Gage's suggestion appalled Carleton, a humanitarian. The idea lay in abeyance until Guy Johnson, who had succeeded his brilliant uncle William Johnson as superintendent for the Northern Indian Department, sought refuge with several hundred Loyalists and Iroquois at Montreal on July 17, 1775. Patriots had driven them from their homes in the lower Mohawk River valley, and they were eager for vengeance. Johnson called a council of the Saint Lawrence valley Indian tribes, ostensibly to rally them to a frontier war, but Carleton forbade that act.

At this point, William Legge, Earl Dartmouth, then the colonial secretary, led the government's effort to crush the rebellion. Gage had shared with him his idea of mustering the Indians to that end. On July 5, 1775, Dartmouth wrote Superintendent Johnson, instructing him to ensure that the Indians remained "in a state of affection and attachment to the King." Three weeks later, on July 24, he authorized Johnson to rally the Indians for war against the rebels.[2] Fortunately, the orders reached Canada too late for action that year.

A debate flared as word of the policy spread through Britain's military and colonial hierarchy. The practical question was whether launching an Indian war against the American frontier would help smother or empower the rebellion. Then there was the moral question. Even if the Indians crushed the rebellion on the frontier, did the means justify the end? Although the policy disturbed many British officials and officers on both practical and ethical grounds, most wearily shrugged and carried on with their duties. One of the few protests came from Captain Edward Abbott, the lieutenant governor for the region surrounding Vincennes on the lower Wabash River. In a letter to Governor Carleton, he condemned the policy as disastrous for Britain on strategic, political, and moral grounds: "Employing Indians on the Rebel frontiers has been of great hurt to the cause, for many hundreds would have put themselves under His Majesty's protection was there a possibility; that not being the case, these poor unhappy people are forced to take up arms against their Sovereign, or be pillaged & left to starve; cruel alternative. This is too shocking a subject to dwell upon; Your Excellency's known humanity will certainly put a stop if possible to such proceedings."[3]

Carleton shared Abbot's abhorrence of the policy, but his hands were tied. He was merely following His Majesty's will. Lord Germain superseded Dartmouth as the war's chief director in late 1775. Well aware of the governor's sentiments, Germain issued on March 26, 1777, a direct order to Carleton to implement the strategy:

> It is His Majesty's Resolution that the most vigorous Efforts should be made and every means employ'd that Providence has put into His Majesty's hands for crushing the rebellion. It is the King's Command that you should direct Lieut. Governor Hamilton to assemble as many of the Indians of his District as he . . . can, and placing proper persons at their Head . . . to conduct their Parties, and restrain them from committing violence on the well affected and inoffensive Inhabitants, employing them in making a Diversion and exciting an alarm upon the frontiers of Virginia and Pennsylvania.[4]

Carleton reluctantly passed on the order to Henry Hamilton and his other field commanders who would be responsible for directing the frontier war.[5]

Jubilation must have filled Hamilton on June 16, 1777, as he read the order to launch a war against the American frontier. Despising Carleton's policy of restraint, Hamilton was in full accord with the new policy. The previous September, he had written Dartmouth that, acting under Carleton's orders, he had so far held back the Indians, but warned that "their inclination is for War [and] . . . I hope the colonists will open their eyes before the clouds burst that hand heavy over their heads."[6] Shortly thereafter, he outright advocated "making a Diversion on the Frontiers of Virginia and Pennsylvania by Parties of Indians conducted by proper Leaders."[7]

Upon receiving Carleton's orders, Hamilton sent runners to the neighboring tribes calling them to a grand council. Hundreds of Ottawas, Pottawatomis, Ojibwa, Hurons, Miamis, Shawnees, and Delawares crowded into the council from June 17 to 30. The opening day was devoted to standard Indian diplomatic etiquette of greetings, praise, and gifts to cover the graves of those who had died since their previous get-together. Over the following days, Hamilton worked to forge a consensus on war against the Americans. Each chief had his say. When Hamilton felt the time was ripe, he brandished "the Hatchet" and "Sung the War Sung." He reassured his superiors that while he had "exhorted them to act vigorously," he reminded them that "they were men & were desired to make war against men, and not against women or Children, and to forbear to dip their hands in the blood of the two latter."[8] Few warriors who strode off to the settlements would heed his admonition.

By the time the council ended, "most of the Nations had brought in their Sticks for the numbers of Warriors." Hamilton would exchange an appropriate amount of gifts for the number of sticks he was handed. By late June, he had equipped and dispatched 15 war parties with 289 warriors and 30 white officers, an average of 19 Indians and 2 Britons. They carried with them more than weapons and a desire to reap war's cruel harvest. Occasionally, the British would read aloud to a besieged fort—or more often nail up at a clearing or burnt cabin littered with mutilated dead—a proclamation. In stirring prose, Hamilton condemned the rebels and urged all Loyalists to hurry to safety at a British post; His Majesty would reward those men who joined his forces with a bounty of two hundred pounds sterling.[9]

The war parties soon began to return laden with loot, scalps, and prisoners. By September, Hamilton could report triumphantly that "eleven hundred and fifty warriors are now dispersed over the Frontiers." Even that did not satisfy his ambitions. He fired off a proposal to Carleton for a campaign that first captured Fort Pitt, then descended the Ohio valley to overrun Kentucky, and, finally, invaded the Mississippi valley to vanquish Spain's settlements all the way to New Orleans.[10]

Congress responded to the worsening frontier war by splitting that vast swath of land into northern, western, and southern commands. The western command encompassed the entire Ohio River watershed and the upper Great Lakes starting with Lake Erie. In April 1777, Congress tapped Brigadier General Edward Hand to head that district. Hand reached his Fort Pitt headquarters on June 1, 1777. On the surface, he seemed a good choice. He had arrived in America in 1767 as a surgeon with the Royal Irish regiment, and served at Fort Pitt until 1772; he purchased the rank of ensign in the regiment, but resigned in 1774. He settled in Lancaster, Pennsylvania, where he practiced medicine and married. When the war broke out, he was appointed a lieutenant colonel of the First Pennsylvania Riflemen. He fought at the siege of Boston, and in the Long Island, Trenton, and Princeton campaigns. But controversy would plague Hand's tenure as the western frontier commander. Contrary to the hopes of those who appointed him, he had apparently learned little about Indians during his first stint at Fort Pitt. Indeed, he proved to be an inept diplomat with virtually everyone. Nor had his previous military experience ingrained in him any ability to command, organize, train, supply, and embolden men to search for and destroy the enemy. His only foray from Fort Pitt's safety would be derided as the "squaw campaign" whose sole "victory" was the murder of half a dozen people, mostly women and children, at a hunting camp. What Hand lacked in military or diplomatic skills, he made up for with the ability to pocket a portion of the money, contracts, and supplies that flowed through his headquarters. His incompetence and greed was illy disguised beneath a garrulous and ingratiating personality. George Rogers Clark was Edward Hand's foil, and they would clash bitterly.

By December 1777, Kentucky consisted of only three settlements— Harrodsburg with sixty-five armed men, Boonesborough with twenty-two, and Logan's with fifteen. Colonel John Bowman sent an urgent message to General Hand that Kentucky teetered on the brink of collapse after a series of Indian attacks: "They have left us almost without horses sufficient to supply the stations, as we our obliged to get all our provisions out of the woods. Our corn the Indians have burned . . . At this time we have not more than two months bread—near 200 women & children . . . are left desolate, widows with children destitute of necessary children." He asked for an emergency shipment of corn to tide them over until the next year. Hand would have to deny that request; he had nothing to spare.[11] The attacks were so terrifying and destructive that Clark "feared the settlers would consider making peace with Detroit and suffer themselves and families to be carried off. Their distress may be easily conceived from our situation; ye they remained firm in the hope of relief, which they received by the arrival of a company of men under Colonel John Bowman on the second of September."[12]

Clark's vision had expanded during that long, bloody, terrifying summer of 1777: "The whole of my time when not thus employed was devoted to reflecting upon things in general: particularly whether or not it accorded with the interest of the United States to support Kentucky. This led me to a long train of thinking, the result of which was to lay aside every private view and engage seriously in the war, having the interest and the welfare of the public my only concern until the fate of the continent could be known; divesting myself of prejudice and partiality in favor of any particular parts of the country, I determined to pursue what I considered to be the interest of the whole."[13] In sum, it was around that time that being an American may have edged ahead of being a Virginian in how George Rogers Clark saw himself.

Tension constantly gnawed away in the guts and minds of Clark and other pioneers that at any second war cries and gunshots could shatter the air. Reasoning that the danger was sporadic rather than constant did little to ease that tension. Safety was uncertain even with scouts constantly prowling the forests and with lookouts posted at the settlements and beside the cornfields and livestock pastures. After a few weeks of peace, Clark recorded a terse entry in his diary for August 5, 1777: "Surrounded ten or twelve Indians near the fort—killed three and wounded others; the plunder was sold for upwards of seventy pounds."[14] Unfortunately, Clark neither clearly states whether he led the force that achieved the rare feat of ambushing a war party nor specifies how many men were in the patrol.

All along, Clark dispatched scouts to spot any approaching raiding parties and, ideally, to find out the enemy's plans. None of his scouts was more skilled, daring, or lucky than Simon Kenton. Even then, Kenton was well on his way to becoming a frontier legend. He commanded near awe not just from his exploits; he was well over six feet tall, and his body and limbs were tautly muscled. In 1771, at the age of sixteen, he had fled his Virginia home to the wilderness after mistakenly believing he had killed a rival over the affections of a local lass. By the time he learned the truth, he felt so at home in the Ohio valley frontier and was such a master of woodlore that he had no desire to return. Kenton had been a professional scout since Dunmore's War and had warned the settlers of numerous would-be ambushes or raids. During an attack on Boonesborough, he saved Daniel Boone's life, who fell when a bullet struck his foot, by hoisting him over his shoulder and dashing toward the fort.

Sending out scouts was standard frontier procedure. What was uncommon was for a commander to run a spy network. George Rogers Clark proved to be as able a spymaster as he was a fighter. He had at least five informants in the Illinois country: Thomas Bentley, Daniel Murray, Richard McCarty, Richard Winston, and Hypolite des Ruisseaux. Of them, Bentley was the best placed since he was among Kaskaskia's most prosperous merchants, had married into a prominent local French family, and worked closely with British authorities. Murray was also a leading merchant who counted Bentley among his friends and business associates. McCarty lived in Cahokia, fifty miles north of Kaskaskia and across the river from Saint Louis. Winston was a business associate of George Morgan and would later accept a captain's commission in the Virginia militia from Clark. Ruisseaux is the least documented of the five, but would later confess to Lieutenant Colonel Hamilton that "he had intimation of the design of the Americans."[15]

How Clark wove his web of spies remains a mystery. No revealing documents survive and most likely never existed. Clark himself would not set foot in Kaskaskia until July 4, 1778. The most likely explanation is that he met one of those men or their agents either in Kentucky or at some point along the Ohio River from Pittsburgh on down, quickly assessed that man's patriot leanings, and sent him back to recruit a spy network. That may have happened in 1776 when Thomas Bentley dispatched a trading party to Kentucky. The next step in nurturing those assets occurred after Lieutenant Linn, his forty-three men, and their barges fill with gunpowder reached the mouth of the Ohio River on March 3, 1777. Awaiting them was Bentley. As his expedition approached that confluence, Linn sent word to Bentley for the rendezvous by powerful paddlers in a dugout canoe. The meeting was ostensibly to trade goods, although intelligence was the crucial transaction. Linn would later pass on what he learned to Clark. The British official in Illinois, Philippe de Rastel, chevalier de Rocheblave, heard of that meeting and accused Bentley of being a rebel spy and selling war supplies to the Americans; Bentley would eventually be incarcerated on those charges.[16]

A parallel channel was with George Morgan, Congress's Indian agent for the trans-Allegheny West. For five years before the war, he had lived in Illinois as the trade and land agent for the Philadelphia firm of Baynton, Wharton, and Morgan. During that time, he employed Richard Winston and other locals, and continued to correspond with them after the war erupted. Though the surviving letters reveal no direct appeal or exchange of critical information, any secret message that passed between Morgan and Winston were likely either verbal or burned after reading. Clark probably did not directly tap that channel. No extant letters exist between Clark and Morgan, and it is unlikely they would have conspired together given the rivalry between their respective states of Virginia and Pennsylvania. Patrick Henry, however, did correspond with Morgan and quite likely was the linchpin between Morgan's assets and Clark's ambitions.[17]

What induced those American transplants in Illinois secretly to side with the rebel cause and thus betray their king? As with all other American-born British subjects, the motives of each were undoubtedly complex. Yet one appeared dominant. Factions splintered Illinois's population. The largest was between the original French inhabitants and the American newcomers. Trade followed the flag. In 1763, following its victory in the Seven Years' war, Britain took title to France's empire east of the Mississippi River. American traders soon arrived with superior quality and lower-priced goods to sell to the French and Indians alike, and swiftly cornered the market. The French naturally resented that intrusion and did what they could to resist the American carpetbaggers. The power balance between the factions shifted toward the French in 1772, when the British garrison at Fort Gage was withdrawn and Rocheblave replaced Captain Hugh Lord as the local magistrate. Rocheblave blatantly favored the French and persecuted the Americans until Bentley, Murray, and Winston petitioned Carleton for his recall.[18] Carleton ignored that plea, and conditions for the American merchants worsened. Clark exploited those animosities both before and after his invasion.

How would Clark use those assets? He mulled several options of which one loomed above the rest. Although he was primarily concerned about the immediate Indian threat just north of the Ohio River, he conceived a plan to outflank those tribes by striking British posts in the Wabash and Mississippi valleys. His spies in the Illinois country would be instrumental in realizing that ambition. But he had to reopen contact with them and get the latest word on troop strengths and popular sentiments.

For that mission, he had two outstanding volunteers. Benjamin Linn,

William Linn's brother, had spent half a dozen years in the Ohio valley, with four years among the Shawnee, Delaware, Miami, and Kickapoo tribes, and spoke their dialects of Algonquin. During that time, he married a white woman who had been held captive for six years. Less is known about Clark's other spy, Samuel Moore, except that he too had spent years in the region and was an able frontiersman.

Linn and Moore operated undercover as hunters and carried enough beaver and other pelts to back that claim. They followed the Salt River to the Ohio River, where they stole a canoe and paddled downstream. They landed near the confluence with the Mississippi, and headed north to Kaskaskia, the southernmost settlement in the Illinois country. Along the way, a third man joined them, but his name was not recorded.

The men initially roused little attention when they strode into Kaskaskia. Stray hunters frequently if sporadically appeared with skins to barter and powder horns and shot bags to replenish. But suspicions soon arose. Linn and Moore both sported white hats, which were known to be popular in Kentucky. Much more damning, one of Clark's spies decided to play a double game. McCarty had second thoughts about working for the Americans. He revealed Linn and Moore as spies in a letter to his friend John Askin, a Detroit merchant who was then plying his trade at Fort Michilimackinac. That letter took months to reach Askin, but when he received it he promptly informed Major Arent Sylvester de Peyster, the fort's commander. De Peyster thought little of the accusations. He did not bother to inform Rocheblave, Kaskaskia's magistrate. Had he done so, Linn and Moore would have been long gone by the time that word arrived. McCarty counted on that time lag and perhaps de Peyster's indifference. He wanted the American spies to get back to Clark and count him among their most valuable informants. Thus did McCarty hope to solidly plant a foot in each camp and reap the rewards for his collaboration no matter who eventually controlled Illinois.[19]

Shortly after reaching Kaskaskia, Linn and Moore contacted Murray, who, on May 25, sent word to Bentley in Cahokia that "the hunters you write of there is three of them, one of which was here before, his name Benj Lynn but they bring no news that I can here of worth your hearing."[20] After quizzing their hosts on the array of political and military questions, Linn and Moore slipped away for the long trek back to the Kentucky settlements.

They got out just in time. The British arrested Bentley on charges of espionage and took him to Montreal for trial. Did McCarty tip off the authorities about Bentley? In doing so, he would at once have eliminated a rival and further ingratiated himself with the crown. The authorities kept Bentley in prison even though they lacked enough evidence to convict him.

Linn and Moore reached Harrodsburg on June 22. Clark's excitement grew as he debriefed them. Kaskaskia was undefended by British regulars. The settlers were mostly French who were increasingly restive under British rule. The militiamen were poorly armed, trained, and motivated. The fort was in ruins. The fort's cannons were useless without gunners to fire them. In sum, the Illinois country was ripe for the plucking. The only trouble was that Clark lacked the men and supplies to reap that harvest.

The only chance Clark had of winning support for his plan depended on his ability to make a direct and convincing appeal to Virginia's governor and his key advisors. However, that effort would have to wait another three months as he supervised Kentucky's defense until early autumn. He intended to set off on September 30, but the horses wandered off, and it took a couple of frustrating days to find them.[21] It was not until the first of October that he departed Harrodsburg with twenty-two other settlers who were fleeing Kentucky's violence. At Logan's Station, other refugees joined them, swelling their numbers to seventy-six. The refugees suffered no Indian attack along the way, only the daily exhaustion of trekking the rutted trail. Provisions were plentiful enough. Those with farms had harvested their crops before they left, and they prodded herds of livestock before them. So they daily devoured johnnycakes, supplemented sporadically by the deer or buffalo that hunters managed to kill, or one of the slaughtered cattle. In late October, three days of rain turned the trail into a quagmire and their journey into a sloppy crawl. After crossing the Cumberland Gap, the party began to diminish as families dispersed to their previous homes or to new ones that would be far safer than what they had left behind in Kentucky. Along the way, both Clark and his horse needed reshodding. His horse threw a shoe that had to be nailed back, and in Charlottesville Clark replaced his worn out moccasins with a new pair of shoes.

Clark joyfully entered his family's home at ten o'clock on the evening of the first of November 1777. He tarried for two days before heading on to Williamsburg, where he would present his plan to the government. It was a two-day ride to the capital. He spent the night at the home of his sister Ann and her husband, Owen Gwathmey. In Williamsburg, Clark felt lucky and bought a lottery ticket for three pounds sterling, a large sum. While the ticket did not pay off, his efforts at the capital would result in extraordinary changes in his own life and in that of his nation.

CHAPTER 7

The Bloodless Conquest

As some Indian tribes . . . have lately, without any provocation, massacred many of the Inhabitants upon the Frontiers of this Commonwealth, in the most cruel and barbarous Manner . . . it is intended to
revenge the Injury and punish the Aggressors by carrying the War into
their own territory.

Virginia's Executive Council

We left our little island and running about a mile up the river in order
to gain the main channel we shot the Falls at the very moment the sun
was under a great eclipse, which caused various conjectures on the
part of the superstitious among us.

George Rogers Clark

George Rogers Clark was a master of politics during the war.[1] He knew
how to turn hearts, minds, and pocketbooks in his favor with network-
ing and carefully crafted arguments that judiciously mingled reason and
emotion. Clark's first overt political task in Williamsburg was not to get a
future campaign approved but to get past expenses reimbursed. On November 7, he presented a bill for Kentucky's defense to the board of auditors and
asked for compensation. The board refused to do so without the executive

council's consent; that body had dismissed for the day. The next day the council accepted the expenses and had the auditors settle the account. Clark's next step was to get approval for his own expenses on Kentucky's behalf. That also took two days of meeting with the auditors the first day and the council the next. He was awarded the extraordinary sum of £726.

Clark supplemented those formal meetings by buttonholing many of Virginia's political elite for intense but discrete talks in taverns and drawing rooms. It was then that he "propos'd the plan to a few Gentlemen, they communicated it to the Governor."[2] The governor was then out of town, so Clark headed back for another sojourn with his parents, this time for two weeks, before returning to Williamsburg.

Clark formally presented his plan to Governor Patrick Henry and the executive council of Thomas Jefferson, George Mason, and George Wythe on December 10, 1777. It was not the idea but the myriad of details that was new to them. Clark carefully explained the strategic, economic, and psychological value of capturing the Illinois country: "The principal inhabitants are entirely against the American cause, and look on us as notorious rebels that ought to be subdued . . . but I don't doubt but after being acquainted with the cause they would become good friends to it . . . If it was in our possession it would distress the garrison at Detroit for provisions, it would flight the command of the two great rivers into our hands, which would enable us to get supplies from the Spaniards, and carry on trade with the Indians . . . I am sensible that the case stands thus—that [we must] either take the town of [Kaskaskia], or . . . send an army against the Indians on Wabash, which will cost ten times as much, and not be of half the service."[3]

Clark's proposal could not have come at a more opportune moment. Not only had the Americans defeated Britain's three-pronged campaign to seize Albany and split New England from the other states, but the army commanded by General Horatio Gates had twice defeated the British army led by General John Burgoyne and then had forced him to surrender 5,500 troops at Saratoga on October 17, 1777. It made perfect sense to follow up that decisive victory with an offensive against a bastion of British power in the Ohio valley.

Governor Henry and his council summoned Clark on January 2, 1778, and declared that they had enthusiastically embraced his plan. They were "determined . . . to be put [it] in Execution as soon as a Bill could be passed to enable the Governor to order it."[4] That would take another a few weeks to arrange. They then asked Clark to command the expedition.

Clark had been politically astute enough to present his plan without an ambition to lead it. In doing so, he once again revealed his mastery of psychology, although there may have been as much genuine modesty as design in that strategy:

> I resolv'd to pursue my other Plans, But being desired by the Governour to stay some time in Town, I wated with impatience; he I suppose believing that I wanted the Command, and was determined to give it to me; But it was far from my Inclination at that time. I was Summoned to attend the Council Board; the instructions and necessary papers was ready for putting in the name of the Person to Command: I believe they expected me to selicit for it, but I resolved not to do [so] . . . However I excepted it after being told the Command of this little Army was designed for me. I then got every request granted and fully impowered to raise as many Men as I could not exceeding a certain number.[5]

That "certain number" was 350 men organized into seven 50-man companies. Clark's recruiting was largely restricted to the upper Ohio and Holston River valleys. He was forbidden to recruit east of the mountains for fear that he might "throw those Counties into great Confusion" by competing with the Continental army for recruits.[6]

Other than that restraint, the governor and council granted Clark broad strategic powers. The campaign's first objective would be Kaskaskia, which would be used as a base of operations for attacks on "the Enemy Settlements above or across, as you may find it proper."[7] Vengeance was an explicit objective: "As some Indian tribes . . . have lately, without any provocation, massacred many of the Inhabitants upon the Frontiers of this Commonwealth, in the most cruel and barbarous Manner . . . it is intended to revenge the Injury and punish the Aggressors by carrying the War into their own territory."[8] As for hearts and minds, Clark was to "show humanity to such British Subjects and other persons that fall into your hands. If the white Inhabitants . . . will give undoubted Evidence of their detachment to this State . . . Let them be treated as fellow Citizens & their person &

property duly secured . . . But if these people will not accede to these rea-
sonable Demands, they must feel the miseries of War."[9]

Secrecy was among the most crucial elements for a victorious campaign. Clark was instructed "to take special care to keep the true destination
of your force secret. Its success depends upon this." The governor also ordered that Clark's two spies to the Illinois country, William Linn and Samuel Moore, be "secured" until the campaign was safely under way. A cover
story was concocted. Governor Henry issued a public order that Clark was
recruiting "Seven companies . . . to act as Militia [in] Kentucky & there to
obey such orders & Directions as you shall give them."[10]

To help facilitate all those ends and means, Henry promoted Clark to
lieutenant colonel in the Virginia militia. There was only one catch. Somehow Clark would have to muster and lead his ambitious campaign on a
shoestring budget of £1,200. He could lure recruits with a promise of 300
acres for each volunteer private, with more land distributed proportionally
to each higher rank.[11] Although he could not know it at the time, that promise would ensnare him in one of his life's most acrimonious, prolonged, and
debilitating conflicts.

Clark's campaign would not be the year's first to penetrate the Mississippi
River valley. One reason why his proposal won such swift and enthusiastic
approval was that it appeared to fit with another mission in that region that
Congress had already launched.

James Willing was a daring, charismatic leader in the mold of George
Rogers Clark. His ill-concealed and overweening greed, rashness, and pom-
posity, however, ultimately provoked a backlash that would destroy most of
what he and his men initially gained, thus complicating American diplomacy
and Clark's tenuous grip on Illinois. Willing was the scion of a rich Philadelphia mercantile family. In 1772, he headed west in search of adventure and
easy money. He ended up in Natchez, West Florida, where over a five-year
trajectory he made and lost a fortune on gambling, women, and risky speculations. Atop his financial losses, he alienated most of the town's elite that he
had at first beguiled. In 1777, penniless and humiliated, he hurried back to
Philadelphia, animated by a scheme designed at once to reap vengeance and
a fortune from the Natchez elite who had scorned his company while eagerly

lightening his purse. It was raw military power that eventually let him realize that scheme first at Natchez then across the rest of West Florida.[12]

West Florida was a rich economic and strategic prize. Its 5,000 British subjects were split into two clusters of settlements, with around 2,500 whites and 600 slaves along the Mississippi River's eastern bank, mostly around Natchez and Baton Rouge, and around 1,000 whites and 600 slaves along the Gulf, mostly around Mobile and Pensacola. The plantations along the river bottoms produced an array of crops, but made the most money from indigo plants and barrel staves. Mobile and especially Pensacola were dynamic trading centers whose merchants enriched themselves buying and selling with both foreign customers and the Creek, Choctaw, Chickasaw, and Cherokee villages along the trails radiating from those ports. That existing economy was of enormous value in itself. But of incalculable potential future value would be to link the Ohio and Tennessee valley settlements to the sea via the Mississippi River. West Florida was lightly defended. A fortress manned by a hundred regulars guarded the bay leading to Pensacola, the capital. The other large towns had only dilapidated stockades within which militias could muster. Given all that, Willing's campaign against West Florida was far more strategically important and militarily challenging than Clark's against Illinois. Yet the expeditions were linked with the success of one aiding the other.[13]

Congress approved and amended Willing's plan—after taking the Mississippi settlements, he was to journey down to New Orleans, purchase on credit vitally needed supplies, and send them back. Willing received a captain's commission, troops, and supplies.[14] On January 11, 1778, he and twenty-six men packed into a large keelboat dubbed "The Rattletrap" and set off from Pittsburgh's landing. After six weeks of hard rowing, they surged ashore at Natchez and forced the inhabitants to take neutrality oaths. Within a few days, the party reembarked and continued down the Mississippi, looting Loyalist plantations and capturing Loyalist boats along the way. Upon reaching New Orleans, Willing and his men would prove to be diplomatic wild cards for America's cause and Clark's efforts far to the north.

Meanwhile, Clark was organizing his own expedition. He issued his first commission on January 3, the day after receiving authorization. He appointed William Smith a major and gave him £150 in bounty money and related expenses for his promise to recruit four fifty-man companies in the Holston River settlements and meet him at some as yet undetermined point on the Ohio River in early summer. Clark had first met Smith in Kentucky in 1775 and clearly reckoned him a fine frontiersman and leader. Armed with money, commissions, and other documents, Clark rode out of Williamsburg on January 4. He tarried a week with his parents before heading on toward Pittsburgh. Along the way, he issued captain's commissions to Leonard Helm, Joseph Bowman, and William Harrod, the brother of James, with each to recruit a company. Clark reached Fort Pitt on February 10.[15]

After three years of war, recruits were tough to drum up. Nowhere did Clark and his officers face greater resistance than in the upper Ohio River region, which Pennsylvania claimed as its own territory. Pennsylvania authorities bitterly resented Virginians like Clark who poached armed men for their own state's ambitions or needs, and they did everything possible to stymie those efforts. Clark angrily recalled the "Conduct of many leading Men in the fronteers, that had like to have put an end to the enterprise . . . and through a spirit of obstinancy they combined and did every thing that lay in their power to stop the Men that had Enlisted, and set the whole Fronteer in an uproar, even condescended to harbor and protect those that Deserted. I found my case desperate, the longer I remained the worse it was."[16]

Major Smith initially reported success in recruiting his two hundred men in four companies in the Holston River region. But then word arrived that a Shawnee war party had captured Daniel Boone and twenty-six of his men at a salt lick in northern Kentucky. That defeat was a terrible blow to the region's defense. Every man was now needed in Kentucky itself. The local leaders forced Smith to divert his recruits to that end. Unfortunately, Clark did not receive the latter message until he acted on the first and was far down the Ohio. As a result, his campaign would have less than half the authorized number of troops.[17]

Although undermanned, Clark's expedition was relatively well equipped. The same day that Governor Henry handed his instructions to Clark, he wrote General Edward Hand, who commanded the upper Ohio region from his headquarters at Fort Pitt. Henry's letter merely hinted at Clark's mission, revealing only that its "benefits will be many. A good understanding with [New] Orleans is a desirable object." To that end, Henry instructed

Hand "to give every assistance which [Clark] . . . may want" and promised that "every other thing furnished by you will be amply compensated by the Major's success." Hand did what he could to provide boats, arms, munitions, provisions, and uniforms for what became known as the Illinois regiment.[18]

What would the Illinois regiment have looked like? The appearance varied from day to day on campaign and week to week in garrison. One thing is certain. There was never a time when the regiment was uniformly clothed or armed. While most of the men carried rifles, the rest either brought or were issued much less accurate smoothbore muskets. Most muskets were seventy-five-caliber British issues, but, after taking Illinois, Clark bought twenty-nine Spanish muskets. As for ammunition, some had leather cartridge boxes, while others made do with powder horns and shot bags. The regiment's "uniform" also varied. In garrison, the men ideally were clothed in a "parade" uniform that included wool breeches and a waistcoat, most likely white; a white or checkered linen shirt; gartered knee-socks; hard, low-heeled shoes, a blue wool "regimental" or long swallow-tailed coat with a white inner lining whose "turn-backs" or "facings" of the coat's underside was exposed and buttoned down the chest and tails; and most likely a tricorne. But quite likely the supply of uniforms fell ever further behind demand, and ever more new recruits wore their eclectic hunter or civilian dress while the uniforms of those lucky enough to get them appeared increasingly threadbare and patched. On campaign, Clark "left behind all of our baggage except enough to equip the men after the Indian fashion," which meant in summer hunting frocks, breech-cloths, leggings, moccasins, and head scarves. In addition, each soldier stuffed items like a tin cup, wooden bowl, fork, extra clothing, flints, and rations in a haversack or large strapped pouch with a buttoned down flap; his blanket was rolled and tied either in a long horseshoe that curved around his body or a short thick roll tied with a strap or tumpline.[19]

By the time Clark set off downstream from Fort Pitt on May 12, he led a couple of hundred men. The flotilla made brief stops at Fort Fincastle at Wheeling and Fort Randolph at the Kanawha River mouth to pick up supplies and possibly more recruits. Joining the expedition for a stretch was Colonel David Rogers, heading all the way to New Orleans with twenty-eight troops to procure vital supplies, and Captain James O'Hara, leading a few troops and a score of families to Kentucky.

The first tough choice Clark faced on the campaign came at Fort Randolph. Captain Matthew Arbuckle, the commander, "informed us that 250 Indians had warmly attacked his post the day before and wounded a few of his men. The Indians had then directed their course to the settlements of the Greenbrier and Captain Arbuckle had sent off an express to warm the settlers. He thought the forces I had, with the addition of part of the garrison, could in all probability overtake the Indians and inflict a total rout upon them." While Clark found the "prospect . . . flattering," he finally decided against it, reasoning that "the uncertainty of obtaining the advantage over the enemy, the loss of time and perhaps a number of the men . . . would cause the destruction of the enterprise upon which I had embarked."[20]

Another strategic choice loomed where the Kentucky River mingled its waters with the Ohio River. Clark originally intended to build a fort there. Upon reflection, he reckoned that the site was too far from his campaign's objectives, so he continued downstream. On May 27, his expedition reached a seven-acre island at the head of the Falls of the Ohio. He disembarked the soldiers and settlers, and set them to work clearing the land, erecting a fort, and planting corn. He appropriately named that refuge Corn Island. There he was reinforced by Captain John Montgomery, who led an understrength company of Kentuckians.

Clark chose Corn Island not just to protect his force from the enemy but also to prevent his men from deserting. He was well aware that morale was dismal, especially in Lieutenant Thomas Hutchins's company. Clark's men grumbled at their fort's remote location far from the stretch of the Ohio River where most war parties passed over to attack the Kentucky settlements. Many of those volunteers regretted the enthusiasm with which they had signed up and the subsequent dangers, fatigue, and drudgery that they had to endure. Most were away from home for the first time and longed for their loved ones and the security of their homes. Morale plummeted even further when word arrived that neither would Major Smith and his couple of hundred men from the Holston River region be coming nor would the Kentucky settlements provide anything more than a small contingent from Harrodsburg. But the worst blow of all was when Clark revealed their mission. Many of the men protested that they had enlisted to defend Kentucky, not to journey to faraway Illinois where they would probably be wiped out by hordes of savages and redcoats.[21]

Among Hutchins's duties was to bolster his men's spirits. Instead, he was just as disillusioned and homesick as the worst of them. The men found a shallow stretch of the river that they could wade from Corn Island to the Kentucky shore. Should they take it? The penalty for desertion was execution. They spent days whispering whether to risk death by desertion now or in the battles to come. Clark's announcement that the expedition was bound for Illinois decided the question. That night Hutchins and a score or so others swiftly waded to the far shore and disappeared into the wilderness. They reasoned that Clark would not delay his expedition to pursue them.

The desertion was detected just around dawn. Roused out of a sound sleep, Clark "was undetermined for a few moments what to do."[22] Should he put off his campaign while he tried to round up the deserters? The longer that task took, the greater the chance that Indians would detect their presence and spread the word. Yet tolerating such a mass desertion would encourage disgruntled others to slip away.

Clark led a pursuit that caught up to the deserters about twenty miles beyond Corn Island on the trail to the settlements. Eight were nabbed, but Hutchins and the others evaded capture and reached Harrodsburg. Those caught were not executed, but were whipped and distributed among the companies. Those who got away suffered the scorn of other settlers for their cowardice. Clark split his remaining 178 men among four companies commanded by Captains Bowman, Helm, Harrod, and John Montgomery.[23] Finally, there were the score of so of settlers on Corn Island, who would later move to the mainland and found a settlement to be called Louisville.

Clark was determined that his campaign would open with joy and enthusiasm rather than regret and fear. On the morning of June 24, 1778, he tapped a rum keg to celebrate the launch of the adventure. He then herded his troops onto the boats, double-manned the oars, and then "we left our little island and running about a mile up the river in order to gain the main channel, we shot the Falls at the very moment the sun was under a great eclipse, which caused various conjectures on the part of the superstitious among us." The Falls were a series of rapids that dropped twenty-six feet over two miles. Somehow they managed to shoot those rapids without a loss despite their blurred faculties. Cheering them from Corn Island was a contingent of Kentucky militia who headed back to the settlements as soon as the expedition was out of sight.[24]

Hard rowing and a swift current brought the troops to the Tennessee River mouth in four days. Just as they were about to set forth from their camp on a nearby island, a party of hunters in a dugout appeared laboriously paddling upriver. Clark dispatched troops in boats to intercept and escort the party to shore. The strangers were Americans who had spent years hunting in the region. They not only freely gave information about Kaskaskia that they had recently left but also volunteered to join the expedition. Their most disturbing insight was that if the French at Kaskaskia were "to get timely notice of us they would collect and give us a warm Reception." "Warm" meant hostile rather than cheerful. In other words, the Americans most likely would have to fight for the town. British propaganda had caused the French "to entertain horrible ideas of the barbarity of the rebels, especially of the Virginians. If, however, we could surprise the place, [the hunters] had no doubt of our ability to master it at pleasure."[25]

Clark recognized that he could turn such lurid British propaganda against its perpetrators: "No part of their information pleased me more than that concerning the inhabitants believing us to be more savage than their neighbors, the Indians. I resolved to make capital of this should I be fortunate enough to gain control over them, since I considered that the greater shock I could give them in the beginning the more appreciative would they be later of my lenity, and the more valuable as friends. This I conceived to accord with human nature as I had observed it in many instances."[26] Clark had mastered the mingled arts of politics, psychology, and warfare.

If Clark ever had a notion of rowing down to the mouth of the Ohio and then up the Mississippi's powerful current to Kaskaskia, he abandoned it then. Traffic was frequent on the Mississippi, hunters ranged the shores, and eventually the first cabins would appear in clearings. Runners would warn Governor Rocheblave of the approaching expedition long before it could reach its target. Instead, Clark reembarked his men for a rapid row downriver to the ruins of Fort Massac, one of the former French empire's more remote posts. There Clark had the boats pulled up a shallow creek and hidden. From there, the men would trek the eighty-mile trail through thick forests and tall grass prairies to Kaskaskia. One of the hunters said he knew the way and would lead them there.

Getting to Kaskaskia overland without being detected would be only slightly less daunting than trying to do so up the Mississippi River. White and Indian hunters ranged the woods. It would be close to a miracle if the expedition were not spotted en route, and the closer they got to the settlements the less likely they would remain unnoticed.

As the troops drew supplies for their trek, a lone man in a dugout appeared upriver. Once again Clark ordered a contingent to scramble into a boat and intercept the passerby. That man turned out to be none other than William Linn, who was carrying electrifying news. The United States and France had signed treaties of alliance and trade on February 6, 1778! The news gave Clark a trump card for the loyalties of the French inhabitants of Illinois, if they believed him. That letter had reached Corn Island the day after the expedition had set forth. Although William Linn had remained behind with the settlers, he had volunteered to carry that crucial news to Clark's party. An ecstatic and grateful Clark rewarded Linn by naming him a captain.[27]

The Americans had another potential asset in wooing the Illinois inhabitants. The acting lieutenant governor of Illinois was neither British nor Canadian. Philippe Francois Rastel, Sieur de Rocheblave was a proud French nobleman who had fought the British at Fontenoy and the Monongahela, and had commanded Fort Massac. Although his official duties were light, the burden of serving the English king weighed heavily on Rocheblave. Keeping the local Indians loyal required frequent councils in which numerous gifts were distributed. He was paying for the English king's diplomacy from his own pocket and a waning hope of ever being compensated. Yet Canada's governor Carleton felt that Rocheblave was not trying hard enough. In one letter, he wondered whether "you have fully explored all possibilities to engage the Ohio Indians to your aid. You are to execute, as quickly as possible, the necessary orders to reassemble the militia under your authority."[28]

The allegiance of Rocheblave and other community leaders could go either way. More often than not, gut emotions like greed and fear trumped more lofty concepts like duty or law in any decision. Having first settled the Illinois region, the French deeply resented the British parvenus, who squeezed into the local communities and markets after the 1763 Treaty of Paris ceded France's empire east of the Mississippi River to Britain. The British in turn disdained the French and especially hated Rocheblave for his corruption and favoritism toward his community. They vainly petitioned

Canada's governor for his removal. American spy Thomas Bentley condemned Rocheblave as completely untrustworthy, "having taken the Oaths of Allegiance to . . . France, Spain, & Great Britain; such a man would not . . . hesitate on the arrival of the Americans to enlist himself under their banner & even to be one of the first that would do so."[29]

Rocheblave was not in Kaskaskia when Clark led his men from Fort Massac's ruins. He was enjoying a visit with his Spanish counterpart at Saint Genevieve, a dozen miles upriver on the western shore in the province of Louisiana. He would get back to Kaskaskia on the afternoon of July 4, just as Clark and his men were nearing the settlement. Weary from his journey, Rocheblave retired early that evening. He would get a very rude awakening later that night.

Clark and his men were exhausted and famished when they finally reached Kaskaskia's outskirts, six days after setting out. Each man could stuff only so much food in his haversack, and he soon devoured that. Fortunately, the trail passed through many a patch of blackberries, raspberries, and dewberries, and the men would break ranks to pluck the fruit into their mouths until the bushes were stripped bare. Yet the greatest challenge was not getting enough to eat. On the third day, they emerged from the forest into a wide prairie where the trail disappeared. John Saunders, the guide, was utterly baffled over which way to head.

Clark feared the worst, that Saunders had deliberately led them astray to the prairie where they would soon be spotted and word rushed to Kaskaskia. "I never in my life felt such a flow of Rage," Clark recalled, "to be wandering a Country where every nation of Indians could raise three or four times our number" and the "certain loss of our enterprise by the Enemie's getting timely notice." Clark threatened to execute the guide if he did not find the proper route by that evening. Saunders begged for a chance to scout ahead and find the proper trail. That appeal only enflamed Clark's suspicions. Whether Saunders was genuinely confused or trying to confuse the Americans, he "in two hours got within his knowledge."[30]

All the stress and anxieties of leading a military campaign through enemy territory did not blind Clark to the natural wonders surrounding him. His enthusiasm for Illinois matched his earlier lyricism for Kentucky. He later described the region as "more Beautiful that any Idea I could have formed of a Country almost in a state of Nature, everything you behold is an Additional Beauty. On the River you'll find the finest Lands the Sun ever shone on. In the high Country you will find a Variety of Poor & Rich Lands with large Meadows extending beyond the reach of your Eyes Variagated with groves of Trees appearing like Islands in the Seas covered with Buff[a]loes and other Game."[31]

On the evening of July 4, 1778, Clark's men were crouched in the woods on the south side of the Kaskaskia River, with the town on the far side. Apparently, the Americans had not been detected. The town emitted no sounds of alarm or muster for an attack. But was that just a ruse to entice the invaders into a trap?

The colonel and his men looked like brigands rather than soldiers. By one account, Clark was "in shirt and breeches, barefooted and bare of limb, with his bedding, provisions, and gun on his shoulder. The troops wore nothing but breeches, powder horn, gun, and knapsack."[32] Days on the trail left them unshaven, filthy, and emaciated. Their appearance alone would terrify the people they intended to subdue.

Scouts brought before Clark a farmer, Nicolas La Chanse, who provided answers to crucial questions. The farmer revealed that in Kaskaskia there was "some suspicion of being attacked," that Rocheblave "had made some preparations" and was "keeping out spies," and that "a few Days before the people were under arms but had concluded that the cause of the alarm was without foundation."[33] Once again, fortune sided with Clark and his men. That false alarm had most likely lulled most of the inhabitants into a deceptive sense of security.

The next question was how to cross a river too deep for wading. Clark sent out scouts along the riverbank to search for boats. Eventually, several were found and rowed to La Chanse's farm three-quarters of a mile upstream of the town. It then took two hours to ferry the men across. Each minute likely seemed like an eternity with each splash of oars, rattle of equipment, or curse of pain or anger emitting from the boats. Clark must have glanced frequently at the dark, silent town, fearing that at any moment excited hollers or the church bell would break the silence, and an armed horde would emerge. At some point, strange sounds did erupt from a distant part of Kaskaskia. Clark demanded an explanation from the farmer. The laconic reply was that he supposed it "was Negroes at a dance."[34]

Once everyone was across, Clark split his command into three groups, with one to seize Fort Gage, another to take the town, and the third to guard the outskirts and ensure that no one escaped to carry word of the attack. Clark led the column that gingerly made its way through the dark to the fort. The men tensed as they crept closer to the dark mass, expecting any moment a challenge and musket shot. But no one was on duty. Clark and his men filed through the gate. One of the hunters pointed out Rocheblave's house. After positioning men around Fort Gage's ramparts, Clark and several others barged into the governor's residence. They startled the governor and his wife in bed. Rocheblave was defiant rather than intimidated. He looked Clark in the eye and said, "I am in your hands, do with me what you wish, the fear of death will not make me change my way of thinking. The King of Great Britain is my Prince. He has nourished me and I have sworn fidelity to him."[35]

At this point, chivalry took precedence over security. Feeling a bit sheepish at his intrusion, Clark apologized and assured the couple that no one would be harmed. He then left the wife alone and escorted her husband downstairs. Unfortunately, in doing so, Clark missed getting his hands on an intelligence windfall. The governor kept his documents in his bedroom. His wife had the good sense to burn them during the night.

Once the fort and governor were secured, Clark gave a signal, and those troops that had scattered through the town screamed war whoops and banged on doors. A few of Clark's men who spoke French shouted explanations that the Americans had taken over the town and that the people were to remain inside their homes until further notice. Only one man called out for his compatriots to resist the Americans, but the others hushed Joseph Brazeau for fear of provoking unnecessary death and destruction.

Through surprise, speed, and audacity, Clark and his men had captured Kaskaskia without firing a shot or harming anything other than perhaps pride. But once that "shock and awe" wore off, how could 180 or so men possibly hold Kaskaskia let alone capture Cahokia and Vincennes, the Illinois country's two other major towns? Diplomacy backed by arms would prove to be crucial in accomplishing those feats.

CHAPTER 8

War of Words

From the time that my friend Colonel Clark arrived in this place, fraternal harmony has reigned between the people from the United
States and the vassals of his Catholic Majesty.... Colonel Clark's
wisdom and affability have made him generally loved by all who know
him.

Governor Fernando de Leyba

I must confess that I was under some apprehension among such a
number of Devils.

George Rogers Clark

As dawn broke on the morning of July 5, 1778, the exhausted troops
slumped against the houses, triumphant, exhausted, and wary.[1] Having
secured the town, Clark then shifted his psychological strategy. Although
the concepts of good cop–bad cop routine and the Stockholm syndrome
would not be articulated for another two centuries, Clark had already
instinctively mastered them. He had terrorized the population during the
night. Now he would shower them with kindness, liberty, and explanations
of why the Americans had rebelled against the British crown and why the
people of Kaskaskia should join them in that struggle. The ideal result

would be relieved, trusting, and informed people who replied with genuine loyalty.

Clark "sent for all the Principal Men of the Town." The half-dozen village elders trembled when they were ushered before him and his officers. Weeks of rowing down the Ohio followed by a six-day overland trek had rendered the Americans bronzed, bruised, scratched, and dressed in filthy rags. Clark explained, "Having left our extra clothing at the Ohio River, we were almost naked; torn by the bushes and briers, we presented a dirty and savage appearance. So shocked were they that some time elapsed before they ventured to speak."[2]

Their spokesman was Father Pierre Gibault, the town's priest since 1770. It took Gibault a while to quell his own terror. He and the townspeople assumed that the Americans would kill or carry off the men, which was how the Indians made war. He humbly requested that his congregation "be permitted to spend some time in the church to take their leave of each other."[3] With soft words, Clark granted that favor and explained some crucial points. The United States and France were now allies. The Americans would harm no one's life or property. The townspeople were free to go about their business. They were encouraged to elect a magistrate and a militia captain to govern their civil and military affairs. Their only restriction for now was not to leave Kaskaskia.

Clark recalled how he began the process of transforming the town's elite and eventually the population from fearful enemies into faithful allies:

I told them I was sorry they had been taught to harbour so base an opinion of the Americans and their cause: Explain'd the nature of the dispute to them in as clear a light as I was capable . . . and that our Principal was to make those we Reduced free instead of enslaving them as they imagined, that if I could have surety of their Zeal and Attachment to the American Cause, they should immediately enjoy all the privileges of our Government, and their property secured. . . . No sooner had they heard this than Joy sparkled in their Eyes and [they] fell into Transports of Joy that really surprised me. As soon as they were a little moderated they told me that they had always been kept in the dark as to the dispute between America and Britain that they had never heard any thing before but what was prejuditial and tended to insence them against the Americans, that they were now convinced that it was a cause they ought to Espouse.[4]

Psychology alone would most likely not have been sufficient to get the inhabitants to transfer their loyalty from the British to the Americans. The occupation was greatly aided by the facts that most of the inhabitants were of French descent and their former country was now allied with the United States. But ultimately it was the nearly two hundred hardened American frontiersmen that kept Kaskaskia and the region tranquil.

Later that same day, after the priest had gathered his congregation for mass and then dispersed them to their homes, he and his delegation reappeared before Clark. They expressed their deep gratitude for sparing them the horrors of war and blamed Rocheblave for any hard feelings or passive resistance that the Americans might experience. They assured Clark that they would be "the happiest People in the World if they were united with the Americans." Clark recalled triumphantly that this "was the point to which I wished to bring them."[5] He quietly asked them to submit to a loyalty oath. With varying degrees of sincerity, they yielded.

One prominent resident, the fur trader Gabriel Cerré, was away on a prolonged trading trip. The elders told Clark that no one knew the region's tribes and could sway their councils better than Cerré. They also warned Clark that Cerré was treacherous and a die-hard British Loyalist. Clark insisted on searching his home. Cerré's wife blocked him with heated words and an iron poker. Once again, a somewhat chastised Clark stopped short of full security measures. He gave a cursory glance through the rooms but did not search under the bed in which the children were lying frightened.[6]

Having secured Kaskaskia's hearts and minds, Clark took the next step. He asked Father Gibault and several elders to accompany Joseph Bowman and thirty men fifty miles north to Cahokia, the region's second largest town, and gain its people's allegiance. They willingly agreed. Within a few days, Clark got word that Bowman had fulfilled that mission on July 6. The Americans now controlled the Mississippi River strip of Illinois that was little more than a half dozen villages anchored by Kaskaskia and Cahokia. Only one other Illinois town was left to take, but it would be quite a hike to get there.

Vincennes lay on the Wabash River's east bank about 180 miles northeast of Kaskaskia, and was in present-day Indiana. Clark dispatched Simon Kenton, Shadrach Bond, and Elisha Batty "for the purpose of viewing Fort Vincennes." Those men trekked the well-trod trail to Vincennes without being suspected, then cached their rifles, wrapped themselves in blankets, and casually strolled through the town as they carefully noted anything of military value. As if that were not daring or foolhardy enough, they repeated their promenade the next two evenings. While Kenton and Batty headed to the Kentucky settlements, Bond carried word of their exploits and the intelligence they had gleaned back to Kaskaskia. Clark was exultant to learn that Vincennes was just as oblivious to the looming danger as Kaskaskia had been.

Indeed, that region's lieutenant governor, Captain Edward Abbott, was not even present. Although he had served at Vincennes little more than a year, Abbott was a frontier veteran. He had first arrived in the region as an artillery officer with British troops at the end of the French and Indian War. He was appointed an Indian agent in 1775, and lieutenant governor of Vincennes in 1777. With his family, Abbott had departed Vincennes on February 3 and, upon reaching Detroit on March 7, had direly warned Hamilton that his French and Indian charges were ever more poisoned against the British and were becoming "arrogant and troublesome."[7] That view was indeed prescient. The Indians were especially restless. The British purchased their tenuous "loyalty" with gifts. But many Indians "despised" the stinginess of British handouts compared to the generosity of their former French "Great Father," who "never spoke to them without a barnfull of goods."[8]

Upon learning that Clark intended to launch a campaign to take Vincennes, Father Gibault offered a bloodless way to do so. Gibault, Dr. Jean Baptiste Laffont, and several others would journey to Vincennes, explain to both the French settlers and the Indians that France had allied with the United States, and encourage them to shift their allegiance. Clark eagerly agreed to the plan. The delegation departed on July 14. They carried with them an address by Clark explaining the reasons for the American occupation and promising that they would enjoy all the liberties and rights of citizenship.[9]

Not long after that diplomatic mission departed, Gabriel Cerré arrived in Saint Louis from months of trading through the Great Lakes all the way to Quebec and back. He was soon informed that the Americans viewed him as their worst potential enemy in the region for his British loyalty and influence over the tribes, and thus guarded his home and warehouse stocked with supplies. Cerré himself was a keen observer of human nature and knew how to manipulate it. To Clark he wrote a carefully crafted letter in which he defended himself with self-confidence, honor, wit, and respect for the American leader, condemnation of his rivals' scurrilous behavior, and appeals for justice: "According to public rumor my enemies, jealous of the efforts I make to obtain a comfortable mediocrity, have profited from my absence to blacken me and destroy me in the opinion of persons to whom I have not the honor of being known. I am well persuaded that, when my past and future conduct are once known to you, you will render me the justice that is due every good and submissive subject . . . I venture to solicit you, sir, to have the goodness to grant me a passport to return home in order that I may be able to clear myself of the accusations."[10]

Clark replied by rejecting any notion of safe conduct and instead insisted that "if he were innocent of all the allegations against him he would not be afraid to surrender himself."[11] Nonplussed, Cerré had himself rowed across the river. Given the distinct possibility that shackles awaited him, his return appeared courageous to his friends and enemies alike. Yet Cerré was probably anything but white-knuckled during his passage and escort to Clark's headquarters. He believed he knew just how the man he was about to meet would act. Cerré was right. Clark immediately recognized not only his courage, but the falseness of the accusations against him. Cerré had many enemies jealous of the wealth and power he reaped from his ability to sway the Indians and curry favor with British authorities. Those enemies were trying to get the Americans to ruin their worst rival.

Yet for now Clark feigned being a stern and unforgiving avenger. The Americans had been able to find a handful of letters that Rocheblave's wife had not destroyed. Among them was one to Cerré from Hamilton, in which the "Hair-buyer" addressed the trader "with much affection." Cerré explained that at Detroit "he behaved himself as become a subject" but "he defied any man to prove that he ever Incouraged an Indn to war."[12] Clark then summoned Cerré's accusers. Wilting before their formidable rival, they denied any charges against him. Clark declared Cerré innocent. His deft handling of Cerré, and Cerré's of him, appeared to have won Clark another grateful ally.

With the French inhabitants backing him, Clark's next diplomatic offensive was designed to sway the region's tribes to neutrality in the war between America and Britain. He dispatched runners to the villages to send representatives to a grand council at Cahokia. He felt no little trepidation before the meeting: "I must confess that I was under some apprehension among such a number of Devils."[13] His uneasiness was understandable. A mostly brutal, merciless frontier had forged him from childhood to manhood. Yet, unlike most frontier whites, he was no mindless Indian hater. Most of the time when he was conducting diplomacy, he displayed a respect for and understanding of Indian culture.

Once again, Clark had an easy audience. Most delegations came from the local Kaskaskia, Illinois, Peoria, Winnebago, and Potawatomi tribes that were culturally among the least disposed to settle differences with violence. Few of their young men had trod the path of war. Geographically, they were far from that swelling, land-voracious tide of whites spilling over the Appalachian Mountains. For generations, the Indians had lived alongside and often with the French. Those two peoples had shared not just trade and the hunt, but often the marriage bed. So if the French gingerly embraced the Americans, then most Indians would naturally follow. The small contingents from distant more aggressive tribes like the Sauk, Fox, Kickapoo, Ottawa, and Ojibwa tribes would for now critically observe the Long Knives. Later at home in their council houses, they would debate whether to war against or with the Americans, or to await the outcome of the struggle between the thirteen Long Knife tribes and the Great English Father so far away.

Clark typically had already mapped out his strategy in his mind, and, just as typically, that strategy was a bold departure from standard procedures: "I had always been convinced that our general conduct of Indian affairs was wrong. Inviting them to treaties was considered by them in a different manner than we realized; they imputed it to fear on our part, and the giving of valuable presents confirmed them in this opinion. I resolved, therefore, to guard against this."[14]

Clark's assessment was profoundly wrong. Indians viewed gift giving as essential to diplomacy in two ways, one symbolic, the other economic. First, good relations between Indians and whites were usually grounded in familial terms, in which the rich white Great Father or elder brother took care of his children or younger brother. Second, Indians expected ample and prompt payment for their loyalty, services, or land rendered. However he justified it, Clark's stinginess came from necessity—he had no gifts to give, so he had to substitute bluster for generosity to keep the tribes in line. It was a high stake and provocative gamble, but he had no other choice.

Clark began by explaining why the Americans had rebelled against the English king. George III embodied evil exploitation and rapaciousness. The thirteen Long Knife tribes had no choice but to unite in one council house that had declared independence and would fight until they defeated the British. He then offered the Indians a stark choice between war and peace. He asserted, "I am a man and a warrior. . . . I carry War in my right hand and in my left hand peace. . . . Here is a bloody belt and a white one. Take whichever you please. Behave like men. . . . If you take the bloody path you shall go from this town in safety and join your friends, the English."[15]

Clark's bold gamble paid off. Nearly every delegation pledged loyalty to the Long Knives. Clark was pleased with his work. He reckoned his speech "had a greater effect than I could have imagined and did more service than a Regiment of Men cou'd have done."[16] Oratory was crucial to his diplomacy because he had nothing more to share. Without gifts to buy peace, Clark could only promise protection for his friends and threaten fire and sword against his enemies. His stunning words spread rapidly through the Indian grapevine. Village councils met to discuss their meaning, and most agreed to send a delegation to hear for themselves what flowed from the mouth of the red-haired chief.

Clark's diplomacy did not inspire or intimidate everyone present. The Winnebagos plotted to capture Clark and spirit him away to Hamilton at Detroit for a generous reward. They camped on the grounds of a trader named Bradley, whose home was just a hundred yards from Clark's head-quarters. Clark, however, was ready for that possibility, having gotten wind "of a bad report of them."[17]

The second night of the council, some Winnebagos slipped across the shallow Cahokia River, fired a few shots, then dashed across shouting that enemies were near. Their plan was to nab Clark, confused after being aroused from his sleep, by acting as his protectors. But when the shots erupted, Clark was already awake, "having too many things to think about to sleep much."[18]

His sentry was alert as well. When he saw dark figures rushing toward him through the night, the sentry lowered his firearm and shouted for help. The guards ripped off their blankets and grabbed their weapons, and their officers formed them into line before Clark's headquarters.

Seeing those men massed before them, the Winnebagos turned and scattered. The French militia mustered. Queries were made at the Indian camps. Rumors fingered the Winnebagos as the perpetrators. The militia rushed to the Winnebago camp and the men pointed their muskets as the warriors tried to slip back. Clark appeared with an escort and demanded where they had been. The Winnebagos claimed that they had chased off the unknown attackers.

Clark asked the French militia to clamp the Winnebago chiefs in irons until he decided their fate. Every day thereafter, Clark let the Winnebago chiefs join the council but forbade them from speaking. Then one day in council he had the chiefs brought to the center of the council circle.[19] Clark sternly explained that he could have them executed for their treachery. Instead, he had chosen to release them, but castigated them as nothing better than "a set of Villians, that they had Joined the Inglish and they were welcome to continue in the Cause they had espoused." The Winnebagos begged forgiveness and assured the red-haired chief that from now on they would be loyal allies of the Long Knives. A chief presented a wampum belt and pipe on the council table. Clark leapt to his feet, drew his sword, and smashed the pipe. That shocked not only the Winnebago but all the participants, red and white alike. Clark proclaimed that he "never treated with women and did not care who was my Friends or Foes; and had no more to say to them."[20]

As chiefs from other tribes asked Clark to take pity on the miscreants, the Winnebago delegation fearfully conferred among themselves. Suddenly, two of their youngest men detached themselves, entered the circle, sat, pulled blankets over their heads, and begged for forgiveness. The chiefs announced that they were offering the two as sacrifices to atone for the tribe's collective guilt. The dramatic gesture briefly stunned Clark: "I had intended all along to let myself be finally persuaded to grant peace to these people, but this action on their part astonished me. I hardly knew whether or not it was sincere although everything indicated that it was. Every person appeared anxious to know what would be done, and a general silence fell upon them and for some time all were in a state of silence."[21] Clark was so moved by the brav-ery of the young warriors who were willing to sacrifice themselves for their people that he ordered them to pull off their blankets and stand. "There was men among all Nations," he proclaimed as he "took them by the Hand as my Brothers and chiefs of their Nation."[22]

Once again Clark proved himself to be a master of diplomacy. He had deftly manipulated the emotions not just of the Winnebago but of everyone present. For days, he had let the Winnebago mull their possible fates and hinted that execution was likely. He then announced that he would not kill them, but would release them to join the English. When the chiefs had begged for forgiveness and peace, he smashed with his sword the most po-tent symbol that they offered. That so terrified them that they offered two of their men as sacrifices. Having contemptuously denigrated the Winnebago as women, he then embraced their two courageous warriors as men.

All along, Clark carefully tacked back and forth across the middle ground between violence and appeasement. The Winnebagos had been punished for their treachery, but lightly enough so that the tribe was not consumed with hatred and an undying lust for vengeance. At no point had any blood been shed or any shot fired. The French militia had unflinchingly supported Clark and his men. Neither the Winnebago nor any tribe present would contemplate let alone mount another attack against such a vigilant, united force led by such a dauntless warrior. Clark's reputation for wisdom and compassion as well as courage and ferocity would not only further strengthen among the Winnebagos and other tribes at council but also would spread as far as legs and mouths could carry it.

The Winnebagos were not the only people teetering between war and peace with the Americans. Among the Potawatomi delegation was Big Gate, who had led three war parties against the Big Knives. He had earned his name as a teenager when he shot and scalped a British sentinel at the en-trance to Fort Michilimackinac during the Indian revolt of 1763.[23] Day after day, Big Gate sat glaring and wordless in the council's inner circle.

Clark was well aware of Big Gate's history and sentiments. But he also understood that Big Gate's mind seethed between hatred and respect for Clark and his fellow Americans. So at one point, Clark addressed Big Gate before all the delegates: "I said it was customary among white people that when officers met in this manner, even though they were enemies, they treated each other with greater respect than they did common people, and esteemed each other the more."[24] He then shared his hope to enjoy Big Gate's company for dinner that evening after the council adjourned. As Big Gate considered the implications of that invitation, Clark's face and voice hardened as he expressed an even greater hope eventually to meet him as an enemy in battle.

Clark's acute ability to whipsaw a warrior's emotions brought the latest conversion; by embracing an enemy, Clark converted him into an ally. As Clark spoke, Big Gate "appeared to be on nettles." Suddenly, Big Gate leapt to his feet, flung to the ground a small Union Jack that he had secreted beneath his shirt, and trampled it. He then stripped off all his clothes except for his loincloth. He denounced the redcoat lies and promised that from now he was the ally of the Big Knives. Big Gate powerfully shook hands with Clark and "the whole company, as his brothers. A great deal of merriment ensued. . . . Big Gate, being a merry fellow himself, kept up their good humor by speaking to them as a new man and a Big Knife. But as our new brother was now naked, it was necessary that he should be clothed." Clark had him dressed in a fine gentleman's suit fringed with lace, and that night at the banquet Big Gate "was much the finest man at the table."[25]

Then after dinner, Big Gate did something that again provoked Clark's fears. Big Gate "told me he wished to have some private conversation with me, and pointed to a room that had a large window opening into a back street. Being always suspicious, I did not know whether my new brother intended to stab me and make his escape through the window." Clark agreed but discreetly posted several of his men beneath the window. Big Gate shared his knowledge of conditions at Detroit and other British posts, and promised to return within forty days with a redcoat scalp. Clark replied by explaining that the Americans wished only that all Indians remain at peace, and presented him with a medal and a captain's commission.[26]

Later, after the council ended and as Big Gate and his followers strode away, Clark ordered a squad of troops to fire a salute. Big Gate abruptly "stopped, and saying he supposed those poor soldiers were hungry for a dram, he ordered one of his men to go to a trader with whom he was acquainted . . . and get a little keg of rum and give it to them to drink to his health."[27]

Then there was Blackbird, an Ojibwa chief who happened to be trading in Saint Louis with some of his people when Clark's expedition took over Illinois. The Ojibwas were split among half a dozen villages. Like other tribes in the region, they naturally leaned toward the British in their war with the Americans; Blackbird's village on the Saint Joseph River was one of the closer Ojibwa bands to the frontier, and many of its warriors had returned home with scalps and plunder from the Ohio valley settlements.

Learning of their presence, Clark invited the Ojibwas to council. Most of his people stayed rooted on the Mississippi River's western shore, but Blackbird crossed over, declaring that had he "been so near them and did not go see them they would think he had run away through fear." He desired no formal council in Indian style but instead sought a private meeting with Clark. He expressed a desire to hear the American side of the war with Britain. Clark was happy to comply. Blackbird was convinced and declared that he and his people would fight no more against the Long Knives. Clark sent him on his way with two packhorses heaped with gifts for himself and his people.[28]

Thus did Clark forge a series of peace treaties with envoys of various tribes from the region and far beyond.[29] Meanwhile, he nurtured a relationship with Governor Fernando de Leyba at Saint Louis just across the Mississippi River from Cahokia. Like Clark, de Leyba was a newcomer to the region. He, his wife, and two young daughters set foot in Saint Louis on June 10, 1778, after a tedious ninety-three-day row up the Mississippi. The governor was as pleased as he was astonished that Clark had supplanted British rule in the region. The two men's first direct communication was a July 8 letter penned by de Leyba. He wished "to congratulate you on your happy arrival at the Kaskaskia." Clark was gratified enough by that warm welcome but was doubtlessly ecstatic to learn that de Leyba was holding "goods turned over by Mr. Pollock of New Orleans which shall be delivered whenever you may be pleased to dispose of them."[30]

Although the governor had not yet met Clark, what he had heard of that dauntless man deeply impressed him. He wrote glowingly to Louisiana governor Bernardo de Galvez that "Colonel Clark deserves the greatest courtesy from all the inhabitant of his district since they are debtors to him his pleasant manner, clemency, and upright administration of justice. Although his soldiers are bandits in appearance, he has them under the best of control. I am expecting this gentlemen's visit from day to day; I shall show him all the courtesy I can and expect to have the best of dealings with him."[31]

The governor spared no expense in celebrating Clark's first visit: "There was a great consuming of powder at his arrival as well as his departure. I entertained him at meals and laid thirty covers [dishes] on his first visit which lasted two days. Dances were given for him both nights and a supper to the ladies and dancers, and lodging in my house with as much formality as was possible." From their first meeting, they formed a deep and lasting bond that endured ever-worsening strains. In November 1778, de Leyba informed Galvez that the "good harmony which Colonel Clark and I keep makes me think that our reactions are in harmony; that is he has from his superiors with regard to us similar instructions. . . . If it were not so, I believe that some small differences which have occurred and which we have ended in friendly fashion would have irritated us. As it is they have served only to strengthen our friendship the more."[32] In April 1779, de Leyba wrote Governor Patrick Henry that "from the time that my friend Colonel Clark arrived in this place, fraternal harmony has reigned between the people from the United States and the vassals of his Catholic Majesty. . . . Colonel Clark's wisdom and affability have made him generally loved by all who know him, and I give your Excellency a thousand thanks for having given me a neighbor who by his friendly manners has made him his debtor for the greatest courtesies."[33]

Clark was just as enamored of de Leyba. "Our friends the Spanyards," he reported, are "doing every thing in their power to convince me of their friendship." And the governor did so enthusiastically. Clark was "much surprised in my expectations" that de Leyba was not a stereotypical Spaniard: "Instead of finding that reserve thought peculiar to that Nation, I here saw not the least symptoms of it, freedom almost to excess gave the greatest pleasure."[34]

Yet there was a limit to how far the governor would aid the Americans—he would not bend the law. One day two of de Leyba's officers "came to this post with orders from their colonel to arrest and take to their side the American deserters that they found on mine. These officers came with orders from their chief not to so without my permission. . . . I answered them that I could not consent . . . because it was against the rights and privileges which my sovereign's domains enjoyed. They replied that they did not know the matter was so delicate and that no offense was intended, and Colonel Clark gave me the same answer in person."[35]

While de Leyba's commitment to their relationship was undoubtedly sincere, by one account, love may have elevated Clark's pleasure at the relationship. According to legend, Clark was smitten with Teresa, the governor's beautiful sister, and courted her during his visits with de Leyba and his family in Saint Louis. He promised to marry her as soon as he was wealthy and famous enough for a woman of such lofty noble status. But war, which first brought them together, eventually tore them forever apart. Clark was drawn back east to defend Kentucky against a series of Indian and British onslaughts and then to lead his campaigns across the Ohio River. Meanwhile, death claimed first the governor's wife and then de Leyba himself. Teresa, crushed by the loss of her family and despairing that she would never reunite with her lover, retired to an Ursuline convent in Spain. Learning that she had departed, Clark too was heartbroken, so much so that he would never again fall in love.

Although a lovely romantic story, it is almost certainly nothing more than a myth. In a fine piece of detective work, historian Nancy Carstens deconstructs the story and its variations.[36] Her key finding was that de Leyba did not have a sister, let alone one named Teresa who lived with him and his family in Saint Louis. He did, however, have two pretty daughters named Pepita and Rita. The girls certainly charmed Clark. In postscripts of three of his surviving letters to de Leyba, he sent his best to the governor's wife and "my two favorites the little Misses," "the young ladies," and "your ladies."[37] Although the age of the girls has been lost, they were probably in their early teens. If Clark and one or both girls flirted, it was undoubtedly of a teasing familial type. Anything serious would have offended the propriety of the straitlaced aristocratic Spanish society that strictly guarded the honor of men, women, and family above all else.

Nonetheless, a woman named Teresa, or Terese, as the name was actually spelled, did exist, and Clark apparently fancied her. A letter from Lieutenant Colonel John Todd to Clark, dated October 3, 1779, bluntly reports that the governor's wife is dead and "Madame Terese still a Maid. . . . If I could get an oppy [opportunity] of sending you some thing good to Toast your Sweet Heart I would."[38] Unfortunately, Terese's identity has been lost to history. How did Clark meet and fall for her? Were his feelings toward her animated by love or just pure lust? Answers to such tantalizing questions will likely never be known. Most likely Teresa was either a friend or, more likely, a trusted servant of the de Leyba family.

The origin of the mythical version of the Clark-Teresa relationship is much more accessible. As with most myths, its sources are diverse. They start with nineteenth-century historian Lyman Draper, who had heard the story and asked survivors of Clark's expedition and their descendants for corroboration. All they could do, however, was pass on versions of what they had heard. Draper accepted those stories as fact rather than hearsay, and constructed the most consistent versions into the best-known narrative. His key mistake was assuming that Clark's beloved Teresa was the governor's sister.

The most seemingly viable of Draper's sources came from the Clark family. In 1848, Clark's niece Diane Gwathmey Bullitt sent Draper two accounts. In her first letter, she recalled, "I was with Gen. Clark a great deal until I was twenty years of age. . . . I never heard him allude to the lady or the affair except when he was intoxicated. He would then frequently say to me that if he had been properly treated [by the government] I would have an elegant aunt whom I would have loved very much. I have often seen him shed tears when he would make the above remark. . . . He never mentioned her name." In her second letter, Bullitt identified the mystery lady as the governor's sister. The trouble was that Clark "thought it was not honorable for him to marry a lady educated as she was and accustomed to all the luxuries of wealth, without having any means of supporting her." After Clark learned that his beloved had left him for a Spanish convent, he "was a changed man." The family attributed Clark's "disappointment in addition to the . . . treatment of the state of Virginia as the cause of his deep depression and intemperance."[39]

So Clark was indeed smitten with a Spanish lady probably named Teresa, but at some point suspended his flirtation. His war duties and shaky finances were certainly genuine reasons for doing so until 1783. But what about after the war as he amassed a fortune in land? By then she had likely married or possibly moved to New Orleans or even Spain as some of the stories suggest. Decades later, his tear-filled, drunken confessions to his niece reveal that he still recalled her with affection and regret.

Did Teresa ever return Clark's feelings or did he follow the false trail of countless men and mistake coquetry for true love? That too we will never know. Most women may have been as much repelled by as attracted to Clark. He was certainly physically imposing, with a muscular body and a towering height. His reputation for courage and audacity along with his gifts of leadership and diplomacy were beguiling. At twenty-six, he would never be more filled with energy and exuberance. But there was a downside. His moon face and steadily receding and thinning strawberry red hair were not conventionally attractive. As for status, he was a lieutenant colonel, though in a rebel rabble of armed men rather than an established great power. Even worse, he was of common rather than noble stock. His quick temper and hard drinking would have troubled most women, even as he struggled to check both when he was with any lady.

One result of the relationship between Colonel Clark and de Leyba's family and friends is certain. The initial heady days of aiding Clark and his men in their epic adventure quickly disappeared as the financial and emotional costs mounted. By October 1779, Governor de Leyba had bankrupted himself for the American cause. He reported to Governor Galvez,

> The coming of the Americans to this district has ruined me utterly. Several inhabitants of this town, who put their property in the hands of the Americans to please me, find themselves in the same situation, and those losses are equally a matter of regret to me with my own since I consider myself the immediate cause of them. But what was there for me to do with your Lordship's orders except to come to their aid in view of the fact that even their principal leader [Clark], however many American documents he brought, had no a shirt to cover his nakedness. I accomplished this on my credit with the inhabitants so that they might provide these Americans with whatever I needed. . . . These inhabitants did not want to give up their goods even for Colonel Clark's receipts. They gave them immediately when I pledged mine.[40]

In donating their resources, they like him would be ruined by their generosity as the receipts proved to be worthless. De Leyba not only lost his fortune but his "beloved wife, who to this exile with so many hardships . . . when she saw her hopes" of returning to Spain "frustrated by the labyrinth of debts . . . was overcome by such a great melancholy that after only five days of illness in bed, she passed from this to another life. . . . Therefore in company with my weeping little daughters, I implore your Lordship's protection for the collection of these bills of exchanged."[41]

Clark's diplomacy in the Illinois region was overwhelmingly successful with all but one person. The British official Rocheblave refused to cooperate. His resistance is understandable. Clark took over Rocheblave's home for his headquarters and ordered his slaves sold to pay off his men. Mrs. Rocheblave protested that devastating loss. Stirred by her pleas, several of Clark's officers suggested that the Rocheblaves be allowed to keep their property. Clark returned her slaves. Those same officers tried further to mollify Rocheblave by inviting him to their table. But the governor could not restrain his rage against all that had transpired, and eviscerated the Americans "in a most intolerable manner as Rebels." Rocheblave had turned coat permanently, so any appeals to him as a Frenchman and thus ally fell on defiantly plugged ears. Clark wearily described Rocheblave's attitude as "fixed and Violent," and ordered the slave auction to proceed. He and his men pocketed $1,500 from the sale, divvied up with wide differences according to rank. He had Captain John Montgomery escort Rocheblave and his surviving official documents, along with letters, to Governor Patrick Henry in Williamsburg.[42]

The final target of Clark's diplomacy was his own men. Having accomplished a mission that none had imagined when they had first enlisted, "the greatest part of my Men was for returning." Clark managed, "by great presents and promises," to talk about a hundred of them into reenlisting for another eight months.[43]

As usual, Clark squeezed the most from his latest challenge. So far he had either inspired or browbeat nearly all of the region's whites and Indians to declare their loyalty to him and the United States either enthusiastically or reluctantly. But that loyalty might well dry up as the conquest's initial "shock and awe" and his number of troops dwindled. So in a canny display of psychological jujitsu, Clark wielded his small force to bolster local support for the occupation: "I made a feint of returning to the Falls, as though I had sufficient confidence in the People, hoping that the Inhabitants would remonstrate against my leaving them, which they did in the warmest terms proving the necessity of the Troops at that place that they were afraid if I returned the English would again possess the Country. Then seemingly by their request I agreed to stay."[44]

As for those who demanded to be released, Clark had Captain William Linn return with them to the Falls, where they would be discharged. Linn was then to evacuate the garrison from Corn Island to the south bank of the Falls and set it to work building a new fort. Although a fort on the mainland would be more vulnerable than the fort on Corn Island, its garrison would also be more mobile and better able to command the portage around the Falls.

Clark was determined to mold those who reenlisted into as professional a body of troops as could be found anywhere. He observed, "Strict subordination among the Troops was my first object and I soon effected it. It being a matter of the greatest consequence to Persons in our situation. You must [be] sensible of the pleasure I felt when harangueing them on Perade. Telling them my Resolutions and the necessity of strict duty for our own preservation. . . . For them to return me for Answer that it was their Zeal for their Country that induced them to engage in the Service. . . . In a short time no Garrisson could boast of better order, or a more Valuable set of Men."[45]

Only after achieving that could Clark relax. Taking the Illinois country had been tough enough. The diplomacy vital to holding it had been far more challenging. He had won over first the French, then the Indians, then the Spaniards, and finally his own men. When Clark reflected on the succession of life-and-death gambles he had made and won over the preceding weeks and all those yet to come, he concluded that "more depended on my own Behavior and Conduct than all the troops that I had far removed from the Body of my Country."[46]

It was time to celebrate. On August 14, 1778, Clark requisitioned twenty bottles of rum as the centerpiece of a wild celebration at Kaskaskia among his men for their stunning bloodless victories, and sent four bottles to Captain Bowman and his contingent at Cahokia so they could throw their own party.[47]

CHAPTER 9

Counterpunch

Great things have been affected by a few Men well Conducted.

George Rogers Clark

C lark's diplomacy at Cahokia had no sooner ended when Father Pierre Gibault and Jean Baptiste Laffont returned from Vincennes. They brought good news. On July 20, most of the French had signed an oath of allegiance to the United States and awaited the arrival of American officials and soldiers.[1] Most of the local Indians were interested in learning what the Long Knives had to say and give.

Clark dispatched Captain Leonard Helm with a score of men to journey to Vincennes and occupy Fort Sackville, which they renamed Fort Patrick Henry. As in Kaskaskia, the tough part would not be getting in but staying put. Helm's greatest challenge would be swinging the allegiance of the Piankeshaw tribe at Vincennes and other tribes in the region from Britain to the United States. The trouble was, with Congress and Virginia penniless, the customary piles of goods could neither bury the dead nor buy the peace. Like Clark at Cahokia, Helm would have to subdue the tribes by projecting the myth that the Americans were as invincible and ruthless to their enemies as they were protective of their friends. That would be a tough sell with only twenty armed men to back it up.

Helm's first symbolic act was to gather the Indian inhabitants of Vincennes, haul down the Union Jack, wrap it in a large stone, and toss it in the Wabash River. He then remarked, "Thus we mean to treat your [British] father." Helm was just as weighty in the substance of his diplomacy. The most important local Piankeshaw chiefs were Old Tobacco and his son, known as the Door of the Wabash. Helm succeeded in opening that Door to an enthusiastic acceptance of the Americans in their midst. He did so by strictly following Clark's script. He offered them war and peace belts, and asked them to choose. When one chief protested that stark choice, Helm replied, "You are young men & your youth excuses your ignorance. . . . Our design is to March thro' your Country & if we find any fires in our Way, we shall just thread them out as we walk along." The chiefs bowed to what they saw as a superior force personified by Helm.[2]

Clark's hold on Illinois ultimately depended on a fragile lifeline down the Mississippi River all the way to New Orleans, where the American agent Oliver Pollock was proving himself to be as brilliant a diplomat as he was a merchant. He had talked first Louisiana governor Luiz de Unzaga and then his successor Bernardo de Galvez into selling on credit enormous amounts of vital military supplies that he promptly sent upriver.[3]

Galvez was eager to forge ties with the Americans. On February 24, 1778, George Morgan, America's Indian agent at Pittsburgh, opened a letter from Galvez, dated August 9, 1777. He carried it to Philadelphia to lay it before Congress, in hope that it could find someone in that city of 40,000 people who spoke and read Spanish. On April 26, Morgan was embarrassed to have to reply in English to Galvez that "unfortunately not a Member of that Body understands it nor has any Person been yet found capable & worthy of Trust to translate it." Nonetheless, Morgan assured that distant governor of the American government's intention to reply as soon as a suitable translator was found. That same day Morgan conducted another act of diplomacy. He acknowledged receipt on November 19, 1778, of a letter from Francisco Cruzat, upper Louisiana's governor before Fernando de Leyba. Once again, Morgan had to beg forgiveness for his vague reply on the prevailing ignorance of the Spanish language.[4] These were among the first awkward steps of early American diplomacy.

As governors and other officials struggled to knit a relationship between the United States and Louisiana, Captain James Willing's expedition barged into New Orleans and nearly severed those slender strands. After selling off slaves and other loot stolen from fifteen plantations upriver, Willing spread the proceeds among his men, who cut loose on riotous days and nights of carousing in the town's numerous taverns and brothels. He and the men delighted in taunting any British they encountered in that neutral city, including baring their backsides to the incensed officers and crew of one of King George's warships anchored in the river. It was not quite the image of American "patriots" that Pollock wanted Spain's governor and subjects to witness.[5]

Between drinking and wenching bouts, Willing tried to talk Governor Galvez into backing his plan to capture Mobile and Pensacola. He presented Galvez a letter from Congress's Board of War admitting its inability to support that plan and requesting any aid that the governor could provide Willing. In return, all Congress could offer Galvez was its "thanks for his spirited and disinterested conduct towards these states."[6] Galvez explained that Spain's neutrality prevented him from openly supporting Willing or any other American military efforts against the British.

Willing's expedition was not just an embarrassing international incident for Galvez and Pollock. Strategically, his raid hurt rather than helped the American cause. The crimes he and his men committed upriver provoked a Loyalist backlash that retook those settlements and executed, jailed, or drove into exile the American patriots who seized power. From West Florida's capital of Pensacola, Governor Peter Chester called for reinforcements and eventually received a thousand troops under General John Campbell.

Another American expedition appeared at New Orleans on September 22, 1778. The dignified behavior of Colonel David Rogers and his twenty-eight men helped repair some of the public relations damage inflicted by Willing and his freebooters. Rogers carried £625 with which to buy supplies. He presented a letter from Governor Henry to Governor Galvez. Henry appealed to Galvez for military and financial aid for "an infant State engaged in a formidable war," and asked for help in conquering West Florida from the British. In return, all the Americans could offer was a mutually enriching trade. He shared his plans to build a fort near the mouth of the Ohio River and eventually take over British West Florida.[7]

Those letters from Congress and Virginia spurred a decisive response from Galvez. He recognized that Spain's empire in North America now faced two threats, one British and the other American. He devised an ingenuous policy that would contain both. In his reply, he assured Henry that he was working closely with Pollock to send supplies to the Americans. He shared Henry's belief "that by separating West Florida from British domination we would proscribe the English all communication in the governance of the Gulf of Mexico." He had no objections to an American fort near the confluence of the Ohio and Mississippi rivers. As for Henry's offer of trade to compensate for Spanish aid, he offered an elaborate expression of gratitude while deferring that decision to King Charles III.[8] Galvez would indeed supply increasing aid to the Americans while beating them to the punch by conquering West Florida. However, it would take several years for him to fulfill that grand strategy.[9]

Colonel Rogers would carry Galvez's reply to Henry along with the supplies he purchased with his hard coin. He would join forces with Lieutenant Robert George, who now led what was left of the Willing expedition. Willing had turned over command to George before sailing for Philadelphia, where he hoped to talk Congress into backing even more ambitious schemes. With Pollock's credit, George purchased his own boatloads of supplies. Rogers, George, and their men embarked upriver in a five-boat convoy.[10]

Clark and his men desperately needed any supplies they could get from any source. A load of supplies earmarked for the United States actually sat in a Saint Louis warehouse. Clark resisted the temptation to requisition the provisions. Oliver Pollock had purchased and sent those supplies from New Orleans without designating a recipient. On July 18, Clark sent Pollock a brief letter explaining his takeover of Illinois and the authority vested in him by Virginia, including the power to order goods on the state's credit. Several weeks later, on August 6, 1778, he sent Pollock an order for $5,000 in goods "suitable for soldiers and Indians," with two tons of gunpowder the most crucial element.[11]

Clark recognized that his occupation's success depended greatly on his ability to set up an efficient, legitimate government. He learned that the previous "government had generally been as severe as though under martial law. I resolved to make capital of this, and took every step in my power to cause the people to appreciate the blessings enjoyed by an American citizen."[12] By the end of 1778, Clark had set up an American-style court system with local magistrates at Kaskaskia, Cahokia, and Vincennes. After getting word that Virginia had designated the County of Illinois in October 1778, he established other appropriate offices. Governor Henry would send John Todd to serve as the county lieutenant.

Until then, Clark and his officers ran the show themselves. Those duties took more and more of his time. The populace looked to him to arbitrate numerous disputes. Two surviving cases reveal the diversity of conflicts brought before him. In one complex case, the parties fought over the property of orphan children, allegations of slander, and a business deal gone awry. In another, a man sought approval for splitting his property among the children of his first and second marriages. In deciding what to do, Clark was somewhat handicapped, having never studied English law, let alone French law with its alien values and procedures. Yet he compensated for that with a firm sense of justice and command.[13]

Meanwhile, Captain Montgomery and his men escorted Rocheblave into Williamsburg in November 1778. Upon receiving Rocheblave and a barrage of complaints, Governor Henry paroled him and fired off a letter to Clark. That letter contained a gentle rebuke: "From matters of general concern you must turn occasionally to others of less consequence." Henry then called on Clark to pay "particular attention to Mrs. Rocheblave and her children, and that you suffer them to want for nothing. Let Mr. Rocheblave's property, which was taken, be restored to his lady so far as it can be done." One sentiment and three principals apparently guided that policy. Henry was clearly moved by the plight of Rocheblave and his family. As for principles, first, the laws of war distinguished public from private property; the former could be confiscated, but the latter could not unless the owner committed a crime or was compensated for its full value. Rocheblave's insults to his jailors may have been imprudent but violated no law. Then there was the mistaken notion that just because Rocheblave was a French nobleman he remained a loyal French subject and was thus outside the law for siding with the British. As a declared British subject, he was protected by the laws of war. Finally, the governor did not want to establish a precedent whereby the British could justify confiscating the property, including slaves, of Virginians should they retake the state.[14]

The Rocheblaves were hardly the only Illinois inhabitants insulted and harmed by the foreign occupation. As time passed, a growing number of

people would regret the night the invaders appeared. At first, virtually everyone seemed either resigned or content with American rule. But after the takeover's shock wore off, the Americans steadily wore out their welcome. By far,
the most alienating practice was to pay for requisitions with worthless paper
script. Atop that, some of the Americans, including its commander, could
be boorish and insensitive.

Shortly after taking over the Illinois country, Clark nearly undid all his
deft diplomacy with a display of gross behavior. The French held a ball in
honor of their American guests. Clark's uniform was patched and faded; he
covered up some of the worst excesses by draping a blanket around himself like a cape, pinned with a locust needle. As if his appearance did not set
enough tongues wagging, his gesture after dancing with Mrs. Joseph Brazeau,
the wife of the only man who was willing to resist the invaders, caused a scandal. Probably in his cups, Clark tried to kiss the lady, who reacted by slapping
his face. At that point, quite likely the music died and all eyes stared in disbelief. Likely red-faced from the slap, drink, and shame, Clark apologized
profusely. But the Illinois folks would titter over that story for a long time to
come.[15] (That incident, in part, might explain why his courtship of Teresa
failed.)

Around the same time, a spy scare erupted. Among the Cahokia merchants, Captain Bowman discovered a man named Dennys secretly sending reports to Detroit. It would have been within the laws of war for Clark
to have the spy tried and executed. Instead, he ordered Dennys "branded
on the hand" then "tied to the tail of a cart and driven through the town,
receiving a lash at every door." Clark explained, "This was the first and
severest punishment inflicted by us on any of the inhabitants. It was necessary
at this time to convince the people that we were capable of extremes either
way, and the good treatment we had heretofore shown them was due to the
principles of the government."[16]

Yet the most restive population under American rule was not the elite
or middling or peasant classes, but those at society's very bottom. Rage
among the black and Indian slaves was reaching a boiling point. On one
hand, they were inspired by American notions of liberty, equality, and justice for all. Yet their already-dismal status worsened under American rule.
The French "Black Code" of 1724 made the yoke of slavery less cruel than
it was in most of the thirteen American colonies (or, more recently, states).

The French law forbade masters from breaking up families by selling spouses or children below the age of puberty to different masters, something perfectly legal in nearly all the states, while slaves were given Sundays off and only worked from dawn to dusk. The British, wisely, retained the Black Code after 1763 when they formally took title to Illinois. The Americans were not so wise.

Perhaps things would have turned out differently had New Englanders rather than Virginian plantation owners occupied Illinois, but that did not happen. Fearing to directly confront the Virginians, ever more slaves defied their own masters. An upsurge in assertiveness and crime among Illinois slaves was among the unintended results of the American invasion. The owners petitioned Clark to suppress "the contagion which has developed in the houses of the slaves" that was becoming "injurious."[17]

Clark responded on December 24, 1778, with a proclamation "to remedy the disorders, abuses, and brigandage of too long duration, that has been caused by the too great liberty enjoyed by the red and black slaves and is causing the ruin of the colony." To suppress the agitation, henceforth no "intoxicating liquors" for any reason or of any quantity could be sold to the slaves. Without a permit signed by the master, slaves were forbidden to trade or sell anything or to be out after dark for "dancing, feasting, or holding nocturnal assemblies," or for any other reason. Any slave who violated those rules would be publicly whipped thirty-nine times for the first offense and twice that the second time. Slaves were, however, allowed to continue "dancing on Sundays and feast days provided it was during the day time and the said slaves are furnished with a permit signed by their masters."[18]

Clark's proclamation also dealt with a related and more insidious problem. Clark and several of his officers had brought slaves with them; Clark himself had five. Those slaves must have envied the fewer restrictions borne by their local counterparts. Atop that, Clark and his men participated in the slave trade. Indeed, among their first acts was to confiscate and sell the slaves of Philippe de Rocheblave, the local British agent. They bought other slaves with increasingly worthless script and sent them in chains down to New Orleans in exchange for provisions from Oliver Pollock.[19]

One of Clark's slaves was accused of a bizarre murder in Saint Louis. A petition to Governor Galvez reported that a "Madame Laurent learns that her negro had been poisoned by another negro" owned "by the American

Colonel Clark, being thereby deprived of her sole support and in poverty, overwhelmed by sadness, and bathed in tears, she went to Monsieur Leyba [to ask] that he . . . write in her favor to Monsieur Clark in order to have her negro paid for or have the poisoner put to death. Mr. Leyba . . . writes. Several days go by. No reply. Nothing more is heard of Monsieur Clark or the negro."[20] Just what evidence if any backed up that murder charge against Clark's slave has been lost. What is clear is that the growing weight of real and imagined crimes prompted Clark's proclamation.

Clark justified his proclamation on security grounds. The reality, of course, was that his new rules actually undermined Virginian rule. There was one slave for every two white inhabitants. Like the white settlers of Illinois, the slaves had a breaking point. Squeeze them jointly too hard and they might rebel united against their common oppressor. As Clark and his officers struggled to rule an alien land and people, they were ignorant of a worsening threat far to the northeast.

Henry Hamilton will forever be damned as one of the more detested villains of American history. He earned the sobriquet the "Hair-buyer" for his practice of paying Indians for the scalps they ripped from Americans. But the man who emerges from his journal, report, and autobiography is far more complex than that caricature.[21] Hamilton was a most worthy enemy for George Rogers Clark, a serious rival in intelligence, courage, enterprise, and ruthlessness. Most important, Hamilton, like Clark, was an outstanding military leader. As the third son of an Irish viscount, an officer's commission was an all but inevitable profession. When Hamilton was twenty-one, his father purchased him an ensignship in the Fifteenth Regiment. He fought in the French and Indian War, notably during the Louisbourg campaign, on the Plains of Abraham, and at the battle of Saint Foy before Quebec, where he was captured. His experiences in North America were not confined to army life. On leave, he traveled to Boston, New York, and Philadelphia, and thoroughly enjoyed his journeys. From 1763 to 1775, his father bought him a series of ranks up to lieutenant colonel.

Until then, Hamilton had been a dutiful enough officer, but had not revealed the full extent of his leadership potential until after he arrived at Detroit, to serve as its lieutenant governor. In command there and later in his campaign to take Vincennes, he proved to be an outstanding field officer and diplomat with the Indians. A vital reason for that was that Hamilton, like Clark, avidly studied what made humans and their respective cultures tick, and made excellent use of his findings to inspire loyalty or fear in his subjects. He was an especially sensitive and open-minded observer of the Indians, and saw much in them to admire.

Yet dark urges lurked in the recesses of Hamilton's mind. Laudably, he found an outlet for his turbulent passions in sketching. However, one surviving sketch is especially revealing, a gruesome scene of an Indian hacking a woman apart with his tomahawk. In 1778, a grand jury in Montreal indicted Hamilton, along with local magistrate Philip Dejean, on charges of miscarriage of justice in a trial in which a man was executed by hanging; Clark's capture of them both at Vincennes would render that judicial proceeding moot. Like his equally notorious colleague Banastre Tarleton, Hamilton was both a ferocious soldier and a ladies' man. He might have disputed Tarleton's boast to have "butchered more men and lain with more women than anyone in the army."[22] While just how many women submitted, willingly or not, to either man is murky, their military records are clear enough. Tarleton's "butchery" occurred at his command before his eyes and at times with his own hands. Hamilton's was more abstract, mostly inspired and subsequently rewarded at Detroit hundreds of miles from the resulting mayhem on the American frontier.

Victorious war parties strode frequently into Detroit, whooping at the top of their lungs, shaking scalps at the ends of muskets and lances, and prodding exhausted captives before them. Hamilton had those warriors and their spoils ushered before him, whereupon he would deliver a rousing speech of gratitude for their efforts. He would then nod to an orderly to distribute an appropriate amount of gifts. Any type of an array of goods could be handed out. The most common were sharp new knives that were perfect for scalping among other uses. During Hamilton's tenure, 8,640 knives were distributed to the Indians.[23]

Although Hamilton rewarded both scalps and captives, he did note his preference for and paid more for the latter. He was well aware that it was much easier to convey scalps than captives all the way to Detroit. The statistics bear out that grim reality. In the first four months of 1778, Hamilton recorded 129 scalps and 21 prisoners. Then, from May to September, he reviewed 81 scalps and 34 prisoners, and ransomed 17 of the latter. Daniel Boone himself along with his twenty-six comrades that Blackfish and his warriors captured were paraded before Hamilton. Although Hamilton offered to buy Boone, Blackfish refused to sell the man whom he intended to adopt as his son.[24]

Hamilton first learned that the Americans had taken Illinois on August 6, 1778, when Francois Maisonville arrived and insisted to the guard that he had urgent and confidential news to share with Detroit's lieutenant governor.[25] Hamilton immediately resolved to retake Vincennes as the first step to replanting the Union Jack in every village of Illinois. The question, of course, was how. Hamilton was the civil administrator for Detroit and the surrounding region. Captain Richard Lernoult actually commanded the town's understrength garrison, and he had no troops to spare.

Two days later, Hamilton sent off letters to Lord George Germain, the architect of the war to suppress the rebellion, General Guy Carleton, Canada's governor, and Lieutenant Colonel Mason Bolton, Fort Niagara's commander, informing them of the American takeover and urgently requesting more troops and supplies.[26] As always, time was a critical factor. Hamilton could expect a relatively quick reply from Bolton in a few weeks, but the round-trip for a message and a reply would take more than a month via Quebec and several months via London. By the time he received any authorization and reinforcements, the weather might well be too cold and wet, thus forcing the expedition's postponement until the following spring. By then, Clark's ranks might swell with enough fresh troops and Indian allies not just to defeat any counterattack but to march against Detroit itself

The time to act was now. Hamilton charged Maisonville with organizing a flotilla of enough boats and rowers to convey several hundred men on the expedition. He gathered the militia captains and asked them to enlist volunteers. He had his quartermaster begin setting aside enough supplies to sustain the campaign for half a year. Those provisions would include not only enough food for the troops but also enough gifts to keep the various Indian tribes along the way loyal and, ideally, enthusiastic allies. On September 27, Hamilton dispatched fourteen militiamen, twenty horses, and tools under Captain Alexander McKee to ascend the Maumee River to its rapids and repair the portage road.

Hamilton sent runners to local and more distant tribes, calling them to council. As various Indian delegations appeared, he performed all the requisite rituals. He symbolically buried the dead with gifts. He made long poetic speeches extolling British and Indian valor, and justifying his expedition. He brandished the tomahawk and sang the war song.

News of Clark's takeover of Illinois had thrown off Hamilton's plan to launch his own campaign against Fort Pitt. He had asked Governor Carleton to approve his plan and had been eagerly awaiting a response. He would not hear from Carleton—Canada now had a new governor. Carleton had finally received permission to resign a post whose incessant demands and moral dilemmas far surpassed its prestige. Brigadier General Frederick Haldimand replaced Carleton in July. Hamilton's proposed campaign against Detroit was among his first orders of business. On the same day that Hamilton learned that the Illinois country had been lost, Haldimand wrote him that he was cancelling the Fort Pitt campaign for what he believed was the diversion of essential resources to a sideshow of paltry strategic worth.[27]

Several weeks later, Haldimand read Hamilton's letter reporting that the rebels had taken Illinois and requesting more men and supplies. He replied with the promise to back any action that Hamilton might take and promised reinforcements. Haldimand was good to his word. He sent orders to Lieutenant Colonel Bolton, at Fort Niagara, to divert a company of troops and supplies to Detroit, and to the commanders at Fort Michilimackinac and Saint Joseph, to rally the Indians and send them to Hamilton.[28]

Drumming up enough reliable recruits was a major headache for Hamilton. After several militia officers and scores of men flatly refused to serve, he felt compelled to re-administer the oath of allegiance to the British crown for those who did volunteer. He was heartened on October 6, the expedition's eve, when Captain Henry Bird and fifty troops arrived from Fort Niagara. They would join Detroit's garrison, both to intimidate those locals who leaned toward the Americans and to act as a strategic reserve that Hamilton hoped to tap in the spring.

Despite the questionable loyalties of many French, Hamilton was optimistic as he anticipated his campaign. The war's military and political conflicts were inseparable. In assessing the broad political landscape as favoring Britain, he was confident of military victory: "The Spanish are feeble & hated by the French, the French are fickle & have no man of Capacity to advise or lead them, the Rebels are enterprising & brave but want resources,

& the Indians can have their resources but from the Inglish if we act without loss [of] time in the favorable conjuction."[29] But only decisive action could exploit that advantage.

The scale of frontier war was a fraction of that along the Atlantic Seaboard. The force Hamilton mustered was formidable by the region's standards. He got permission from Captain Lernoult to take three officers and thirty men from Detroit's garrison. The local militia supplied fourteen officers and seventy-one volunteers, of whom most would serve until Vincennes was retaken and then head home. Of the militiamen, Captain Guillaume La Mothe led a company of five officers and thirty-one soldiers that would serve for the campaign's duration. Seventy Indians also joined the 162 soldiers on the expedition. As for artillery, Hamilton took only one six-pounder field cannon, but it would be powerful enough to batter down the walls of any palisade. Three Indian agents accompanied the expedition, with Major Jehu Hay in charge. The expedition would proceed on water with thirteen flat-bottomed bateaux "calked and fitted with oars" and "capable of carrying 39,300" pounds, and "17 pirogues and canoes to carry 33,700" pounds, for a total capacity of 73,000 pounds.

The expedition set forth from Detroit at a quarter past two on the afternoon of October 7, 1778. Ahead lay a grueling 450-mile journey. The campaign did not get off to an auspicious start. Indeed, the superstitious among the men could later look back and cite an accident as a decidedly prescient omen. The six-pounder was mounted on a gun platform at the bow of the bateau commanded by Lieutenant Henry du Vernet. It is unclear whether Vernet ordered the cannon fired on his own initiative or from Hamilton's instructions, and if it was fired to salute the campaign's inauguration, to test the piece, or both. What is clear is the result. Any hope of using that gun for naval combat dissolved as soon as the gun smoke drifted off. The recoil split the bateau's seams. Water gushed in. The crew jumped off and splashed their way to shore. The boat sank in shallow water, so the men were able to salvage the cannon and most of the supplies and cram them into the other boats. Nothing was hurt but pride and Hamilton's timetable.

The journey ahead from Detroit to Vincennes was studded with obstacles that could only be surmounted with hard muscle and ingenuity. The first and last legs were the easiest with their deep waters. It took only seven days to row down the Detroit River, across the western stretch of Lake Erie, and up the Maumee River to the first of its series of eight rapids bypassed via a fourteen-mile portage. It took five days to portage all the men and supplies around and pull the boats by rope up those rapids. More days were consumed caulking the bottoms of the boats battered by being dragged over the rocks. The artillery boat alone demanded fifty men straining at long ropes from dawn to dusk. From the top of the rapids, it was just a few days more paddling until the expedition reached the nine-mile portage between the headwaters of the Maumee and Wabash Rivers. There the boats had to be emptied and dragged on rollers. To the men's dismay, unusually low water lengthened that already-grueling portage.

Hamilton resolved that problem in a novel way. He discovered "that at the distance of 4 miles from the landing . . . the Beavers had made a dam which kept up the water, this we cut through to give a passage to our boats." Their miseries did not end their trials: "The floating ice cut the men as they worked in the water to haul the boats over shoals and rocks, our Batteau were damaged, and" had "to be repeatedly unloaded [and] calked. . . . It was sometimes a day's work to get the distance of half a league."[30]

Incidents broke the tedium of the expedition's daily exertions. One was tragic—a lieutenant shattered his knee when he accidentally discharged his musket as he stumbled from his tent one morning; he was taken by pirogue back to Detroit where he died of gangrene. A militiaman was court-martialed for sleeping at his post. The Indians and some of the militiamen hunted along the way, bringing in the dressed carcasses of deer, bear, turkeys, and ducks. At one point, to reward his men for their exertions, Hamilton ordered three oxen slaughtered, one each for the redcoats, militiamen, and Indians.

The days shortened and grew colder; the men huddled around the fires during the long nights. The first snow fell on October 15; thereafter, the snow swirled down and ice spread across the waters frequently. On November 26, the "frost being very severe, the wind high, and the water being very shallow, we had great difficulty. . . . The roughness of the water prevented our finding the channel—The Men suffered much, many of them having their legs cut by the floating ice. . . . After getting 1/2 a mile we were obliged to land, make fires, and recruit the men with a dram each. About 3 P.M. we found the river completely barred with ice."[31]

Like Clark, Hamilton found much to admire in the Indians, especially alongside his fellow whites. He was surprised to learn that their language harbored no "oath or a curse—terms of reproach they have few—Hog is most common—to call a Man woman is highly injurious, which they express by saying, You are only fit to wear a . . . pettycoat—to spit in a man's face is the penultimate indignity, to bit off his nose is an ultimatum, but this usually is done when liquor has possession of them and happens more commonly among the soft sex than among the men."[32]

The Indians' religious practices intrigued Hamilton. He noted that their priest first addressed "the Master of Life . . . imploring his protection in their present undertaking and besought the inferior spirits presiding over rivers, Woods, Mountains. . . . The deepest silence and most serious attention was observable during the prayer, no such thing as laughing or whispering so common in our places of Worship—It was a clear star-light night, and I was affected by the humble and reverential worship."[33] Hamilton marveled that some of the scenes he witnessed were truly sublime: "The priest goes in front of the encampment and begins his incantation . . . in a tone between melancholic and terrific—The various tunes in various languages bellowed aloud by these Heralds of the night, the thickness of the Woods and darkness of the Weather with the blaze of a great many large fires extending along the Savage camp . . . the intervals of silence from time to time broken by these . . . Songs . . . formed a very strange but striking melody."[34]

Indians believed that spirits animated all living and nonliving things in the web of existence. In that interrelated world, each human had one or more spirits to guide his or her path in life, and one's spirit most vividly expressed its guidance through dreams. Like modern psychoanalysts, shamans interpreted dreams. The crucial difference was that shamans believed that dreams revealed spiritual as well as psychological truths about that individual and his or her community. At times, life and death literally hung on a dream's interpretation. A favorable analysis would bolster a war party's enthusiasm and daring; a negative analysis could pivot a war party for home. But each was free to interpret his or her own dreams, with the same potential to dramatically change one's course: "Should any one have a dream which bodes something favorable, or the contrary he relates it to his comrades, and their reliance on omens is such, as frequently to defeat an enterprise—Sometimes a man who is disposed to return from war, makes known a dream which calls for him to quit his comrades, no one pretends to dissuade him."[35]

Hamilton's open mind greatly aided his diplomacy. He held frequent evening councils with the chiefs who accompanied him, passed the pipe, and spoke eloquently of their shared mission and other interests. Along the way, he held councils at Ojibwa, Ottawa, Wyandot, Potawatomi, Miami, Shawnee, Wea, Kickapoo, and Mascouten villages. He enthusiastically joined them in their war dances and whoops. Hamilton was generous with his gifts, distributing heaps of blankets, scalping knives, gunpowder, musket balls, silver ornaments, and paints. To salute his esteem for his Indian brothers, he ordered the six-pounder fired three times at each council's conclusion.

Ouiatenon, near present-day Lafayette, Indiana, was the main Wea town that, along with nearby smaller Kickapoo village, comprised the most populous site between the Wabash headwaters and Vincennes. On December 1, Hamilton gathered the local peoples, along with the usual mélange from other tribes across the region, for the first of four days of formal talks and feasts. Eventually, over 960 Indians participated in the proceedings, and a couple hundred warriors joined Hamilton and his men when they pushed off downriver on December 5.

The expedition finally reached deep waters below Ouiatenon and thereafter made good time. On December 12, the men found beached on the west bank a raft with a small campfire smoldering on sand atop it. One or more occupants of that raft had spotted them and fled. Hamilton ordered his Indians to try to track down what were most likely American scouts. The Indians came back empty-handed. Whoever they were had gotten too quick a start and were moving too quickly to catch.

Afraid of running into an ambush, Hamilton ordered the Indians to split into two parties with one on each side of the river as the flotilla slowly floated downstream. On December 15, Indians prodded a prisoner, Lieutenant Michel Brouillet, into camp. A search of him revealed commissions from both the American and British armies. Clearly, Brouillet was wielding those documents to spy. That discovery infuriated Hamilton, who "should not certainly have hesitated at the propriety of hanging this fellow on the first tree." But he restrained himself from doing so "for two reasons—I was unwilling to whet the natural propensity of the Indians for blood, and I wished to gain the perverted Frenchman by Lenity."[36]

Instead, likely by metaphorically dangling that noose before Brouillet, Hamilton proceeded to interrogate him. What he learned came as an enormous relief. Captain Leonard Helm, the American commander at Vincennes, had furloughed the American troops and now relied solely on the flexible sword of the French militia for defense. Though the French had taken an oath of allegiance to the United States, it would not take much to convince them that their interest was to realign themselves with His Majesty's forces.

Seventy-one days after leaving Detroit, Hamilton and his men camped a few miles north of Vincennes. Early the next morning of December 17, Hamilton gathered most of the Indians and again split them into two parties. He sent one southeast on the trail to the Falls of the Ohio. The other he pointed west on the trail to Kaskaskia. Their mission was to capture any couriers and discover the number and location of any enemy forces. After the Indian parties disappeared into the forest, Hamilton ordered Major Jehu Hay to lead the redcoats, La Mothe's company, the six-pounder and crew, and his remaining Indians down the trail to Vincennes. Hamilton and the rest of his force would paddle downriver in the flotilla.

Despite his precautions, Hamilton did not surprise Helm. Scouts brought word of the enemy's advance. Honor rather than discretion determined what Helm did with that warning. Rather than prudently flee, Helm chose to stand firm in the fort that he had been entrusted with capturing and defending. He scribbled off a letter to Clark and handed it to a courier. The captain kept his cool despite his desperate predicament:

> At this time theer is an army within three miles of this place. I heard of them comin several days beforehand sent spies to find the certainty the spies being taken prisoners I never got intelligence till they got within 3 miles of the town as I had call'd the militia & had all assurance of their integrity I orderd . . . the firing of a Cannon every man to appear but I saw but few. . . . My determination is to defend the Garrison though I have but 21 men. . . . You must think how I feel, not four men that I can really depend on, but am determined to act brave think of my condition I know its out of my power to defend the town as not one of the militias will take arms there is a small distance I must conclude.[37]

In the end, only three men stayed with Helm. The four men stood defiantly behind a cannon emplaced at Fort Patrick Henry's open gate. Seeing no one else, Hamilton and his officers approached the fort. Helm called out that he would die fighting unless he received honorable terms. Hamilton replied that Helm's "situation did not admit of any other than his being treated with humanity."[38] That was good enough for Helm.

Hamilton immediately ordered his redcoats forward to secure the fort. He posted guards at the gate to prevent the Indians from getting inside and another before Helm's headquarters to guard his papers and a keg of rum. Those efforts mostly came to naught. The Indians massed around the gate and angrily demanded to be let in. Several crawled through cannon ports or clambered over the palisade. When those outside heard the war cries of those inside, they shoved aside the guards, surged into the fort, and scattered to loot anything that appealed to them. The pandemonium frenzied the thirty-two horses penned in the fort. They broke free and dashed around the parade ground and reared or kicked at anyone who tried to seize them. Somehow, no one was trampled. Eventually, the Indians were able to calm the horses and lead them off to their camps. Fortunately, the soldier guarding Helm's headquarters kept the Indians at bay; had they swarmed past and tapped that rum keg, all hell would have erupted.

A couple of Indians also tried to seize Helm. Before advancing on the fort, Hamilton had promised a wampum belt worth three pounds sterling to the warrior who took the first captive. Hamilton handed over the belt to secure Helm's release. Later, he would parole Helm for his promise to stay in the fort and not send word to his compatriots elsewhere.

Fort Patrick Henry had fallen without a shot being fired or anyone killed. Despite their pledges of support for the Americans, no more than three local Frenchmen and not a single Piankeshaw had rallied to Helm. The day's only casualty occurred when an Indian fell into a cellar and dislocated his shoulder. In all, given that at times Indians slaughtered a frontier fort's garrison that surrendered, Hamilton and his officers were enormously relieved at what transpired. The care that Hamilton took to prevent any atrocities reveals a side of him at odds with his ruthless "Hair-buyer" image.

The scouts that Hamilton had sent westward fulfilled their mission. Later that day, they brought in the courier with the letter that Helm had dispatched. Nabbing the courier further swelled Hamilton's confidence. It might well take weeks or months before Clark learned Fort Patrick Henry's fate. By that time, Hamilton and his small army might well be on the way to surprise him and his ragtag followers at Kaskaskia.

To the local Piankeshaws and other tribes in the region, Hamilton sent runners calling for a council on December 20. When the council convened, the Piankeshaw chiefs Tobacco and Tobacco's Son, the Door of the Wabash, were chagrined as Hamilton rebuked them for their betrayal. The chiefs from other tribes joined in the condemnation. To that, the son retorted, "You have 'till now been afraid to come thus far from your homes to encourage me, I was dismayed being so inconsiderable as I am and without advice or support, I am but a young man; When the rebels came into the country I was alarmed, what I have done was from a sense of my own weakness." After venting that frustration, he declared, "Why should I use many words, I am glad to join my hands with yours."[39]

On December 29, Hamilton issued a proclamation designed to cow the inhabitants back into loyalty to the British king. He would "impress on them a due sense of their error in facilitating the entrance of the rebels into their country, in neglecting their duty to their King, and committing an offense against God." He warned them that a "storm which threatens them on all sides is gathering fast, and will soon burst without distinction on the rebels and those who shall support them."[40]

Finally, Hamilton dispatched a thinly veiled warning to Louisiana governor Galvez not to aid the rebels. He first explained that he was fulfilling "my duty to dispossess" the Americans of the Illinois country. He had recaptured Vincennes and would march against Kaskaskia in the spring. Although he was well aware that Galvez was aiding the Americans, he pretended that was not so and blamed his predecessor for "sending . . . supplies of Gunpowder and other stores to the Rebels. . . . Tho' this may have been transacted in an underhand manner by merchants, unknown to the Governor, I must suppose that under your Excellency order's, such commerce will for the future be positively prohibited." From such polite fictions is diplomacy made. However, Hamilton's last point could not have been more blunt. Should the Spanish harbor any rebels in their territory, "It will become my Duty to dislodge them, in which case their protectors must blame their own Conduct, if they should suffer any inconvenience in consequence."[41]

Meanwhile, Hamilton set his men to work transforming the palisade (which reverted to its previous name, Fort Sackville) from "a miserable stockade without a Well, barrack, platform for small arms, or even a lock to the gate," into a genuine military stronghold. Over the next two months, the men "build a guard-house, Barracks of four companies, sunk a Well, erected two large Blockhouses of oak, musket proof with loopholes below and embrasures for 5 pieces of Cannon each, alter'd and lined the Stockade, [and] laid the Fort with gravel."[42] That transformation would be completed just in time for Hamilton to surrender the fort to Clark.

Hamilton's vision of a two-step bloodless reconquest of the Illinois country was bolstered a few days later when a patrol brought in Francis Vigo, a Saint Louis merchant and business partner of Governor de Leyba, whom Clark had dispatched with five hundred dollars' worth of supplies to deliver to Helm. Under interrogation by Hamilton, Vigo revealed how vulnerable the Americans were at Kaskaskia: "There was no discipline or regularity observed by the Americans, that they were billeted upon the inhabitants, and squandered at large thro' the settlements."[43] He explained that he was a Spanish subject and peddler who was on his way to sell his wares in Vincennes. He requested the return of the "merchandise" that the Indians had stolen from him. That was beyond Hamilton's power, but he could release Vigo if he promised not to reveal that the British had retaken Vincennes while he was on the way back to Saint Louis. Vigo promised and was soon headed westward. Strictly keeping his promise, he would reveal nothing on the way to Saint Louis, but, after a short sojourn during which he briefed Governor de Leyba, he recrossed the Mississippi River. On January 29, 1779, Vigo was seated across from George Rogers Clark at Kaskaskia.

Until then, Clark had confidently assumed that the war was largely won not just in the Illinois country but in the entire Ohio valley. Indeed, he hoped any day to receive word that General Lachlan McIntosh's expedition from Fort Pitt had captured Detroit. Although Helm was supposed to dispatch a courier every two weeks and none had appeared for a month, he continued to assume that all was well.

So when Clark headed north with half a dozen companions one day during the last week of January, he mostly had pleasure in mind. The first stop would be Prairie du Rocher, a dozen miles away, where a ball would be held that night. The next day they would proceed to Cahokia for another ball, and thereafter perhaps a visit to Governor de Leyba in Saint Louis across the Mississippi. Although Clark and most of the group rode horses, a driver rode a horse-drawn cart, most likely filled with provisions. Just a mile or so short of Prairie du Rocher, the cart got stuck in a snow drift. As bad luck would have it, Clark's group had floundered just where a war party had set up an ambush.

A couple of weeks earlier, Hamilton had dispatched an expedition composed of a score of Ottawas and Canadians led respectively by Ottawa chief Egushawa and Charles Beaubien. The expedition had two missions. One was to get a message to Gabriel Cerré to spread the word among the community that the British were coming and not to resist. The other was to capture George Rogers Clark. The expedition had set up a camp a half mile from the road and had sent forward half a dozen Ottawas to scout. Those Ottawas now lay hidden in the woods within musket shot of Clark and his men.

The Ottawas faced a dilemma. They had a good idea that Clark was among the party digging its cart from the snow. If they rose and fired through the trees and then charged screaming war cries, they might initially drop some of the Americans and capture or scatter the rest. But what if a bullet killed Clark or he escaped? As they debated in whispers what to do, Clark and his men remounted, the cart driver urged on his horses, and the party moved rapidly up the road, completely oblivious to the mortal danger they had escaped.

Meanwhile, a hunter spotted the enemy's camp and hurried back to Kaskaskia to warn that raiders skulked in the woods. The Ottawas captured two slaves who were cutting wood along the Kaskaskia River. Once again, they faced a dilemma. If the slaves did not return by evening, the garrison would most likely send out patrols to search for them. If the slaves were released, they would likely inform the garrison of the lurking enemy. The Ottawas finally decided to let the slaves go with their promise to keep silent. Upon reaching safety, the slaves breathlessly reported what had happened. The officer in charge of Kaskaskia's garrison sent a courier galloping north to carry the alarm to Clark.

Clark and his entourage had been enjoying the ball when around midnight the courier burst in and bent his mouth to the lieutenant colonel's ear. Clark quietly ordered the horses saddled while trying to "appear as unconcerned as if no such thing was in Adjutation." He calmly explained that the report of enemy raiders required him and his men to return to Kaskaskia, but he expressed his hope that "they would not let the news Spoil our

Divirsion sooner than was necessary, that we would divirt ourselves until
our horses was ready." He then called on the musicians to strike up a tune
and encouraged everyone to join in dancing. He dispatched a courier with
orders to Bowman to ready his men for possible action. When an orderly
informed Clark that the horses were ready, he and his men exited, "politically making very merry."[44]

Here is yet another example of Clark's understanding of psychology. A
leader's mood was infectious. If he exuded the notion that war was a grand,
joyous lark with victory just a matter of time and determination, his soldiers
and the population he was trying to win over would share that enthusiasm
unless experience taught them otherwise.

The merry faces of Clark and his men likely tightened into taut masks as
soon as they began trotting down the road. The closer they got to Kaskaskia,
the greater the chance that musket shots, war whoops, and a rush of warriors
could break the night's snowbound silence. The men frequently reined in
and peered through the dark whenever someone harshly whispered a warning. But eventually they spied the black jumbled mass of Kaskaskia ahead
and hollered out their arrival to the sentinels posted at the edge of town.

Clark was pleased to find the garrison and militia armed and ready, but
was concerned and disappointed when a council with the village elders revealed their preference for neutrality should the British and Indians attack.
He grimly reckoned that only an even worse threat could pressure them
back into allegiance with the Americans: "I pretended to be in a passion,
and ordered them to their homes, saying I had no further business with
them, and that I expected they would soon see their towns in flames." Clark
was good to his word. He had his men burn several buildings close to the
fort. Clark was stone-faced as he watched the flames, but his mind and
stomach were seething: "All was now confusion, the town on fire, the women
and children screaming, and the inhabitants moving out. I keenly felt their
distress." In a panic, the elders approached him and asked how much of the
village he intended to destroy. Clark stoically announced his intention to
burn every house with provisions that the enemy could requisition. The elders then hurriedly scattered to spread the word among the people to carry
all their excess grain and dried meat to the fort. Clark soon saw that his
ends justified his harsh means: "Within two or three hours we had upwards
of two months provisions in store. Our policy was, aside from getting the

provisions, to make ourselves as daring as possible."[45] As "the inhabitants now wished that they had behaved in another manner," Clark shifted back to his magnanimous role: "I took the advantage of the favourable opportunity to Attach them entirely in my Interest, and instead of Treating them more severe . . . I altered my Conduct towards them and treated them with the greatest kindness, granting them every request."[46]

Clark was most disappointed with Father Gibault, who was terrified that Hamilton would retaliate against him when he learned that the priest was crucial in swaying the communities of Kaskaskia, Cahokia, and Vincennes to back the Americans. Clark sent him along with his force's papers and cash to safety on the Spanish side of the Mississippi.

The following morning scouts returned from the enemy camp to report that the raiders had numbered about forty and had withdrawn. After realizing that their presence had been discovered, the raiders had made haste to avoid being encircled and destroyed by Clark's superior numbers of troops.

When Clark pondered just where those raiders had come from and returned to, he could only reach a chilling conclusion—"It was now conjectured that Vincennes was in the hands of the enemy." That was confirmed on January 29, when Francis Vigo appeared and urgently requested a meeting. The news that Hamilton had taken Vincennes was alarming enough, but Vigo's initial estimate that he commanded eight hundred men jolted Clark. After Clark pressed him on that figure, Vigo halved it to four hundred Indians, thirty redcoats, fifty French volunteers, and a few Indian agents. Those were still formidable odds, with Hamilton's men outgunning his own by two to one. Hamilton's artillery included the six-pounder he had brought along with two smaller cannons, probably three-pounders, and two swivel guns that were already at the fort.[47]

The following day, Clark convened his officers in a council of war. Holding nothing back, he tersely explained the threat and their options to counter that threat. His officers "now saw we were in a very critical situation," indeed so critical that Clark declared he "would have bound myself seven years a Slave to have had five hundred troops."[48] But no possible source of reinforcements—the Kentucky settlements, Fort Pitt, Virginia—had any to spare. Indeed, Clark most likely could not get a message to his compatriots elsewhere because Indians would probably waylay any couriers paddling slowly up the Ohio River's powerful winter current.

Given those apparently overwhelming odds, a conventional commander would have seen two choices. He could sit tight, strengthen the defenses, send desperate appeals to Kentucky, Fort Pitt, Williamsburg, and Congress for reinforcements, and steel himself and his men for the enemy onslaught in the spring. Or he could try to withdraw his force to the fort at the Falls of the Ohio and await Hamilton there.

George Rogers Clark was not a conventional commander. In a letter to Governor Henry, he explained his dilemma and the strategy that might just resolve it: "Being sensible that without a Reinforcement . . . I shall be obliged to give up this Cuntrey to Mr. Hamilton without a turn of Fortune in my favour, I am Resolved to . . . Risque the whole on a Single Battle. . . . You must be Sensible of the Feeling I have for those Brave Officers and Soldiers that are Determined to share my Fate. . . . I know the Case is Desperate but . . . Great things have been affected by a few Men well Conducted."[49]

CHAPTER 10

Purgatory

They really began to think themselves superior to other men and that neither the rivers or seasons could stop their progress their whole conversation now was what they would do when they got about the Enemy and . . . wound themselves up to such a pitch that they soon took St. Vincennes divided the spoil and before Bed time was far advanced on their route to Detroit.

George Rogers Clark

How could Clark and 170 or so men possibly take Hamilton and his troops in Fort Sackville at any time, especially during a harsh winter? Clark reasoned that his greatest ally was the very notion that trying to do so would be suicidal and thus would never be attempted. He explained that the "season of the year was also favorable to our design since the enemy could not suppose that we should be so mad as to attempt to march eighty leagues through a drowned country in the depths of winter."[1]

After discussing his plan with his officers, he dismissed them to ready their men for the campaign. A courier galloped off to Cahokia, with orders to Captain Richard McCarty to quickly march down his company. A company of volunteers was organized among the Kaskaskia militia by Captain Francois Charleville. It did not take much time or effort to distribute what few supplies of munitions and rations were available. But any campaign, especially the daunting one that lay before the men, demanded another element even more vital than equipment and organization.

Of all the ingredients of a military victory, none is more crucial than leadership. That involves not just planning, training, organizing, and implementing but, above all, inspiring. A leader must reach deep into the minds of his followers and convince them to zealously and unquestionably do whatever he commands them to do. A true leader leads from the front, at times physically, always symbolically.

Clark epitomized great leadership. He mastered the dynamic relationship between mind and matter or soft and hard power. He later explained, "I conducted myself as though I was sure of taking Mr. Hamilton, instructed my Officers to observe the same rule. In a day or two the Country seemed to believe it." He understood the interwoven emotional ties between soldiers and civilians, men and women. He immersed each community in the passion of his vision, and in doing so he stirred waves of enthusiasm surging from one to the next: "The Ladies began also to be spirited and interest themselves in the Expedition, which had great Effect on the Young men." That rising tide even carried with it those who had previously passively resisted the invaders but were now "anctious to retrieve their characters."[2]

Clark's strategy was to hit Vincennes from two directions, one by land and the other by river. Clark himself would lead 130 men and a dozen packhorses overland. For the water route, he bought a keelboat, christened it the *Willing*, and had his men convert it into a war vessel. Captain John Rogers would command the *Willing*'s forty-six-man crew, two four-pounders, two swivels, and hull crammed full of munitions, rations, and other vital supplies. Their mission would be to run the Mississippi down to the Ohio and then laboriously pole upstream to the Wabash and finally up it to ten leagues below Vincennes, where they would await further orders.[3]

If Clark achieved surprise, he could circle Fort Sackville by land and water, trapping Hamilton and his men inside. The Wabash's current would make it difficult for Hamilton and his men during the night to sneak out of the fort and paddle their way upriver without being detected and raked with rifle fire. The *Willing* would cut off any attempt by Hamilton's force to ride the swift current downstream to refuge in then-neutral Spanish territory. Clark saw the latter as a genuine possibility and instructed Rogers, "If you should meet him, never quit him as long as you have the least chance to take him."[4]

Rogers and his crew cast off from Kaskaskia on February 4, 1779. Clark had picked Rogers for that independent command because he had proven himself to be a top-notch leader. He was described as "common sized, well formed, & very handsome. A good & very kind & popular with his men— careful of them."[5] Nonetheless, getting the *Willing* to Vincennes in time to reinforce Clark would be a Herculean labor.

Clark and his men set forth midafternoon the following day after receiving the blessing of Father Gibault and the cheers of the people who turned out to see them off. The late start and nasty weather prevented them from trekking more than three miles before nightfall. For the next eighteen days on the trail, more often than not, rain either drizzled or poured. Virtually each step of that 180-mile trek was sodden and often flooded ankle-deep or higher. The mud sucked at their feet, constantly devouring the men's energy and spirits and occasionally a moccasin. No streams were bridged. Holding their rifles, powder horns, and blanket rolls over their heads, the men waded across the frigid waters. The men were constantly soaked, trembling from cold, and aching with fatigue and hunger.

Clark labored ceaselessly to boost his men's spirits. On the march, he was in perpetual motion up and down the line, ready with a helping hand or encouraging word to those in need: "I myself and my principal officers conducted ourselves like woodsmen, shouting now and then and running through the mud and water the same as the men themselves. Thus, insensible of their hardships and without complaining, our men were conducted through difficulties far surpassing anything we had experienced before."[6]

His infectious enthusiasm and energy glowed especially bright during the long winter nights as the exhausted men huddled around smoky fires. Each evening a different company was charged with hosting a feast. Usually, there was fresh meat. Scouts doubled as hunters and left gutted deer, turkeys, and other game hanging from tree limbs on the trail. Stories, songs, war dances, high jinks, and hearty laughter shoved aside the gloom, fear, and fatigue, at least for a while. As Clark put it, "The divertions of the night wore off the thought of the preceeding Day."[7]

The party reached the confluence of the Embarrass (then known as the Little Wabash) and the Wabash Rivers on February 17. What they saw disheartened even Clark, although he never let on. The rivers had spread far beyond their banks in all directions and mingled in one vast flow. Somehow, they would have to cross those surging, bone-chilling waters. Clark sent a courier down the Wabash valley to find and urge on Captain Rogers and his men. He ordered the men to chop down small trees, trim the branches, and lash the logs into rafts. They piled their supplies and the exhausted on the rafts and pushed them across the Embarrass River, while swimming the horses alongside. A diminutive fourteen-year-old drummer boy lightened spirits when he used his instrument as a flotation device and sang comic songs of their predicament. If a lad could be so lighthearted at such a daunting challenge, then every man's pride dictated that he be at least as insouciant.

Once across the Embarrass River, the men "really began to think themselves superior to other men and as persons whom neither the rivers nor seasons could stop. All their conversation was now what they would do when they could charge the Enemy and now began to talk about the main Wabash as a creek, not doubting but such men as they were would find a way to cross it. Their spirits rose to such a pitch that they soon took St. Vincennes and divided the spoil and before bed time were far advanced on the road to Detroit."[8] But they still had to cross the Wabash River, swollen five miles across.

The men camped about nine miles below Vincennes on February 18. After dark, Clark sent out two parties to reach Vincennes by different routes, spy, and, ideally, steal boats and bring them downstream. Captain Richard McCarty and three men embarked in a battered dugout canoe that had been found bobbing in a backwater. They paddled a few miles upstream but turned back when they spotted four large fires on shore. Four other men tried to paddle their way across the river on a raft with the mission of hiking north to Vincennes. They never reached the far shore. The current was too swift, and the floodwaters were too wide and deep through the forest. Indeed, they were lucky to make it back to camp shortly after dawn.

What McCarty and his men saw was a British patrol that was searching for an American, William Williams, who had escaped from Vincennes along with Drury Bushe, a deserter from Captain La Mothe's volunteer company. Any joint escape and desertion would have been upsetting enough to Lieutenant Colonel Hamilton, but the disappearance of Williams must have been particularly vexing. Hamilton had ransomed Williams from Methusaagai, an Ojibwa chief who had adopted Williams to replace the son he had lost the previous year. Had Hamilton not done so, in the spring Williams most likely would have been taken north to a very distant village. But Hamilton had ransomed Williams in return for his pledge to be loyal to the British crown. Now, if Williams were caught, he would face a noose for breaking his parole to Hamilton. And Bushe would quite likely dangle besides him for desertion.

As they slogged their way from Vincennes all the way to the Ohio River, Captain Francois Maisonville and his men did not catch Williams and Bushe. However, on the north bank of the Ohio River they did capture two Americans, Captain William Shannon and another man, who most likely were returning from Fort Pitt to join Clark but claimed they were on a long scout. On their way back to Vincennes, they spotted the fourteen campfires of Clark's force far across the flooded Wabash. Though Maisonville "could not tell whether . . . Virginians or savages" warmed themselves beside those flames, he had no means of crossing the river to find out. He sent a courier trotting ahead to report the sighting to Hamilton.

Upon hearing of those mysterious campfires, Hamilton dispatched Captain La Mothe, Lieutenant Jacob Schieffelin, and twenty men to discover who had kindled them. Maisonville was just getting back with his patrol as La Mothe's set forth. Despite his exhaustion from a week's trek through the sodden wilderness, Maisonville agreed to guide them to the spot.

Clark, meanwhile, secretly despaired over the *Willing*'s failure to appear. If that keelboat filled with supplies did not soon reach Clark and his men, not only would it be impossible to capture Fort Sackville but they would face a grim fate. They had devoured the last of their rations and, apparently, the horses. Hunger tightened their bellies and sapped their energy and morale. That "starving," Bowman wrote, rendered "Many of the Men much cast down particularly the Volunteers, no provisions of any Sort now two days hard fortune . . . Camp very quiet but hungry some almost in despair Many of the Creols [French] Volunteers talking of returning."[9]

Clark crowded Captain McCarty and several men into the dugout on February 19 and sent them downstream in a grim search for the *Willing*. He directed each company to chop down trees and begin shaping the trunks into dugouts. He had hunters scour the woods. For the time being, that was all he could do. But if help did not arrive soon, his men might well have forced Clark to surrender to Hamilton rather than starve to death.

Help appeared the following day, but from an unexpected direction. A patrol brought in a boat with five Frenchmen. What the guests revealed was encouraging. The British were unaware that an enemy force was lurking nearby. The villagers leaned toward supporting the Americans. Two dugouts were adrift upstream. Clark had the French retrieve those canoes. Around that time, a hunter staggered into camp with a gutted deer slung over his shoulders. Sliced up and hastily roasted, that venison yielded each man a chunk of desperately needed protein. He sent the French back to Vincennes to secretly spread the word among the villagers that the Americans would soon arrive and would need their aid in taking Fort Sackville. Clark told his men to clean their rifles then get a good night's sleep for tomorrow's crossing.

By the first glimmer of light, Clark and his men were up peering across the vast expanse of river surging past. Each of the two canoes could only take a few men at a time across those roiling waters and deposit them on a low distant rise wistfully dubbed either the "Bubbie" or "Mammelle," depending on one's native tongue.[10] Although the crossing through a steady drizzle began at dawn, the last man did not step ashore until midday. Even then, the river still hemmed them in. The men had to wade in water up to their armpits across to the island. As they crossed, a canoe appeared coming downriver. Clark dispatched men in the two canoes to intercept it, but its paddlers turned their craft and pushed upstream until they disappeared from view.

That incident was deeply worrying. Had they been French, they would have likely joined them. But the flight of those canoeists meant that they were probably British and would sound the alarm at Fort Sackville. And that could lead to the expedition's destruction. Clark and his men were soaked, trembling, and exhausted; their bellies were pinched with hunger; the drizzle or stumbles in the river had dampened most rifle loads. They would be cut to pieces if a British and Indian force suddenly appeared on the road somewhere ahead. But they still had to get to that road.

Another vast stretch of floodwaters separated the Mammelle from the next patch of land known as the Sugar Camp. Clark and several men climbed into a canoe and paddled across to see if they could wade it or would have to spend more miserable hours crossing in the canoes. The men were at their breaking point. All eyes were locked on Clark when he returned. His face was hardened, and he "unfortunately spoke in a serious manner to one of the officers." That snapped the final thread holding back the men from utter despair. They ran "from one to another . . . bewailing their situation."[11]

That collapse of morale threw the expedition into its latest and worst crisis of all. The uproar bewildered Clark, but only for a few moments. Suddenly, he ordered his officers to do exactly as he did. He poured some gunpowder in the palm of his hand, doused it with water, and then smeared his face black until only his cold blue eyes shone. As he and his officers did so, one after another of the men grew silent and warily watched them. Suddenly, Clark threw back his head, screamed a war whoop at the top of his lungs, and plunged into the water. His officers and men stoically waded in after him. To dilute some of their misery, Clark had his men sing their favorite songs. When a man stumbled, fell beneath the water, then shot to the surface sputtering curses, he turned "such a mishap . . . into sport to inspirit the men."

The men did not reach the Sugar Camp until nearly nightfall. Profanities erupted as they learned it was yet another island. Clark scattered the men to different tasks. Most chopped or hauled firewood. Others cocked their rifles and tramped through the brush or thumped hollow trees in search of game. A few scrapped steel against flint and unleashed sparks onto tinder packed within teepees of twigs. The hunters spooked from lairs and killed a fox and several opossums; each man got a bit or two of the gamy meat. Then they crowded around the fires and trembled away the seemingly endless night.

At dawn, Clark gathered his men and wielded every possible appeal to their manhood, patriotism, and desire to just stay alive that might coax them into following him across that last long, agonizing stretch of drowned wilderness. Then he turned, jumped in, and vigorously pushed through the deepening waters. His officers and most of the men followed, but a few hesitated. Clark ordered Captain Bowman to fall out with his company and "put to death any man that refused to march."[12] Soon everyone was wading through the frigid watery hell except the sick who were packed in the two canoes. But after a hundred or so yards, men began to falter, slump against trees, and mutter to be left to die. Those less exhausted locked arms around the laggards and dragged them onward.

The sight of another island through the trees ahead stirred another burst of hope and energy. One by one, the men stumbled ashore. As they lay trembling on the ground, someone spotted a canoe full of Indian women and children in an expanse of water on the island's far side. Clark ordered able-bodied men to scramble for the canoes and intercept them. The women submitted without trying to flee. In their canoe was a "nearly half a quarter of buffalo . . . some corn, tallow, and kettles." Firewood was gathered and ignited. The meat and corn was divvied up among the kettles and boiled. Clark ensured that "with great care most of the men obtained a little, but many of them would not taste it, giving it instead to the weaker ones and saying something encouraging to their comrades."[13]

After he felt the men had rested enough, Clark spread the word for each to ready himself for the final push. Vincennes was just beyond the northern horizon.

George Mason, by Dominic Boudet from original by John Hesselius. © Courtesy of the Board of Regents of Gunston Hall, Home of George Mason, Mason Neck, Virginia.

Patrick Henry by George Bagby Mathews. Courtesy U.S. Senate Collection.

Thomas Jefferson by Charles Willson Peale, from life, 1791–1792. Courtesy Independence National Historical Park.

Henry Hamilton. Courtesy The Filson Historical Society, Louisville, Kentucky.

Joseph Brant/Thayendanegea by Charles Willson Peale, from life, 1797. Courtesy Independence National Historical Park.

William Clark by Charles Willson Peale, from life, 1807–1808. Courtesy Independence National Historical Park.

Meriwether Lewis by Charles Willson Peale, from life, 1807. Courtesy Independence National Historical Park.

William Croghan by John Wesley Jarvis. From the collections of Historic Locust Grove.

Lucy Clark Croghan by John Wesley Jarvis. From the collections of Historic Locust Grove.

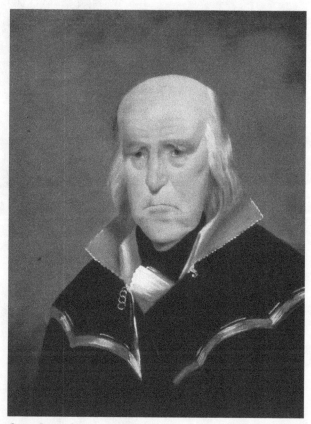

George Rogers Clark (around 1814) by Joseph Bush. From the collections of Historic Locust Grove.

Locust Grove, photograph by Courtney Novak. From the collections of Historic Locust Grove.

CHAPTER 11

Caging the Hair Buyer

You and all your men are prisoners of George Rogers Clark.

Leonard Helm

Could I look upon you Sir as a Gentleman I would do the utmost of my power, but on you Sir who have embrued your hands in the blood of our women and children, Honor, my country, everything calls on me aloud for vengeance.

George Rogers Clark

The last water barrier for Clark and his men was a creek that winter rains had swollen into a river. It was too deep to wade, but with three canoes and only a few hundred yards of passage, the men were crouched on the far shore by early afternoon. Before them was a vast sodden rolling prairie that stretched to Vincennes a couple of miles away. The men must have gazed in disbelief at that distant cluster of tiny buildings as if it were some bizarre mirage. Some may have refrained from blinking for fear that Vincennes would dissolve back into that endless bone-chilling flooded wilderness purgatory into which they had so eagerly plunged several weeks earlier.

Though the men were then too far off to be seen by anyone in Vincennes, the odds of being spotted would rise steadily the closer they got to town. And that could provoke their worst peril yet: "Our situation was now sufficiently critical. We were within full view of a town which contained upwards of six hundred men, counting soldiers, Indians, and inhabitants, with no possibility of retreat . . . in case of defeat. . . . In the event of capture [we] looked forward to being tortured by the savages. Our fate was now to be determined within the next few hours, and we knew that nothing but the boldest conduct would ensure success."[1]

All the men could do was sit tight among the trees fringing the prairie, clean their rifles, and wait for dark. Clark recalled to their hearts and minds the whole point of their campaign. Sitting cozy in his headquarters just a few miles yonder was the evil "Hair-buyer," Henry Hamilton, who had inspired the brutal murders, tortures, and captures of hundreds of their compatriots, friends, and loved ones. Rage and a lust for vengeance trumped misery as "everyone feasted his eyes and forgot that he had suffered any thing."[2]

Someone pointed to riders trotting across the prairie from Vincennes. The horsemen angled over to a shallow backwater of the Wabash River, where they dismounted and took potshots at ducks. Clark had several French volunteers stride over and hail them. The plan was to capture the hunters if they were British and try to entice them if they were French. Fortunately, they were French and agreed to help when they learned of the expedition. Upon being brought to camp and debriefed, the Frenchmen revealed one bit of ominous news. Fort Sackville had been a dilapidated, rotting structure when Hamilton and his men took it in mid-December. Since then, Hamilton had daily deployed his men to strengthen the fort. They had finished the final repairs earlier that very day.

Clark scribbled a proclamation for the hunters to take back to the village and have someone translate and circulate among the French villagers. The proclamation read:

> To the Inhabitants of Vincennes
>   Gentlemen: Being now within two miles of your village with my army determined to take your fort this night, and not being willing to surprise you, I am taking the measure of requesting such of you as are true citizens and desirous of enjoying the liberty I bring you to remain quietly in your houses. If there are any friends

of the King of England I desire them instantly to repair to the fort and there join his troops and fight like men; and if any that do not repair to the garrison shall hereafter be discovered they may depend upon being severely punished. Those, on the other hand, who are true friends of Liberty, may expect to be well treated. I once more request that they keep out of the streets, for every person found under arms upon my arrival will be treated as an enemy.[3]

Once again Clark revealed his mastery of psychology. With those words, he symbolically brandished his sword and drew a line through the emotional, ideological, and ethnic landscape. On one side were the Americans who championed the liberty of all those who shared their love of freedom. Their enemies were those who defended the tyranny of the King of England. Those who loved freedom should wait safely in their homes for their liberation. Those opposed should immediately withdraw to the fort or else suffer "severe punishment." Clark later explained that he intended his proclamation to "encourage our friends, cause those who were lukewarm to take a decide stand, and astonish our Enemies."[4]

Clark sought to magnify the amount of troops under his command in his enemy's minds—he kept them hidden and circulated the fiction that they had marched from Kentucky rather than Kaskaskia. Hamilton knew the American forces in the Illinois numbered no more than a couple of hundred. He did not know how many Kentuckians could muster but might well reckon they numbered two or three times those actually before him.

Clark and his men watched anxiously as the hunters returned to Vincennes with that startling proclamation. Soon "we could perceive with the aid of our glasses a stirring about in every street and large numbers running or riding out into the commons, intent as we supposed upon viewing us."[5] Yet Fort Sackville remained quiet; no cannon shot or drumroll sounded the alarm. The Americans assumed that meant the garrison was already alert and waiting. Actually, Hamilton and his troops were oblivious to the danger hovering just on the horizon. Clark had achieved complete surprise.

As the sun set far to the southwest, Clark split his men into two divisions, with the companies of Captains John Williams and Edward Worthington, and the Kaskaskia volunteers of Captain Francois Charleville in the first, the company of Captain Joseph Bowman and the Cahokia volunteers of Captain Richard McCarty in the second. Clark would command the first and Bowman the second division.

Clark then led his men across the prairie. Each company's flag was unfurled atop a tall pole and waved defiantly by the bearer. Deception remained essential to Clark's plan: "We advanced slowly in full view of the town but as it was a matter of some consequences to make ourselves appear as formidable as possible, on leaving our place of concealment we marched and countermarched in a fashion calculated to magnify our numbers. . . . Since the plain through which we advanced was not perfectly level but was dotted with elevations rising seven or eight feet above the common level . . . we took advantage of one of these to march our men along the low ground so that only the colors . . . could be seen above the height."[6]

Upon reaching the town, the men spread out to secure it and then devoured platefuls of food passed from the thresholds of grateful or fearful families. Meanwhile, the local militia leaders handed out gunpowder and lead that they had secreted from the British when they arrived and demanded that the inhabitants surrender their arms and ammunition. The local Piankeshaws, led by the Door of the Wabash, eagerly rallied to the Americans. Clark was grateful but "told him the Ill consequence of our People being mingled in the dark; they might lay in their quarters until light."[7] Astonishingly, no one had warned the fort, and the garrison's sentinels had not spotted their enemy's advance.

Fort Sackville was sited atop a twelve-foot bank overlooking the river. At Vincennes, the Wabash River actually breaks its long north-to-south flow to twist westward before curling south again a mile beyond, so the fort and the town actually lay south of the river. Fields spread away from the fort's three land sides. The town's closest prominent building was the Catholic church, sixty yards south. Fort Sackville was trapezoid-shaped, with a ten-foot split-log palisade running 222 feet on the north wall, 195 feet on the east, 208 on the south, and 168 on the west. A gate opened on the east side; blockhouses stood at the northwest and southeast corners. A narrow firing platform ran along each wall. Within the fort stood two barracks, a headquarters, a guardhouse, and a magazine partially dug underground.[8]

Surprise and deception alone were not enough to take the fort. Firepower was essential. That, however, was in short supply. Without the *Willing* and its men, munitions, supplies, and, most vitally, cannons, Clark and his men could raise only their rifles against the redcoats within the palisade. While the riflemen might pick off careless defenders, the British were unlikely to yield unless cannon balls were systematically blasting the palisade to splinters. To make up for that deficiency, Clark once again deployed his most powerful weapon—psychology. He spread the word for his men "to appear as Darring as possible, that the Enemy might conceive by our behavior that we were very numerous and probably discourage them."[9]

Clark was spoiling for a fight. After his men had satiated their hunger, he ordered Lieutenant John Bailey and his fourteen fighters to creep close to the fort, scatter around its three land sides, and open fire at the palisade silhouetted against the night sky. Even then, no excited calls to assemble and drumrolls sounded from within the fort. Apparently, "drunken Indians often saluted" the fort with gunfire "after nightfall."[10] When the shots erupted, Hamilton and all his men except a few inattentive sentinels were resting from their own exertions. To celebrate the completion of the six weeks of steady labor that finished the fort's defense, Hamilton had his officers organize games and then a feast. At that very moment, Hamilton and Helm were enjoying hot apple toddies and a card game of piquet. Hamilton leapt up from his chair and demanded the meaning of the gunshots. Helm reputedly offered a laconic but pointed reply: "It means that you and all your men are prisoners of George Rogers Clark."[11]

Hamilton dashed out to the parade ground and "heard the Balls sing, still I could not conceive otherwise than some drunken people were amusing themselves." He finally understood that the fort was suffering an attack only after hearing that one of his sergeants was "mortally wounded," but it proved only a contusion, a metal button having saved his life.[12]

Hamilton ordered his officers to assemble the troops. With their adrenaline doubtlessly pumping from the sudden gunshots and alarm, the redcoats stumbled from the barracks onto the parade ground and then, according to their assignments, either lined the parapet or crowded into the blockhouses. Each side fired at shadows and gun flashes in the dark. But the British only fired a few musket and cannon shots before they received an order to cease-fire and keep their heads down. That order reputedly came after Hamilton acted on Helm's warning that the frontier marksmen were so skilled they could shoot out their eyes. To deny those sharpshooters a silhouette, all candles and fires were doused.[13]

Clark sent over another dozen men to relieve Bailey and, after that detachment had fired half a dozen or so shots, replaced them with another dozen men, and so on. That way he could "keep the garrison eternally alarmed," while letting his men scatter within the homes, stretch before roaring fires, and rest. To further eat away at the enemy's morale, Clark had his men catcall insults and howl with mocking laughter at the British.

All along, Clark emphasized his men's safety, both from humanitarian concerns and the hard reality that with so few troops, each was precious: "Since we could not afford to lose any of our men, great pains were taken to keep them sufficiently sheltered and to maintain a hot fire against the fort in order to intimidate the enemy as well as destroy them." It was far easier to cow than kill the enemy—indeed the former all but prevented the latter: "The embrasures for their cannon were frequently closed, for our riflemen finding the true direction would pour in such volleys when they were open that the artillerymen could not stand to the guns. Seven or eight of them were shot down in a short time. Our men frequently taunted the enemy in order to provoke them into opening the portholes and firing the cannon so that they might have the pleasure of cutting them down with their rifles."[14]

It was certainly far safer to fire at rather than from the fort. The garrison's cannons were all but useless as they were deployed "on the upper floors of the blockhouses located at each angle of the fort eleven feet above the ground, and the portholes were so badly cut that our troops lay under their fire within twenty or thirty yards of the walls. The enemy did no damage except to the buildings of the town, some of which were badly shattered."[15] The garrison's small arms were just as ineffective. The redcoats were armed with muskets, notoriously inaccurate beyond a score or so yards even when deliberately aimed in daylight. By contrast, the Americans mostly cradled rifles and many were crack shots. They fired at every figure that passed by a porthole or who raised his head above the palisade.

When Bailey and his men first opened fire, John McBeath, the garrison's surgeon, was visiting a Frenchwoman in the village. He too had been oblivious to the American parade across the prairie followed by their noisy entrance into the village. If he heard any commotion, he likely dismissed it as a returning hunting or scalp party. The first volley of gunshots puzzled him as it had Hamilton and the other British. The hostess cried excitedly,

"There Colonel Clarke is arrived from the Illinois with 500 men." Though he was cut off from the fort, McBeath obeyed his duty to his imperiled comrades. Somehow, he was not hit in his mad dash from the village to the palisade, although a ball clipped one of his leggings.[16]

Among the fort's defenders was militia captain Francois Bosseron. The governor knew from an intercepted letter that Bosseron had previously pledged allegiance to the Americans, even though he held a crown's commission for his rank. Yet, until the burst of gunshots, Bosseron's conflicted loyalties had not worried Hamilton because he believed that the distant enemy had lost their influence over the French.

Indeed, not all of the French inhabitants either enthusiastically or reluctantly sided with the Americans. Isadore Chene had joined war parties against the Kentucky settlements along with the expedition to capture Clark at Kaskaskia. He too somehow was unaware of the enemy's presence until the first gunshots. When he learned their significance, he gathered several other Loyalists, including Ottawa Chief Egushawa and his few men, and they headed for safety not in the fort, but in the woods.

Meanwhile, another British force was trying to slip into Fort Sackville. Captain La Mothe and his detachment were returning from their grueling patrol when the gunshots began popping in the pitch darkness far before them. Upon reaching the outskirts of Vincennes, they sheltered in the barn of a villager they trusted. There they would sit tight and await word on the enemy's strength and disposition.

Among La Mothe's party was Francois Maisonville. It was Maisonville whose patrol had spotted the mysterious fires of Clark's party and who had no sooner arrived back at Fort Sackville when he agreed to guide La Mothe's patrol to the distant flames. A couple of grueling weeks in the wilderness had exhausted him. Earlier, he had informed La Mothe that he was going to stay in his own bed that night. He would regret that decision.

The Americans nabbed Maisonville and, after learning his notorious identity, roughly interrogated him. Not only was Maisonville fingered as the Kaskaskia resident who had escaped to carry word of the American conquest to Hamilton, but he was also said to be a merciless and frequent participant in war parties against the Kentucky frontier. His confession to those charges enraged Clark, who ordered Maisonville scalped. A soldier pulled a butcher knife and carved "two pieces of the Skin of the size of a sixpence." Maisonville's courage in the face of excruciating pain impressed Clark, who ordered him released.[17]

Some mix of pain, terror, and gratitude prompted Maisonville to reveal the whereabouts of La Mothe and his men and their intention to join their comrades inside the fort. That intelligence posed a tough choice for Clark. Should he send a company to encircle and attack that lurking enemy? Or was it better to let them slip into the big trap rather than spring a smaller one on them? Clark noisily ordered a cease-fire and withdrawal of his snipers from around the fort. After hearing that command followed by a prolonged silence, La Mothe and his men crept out of the barn and toward Fort Sackville. The Americans did not fire as they hurried past, and neither did the British as they crouched outside the gate, identified themselves, and demanded to be let in. After La Mothe and his men were safely inside, the Americans "loosened a barrage of catcalls and . . . of our stratagem . . . for suffering them to enter the fort." Then "firing immediately recommenced with redoubled vigor and I do not believe that more noise could possibly have been made by an equal number of men. Their shouting could not be heard amid the discharge of the muskets, and a continual line of fire around the garrison was maintained until shortly before daylight when our troops were withdrawn to positions that had been prepared for them sixty to one hundred yards from the fort."[18]

With La Mothe and his men inside, Fort Sackville was defended by thirty-three British regulars and thirty-six French militiamen, commanded by ten officers. Hamilton grimly noted the difference between the two. With the militia, "I could not find that those . . . had acted with spirit from the first. On the contrary the men of the King's regiment behaved with the greatest alacrity, and even exposed themselves more than I wished."[19]

As dawn broke on February 24, Clark withdrew his men beyond accurate musket range and deployed them behind solid cover. Now the deadliness and range of Clark's riflemen could take full effect. Yet it was no time for complaisance. A lucky shot from the fort severely wounded an American in the head who was nonchalantly strolling to the village blacksmith to get his rifle repaired. Clark ordered a cease-fire around eight that morning and sent a message to Hamilton under a flag of truce. While he awaited Hamilton's reply, Clark had the villagers distribute food to his men.

Hamilton must have blanched at Clark's fiery words: "Sir, In order to save yourself from the Impending Storm that now Threatens you I order you to Immediately surrender your self up with all your Garrison Stores &c. &c. for if I am obliged to storm, you may depend such Treatment justly due a Murderer beware of destroying Stores of any kind or any papers or letters that is in your possession or hurting one house in the Town for by heavens if you do there shall be no Mercy shewn you. signed G.R. Clark."[20]

Clark's threat to assault the fort was a bluff. Without cannon to blast holes in the palisade, the attackers would have had to carry ladders, place them against the wall, and then scramble to the top. The defenders likely would have cut his men to pieces before they reached the foot of the palisade. If Clark's men recognized that reality, it did not faze them. After they learned Hamilton's reply, Clark had to restrain their being "greatly animated" and desire "to put an end to the business at once."[21]

Hamilton called Clark's bluff with a curt reply: "Lieutenant Governor Hamilton acquaints Colonel Clarke that neither he nor his Garrison are to be prevailed upon by threats to act in a manner unbecoming the character of British subjects."[22] Yet Hamilton's response was also a bluff. He was well aware that the seemingly miraculous appearance of Clark and his men followed by the storm of lead had demoralized the French militia, if not the British regulars. He gathered his troops, read them Clark's demand and his reply, and asked if they would defend the decision of his officers and himself to defy the rebels. The reaction of the redcoats was deeply gratifying: "The English to a man declared they would stand to the last for the honor of their Country, and as they expressed it, would stick to me as the shirt to my back. They then cried 'God Save King George, and gave three Huzzas.'" The French, understandably, were hardly as enthusiastic. They "hung their heads, and their sergeants first turned round and muttered with their men, some said it was hard they should fight against their own Friends and relations who they could see had joined the Americans and now fired against the fort."[23]

Meanwhile, Clark reacted to Hamilton's defiance by ordering the truce flag lowered and his men to open fire and holler warnings that the redcoats would be butchered unless they capitulated. Rifle balls wounded several more British soldiers. That barrage of lead and threats doused the earlier enthusiasm of the redcoats. Sergeants informed their officers that their men feared being put to the sword if they continued to hold out, and the officers in turn explained that to Hamilton. Undoubtedly, the Hair-buyer himself worried that he would be subjected to frontier justice for the hundreds of atrocities he had instigated and underwritten.

Around noon, a white flag appeared above the fort. Helm strolled out with the message that Hamilton would surrender if he and his men could withdraw to Detroit with honors of war. That must have provoked a triumphant grin from Clark. He returned Helm with word that Hamilton had no more than half an hour to give up with discretion or else face the horrific consequences. To surrender with discretion meant to do so unconditionally.

Helm soon returned with a counterproposal for a direct talk with Clark inside the fort followed by a three-day truce. Clark instantly rebuffed that offer. Did Hamilton think he was a fool? Clearly, the Hair-buyer hoped to lure Clark into a treacherous seizure or, at the very least, play for time as a scheduled supply boat ground ashore on the fort's riverside and unloaded desperately need munitions and provisions. Having learned from villagers of the approaching supply boat, Clark intended to intercept it before it could be rowed to safety beneath the fort's guns. He sent Helm back with his message that he would speak with Hamilton before the east gate, but would certainly not enter the fort.

Regardless of what Hamilton intended, the choice he faced was starkly clear—either surrender now or most likely be slaughtered with his men later. So far no one had been killed, although gunshots had wounded seven redcoats and one American. That was about to dramatically change.

Distant war whoops and gunshots erupted from the prairie. Striding toward Vincennes was a war party fresh from the Kentucky settlements and oblivious that the Americans were now besieging Fort Sackville. The raiders included eight Ottawas, two Wyandots, two Miamis, two sergeants from the garrison, and two prisoners. Clark ordered Captain John Williams to lead his company out with smiles and hurrahs as if welcoming back the raiders. The two parties were "hooping, hollowing, and Striking each others Breasts as they approached in the open fields each seemed to try to out do the other in the greatest signs of Joy." Clark was "highly pleased" as he watched Williams and his men circle the raiders, lower their rifles, and open fire: "The Poor Devils never discovered their mistake until it was too late."[24] The volley killed six of the raiders, and the rest threw down their arms and begged for mercy. The survivors—four Indians and four whites—were shoved toward Clark. It was soon discovered that two of the whites were themselves captives and were released.

Once again, Clark swiftly assessed a situation and acted on the option with the most powerful psychological impact. As he put it, "I had now a fair oppertunity of making an impression."[25] He ordered the prisoners to line up and kneel facing the fort's east wall. He then grimly announced that they would die for their crimes. Macutte Mong or Muckeydemengo, the Ottawa chief, began to sing his death song, inspiring his warriors to utter their own chants.

Not all of the prisoners would die. Captain Richard McCarty, who commanded the Cahokia company, recognized one of the Indians as Pontiac's son. As the father Pontiac had once spared McCarty's life, the captain now asked that the son be spared. Clark reluctantly nodded his approval. Then McCarty's lieutenant was stunned to recognize that beneath the sergeant's garish war paint was his only son, Jean Baptiste Romain Sanscrainte. He begged Clark to revoke his son's sentence. Clark again demurred.[26]

A hundred yards away, Hamilton and his men lined the parapet and viewed with horror the fate of the Indian captives. Hamilton's mind and stomach must have churned with guilt. Just weeks earlier he had exhorted and supplied those raiders and now would have been amply rewarding them had Clark and his men never appeared. What was unclear was the executioner's identity. Hamilton could not tell if it was Clark or another officer. Lieutenant Schieffelin insisted that it was Clark.[27]

Whoever the executioner was stepped behind one of the captives, raised his hatchet, slammed it into the victim's skull, then moved on to the next. He had caved in five skulls before nearing Macutte Mong, the scalping party's leader, who was saved for last. By now, either the executioner's arm or blood-lust was spent. His blow stuck in the Ottawa chief's skull without killing or even dropping him. Macutte Mong bent his head, reached up, yanked the hatchet from his skull, and offered it. His executioner stepped back in astonishment before seizing it. He then stepped behind the Ottawa chief and again swung his hatchet, but Macutte Mong survived not just that but a third blow. He was still breathing when a rope was looped around his neck and he was dragged to the Wabash and thrown into the surging brown waters.[28]

As his men hoarsely cheered the executions, Clark dipped his hands in a swelling pool of blood, "rubbing it several times on his cheeks, yelping as a savage."[29] He then strode toward the fort and called on Hamilton to come out and discuss terms. The executions horrified Hamilton. He refused to recognize himself as someone who had instigated countless similar or worse deeds and, in the eyes of most Americans, now deserved the same fate. Instead, he would thereafter sarcastically refer to "the courage and Humanity of Colonel Clarke" whenever he recalled the horrifying scene.[30]

Yet Hamilton had little choice but to submit. He knew that his soldiers were terrified that they would suffer the same fate without an immediate surrender. To his credit, the Hair-buyer somehow retained his composure as he walked out to meet Clark. He had likely slept little if at all throughout the long night since the first gunshots had erupted. He had just witnessed six grisly executions. And now he was standing before Clark who, "bloody and sweating, seated himself on the edge of one of the bateaus, that had some rainwater in it, & while he washed his hands and face still reeking from the human sacrifice in which he had acted as head priest," described the executions "with great exultation."[31]

Accompanying Clark was Captain Joseph Bowman; Captain Jehu Hay and captive Captain Leonard Helm stepped beside Hamilton.[32]

Clark loudly announced, "I will give no other terms but to submit yourself and Garrison to my discretion and mercy." If Hamilton did not promptly surrender, "not a single man should be spared."

"Sir," Hamilton replied, "my men are brave and willing to stand by me to the last. If I can't surrender upon Hon. terms I'll fight it out to the last."

Clark retorted, "Sir this will give my men infinite satisfaction and pleasure for it is their desire."

Hamilton's steely reserve began to break. "Col. Clarke why will you force me to dishonour myself when you cannot acquire more honor by it?"

"Could I look upon you Sir as a Gentleman," Clark replied, "I would do the utmost of my power, but on you Sir who have imbued your hands in the blood of our women and children, Honor, my country, everything calls on me aloud for vengeance."

At this point, Helm interrupted: "Gentlemen don't be warm, strive to save many lives which may be useful to their country which will unavoidably fall in case you don't agree."

Clark then stated that if the British surrendered at discretion, they might just receive better treatment than if they "articled for terms."

Hamilton refused to yield. They agreed on a half-hour break. Hamilton, Hay, and Helm disappeared inside the fort while Clark gathered his officers to explain what had been said and to solicit their advice.

The next round of talk was held near the church, but was just as heated and deadlocked. After condemning "Indian partisans," Clark coldly explained that Hamilton's intransigence was giving him the "excuse to put them to death."

That prompted Captain Jehu Hay, who himself had organized and led war parties, to nervously ask, "Pray Sir, who is it that you call Indian partisans?"

"Sir," Clark replied, "I take Major Hay to be one of the principle ones."

That condemnation caused Hay to react just as Clark intended. He recalled, "I never saw a man . . . so stricken as he appeared to be, pale and trembling, and scarcely able to stand. Governor Hamilton blushed and was . . . much affected at this behavior."

The two parties then turned and strode away. But upon reaching the gate, Hamilton called out to Clark, "Is there nothing to be done but fighting?"

"Yes Sir," Clark replied. "I will send you such articles as I think proper to allow, if you accept them . . . I will allow you half an hour to consider on them."

With that stance, Clark abandoned his demand for unconditional surrender. But having yielded a symbol, he insisted that the fort, troops, weapons, and supplies be entirely given up. He would permit the redcoats to march out with their arms and ceremonially stack them. Officers could retain their personal baggage. Each man had three days to pay up any accounts in the village stores. Then they would be herded off to captivity in faraway Virginia. As for the French militia, those from Detroit were required to sign a neutrality oath and then were allowed to go home; those from Vincennes had to sign a loyalty oath and then muster to the American cause when called upon. The surrender document's last line must have been especially galling to Hamilton. It read, "The Hon'ble Terms allw'd and lastly confidence in a Generous Enemy."

The formal surrender took place at ten o'clock the following morning of February 25. With the two companies of Illinois volunteers lined up on opposite sides of the gate, the two American companies marched between them into the fort and onto the parade ground. The British soldiers and French militia were lined up on the opposite side. Between them stood the bare flagpole. Hamilton had given orders that "the colors not be hoisted this morning, that we might be spared the mortification of hawling them down." An American color guard marched forward and raised the stars and stripes. Clark's men cheered lustily. For Hamilton and the redcoats, "Mortification, disappointment, and indignation had their turns."[33] Fort Sackville reverted to its American name, Patrick Henry.

Clark ordered his men to fire a thirteen-gun salute for the United States with the captured cannons. All went well until the ninth round, when a spark ignited a box of six-pounder cartridges that exploded with a deafening roar. The explosion severely burned Bowman, five other Americans, and a British gunner assisting them. It was a tragic end to a glorious victory.[34]

Humiliation for the Hair-buyer and his officers did not end with the surrender. Clark was determined that those who had committed war crimes would suffer. He had Jehu Hay, Francois Maisonville, and Guillaume La Mothe clamped in "neck-irons, fetters, and handcuffs." Hamilton protested that his officers had merely followed his orders and thus were innocent of any crimes, and demanded that Clark "throw me into prison or lay me in irons rather than the others." Clark "smiled contemptuously, turn'd away . . . The scalps of the slaughter'd Indians were hung up by [our] Tents."[35]

Two days later, the *Willing* finally arrived, packed with forty-six men and several tons of supplies. The crew learned with "great mortification . . . that they had not the honor to assist" Fort Sackville's capture.[36] Clark now commanded nearly three hundred armed men, including both those who had slogged or sailed from Kaskaskia and the local Vincennes militia.

Clark learned that the seven-boat convoy loaded with supplies was due at Vincennes any day. Fearing that the convoy's leader would order a withdrawal upriver should word reach him of Fort Sackville's fall, Clark sent Helm, Bosseron, and fifty men packed in three boats upriver to capture those vital supplies. On the night of February 27, Helm and his men spotted campfires ahead and swiftly rowed ashore. Helm waited until the boatmen had bedded down and had his men surround the camp. He then shouted through the darkness a demand that the boatmen give up. They promptly did so without a shot being fired. The Americans captured another forty men and six tons of supplies worth £10,000, including clothing, blankets, food, coffee, tea, rum, wine, munitions, arms, an array of tools, and Indian gifts.[37] Helm and his men brought the flotilla, prisoners, and supplies down to Vincennes.

Most of the prisoners would not suffer long in captivity. "Having more prisoners than I knew what to do with," Clark "was necessitated to discharge a greater part of them on parole."[38] The French militia were all paroled, except for those officers accused of war crimes. The redcoats would remain prisoners, with the wounded staying at Fort Patrick Henry and the rest sent to Virginia.

Between the fort and flotilla, the Americans seized an enormous amount of vitally needed supplies. Clark diverted a generous portion of that hoard to his men. His first step was to issue goods to each man equivalent in value to what he was owed in months of deferred back pay, along with a generous bonus. Tailors got busy transforming woolen cloth into uniforms to replace the troops' tattered versions. The men could also rely on regular daily food rations of dried biscuits, salted meat, and rum for as long as the supplies lasted. The small mountain of gifts earmarked for the Indians would render Clark's diplomacy much less parsimonious than before. Excess goods could be traded to the local inhabitants for critical needs. And for once the Americans had an abundance of gunpowder and lead.[39]

Hamilton condemned Clark and his men as nothing more than "unprincipled motley banditti."[40] Clark, however, was much more charitable in viewing his captive. The evening after the surrender, possibly after many a cup of spirits, he exclaimed, "Sir I find I have been mistaken in your character & facts have been grossly misrepresented." Clark later wrote that "every man had conceived a very favorable opinion of Govr Hamilton (and I believe that what affected myself made some impression on the whole). I was happy to find that he never deviated while he stayed with us from that Dignity of Conduct that became an officer in his situation."[41] Of course, it was much easier for Clark to be magnanimous in his glorious victory than Hamilton in his ignominious defeat.

Clark and his men watched in triumph on March 8, 1779, as Hamilton and twenty-six other prisoners were herded into boats for the first stage of their long route to captivity in Virginia.[42] Captain John Williams and twenty-three guards would escort the prisoners as far as the Falls of the Ohio, and then Clark's cousin Lieutenant John Rogers would lead them overland to Williamsburg. Along the way, the captives would run gauntlets of taunts and threats in most villages they passed through or tarried in, although they would suffer no physical abuse. In Virginia, the redcoats were mixed with thousands of other British and German troops taken at Saratoga and other battles. The officers would be incarcerated in various jails.

Governor Thomas Jefferson was just as grimly determined as Clark to have Hamilton and his officers suffer for their crimes. Hamilton bitterly recalled that after reaching Williamsburg on the evening of June 16, they "were conducted to the Palace where we remain'd about half an hour in the street at the Governor's door, in wet cloaths, weary, hungry, and thirsty, but had not even a cup of water offered to us—During this time a considerable Mob gather'd about us, which accompanied us to jail—On our arrival there we were put into a cell, not ten feet square."[43]

Jefferson and his council found Henry Hamilton guilty of "inciting the Indians to perpetrate their accustomed cruelties on the citizens . . . without distinction of age, sex, or condition, with an eagerness and activity which evince that the general nature of his charge harmonized with his particular disposition." Although Hamilton was ultimately the most responsible for those crimes, his subordinates Philip Dejean and Guillaume La Mothe were also guilty for behavior "savage and unprecedented among civilized nations." For that, the three would be "put in irons, confined in the dungeon of the public jail, debarred from the use of pen, ink, and paper, and excluded from all converse except with their keeper."[44]

Hamilton vehemently rejected those charges, dismissing them as "odious falsaties propagated by the Rebels." Regardless, he was just following orders with "a most strict adherence." When he presided over Indian councils, he insisted that he issued "every dissuasive against cruelty." When he dispatched war parties, he ensured that each was given "strict injunctions to discourage and restrain them from their usual barbarities."[45] Hamilton's depiction of his policy reflected the official British position. Governor Guy Carleton, renowned for his own humanitarianism, and General William Phillips, who was captured at Saratoga and soon paroled, wrote protest letters to Virginia's governor.[46]

Jefferson offered a sharp retort to Carleton: "We think ourselves justified in Governor Hamilton's strict confinement on the general principle of national retaliation." He then condemned the British for their "confinement and treatment of our officers, soldiers, & seamen . . . so rigorous and cruel . . . that a very great proportion . . . have perished miserably." Finally, he detailed the war crimes of Hamilton and his underlings, describing him as "the butcher of men women & children." While Jefferson confessed his ignorance of how far "the fair rules of war would extend the right of punishment against him . . . I am sure that confinement, under its strictest circumstances, as a retaliation for Indian devastation & massacre, must be deemed lenity."[47]

Though Jefferson had asserted a definitive answer, the issue raised a swirl of legal and moral questions in his mind as to what constituted justice. He wrote George Washington for his advice.[48] The general's initial reaction expressed the almost universal patriot feelings that there was "no doubt of the propriety of the proceedings against Governor Hamilton, Deejan, and Lamothe. Their cruelties to our unhappy people who have fallen into their hands and the measures they have pursued to excite the savages to acts of the most wanton barbarity, discriminate them from common prisoners, and most fully authorize the treatment decreed in their case." Washington's view, however, softened with time and reflection. Several weeks later, Washington made two suggestions to Jefferson. First, he proposed that "it may be proper to publish all the Cruelties he has committed or abetted." Second, given the likelihood that the British would retaliate with similar treatment against captured American officers, he thought it might be better if the prisoners "be confined in a Room."[49]

Jefferson responded by offering parole to the prisoners on October 1, 1779. The three initially refused, although LaMothe and Dejean soon changed their minds and won liberty by accepting parole on October 11. Two of Hamilton's other officers found different paths to release. Jacob Schieffelin escaped along with Philippe Rocheblave in April 1780. Francois Maisonville committed suicide on June 1. Henry Hamilton and Jehu Hay remained defiant until October 10, 1780, when they signed a parole. They were then sent to New York, where they were formally exchanged on March 4, 1781.[50]

Were Henry Hamilton and his officers guilty of war crimes? It was British frontier policy to subsidize the raids of their Indian allies with arms, munitions, and other goods, and to pay extra for scalps and captives they brought back. Hamilton may have practiced that policy more enthusiastically than his colleagues at other frontier posts, but ultimately he was following a policy devised by Whitehall and ultimately approved by King George.

That policy, however, violated international law. Eighteenth-century laws of war forbade the looting or destruction of civilian property and the murder of civilians. Hamilton authorized and rewarded Indian war parties, often joined by British officials and soldiers, to commit those very crimes. During their incarceration, Hamilton and his officers got off lightly compared to British standards. Over seven thousand American officers and enlisted men died from brutality, disease, and malnutrition in British captivity during the war, as many as those who died in battle. That was the nature of the war the British wielded against the Americans, but nearly all those responsible got away with their crimes.

CHAPTER 12

Crossroads

I knew that to excel them in barbarity was and is the only way to make war upon Indians and gain a name among them.

George Rogers Clark

Detroit lost for want of a few Men.

George Rogers Clark

Clark would have loved to have followed up his victory at Vincennes with an advance northward that eventually took him to the gates of Detroit itself. But he lacked enough men to intimidate or fight his way through four hundred miles of wilderness just to get there and then overwhelm that fort's defenders into surrendering. He fired off a letter to Governor Patrick Henry explaining that he could decisively win the war in the west with enough troops: "This stroke will nearly put an end to the Indian War, had I but men enough to take the advantage of the present confusion of the Indian Nations, I could silence the whole in two months. I learn that five hundred men is ordered out to reinforce me. If they arrive with what I have in the country, I am in hopes . . . to do something clever."[1] What that "something clever" was, of course, was capturing Detroit.

But Clark soon learned to his dismay that any fresh troops would go not to him at Vincennes but to General Daniel Brodhead, the Western Department's latest upper Ohio valley commander at Pittsburgh. Likely with envy, he wrote Henry that a "small army from Pittsburgh conducted with spirit may easily take Detroit and put an end to the Indian war."[2] Yet he may have wondered if Brodhead harbored the "spirit" vital for doing so. He was certainly confident that if Brodhead faltered, he would take Detroit later that year if he could amass enough men and supplies.

Clark would not only fail to muster what he needed that year but thereafter. Eventually, Detroit would change from British to American hands, but that would happen peacefully and Clark would have no role in the event. Of course, he had no way of knowing that. Instead, his dream would animate him until the war ended.

If Clark could not then take Detroit, he hoped to goad Detroit's commander, Captain Richard Lernoult, into trying to retake Vincennes. To Lernoult, he composed a letter in which, as usual, he played mind games designed at once to provoke and intimidate: "I learn by your letter to Gov Hamilton that you were very busy making new works, I am glad to hear it, as it saves Americans some expences in building. The Officers of Fort Pat. Henry solicit Captain Lernoult to present their compliments to the Officers of his garrison."[3] Thus did he insinuate that his officers held equal status with their British counterparts, that his soldiers were superior to the redcoats, and that Detroit's fall was just a matter of time. With luck, he could taunt Lernoult into attempting to recover Britain's honor and strategic position in the Ohio valley. If Clark could bag yet another British force, he could cow the tribes into neutrality or outright alliance, and then march triumphantly against a weakly defended Detroit.

On paper, Lernoult commanded formidable forces. Detroit was a large bustling town of 2,144 people, with 564 on the militia muster rolls in 1778, up from 1,400 with 298 militiamen in 1773.[4] War swelled the population with refugees during those five years. With the town in the middle, farms spread a dozen miles along the Detroit River, while nearby were Huron, Ottawa, and Potawatomi villages. Skilled diplomacy could rally hundreds of local militia volunteers and hundreds more Indians from across the region for a campaign against Vincennes.

Yet even with such numbers, Lernoult never mulled taking Clark's bait. He now faced twin potential threats from Forts Patrick Henry and Pitt.

Rumors and fears exaggerated the number of American troops at both posts. The return of Hamilton's paroled French volunteers to Detroit further undermined his position. They extolled Clark's ferocity in battle and magnanimity in victory, and assumed that sooner or later he would appear before Detroit. Lernoult fatalistically shared that belief. He wrote, "If the fortune of war Turns on Col. Clarks side and I am taken prisoner I had Rather be taken by him than any other person."[5] That was quite a tribute.

Lernoult revealed his plight in a letter to Lieutenant Colonel Mason Bolton, Fort Niagara's commander. Clark's capture of Vincennes and Hamilton "has greatly damped the spirits of the Indians" and "opens a new road for the Virginians to this place. . . . The Canadians, exceedingly assuming on our bad success and weakness, not one of them will lend a hand." He found his duties a "burthen heavy without assistance. It requires, I confess superior abilities and a better constitution. I will do my best, however. I beg leave to repeat to you the necessity of a reinforcement being sent, as the consequences may be fatal."[6] For now, Lernoult's only sensible strategy was to keep both Clark and Brodhead on the defensive by launching more Indian attacks all along the Ohio valley frontier. But that was an increasingly difficult challenge as war weariness afflicted the tribes.

Lernoult was not alone in worrying about Detroit's vulnerability. General Henry Clinton, who commanded British forces in North America, expressed his concern to Canadian governor Frederick Haldimand. The governor assured the general that he had "reinforced Detroit" and was confident that it would hold "unless the Rebels should be able to make their way to it in great force, which the growing slackness of the western nations . . . may perhaps enable them to make."[7]

Meanwhile, Lernoult set his troops to work strengthening Detroit's defenses. A dilapidated stockade defended the town itself. The stockade was 15 feet high, 1,500 feet on each side, and studded with 11 blockhouses or batteries. Within the town was a "citadel" or stockade with a headquarters building, barracks, and magazine. On a low hill several hundred yards from the town beyond Savoyard Creek, sat Fort Lernoult. The upright logs of each fortification were rotting; many had toppled over and had been sawn up for firewood.

Clark knew that enticing Lernoult to Vincennes was, at best, a long shot. Spies reported no more than a hundred redcoats at Detroit, barely enough to garrison the town, let alone launch a campaign. If neither the Americans nor the British were strong enough to reach the other, then what could break that deadlock?

When Clark dreamed, he dreamed big. Why not head in a completely different direction? After consolidating his position in Vincennes, what if he led his best men downstream all the way to British West Florida? After overwhelming the lightly defended posts along the Mississippi, he might be able to wrangle enough supplies and volunteers from the Spanish at New Orleans to march on and take Mobile and Pensacola. To ascertain British strength in the region, Clark sent out spies and solicited information from Oliver Pollock, America's envoy in New Orleans. Clark eventually recognized that such an expedition would demand even more troops and supplies than a march against Detroit. Ultimately, that scheme never got past the speculation and spy stage.

Clark would soon learn that Bernardo de Galvez, Louisiana's energetic governor, beat him to the punch. In July 1779, word reached Galvez that Spain had declared war on Britain on June 17. He was not content to sit back and defend Louisiana from the British. On September 6, 1779, he launched the first of three campaigns over three years that would conquer West Florida from Britain and seal off the United States from the Gulf of Mexico until 1803. During the first stage in the autumn of 1779, his troops headed up the Mississippi River and captured in swift succession the British posts at Fort Manchac, Baton Rouge, and Natchez. The Mississippi River was now clear of British forces all the way from New Orleans to Prairie du Chien far north at the Wisconsin River mouth. But British Indian allies still straddled segments of that long route.

For now, Clark's most important mission was diplomacy with the Indians, with the vital task of convincing them to stop sending war parties against the frontier. He invited Piankeshaws, Kickapoos, Miamis, Ojibwas, and Potawatomis to Vincennes for a council that opened on March 15, 1779. He explained why the Americans were fighting for independence, denied any desire for Indian lands, and asked the Indians either to be neutral or join him in war against the redcoats.

Once again, Clark's diplomacy succeeded. The chiefs "were convinced from what they had seen and heard that the Master of Life had a hand in all things. They said their people would rejoice on their return, and that they would take pains to diffuse what they had heard throughout all the tribes and they had no doubt of the good it would produce. After a long speech in the Indian fashion, calling on all the spirits as witnesses, they concluded by renewing the chain of friendship, smoking the sacred pipe, and exchanging belts with us."[8] Those who appeared at the council were either already peaceful or so inclined. Those then on the war path stayed away. To the hostile or more distant villages, Clark sent a warning whose essence included these words designed to provoke and terrify:

> To the Warriors of the Different Nations—Men and Warriors; it is a long time since the Big Knives sent Belts of peace . . . soliciting of you not to listen to the bad talks and deceit of the English as it would at some future day tend to the Destruction of your Nations. You would not listen but Joined the English against the Big Knives and spilt much Blood of Women & Children. The Big Knives then resolved to shew no mercy to any People that hereafter would refuse the Belt of Peace which should be offered, at the same time One for War; You remember last summer a great many People took me by the hand, but a few kept back their Hearts. I also sent Belts of Peace and War among the Nations to take their choice. Some took the Peace Belt; others still listened to their great Father (as they call him) at Detroit, and Joined him to come to War against me. The Big Knives are Warriers and look on the English as old Women and all those that Join him.
>
> I Glory in War and want enemies to fight us, as the English cant fight us any longer, and are become like Young Children. . . . This is the last Speech you can ever expect from the Big Knives. The next thing will be the Tomahawk. And you may expect in four Moons to see Your Women & Children given to the Dogs to eat, while those Nations have kept their words with me will Flourish under the care and nourishment of their father the Big Knives.[9]

The Piankeshaws conveyed their gratitude and respect for Clark by granting him a nearby tract of land of nearly forty square miles. They announced their gift in a council with him on July 16, 1779.[10] He would never take title to that territory. To curb a potential source of corruption, Congress had passed a law that forbade any American from directly receiving land from any Indians. Only the states could buy or take land from Indians and give or sell it to citizens.

Clark took measures to ensure that the American position in Vincennes was powerful enough to defeat another British and Indian attack. He named Captain Helm as both the governor of Vincennes and Indian superintendent for the local tribes. Moses Henry would be the deputy Indian agent. Left in command of Fort Patrick Henry's forty-man garrison was Lieutenant Richard Brasher, ably assisted by Second Lieutenants John Bailey, whose men had fired the first shots at Hamilton and his men, and Abraham Chapline, a former Shawnee captive who knew and respected Indians. Supplies, for the time being, would not be a problem with so much taken from the British.

With enormous satisfaction, Clark led the rest of his men back to Kaskaskia, this time by boat. He boarded the *Willing* on March 20, 1779, and, with seventy men squeezed aboard that vessel and five dugouts, pushed off for Kaskaskia.

Important letters from Governor Henry and Virginia's executive council awaited Clark at Kaskaskia. While Clark would retain his military powers, his civil authority would go to John Todd, who would soon arrive with his commission. Clark was "happy in his appointment as the greatest intimacy and friendship subsisted between us." Until Todd arrived, Clark would continue to exercise both civil and military powers. And in exercising his military duties, he would enjoy complete discretion. Perhaps the best news was that Lieutenant Colonel John Montgomery would soon arrive with reinforcements and £10,000 with which to pay off some of the mounting debts owed to the troops for their service and the merchants for their supplies.[11]

The executive council asserted observations that mingled sympathy and warning: "Your situation is critical. For detached from the Body of your Country, placed among French, Spaniards, & Indian Nations strangers to our people, anxiously watching your actions & Behaviour, & ready to receive Impressions favourable or not so of our Commonwealth & its Government, which Impressions will be hard to remove & will produce lasting good or ill Effects to your Country: These Considerations will make you cautious & Circumspect. . . . I doubt not your virtue will accomplish the arduous Work With Honor to yourself and advantages to the Commonwealth."[12] The council's message likely irritated Clark. Beneath a courteous veneer, the council's tone was patronizing and condescending. Clark was well aware of how "critical" his situation was and the delicate diplomatic tightrope that he had to constantly navigate.

Clark soon had to assert both his diplomatic and military powers. A war party of White River Delawares murdered and plundered a group of Americans at the Falls of the Ohio. The very mixed feeling that atrocity provoked in Clark displayed his character's more ruthless side: "I was sorry for the loss of our men but for the rest pleased over what had happened, since it would afford me an opportunity of showing the other Indians the horrible fate of those who dared make war on the Long Knives; and I knew that to excel them in barbarity was and is the only way to make war upon Indians and gain a name among them."[13]

Clark fired off orders to Vincennes to unleash a merciless campaign against the White River Delawares. The results grimly pleased Clark: "This order was executed without delay. Their camps were attacked wherever they could be found. Many were slain, while others were brought to Vincennes and there put to death and the women and children taken captive."[14]

The surviving Delaware chiefs begged for peace. Clark agreed to a truce but not peace. He sent Captain Helm detailed instructions on how to conduct the diplomacy and a speech he was to read to the chiefs. Through his mouthpiece, Clark declared that "We never trusted those who had once violated their faith; but if they were disposed to be quiet and if they could induce any of their neighboring Indians to be responsible for their good behavior, I would let them alone."[15]

These efforts were the latest strands in the diplomatic web that Clark had been knitting across the region since taking Kaskaskia on July 4, 1778. Each strand was itself an entangled mix of hope, fear, honor, shame, and sublimated aggression. Clark would never come close to finishing that web. Indeed, the combined forces of warrior cultures, British inducements, and American blunders constantly frayed, unraveled, or outright snapped his efforts. Yet Clark had no choice but to keep trying. He had shouldered the diplomatic equivalent of the rock of Sisyphus.

Clark faced the same "hearts and minds" dilemma that all conquerors have faced throughout history. The honeymoon between the Americans and the French in Illinois was long past, and ever more locals whispered in favor of divorce. Not surprisingly, Clark breathed a huge sigh of relief at passing the burden of governing that increasingly resentful and defiant population to Todd: "I now saw myself happily rid of a piece of trouble that I had no delight in."[16]

Clark tried to take advantage of the transfer of power to Todd to revive French enthusiasm for American rule. He introduced the people to their new civil leader with a ringing proclamation: "I present to you Colonel Todd, my good friend, as your governor. He is the only person in the state whom I wished to have fill this post. . . . I am fully persuaded from my knowledge of his capacity and diligence that he will render you justice and at the same time make you happy."[17]

Unfortunately, Todd would not fulfill a single one of those promises that Clark made for him.[18] Relations between the occupiers and occupied would deteriorate to the point of collapse under Todd's heavy-handed rule. Then relations would worsen after Todd was recalled and he passed the baton of rule to his even more incompetent successor, Richard Winston.

All that lay in the future. For the time being, Clark tried to reconcile the inhabitants to "the American system which you will find, perhaps in the beginning, a little strange; but in the course of time you will find so much peace and tranquility in it that you will bless the day that you espoused the cause of the Americans."[19] Todd reinforced that theme in his inaugural address: "The Republic of Virginia has had very noble motives in coming here. It was not for the love of conquest, but to invite you to enjoy, with her citizens, the blessing of independence, free and equal, and to be judged and governed by officers who will be placed in power by the people."[20]

Thomas Jefferson, who replaced Patrick Henry as governor of Virginia in 1779, offered the most eloquent and profound explanation of Clark's mission that eventually would become a perennial American crusade around the world: "We are in hopes . . . to introduce our Laws and form of Government among the people of the Illinois as far as their temper & disposition will admit. . . . We wish for their own good to give them full participation of the benefits of free and mild Government." To his credit, Jefferson did temper that crusade's idealism, indeed arrogance, by admitting "the difficulties attending this" attempt to "perfectly incorporate them into the American body."[21]

George Rogers Clark was the first American to try to impose democracy on an alien people with authoritarianism deeply rooted in their culture.

For better or for worse, he would hardly be the last. Since then, countless American officials, soldiers, and humanitarians have learned to their chagrin that democratic ideals offend a population whose livelihoods, culture, and pride are trampled in their "liberation." As for the Illinois people, they were not so much disgusted by the "strange" notion of political rights and representation as by the occupiers' habit of not paying for what they took.[22]

What Clark and other officials inspired was not liberalism but nationalism, expressed in ever-fiercer resistance to the foreign rulers. A mere nine days after Todd's speech, a group of prominent Illinois inhabitants presented him a petition in which they expressed their "sorrow" that "the soldiers of the company of Fort Clark . . . get the animals . . . without paying any attention . . . to whom they might belong. . . . They penned these in the said fort and killed them." The petitioners noted the irony that the foreigners "announce to us that this is a free country, where each one should be master to do with is property as he pleases . . . yet they have killed plowoxen, milch cows, and other animals which belonged to . . . people who could not get along without them. . . . If similar abuses continue, which tend to the general ruin of the colony, what will become of the colonists?"[23] The people at Cahokia were just as outraged by the American occupation. In September 1779, Clark received a report that there Captain Richard McCarty "has lost most part of his French Soldiers and the Inhabitants is So Saucey they threaten to drive him and his soldiers away, tells him he has no business there nobody Sent for them. They are very discontented the Civil Law has Ruined them."[24] For the Illinois people, the only "right" they witnessed was asserted by American "might."

Money, or the lack thereof, was the root of most of that American "evil." For Clark, the frustration, indeed agony, of a lack of vital resources would plague him to his grave. Every commander faced an array of duties. Of those, battle was as rare and fleeting as the need to properly feed, clothe, shelter, and arm his men was constant. And all that had to be paid for. The trouble was that Congress, Virginia, and all the other state governments were bankrupt. They could merely issue ever-depreciating paper notes to "pay" for requisitions. The British gleefully accelerated that plummet in value by arming a skilled forger with a printing press lent from newspaper owner James Rivington aboard the HMS *Duchess of Gordon*, anchored off New York City, and by then distributing the phony money as widely as possible.

Clark was authorized to pay for local supplies by filling out certificates issued by Congress and the State of Virginia. He also wrote out his own IOUs, expecting that the government would later reimburse him. Such notes were a novelty in the Illinois country. Coin was scarce. Most goods changed hands through barter rather than money. People initially accepted those notes not knowing that their value would plunge in the months and years to come. By January 1779, it took eight Continental dollars to buy one Spanish dollar. Then, a mere year later, a Spanish dollar was worth seventy-seven American dollars! People complained bitterly as their certificates declined in worth and they "look on our Monney and bills to be of no More a Count then So Much Blank paper."[25]

As the dollar's value plunged, Clark received word that merchants in New Orleans were disputing $25,000 worth of his notes. That cast a very dark shadow on the thousands of dollars' worth of Clark notes held by local Illinois merchants. Only one man might be able to alleviate that crisis. Clark explained to Oliver Pollock, America's unofficial envoy and financier at New Orleans, that "although our credit appears to be low (perhaps our own fault), I am Determined not to wait until some Person appears with a longer Sword than I have" for launching the campaign. But to do so, Clark would have to run up yet another huge bill on credit with Pollock. Yet Pollock should not worry since "Virginia State will never let you suffer long for what you have done for her."[26] Anyone familiar with the years of spiraling mounds of unpaid, increasingly exorbitant bills might well have questioned the sincerity of Clark's assertion.

Oliver Pollock's credit was near rock bottom. In July 1779, he wrote Governor Henry that he was "already drained of every shilling I could raise for the use of yours and the rest of the United States. I went first to the Governor of this place, and then to every merchant in it, but could not prevail upon any of them. . . . I have voluntarily mortgaged part of my Property."[27] He would soon be forced to mortgage the rest of it as well as to sell off his slaves.

As if Clark's duties were not demanding and exhausting enough, Governor Henry dropped another task atop the heap. In three urgent letters, he asked Clark to do all he could to acquire and send him "two of the best stallions that could possibly be found at the Illinois," along with "eight of the best mares." He not so subtly linked his request to a quid pro quo "towards securing the Land you wanted."[28]

Clark replied that although "nothing could give me great pleasure . . . at present it is out of my power. . . . I have so much publick business to do especially in the Indian Department. . . . [Besides,] I find that you have conceived a greater oppinion of the Horses in this country than I have." Though the horses bred by the Pawnees and Chickasaws were "very good and some of them delicate . . . the common breed in this country is trifling as they are adulterated." Having said that, Clark had good news. He had bought the region's "finest Stallion . . . and rode him on this Expedition, and resolved to make you a Compliment of him, but to my mortification I find it impossible to get him across the drown'd lands of the Wabash . . . but you [can] depend that I shall buy the first opportunity send him to you." Clark's stallion originated neither among the Chickasaws nor the more distant Pawnees but from New Mexico. He promised to procure some mares from either the Chickasaws or Pawnees. And as for that land deal Henry mentioned, Clark reminded him that he had purchased three thousand acres and feared losing it without a clear title if the government intended reserving that land for veterans. Finally, Clark mentioned his purchases of land in Illinois and promised to send Henry a map of the region.[29]

The exchange is revealing in several fascinating ways. One is the vastness and sophistication of the trade network. The Chickasaws lived in villages in what is now western Tennessee and northern Mississippi. The Pawnees were even farther away, living in a string of mound villages along the Platte River in the northern Great Plains. And then there was New Mexico with its cluster of settlements in the northern Rio Grande valley beyond the Sangre de Cristo chain of the Rocky Mountains! Those three far-flung cultures were tenuously linked by a trading system that stretched across the continent. The Chickasaws, Pawnees, and New Mexicans had separately developed breeds of horses so renowned that wealthy Virginia planters dreamed of acquiring them to bolster their own stock.

Additionally, the Spanish monarchy had forbidden its colonies to trade with anyone other than the mother country; that taboo apparently did little to inhibit New Mexico and Louisiana merchants. The most blatant violations of that ban occurred where settlements of the Spanish and British empires—Saint Louis and Cahokia, Saint Genevieve and Kaskaskia— faced each other across the upper Mississippi River. Horses were among the array of goods that passed hands from one shore to the other, at times with payoffs to the appropriate officials.[30]

The exchange offers insights into Clark himself. He clearly had a discerning eye for horses. He had eagerly bought the region's finest stallion probably after falling in love at his first critical glance. He was likely a natural rider whose skill, confidence, and sheer joy emerged at a young age.

Finally, contemporary readers might be surprised at the unabashed fashion in which Henry and Clark mingled their public and private interests. Actually, it would have been notable had they abstained from doing so. Conflict of interest was a fuzzier notion then than now. It existed, but an aloofness from exploiting one's public office for private gain was more one of style than substance. One feigned disinterest while wielding one's wealth and power to garner more of the same.

Despite Clark's strenuous efforts, the lower Ohio valley would be even more of a strategic sideshow that year. General George Washington had decided on launching a knockout blow against the Iroquois. Three columns would attack different parts of the Six Nation empire that sprawled across central New York state and the Allegheny River valley of northwestern Pennsylvania. Generals John Sullivan and James Clinton would march against and gut the Iroquois heartland; General Daniel Brodhead would attack the Iroquois villages up the Allegheny valley. Although the Americans fought only one battle and a few skirmishes and killed only a handful of Indians, they burned about forty villages and drove several thousand Iroquois refugees to shelter in hovels beneath Fort Niagara.[31]

In launching that campaign, Washington did not ignore the Ohio valley front, but he was confident that with Clark in the field, he could divert Brodhead's forces northeastward. Washington instructed Brodhead that even on his campaign he was to communicate regularly with Clark and help him if he could. Washington recognized the inherent problem in any coordination between the two frontier commanders: "Clark is not an officer in the Continental line—nor does he act under my instructions. He is in the service of the State of Virginia. I make no doubt however that the Instructions he has received are calculated to promote the general good—and from the character he seems justly to have acquired I should suppose he will act with the caution and prudence—and do nothing that will not be primitive of it."[32]

Meanwhile, Clark threw himself into preparing for his campaign against Detroit. All troops and supplies were massed at Vincennes by late June. He made rapid progress in gathering men. On May 21, he commanded 318 troops in 5 companies at Kaskaskia. Then by June 2, he had commitments from various sources for 813 men in 10 companies to join him; that was 300 more troops than the 500 he reckoned were enough to get the job done. His officers and most men were eager to get underway. From Cahokia, Captain Bowman wrote Clark, "I begin to be Impatiant to start and am in hopes by Next Monday to make a move with every thing from her with hoops of finding you all in Readiness. . . . The weather begins to grow warm & the waters Low so that no time Ought to be lost with regaud to prepareing Every Necessarry requird for our Expedetion, pray make Every officer Exert himself as I have been obligd to do, as much depends on Industery."[33]

So what had happened? The militia captains found that mustering then retaining the men on their rolls was as slippery a task as grasping quicksilver. A growing number of the men, disgruntled with the harsh conditions of being soldiers, escaped to the Mississippi River's far side. To deter that, Clark issued on June 19, 1779, a decree that forbade any "Protection . . . to any deserter, from his Catholic Majesty's troops, and those that had heretofore Received Protection from me, are . . . Ordered to quit this Shore."[34] Elsewhere at Vincennes and the fort at the Falls of the Ohio, scores of men slipped away to their distant homes.

Meanwhile, the five-boat supply convoy commanded by Colonel David Rogers and Lieutenant Robert George was slowly making its way up the Mississippi River valley. That journey took much longer than usual. The British had retaken Natchez. To avoid capture, Rogers led his convoy up the Red River, transferred his supplies to pack animals for the trail across to Arkansas Post near the confluence of the Arkansas and Mississippi Rivers, repacked the cargo on boats, and continued upstream. Rogers and his men reached the Falls of the Ohio in August 1779. The supplies were transferred to boats above the Falls.

Clark was at the fort at the Falls when the expedition arrived. He retained a share of the supplies and Lieutenant George for his artillery skills.

He assigned Lieutenant Abraham Chapline and twenty-three men to escort the convoy along with a dozen British prisoners up to Fort Pitt. The convoy now numbered about sixty people.

All went well until the morning of October 4, when Rogers ordered the convoy to land at the Licking River mouth. That would be a fatal act. Simon Girty, Matthew Elliot, and 170 Shawnees, Wyandots, Mingos, and Delawares were hiding in the nearby forest. As Rogers and his men stretched their legs, the warriors burst from cover, shooting and war whooping. They swiftly cut down a dozen men, including Rogers, and captured four of the boats. Thirteen Americans managed to scramble aboard the fifth boat and row frenziedly downstream; they reached the Falls five days later.[35] Clark reckoned the capture of Rogers's boats, supplies, letters, and men as "a very great loss, and will Incourage the Savages much. The Savages on the Ouabash and Wesward would to a man take up the Tomahawk against the Shawnees if we had a few goods to present them with."[36]

Clark led his men and supplies to Vincennes, the launch site for the campaign against Detroit. As always, his first task was diplomacy. He called a council of all the local chiefs and gave a typically powerful speech for peace that deftly mixed reason and emotion. The Door of the Wabash, the son of Piankeshaw chief Old Tobacco, delivered a response that could not have pleased Clark more. With poetic eloquence, he expressed the anguish that their "once Peaceable Land hath been put in confusion by the English encouraging all People to raise their Tommahawk Against the Big Knives. . . . But as the Sky at our Councils was always Misty and never Clear we still was at a loss to know what to do, hoping that the Master of Life would one Day or other . . . put us on the right Road. He taking Pitty on us sent a father among us (Colo. George Rogers Clark) that has cleared our eyes." As a result, the Piankeshaws and other tribes near Vincennes not only committed themselves to peace but also to convincing all hostile tribes to bury their hatchets against the Big Knives.[37]

Atop the chronic money and supply worries was Clark's growing frustration that only a fraction of all the force promised him would show up. Lieutenant Colonel John Montgomery brought only 150 of the 500 men he was authorized to raise. A minor compensation was the presence of the gunners Captain Robert George and Lieutenant Richard Harrison. Those men had formerly served with Captain Willing on his campaign down the Mississippi River to New Orleans. Skilled and experienced artillerymen were in short supply in the American army, especially on the frontier.

Clark was enraged to learn that Colonel John Bowman had disobeyed orders to bring his 296 men to Vincennes. Indeed, Bowman spurned Clark's campaign for his own.[38] He did so not only because he disliked Clark and sought his own glory but also because he justified his act on what he and most Kentuckians believed were sound strategic reasons. For settlers in central Kentucky, the primary Indian threat was due north in the Shawnee, Mingo, and Wyandot villages of today's Ohio, not the various tribes living far away on the upper Wabash River in today's Indiana. So on May 27, Bowman led his men across the Ohio River at the Licking River mouth.

The target of Bowman's unauthorized campaign was Chillicothe, sixty-five miles up the Little Miami River. The footsore frontiersmen warily approached Chillicothe on June 1. Shawnee scouts had long warned of the Long Knives' approach. While nearly everyone in the village had fled along the trail to Piqua, a dozen miles northwest, about forty warriors stayed behind to fight. Although outmanned more than seven to one, the Shawnees were fortified in cabins with loopholes. Bowman and his men were able to torch part of the town but could not dislodge the warriors. The Shawnees repulsed the attack and killed ten Kentuckians, but among their dozen losses was Chief Blackfish, who was mortally wounded in the fighting. The raiders did succeed in rounding up 163 horses, of which most were previously stolen from their own settlements. That campaign satiated the Kentuckians' lust for blood and loot, and Bowman yielded to their demands that they return to their farmsteads. Only thirty of his men were willing to journey with him to Vincennes.

Despite the lack of men, Clark was still eager to launch his campaign. He "wanted men sufficient to make me appear Respectable in Passing through the Savages by which means I could on the March Command those friendly at my ease, and defy my Enemies. Three hundred Men being at this time sufficient to Reduce the Garrisson at Detroit, as the new Works were not Compleat, nor could not be . . . before my Arrival."[39] That may well have been a gross underestimate. Although the garrison numbered less than a hundred men, the British could count on hundreds more local militiamen and Indians rallying to the defense.

As Clark prepared his campaign, he authorized a daring raid that he hoped would divert the enemy's attention, mask his own intention, and gain intelligence. Captain Godefroy de Linctot led a hundred men from Cahokia up the Illinois River to visit friendly villages, then cut across to the middle Wabash to attack a cluster of hostile Wea villages at Ouiatenon, and finally descend the river to Vincennes. Linctot's raid was at once a brilliant tactical success and strategic failure as it kicked in a hornet's nest along the Wabash route toward Detroit. Clark and his officers came to the bitter realization on July 1 that they would need hundreds more men just to battle the enraged villagers on the first leg of the journey. The dream of taking Detroit was nothing more than a mirage, at least that year. Clark "now regretted that," after capturing Fort Sackville, "we had not marched from Vincennes upon Detroit at once." "Never was a person more mortified than I was at this time, to see so fair an opportunity to push for victory; Detroit lost for want of a few Men."[40]

Clark dispersed his men to various posts on August 5. Lieutenant Colonel John Montgomery was to return to Illinois and garrison Fort Clark at Kaskaskia with three companies while Captain Richard McCarty proceeded to Cahokia; Captain Godefroy de Linctot would be the region's Indian agent. Four companies under Lieutenant Colonel John Todd's command would garrison Fort Patrick Henry at Vincennes, while Captain Leonard Helm served as its Indian agent. Clark would establish his headquarters at the Falls of the Ohio, accompanied by five captains and their companies along with Captain Robert George's artillery company. He dispersed a half dozen lesser officers across Kentucky to drum up recruits.[41]

Clark felt increasingly at home at the Falls of the Ohio. The setting was as beautiful as it was strategic, and he had founded both the fort and Louisville, named in gratitude for the French king who had allied his nation with the United States. The palisade and village now stood beside each other, respectively occupied by several score troops and a hundred or so settlers. A score of families had staked out claims along Beargrass Creek, which flows into the Ohio River just above Louisville.

To celebrate his and his men's victories, Clark threw a ball. Invitations were sent not just to the inhabitants of Louisville but to all the Kentucky settlements. One party of twenty men and six women were determined to journey all the way from Harrodsburg to attend. They had gone no more than a mile when Indians were spotted "running to Get before us." The party hastily retreated to Harrodsburg's safety. The next day fifteen men and three women once again set forth on that eighty-mile trek to Louisville. Along the way, "Mistress Harrod killed a Buffeloe. We got safe to the falls of the Ohio."[42]

The ball was that year's social highlight for Kentucky. For the ball, Clark had his men erect in the fort "a large new room" of "hewed logs in the inside, a good plank . . . Floore." Nearly everyone had a grand time. The women from Harrodsburg were especially extolled for their courage and beauty: "When these Fort Ladys come to be Dressed up they did not look like the same every thing looked anew we enjoyed ourselves very much Col. Harrod & his Lady opened the ball by Dancing the first Gig we had a plenty of rum Toddy to drink."[43]

The only killjoy was the French violinist who was miffed at how the minuet was being danced, apparently with far more enthusiasm than grace. He refused to play any more tunes and placed a black fiddler named Cato in charge of the music. Although Cato's rhythms and songs enhanced the festive mood, he would later cast a macabre shadow on memories of the evening—he was hanged for murdering his master.[44]

Clark was now at the height of his popularity, nearly universally renowned for his drive, daring, and vision. Captain Helm spoke for countless Kentuckians when he expressed his "Great Satisfaction to think of your Intention against Detroit, you must be the man to take that place . . . you may be assur'd your Name Strikes Terror to both English and Indians."[45] Indeed, Clark's reputation was so great that he aided the American effort merely by the reports to British commanders of his presence at various places like Vincennes, Kaskaskia, and Louisville. That news diverted British attention and sometimes troops from more pressing needs. General Henry Clinton, who commanded of His Majesty's forces in North America, was kept informed at his New York City headquarters of Clark's exploits. He described that "rebel general" as "a very enterprising man."[46]

But living up to that popularity and those expectations was itself a burden. The pressure was getting to Clark. He confessed to his father that "Circumstances appear more [serious] at present than for some time past but I hope to Extricate myself as formerly no person Commanding on this Continent is in a more Critical Situation than I am surrounded on all Sides by Numerous Nations of Indians with English officers among them Incouraging them to war." He did proudly recount one success. Having given his younger brother Richard a lieutenant's commission, he expressed the hope that "if I can get him to Imbrace the Air of an officer I don't doubt but he may make a good appearance in a short time. I think he already improves."[47]

The specter of death hovered at Clark's elbow. He asked his father, "If Dicky and myself should be lost . . . Trouble my Brothers to Seek after my Fortune which at this time Cant be less than Twenty Thousand Pounds Sterling as my success in Trade has been Equal to that of war." Clark's foreboding for his brother and himself would be half realized. After the war, Richard mysteriously disappeared while journeying by himself from Louisville to Vincennes and was never seen again. Clark noted that his father has "known the height of my ambitions . . . I did not Expect to arrive at that so much determined Moment in so short a time." He gratefully acknowledged that his success was due to more than just his own relentless efforts: "Fortune in Every Respect has as yet hovered Round me as if determined to direct me." In return, Clark acknowledged that his "greatest glory is to addore the Suppreme director of all things."[48]

At the age of twenty-six, Clark was promoted by Virginia to full colonel. That was not the only official recognition of his astonishing feats. On June 12, 1779, Virginia's assembly voted to grant him a sword "as proof of their Approbation of your Good Conduct & gallant Behavior." It was not, however, a new sword especially made for Clark, but a secondhand sword. Yet Virginia lieutenant governor John Page assured Clark in a letter that the sword had been used "but a little" and was "elegant & costly."[49] His cousin John Rogers conveyed that gift from the assembly to Clark. Alas, according to one possibly apocryphal account, the timing could not have been worse. He presented the sword just after Clark received a huge bill for requisitions from Oliver Pollock in New Orleans. Enraged that he rather than Virginia or Congress was responsible for payment, "Clark took the fine sword, walked out on the bank of the river with none present but his servant, thrust the blade deep into the ground, & gave the hilt a kick with his foot, broke it off, & sent it into the river, & sent word to the Governor of Virginia that he would have no such hollow-heart insignias while they refused his starving soldiers the common necessities of life."[50]

CHAPTER 13

Forting Up

The same world would scarcely do for them and us.

Thomas Jefferson

C lark lingered at Louisville from late 1779 until early spring 1780. He did so ostensibly because "the interest of the Department required me to spend a few months at the Falls of the Ohio." There, he mulled seeking a secondary prize after falling short of mustering what it took to capture Detroit. He was "Induced . . . with the hopes of giving the Shawnees a Drubing in case a sufficient force Could be again raised at Kentucky."[1] That hope would also disappoint him. He could not gather enough militiamen for even that.

It was not that Kentucky lacked armed men. Indeed, despite six years of brutal frontier war since James Harrod had founded the first settlement in 1774, a greater number of new people arrived in Kentucky than were killed or scared off. The only exception was in 1778 when more fled than came. But there was a surge of new settlers in 1779, either by dugout or flatboat down the Ohio River or by foot and horseback over the Wilderness Road. The biggest influx was in 1780. By that year's end, Kentucky had over twenty thousand people scattered among scores of new settlements.[2]

A new law was the sharpest spur to that human tidal wave. The state of

Virginia promised four hundred acres outright and another one thousand acres by preemption to each pioneer who sowed and reaped a corn crop by the end of 1780. The veterans among the migrants were lured westward by land grants distributed according to their rank. Those were the pulls. The push was terrorism, either from redcoats or rebels. Swelling the ranks of those pioneers were countless refuges who had witnessed or had been victims of homes looted and burned, beatings, rapes, and murders by rampaging armies, gangs, or lone criminals.

Once the newcomers found and cleared a patch of land, the last thing they wanted to do was march off to war. Yet even as they stayed put, an unbridgeable chasm often lay between occupying and owning a homestead. Virtually all those who sought land would be bitterly disappointed when red tape, conflicting claims, and shoddy or lost records denied them that desire. To sort out that mess, Virginia dispatched four commissioners—William Fleming, Edmund Lynne, James Barbour, and Stephen Trigg. They convened a meeting at Harrodsburg on October 13, 1779, and assured those who had settled before January 1, 1778, that they would be entitled to land, although just where and how much remained to be seen. As for those who came later, the commissioners promised to do their best to find them land somewhere.

Even without that thickening Gordian knot of disputed land claims atop the frontier war's death, destruction, and terror, Kentucky was hardly the arcadia peddled by eastern promoters. Both getting there and being there must have seemed like a sojourn through Dante's circles of hell to those few with a love of literature and just plain hell to everyone else.

The journey to that promised land was harsh enough. Pioneer John May recalled with disgust that the Wilderness Road was "the most rugged and dismal I ever passed through, there being thousands of dead Horses, Cattle on the Road Side which occasioned a continual Stench; and one Half the way there were no Springs, which compelled us to make use of the water from the Streams in which many of the dead animals lay: and what made the Journey still more disagreeable was the continual apprehension we were under of an Attack from the Indians, there not being one Day after we left Holston but News was brought us of some Murders being committed by those Savages."[3]

Forts had all the charm of feedlots. Fort Harrod was especially wretched since its spring was located in the lowest corner. According to Colonel

William Fleming, who was also a doctor, "The whole dirt and filth of the Fort, putrefied flesh, dead dogs, cow hog excrements and human odour . . . the ashes and sweepings of filthy Cabbins . . . the dirtiness of the people," and "the washing every sort of dirty rags and cloths" drained into the spring. The result was "the most filthy nauseous . . . water imaginable and will certainly contribute to render the inhabitants of this place sickly."[4]

Atop all the unsanitary conditions, of course, was the nagging fear that at any moment war cries and gunshots would fill the air and a horde of Indians and white renegades would swarm over the fort to murder, torture, loot, and kidnap. That fear was exacerbated by the Loyalists living secretly amid the patriots and fence-sitters. Loyalist "plots," some dangerous, others exaggerated, and still others purely imagined, were periodically uncovered, and stern measures of arrests, exiles, beatings, or humiliations were inflicted on the accused.[5]

Virginia's distant government became a scapegoat for the array of problems afflicting Kentucky. A swelling majority of Kentuckians agreed that they were better off governing themselves. Six-hundred seventy-two men signed a petition for Kentucky statehood, dated May 15, 1780, and fired it off to Richmond. That campaign would not succeed for another dozen years.

A group of statehood advocates approached Clark to serve as their governor. Although the offer flattered him, he gently rebuffed it. He explained why to his brother: "The partisans in these Cuntries are again Soliciting me to head them as their Governor General as all those from foreign states are for a new Government but my duty obliging me to Suppress all such proceedings I consequently shall loose the Interest of that party."[6]

Though Clark was devoted to fulfilling his military duties, he was finding them increasingly exhausting. An array of obstacles stymied even the most limited military operations. The shortage of all the vital ingredients for a campaign—men, money, and material—exacerbated the rivalry among commanders for what little was available.

As the respective commanders of the upper and lower Ohio River regions, Colonels Daniel Brodhead and George Rogers Clark were supposed to coordinate their plans. Unfortunately, their rival egos and ambitions trumped duty in that regard. In that respect, Brodhead was more guilty. As a Continental army colonel, he outranked Clark with his Virginia commission. Jealous of Clark, Brodhead continually sought to undermine him by reneging on his promises to send him supplies and troops. Instead, Brodhead hoped to steal a march on his rival and take Detroit and all the resulting glory and accolades. In that dream, he would be just as frustrated as Clark.[7]

Governor Thomas Jefferson was well aware of Brodhead's machinations. Rather than confront him directly, Jefferson went above his head. To General Washington, he explained, "The reason of my laying before your Excellency this matter is that it has been intimated to me that Colonel Brodhead is meditating a similar expedition. I wished therefore to make you acquainted with what we had in contemplation. The enterprising and energetic genius of Clarke is not altogether unknown to you. You also know (what I am a stranger to) the abilities of Brodhead, and the particular force with which you will be able to arm him for such an expedition. . . . It may [be] necessary, perhaps, to inform you that these two officers cannot act together, which excludes the hope of ensuring success by a joint expedition." If Washington was to support Brodhead's campaign, then Clark would be diverted from Detroit to an "object, which is also important to this State."[8]

With want of a "sufficient force" once again denying him a march against Detroit or even the Shawnees, Clark soothed his disappointment with a consolation prize. For some time, he had been among those who recognized the potential strategic, diplomatic, and economic advantages of erecting a fort at the confluence of the Mississippi and Ohio Rivers. That site was "a beautifull Situation as if by nature designed for a fortification" that would become "the key of the whole Trade of the Western Cuntrey" as well as "Awing our Enemies."[9] To that end, Clark could not have had a better ally in Virginia's capital. Jefferson had been on the executive council when Clark promoted his Illinois expedition in December 1777. Deeply awed by Clark's vision, energy, and intelligence, Jefferson had since then enthusiastically backed all of Clark's endeavors.

Few men differed as much in temperament and calling as did Clark and Jefferson. Clark was a born warrior, all fiery passion and relentless drive. Jefferson was a born scholar, all buttoned-down reason and study. Yet they shared at least three essential characteristics. Both had an insatiable curiosity about all the wonders of the natural world; growing up on the frontier, they mulled what lay beyond the western horizon all the way to the Pacific. Like skilled chess players, they could scan the political chessboard and spot the array of possible threats and opportunities usually several moves ahead of their opponents. Similar strategic visions inspired them over how to win first the war and then the peace—securing independence, rooting the American republic in the virtues of family farms, and conquering the west were inseparable.

To those ends, it was essential to anchor America's western frontier on the Mississippi River. That had been the ultimate rationale for Clark's Illinois campaign, atop the immediate goal of snatching a swath of British territory. But the grip of the garrisons at Kaskaskia, Cahokia, and Vincennes was steadily weakening. The Americans had worn out the initial guarded welcome of most of the inhabitants. Unable to pay for their occupation with hard silver, they handed out worthless script instead. Merchants and farmers naturally responded by refusing to sell. The Americans then resorted to confiscating what they needed, thus pushing an enraged populace toward the brink of rebellion. Through a mix of desperation, incompetence, greed, and brutality, the Virginians had unwittingly sparked slow-burning fuses to the political equivalent of gunpowder kegs in each of the settlements they ruled. Sooner or later, the flame would touch the powder.

Jefferson saw only one way to defuse those all but inevitable explosions. It was essential to lighten the burden of occupation before it provoked an outright revolt. The garrisons should be reduced and the people granted self-rule in return for their promise to stay loyal to the United States. He advised Clark "to withdraw . . . all the forces not absolutely necessary to sustain the Spirits of the Inhabitants of the Illinois, and for their real defense. This necessity has been inferred by the impossibility of our supporting an armed force where our paper money is not current."[10]

But before that happened, the Americans needed a fallback position. For American interests, no place along the Mississippi River was then more strategically vital than at its confluence with the Ohio River. Building a fort at that spot was the third strategic option Jefferson gave Clark to ponder for 1780 in a letter he penned on New Year's Day. The first two options were the familiar choices of campaigns either against Detroit or the Indians. The decision was solely Clark's to make: "Removed at such a distance as we are, and so imperfectly informed, it is impossible for us to prescribe to you. . . . [W]e must leave it to yourself to decide on the object of the campaign."[11]

If Jefferson let Clark choose what to do, he issued chilling instructions over how to do it. Although he was a humanist, years of war had coarsened him to its horrors. He now reconciled himself to the reality that in war one must either kill or be killed, destroy or be destroyed. Yet the humanist in Jefferson kept him from fully expressing that with others, even his favorite field commander. He deleted the following lines from his 1780 New Year message to Clark: "I think the most important object which can be proposed with such a force is the extermination of those hostile tribes of Indians who live between the Ohio and the Illinois who have harassed us with eternal hostilities, and whom experience has shewn to be incapable of reconciliation. The Shawanese, Mingos, Munsees, and Wiandots can never be relied on as friends, and therefore the object of the war should be their total extinction, or their removal beyond the . . . Illinois." Instead, he presented a choice: "The end proposed should be their extermination, or their removal. . . . The same world would scarcely do for them and us."[12]

Clark affirmed what Jefferson assumed. Expeditions against Detroit or the Indians were not feasible that year. The best that could be done was to build a fort on high ground near where the waters of Ohio and Mississippi Rivers mingled. Jefferson authorized that mission on January 29, 1780. That was about all the governor could do. The treasury was bare, and Virginia's credit was nearly worthless. So Clark would somehow have to organize and sustain the expedition on his own. Jefferson encouraged him to "take such care of the men under you as an economical householder would of his own family, doing everything within himself as far as he can and calling for as few supplies as possible. The less you depend for supplies on this quarter, the less will you be disappointed by those impediments which distances and a precarious foreign commerce throw in the way." He cautioned him to "Purchase nothing beyond the Ohio which you can do without, or which may be obtained from the east side where our paper is current."[13] The only resources Jefferson could provide were land grants to entice potential recruits and settlers. He sent Clark three hundred land warrants to distribute, with the acreage distributed according to rank for soldiers or the number of members for families.

In urging austerity and self-sufficiency, Jefferson departed from his predecessor, Patrick Henry, who had essentially given Clark blank checks with which to pay his way. That was then. Now the state was not only bankrupt but besieged by creditors demanding payment for IOUs signed by scores of officers and officials. To sort out who owed what to whom, Jefferson asked

Clark to "send us a list of all the bills you have drawn on us, specifying where they are drawn in dollars, whether silver or paper dollars were intended, and if paper at what rate of depreciation."[14]

That task was easier demanded than done. Gaps pockmarked the records of Clark and most other commanders. Many of the existing documents were cryptic scribblings, water-soaked and either inadvertent or, at times, deliberate miscalculations. Many had been lost or misplaced. An exact accounting was impossible.

The governor's instructions did not end there. In the four weeks since his New Year's letter, Jefferson had been wrestling with his conscience. He had reconsidered his earlier harsh policy of either annihilating or expelling the Indians. Now he "would have you cultivate peace and cordial friendship with the several tribes." Any treaties, however, would commit those hostile Indians to neutrality rather than alliance with the United States: "As to the English, notwithstanding their base example, we wish not to expose them to the inhumanities of a savage enemy. Let this reproach remain on them, but for ourselves we would not have our national character tarnished with such a practice."[15]

Upon receiving the governor's go-ahead, Clark swiftly carried out his mission. He had actually laid the foundation for such an expedition in late September 1779, when he had not only expressed his vision to Jefferson but, expecting authorization, had issued orders to subordinates to begin drumming up supplies, soldiers, and settlers. That way, once he got official approval, he could accelerate the mission rather than start the preparations.[16]

An essential element of leadership involves explaining the logic behind a plan and then delegating the appropriate authority to fulfill it. Belief and behavior are inseparable; generally, the more one believes in something, the more effort one is willing to expend to realize that belief. John Todd, Illinois County's lieutenant, would render important aid in realizing Clark's latest plan. But before Clark revealed exactly what he had in mind, he sought to convince Todd that the existing strategy was a recipe for disaster. He bluntly stated, "I make no doubt of the English regaining the Interests of many Tribes . . . and their designs agst the Illinois." The English would take advantage of the volcanic rage among the people swelling beneath the voracious alien presence in Illinois. Only a seemingly paradoxical plan could save Illinois: "I see but one probable method of maintang our Authority in the Illinois . . . by Amediately Evacuating our present posts, and let our whole force Center at or near the Mouth of the Ohio."[17] In other words, the Americans had to abandon Illinois in order to save it.

Although Clark's logic won over Todd and his other officers, his plan provoked outrage among Kentucky's settlers. Gaining wind of the expedition, the citizens of Boonesborough and Bryan's Station sent Clark petitions calling on him to wield his resources of men and supplies to help defend them against the relentless Indian attacks.[18] The pioneers of central Kentucky had long resented the establishment of a fort at the Falls far to the northwest from the war party routes that ran south down the Licking River and Limestone Creek directly to their homes. Now, Clark's already-meager forces would be stretched even thinner, all the way to Kentucky's far western edge, where a fort would be set up on the Mississippi River. The settlers' outrage would turn to fury the following year as the deadliest Indian and British campaign yet assailed Kentucky. And George Rogers Clark's magic with most settlers would vanish in the smoke of burned homes, bodies, and gunpowder.

All those horrors lay ahead, and Clark could not foresee them. He brushed off the settlers' petitions with little thought. His mind, however, was not solely riveted on readying his latest campaign. Amid the flurry of preparations, he found time to cut a deal that would vastly expand his and his family's potential wealth. On January 29, 1780, he received title from Virginia to 168,000 acres of yet-to-be-determined western land for himself along with 300 warrants of 560 acres each to issue to recruits and settlers alike.[19]

Clark's expedition set forth from Louisville on April 14, 1780, and fifteen days later landed at Iron Banks, half a dozen miles below the Ohio River mouth and on the north side of Mayfield Creek. Ground was cleared. The outlines of a square fort a hundred feet to a side was paced off and staked out. A dry moat ten feet wide and eight feet deep was dug beyond the lines and piled up. Ten-foot logs were planted atop the earthworks. Square blockhouses with twenty-foot-sides were erected at opposite angles of the palisade; a six-pounder cannon was emplaced in one. Within what was named Fort Jefferson rose storehouses, barracks, a magazine, and a blacksmith shop. Beyond the fort, the settlers cleared land and built cabins for a hamlet they called Clarksville.[20]

Clark was directing the scores of laborers at those construction sites when urgent news arrived. An enemy attack was pending that demanded his immediate presence.

As 1780 dawned, the British did some grim reckoning. Their effort to crush the American rebellion was nearly five years old. Yet all they had to show for the expenditure of enormous blood and treasure was the occupation of New York City and Savannah. Although in the field the British had won more battles than they had lost, a crushing blow had eluded them. Instead, the Americans had scored a decisive military victory in October 1777, which led to a decisive diplomatic victory in February 1778. The rebel capture of General Burgoyne and his army of 5,500 troops at Saratoga encouraged France to ally openly with the United States. Then on June 17, 1779, Spain joined its army and fleet with those of France in the war against Britain. When the British looked ahead, they saw little more than spiraling deaths and debts, capped by ignominious defeat.

Whitehall hoped to reverse that in 1780. Lord George Germain, the minister in overall charge of Britain's war effort, authorized three grand offensives to retake regions of their imploding American empire, one against the southern colonies, another against Louisiana, and the final against the Mississippi and Ohio valleys.

The major effort was in the South, and that offensive would be a great success. General Henry Clinton bagged 5,500 rebels at Charleston on May 12, then handed over his army's command to General Charles Cornwallis and sailed back to New York. Cornwallis routed the American army led by General Horatio Gates at Camden on August 16. By the summer's end, the British controlled most of South Carolina, North Carolina, and Georgia. In stark contrast, the campaign to capture Louisiana, led by General John Campbell, West Florida's governor, died stillborn. Louisiana governor Bernardo Galvez preempted that plan by snatching Mobile then repelling a British attempt to retake it. The following year, Galvez would move against Pensacola with overwhelming force.

Then there was the campaign to overrun the Ohio and upper Mississippi valleys. To that end, Canadian governor Frederick Haldimand devised a two-pronged campaign plan and sent it to his two field commanders, Captain Patrick Sinclair at Fort Michilimackinac and Major Arent de

Peyster at Detroit, to implement. Sinclair ordered two veteran wilderness traders and fighters, Captains Emanuel Hesse and Charles Michael de Langlade, to muster native armies, the former from among the upper Mississippi Indians at Prairie du Chien, and the latter from the Lake Michigan Indians at Chicago, then a tiny trading post. They would join forces at the confluence of the Illinois and Mississippi Rivers, then overrun the cluster of Spanish and American villages, starting with Saint Louis and Cahokia. Meanwhile, Major de Peyster ordered Captain Henry Bird to organize a campaign that would destroy the fort at the Falls of the Ohio and then march against Kentucky's settlements.[21]

Having set that ambitious scheme in motion, Haldimand was pessimistic about its chances for success, especially in the Ohio valley. He informed General Clinton, "Very little is to be expected from the Indians upon the frontiers of Virginia . . . I mean the Western Nations who resort to Detroit and that neighbourhood. Indefatigable pains have been taken, and immense sums lavished to secure their affections, yet they are every day declining, particularly since the American alliance with the French, to whom they have an old and a very firm attachment. Add to this the misfortune of Mr. Hamilton, the disappointments of reinforcements promised to them from year to year; the unwearied pains of the Spanish from the Mississippi to debauch them; and the advances of the enemy on all sides into their country."[22]

Nonetheless, Illinois seemed like an easy conquest. De Peyster reported to Haldimand that Kaskaskia was poorly defended, "the fort being a sorry picketed enclosure round the Jesuits College with two Plank houses at opposite angles mounting 2 four pounders each on the ground floor, and a few swivels mounted on a pigeon house. The militia are about one hundred and fifty men serving much against their inclination." The Indians were also unwilling and restive subjects of the Americans, who "have nothing to give them and treat them with great contempt. Their policy is to intimidate them since they cannot caress them."[23]

The first of the two campaigns to get under way targeted the vulnerable Illinois villages and their neighbors west of the Mississippi.[24] To that end, Hesse rallied about 750 Indians at Prairie du Chien, at the confluence of the Wisconsin and Mississippi Rivers. The largest contingent was a couple hundred Sioux led by Wabasha (Red Leaf) and a hundred Ojibwas led by Matchekewis, along with lesser numbers of warriors from the Menominee,

Winnebago, Ottawa, Fox, Potawatomie, Sac, and Kickapoo tribes. On
May 2, Hesse, a dozen Canadians, and the Indians pushed off their canoes
and dug their paddles deep into the river bound for Saint Louis. That force
would not rendezvous with Langlade, who was having trouble recruiting.
Instead, Hesse and his warriors would head straight to Saint Louis.[25]

At Fort Jefferson, Clark received two alarming messages, one each from
Lieutenant Colonel John Montgomery and Captain John Rogers at Cahokia.
Governor Fernando de Leyba had warned the Americans that a force of
British and Indians would soon descend the Mississippi River. The officers
promptly crossed over to Saint Louis and discussed with de Leyba what to
do. For Montgomery, offense was the best defense. He proposed a spoiling
attack on the enemy Indian villages upriver. De Leyba promised to supply a
hundred militiamen to the expedition. Rogers, however, balked at Montgomery's order to add his company to the ranks since it conflicted with Clark's
order that he stay at Cahokia. For the time being, Montgomery's planned
offensive was on hold for lack of men, munitions, and provisions. Both men
requested their commander's presence to defeat that enemy offensive.[26]

Clark immediately set off from Fort Jefferson with a company of troops
on the grueling hundred-mile row up the Mississippi current. At Kaskaskia,
Clark went ashore and galloped north on horseback while his men continued
pushing upstream. Clark reached Cahokia on May 25, the day before the
enemy would arrive; his reinforcements would appear the day after the battle.
The fort at Cahokia did not amount to much, just a wooden palisade atop
earthworks with a shallow ditch beyond. Clark could call on about a hundred
Americans and local militiamen.

After inspecting the troops and palisade, Clark crossed the river to confer with de Leyba at Saint Louis. The governor must have been deeply somber.
His beloved wife had recently died, and now he faced an enemy onslaught
that might wipe out Saint Louis. Indeed, he was so despondent that he offered Clark command of Spain's forces. Clark politely declined that extraordinary offer. He then asked for the latest intelligence, explained his own
preparations, and learned just what de Leyba had done. Neither had any
men or supplies to spare for the other. Their meeting's chief purpose was to
boost confidence and share information. Clark then hurried back across the

river to Cahokia to ready his men for battle. It is not clear whether Clark raised an issue with de Leyba during their meeting that had irritated him for some time.[27]

The relationship between the Americans and Spaniards on the upper Mississippi was sound, grounded in their interest in defeating a common enemy. But one Spanish policy undercut the effectiveness of those efforts. Clark confessed, "I am not a Sufficient Statesman to Comprehend the Policy of the Spanish Gentlemen, Protecting the Deserters of a People so fond to serve them as we are at Warr against the same Enemy. It cannot be good policy at this time for nothing saves both Spanish & American Illenois from the hands of the English but the Troops we have."[28] Desertion was easy for Americans stationed at Kaskaskia or Cahokia; sanctuary could be bought for a coin or two pressed into the calloused hand of a man with a rowboat or pirogue. Clark asked Oliver Pollock to intercede with Governor Galvez to end that policy. Most likely he shelved raising that issue with de Leyba until after the invasion. If worse came to worse, the question then might be quite moot.

Fortunately, Governor de Leyba had readied Saint Louis for the looming onslaught.[29] As an army captain, he was well-versed in such military fundamentals as command, supply, fortifications, reconnaissance, and tactics. Two electrifying reports provoked his efforts to strengthen the town's defense. On February 9, 1780, he got word from New Orleans that Spain was now at war with Britain. Then, on March 9, a trader arrived to warn of the attack being mustered a couple hundred miles upstream. De Leyba mobilized men and material to build a stone tower at the town's west side, the first of four planned. He called up the militia from Saint Genevieve and other villages down the valley. The governor sent patrols up the Mississippi to provide advanced warning of the approaching enemy. When the attack came, Saint Louis would be defended by as many as 40 soldiers and 220 militiamen. Although the stone tower was unfinished, a cannon was mounted on top with a commanding view of the countryside.

The sentinels in the tower witnessed a nightmarish scene on the morning of May 26. Indians suddenly burst from cover and, screaming war cries, dashed toward farmers tilling the distant fields. The sentinels touched off the signal gun and watched in horror as the Indians ran down and clubbed or shot the terrified peasants, and then, with scalping knives, bent over the inert or thrashing bodies. A group of peasants piled into a cart, and the driver whipped the horse toward town, but the horse could manage no more than a trot with all that dead weight. Indian arrows and musket balls wounded seven people in the cart. An Indian running hard after a black man stumbled and fell. The man turned, grabbed the Indian's musket, and shot him dead. One severely wounded man would lay in thick brush for three days before he was discovered by a howling dog.

The Indians soon lost heart after their initial exhilarating rush. At the loud crack of the signal gun, the Spanish troops and militiamen quickly grabbed their muskets and hurried to their preassigned positions. The Indians gazed across the open fields toward a town bristling with armed men awaiting their advance.

Prudence prevailed. The Indians did not assault the town but instead scattered across the countryside, killing or capturing people either unaware of the attack or unable to reach safety, looting outlying houses, and slaughtering livestock. In all, the Indians killed fourteen whites and seven slaves, wounded six whites and one slave, and captured twelve whites and thirteen slaves. And that was just at Saint Louis. Elsewhere, the raiders killed or captured another forty-six people. Those were terrible losses for a colony with less than a thousand people. But Saint Louis at least had been saved. The following day, Hesse and his followers headed back upriver, their canoes filled with loot and captives.[30]

De Leyba would not have long to savor his victory. He died on June 28. Although his death orphaned his two young daughters, it may have come as a relief to him. He not only was mourning the loss of his wife but also was crushed by debt, his own and that of others who trusted him. He had sacrificed his fortune, family, reputation, and eventually his life for American independence.[31]

The attack that same day on Cahokia had its own surreal moments. Private John Murphy and two comrades were out picking wild strawberries when they heard distant gunshots from across the river at Saint Louis.[32] Reckoning that it was the attack they had been warned about, they headed back to the fort. However, for unknown reasons, they decided to stretch out under a cottonwood tree and doze off. Suddenly, a black woman rushed by and hollered, "Run Bostoni! Run Bostoni! beaucoup des Savages! beaucoup des Savages!" The soldiers glanced around in terror, spotted warriors trotting toward him, and dashed toward the fort. Luckily, the Indians did not run after them but instead murdered two French peasants out tending their fields.

Clark was leading his troops and a six-pounder from the fort as his three stray soldiers panted up to him. He ordered them to fetch their muskets and join the ranks. Clark pushed on up the road at the head of his column then called a halt when Indians were spotted lurking in the trees. He had the six-pounder wheeled, pointed, and fired. The cannon exploded a load of musket balls and scrap metal toward the Indians but hit no one. The Indians scattered. And that was the end of the skirmish. The raiders withdrew across the river to the main force near Saint Louis.

The affair at Cahokia ended on a humorous note that provides insights into Clark's character. Astonishingly, after his narrow escape earlier that day, Private Murphy once again obeyed the commands of sleep deprivation amid danger. That night he dozed off on sentry duty. Fortunately, he heard approaching footsteps and roused himself before whoever it was discovered that he was sleeping on the job, an offense officially punishable by execution.

"Who goes there?" Murphy called out.

"Rounds," was the sharp reply.

Murphy, obviously still befuddled by exhaustion and lack of sleep, replied, "What rounds?"

"Grand rounds," was the likely irritated response. It was an officer inspecting the sentries to ensure that they were fulfilling their duties.

That did not faze Murphy, who warned, "Keep clear of my arms."

The officer halted and then identified himself. It was none other than George Rogers Clark. Apparently, the colonel vented some of his irritation at the private in colorful language.

The next morning, Murphy learned to his dismay that Clark was not done with him. Murphy received orders to report promptly to headquarters. His natural trepidation worsened when he saw Clark sharpening a switch and he assumed he was in for a flogging.

Clark demanded how the private could "talk so saucy to him."

To that, Murphy could only utter words about duty.

To Murphy's astonishment, Clark praised him, shared a glass of wine with him, then sent the lackadaisical but very lucky soldier on his way.

That gesture was vintage Clark. He flared easily with anger. At times, that anger was justified, and at other times it was misplaced. When he realized that he had overreacted, he tried to make amends. The way he dealt with Murphy in their two encounters was multiplied countless times throughout his life.

When Clark learned that Hesse had retreated, he sent Colonel Montgomery with 230 men to shadow him. At the Illinois River mouth, Montgomery chose to veer up that stream rather than follow Hesse up the Mississippi. His expedition rowed all the way to Peoria, where the troops burned several Fox and Sauk villages whose inhabitants had fled at word of the Long Knives' approach.

Meanwhile, Clark headed back downriver to Fort Jefferson, where he arrived on June 4. He nearly did not make it. As his boat passed between an island and the shore, he spied Indians hidden in the trees on both sides. He had the presence of mind to rise up and gesture behind him to imaginary boats upriver. The Indians withheld their fire, and Clark and his men were soon out of danger.

Clark had no sooner put out one fire than he got word of an even more menacing one, this one in the heart of Kentucky.[33]

CHAPTER 14

The Village Burner

I think the most important object which can be proposed with such a force is the extermination of those hostile tribes of Indians who live between the Ohio and the Illinois.

Thomas Jefferson

In the summer of 1780, Kentucky faced its most formidable invasion yet.[1] Captain Henry Bird led south from Detroit about 140 redcoats of the Eighth and Forty-seventh Regiments, around 30 Detroit militia volunteers, and about 800 Indians, including Shawnees, Wyandots, Ottawas, Hurons, and Miamis. Bird's expedition included several score packhorses carrying munitions and provisions, and two field guns, a six-pounder and a three-pounder, dragged by oxen. The trails were usually wide enough to permit the passage of those cannons, but at places the men had to hack a passage. Part of the trip was over water, on bateau from Detroit to the Maumee River portage, and on rafts from the upper Miami River to the Ohio River.

Fortunately, word of Bird's expedition reached Kentucky before he and his men did. Two captives among the Indians escaped separately to warn the settlers of the pending invasion. That intelligence was confirmed by David Zeisberger, the Moravian missionary, and Chief Killbuck and the Delaware council that struggled to stay neutral in the war.[2]

Bird would be unaware that he had lost the element of surprise for some time. But not far down the Miami River a rumor halted his expedition for several days of debate. Word had passed through the Indian grapevine that George Rogers Clark had returned to the fort at the Falls. The rumor was wrong; Clark was then at Fort Jefferson, but Bird would not learn of that until much later. A council of his officers and the chiefs chose to head due south to attack the cluster of settlements in central Kentucky. After crossing the Ohio River, they headed upstream a short way and then south up the Licking River trail. It took the expedition twelve days of hard labor widening that trail before they reached Ruddle's Station, the northernmost settlement.

Aware of the approaching onslaught, the Kentuckians chose to fort up rather than flee. Bird's redcoats and warriors encircled that settlement on the evening of June 21. The settlers passed a terrifying, sleepless night as war whoops, taunts, and musket shots resounded from the surrounding forest. The following morning the gunners opened fire with the three-pounder cannon; the six-pounder was still back down the trail. It took only a few well-placed shots to smash a hole through the palisade. A white flag appeared over the fort. Henry Bird agreed to Isaac Ruddle's plea that his soldiers would protect his followers from the wrath of the Indians, but in return all adults would make loyalty oaths to the king and be taken north to Detroit. Bird and his men then headed to Martin's Station, the next settlement, where the settlers quickly surrendered on similar terms.

At that point, Bird was poised to systematically capture all of the Kentucky settlements. Instead, he called it quits and about-faced for Detroit. That puzzling decision was partly due to the desertion of a growing number of Indians whose arms were filled with plunder taken from the two settlements. Yet even then several hundred Indians remained with the redcoats. Also contributing to Bird's decision were the more than 350 captives he now had to feed and guard. At both stations, the Indians had maliciously slaughtered the cattle, pigs, and other livestock that could have sustained both the campaign and then the long march back to Detroit. The desertions and shortage of food were pressing enough. But the most compelling reason for Bird's withdrawal was his fear that he might suffer the same fate that Lieutenant Colonel Henry Hamilton had suffered at Vincennes. Bird had no idea where Clark was but imagined him leading an army to cut off his rear escape and trap him in Kentucky. So to sidestep that catastrophe, Bird turned tail and swiftly retreated. Along the way, the Ohio Indians dispersed with their loot to their homes. Bird, his redcoats, most of the Great Lakes Indians, and the captives trudged into Detroit on August 4.[3]

George Rogers Clark had indeed learned of the invasion but could only dream of realizing Bird's worst nightmare. On June 5, he and two of his men strode from Fort Jefferson on the long trail east. By the time they reached Harrodsburg, the invaders were far beyond reach. But if Clark could not catch up to Bird, he was determined to reap a bloody vengeance on whatever Indian villages were in striking distance.[4]

If the image of Clark marching at the head of an army bent on vengeance was the greatest fear among the British and Indians, it was the greatest hope among the Kentuckians. By one account, "the great panic occasioned through Kentucky by the taking of Ruddle's and Martin's Stations caused the people to look up to Clark as their only hope. His counsel and advice were received as coming from an oracle."[5]

Yet all that faith and popularity did not translate into troops and supplies. Clark's mission collided with a huge stumbling block when initially no one heeded his command to muster. Greed trumped security as the dominant drive for most settlers who had long awaited the opening of a land office in Harrodsburg to register their claims. In its brief initial days of operation, the office recorded 1.6 million acres of largely overlapping claims!

Prying homesteaders from their dreams would take extraordinary measures. Clark ignited rage among them when he shut the land office until further notice. Then there were the scores of those so traumatized by the frontier war's horrors that they wanted to pull up stakes and hurry back east. Clark enraged them when he forbade anyone from leaving Kentucky and posted militiamen on the Wilderness Road to enforce that order. To the county lieutenants, he sent word to muster four of every five men from their militia companies and rendezvous at the mouth of the Licking River no later than July 31. Many of those who did appear would be sullen and resentful.

There was ample irony in shutting down the land office, although Clark likely was not then aware of it. On June 30, Virginia's government approved Clark's petition for 36,000 acres north of the Falls of the Ohio River. It did so as an award for Clark's "great services to this Commonwealth, not only in reducing the British posts at the Kaskaskias and St. Vincent's, and engaging the inhabitants there to become citizens of this Commonwealth; but also in defeating the machinations of our enemies, by attaching to our interest many heretofore hostile tribes of Indians, and thereby saving the inhabitants of the western frontiers and this and neighboring States from a cruel and destructive Indian war, mediated by the British officers, against them."[6] The land, however, was not a gift. Clark somehow had to scrape up £7,000 to secure the title.

Clark's controversial measures did not end after he and his contingent, the understrength regiments of Captains John Floyd, William Harrod, and William Linn, headed upstream from the fort at the Falls. The flotilla encountered settlers aboard a flatboat. Short of supplies, Clark ordered the requisition of their cargo of corn and several jugs of whiskey, then scribbled them a receipt.[7] While Congress and the state governments empowered their field commanders to requisition supplies from patriots and outright confiscate them from Loyalists, the outrage of the victims tended to target the officers in charge.

Clark needed all the provisions he could garner. During the hard row up the Ohio River from the Falls to the Licking River mouth, water from the leaky boats had seeped into the bags of provisions, ruining all but 1,500 pounds of the 3,130 pounds of flour, all 375 bushels of corn, and 6 of 40 bushels of salt.[8]

That was hardly the only problem. Among the expedition's militia captains was Hugh McGary, who was murderously inept as a Kentucky leader. It was McGary who in 1782 would shout down Daniel Boone's warning of an ambush at Blue Licks and bully the other captains into a blind dash forward that cost the lives of seventy-seven Kentuckians. But his first blunder that got his men killed took place during Clark's 1780 campaign. En route up the Ohio River toward the rendezvous, McGary led his men to the north shore to hunt. Although they passed four burning campfires indicating a large Indian party had just departed, he scorned those who urged caution and pushed his men into an ambush that killed nine of them. The horrors of frontier warfare were epitomized with the death of one man, who "was seen to jump out of one of the pirogues, wade ashore, & take down river, & was pursued by an Indian with a . . . spear elevated & aimed in hand. After following some 20 or 30 yards, the Indian stopped & cast the spear which entered the man between the shoulders & penetrated through, the point sticking out of his breast—he fell forward . . . scrambled up & crawled . . . under some driftwood. He was soon afterward conveyed to the boats . . . died before night, & was buried on shore."[9]

Not all the militia companies were so poorly led as McGary's company. At the mouth of the Licking River, Clark found Lieutenant Colonel Benjamin Logan's force a "delightful sight all good Woodsmen well armed with good rifles and chiefly good marksmen."[10] All the men were militia except for Major George Slaughter and fifty Virginian regulars. Most were dressed in hunting shirts, leggings, and moccasins. It took days before all the companies straggled in. Meanwhile, Clark had two blockhouses built and filled with a company of militiamen, several sick, and all the supplies that could not be carried.[11]

When Clark's army crossed the Ohio on August 2, 1780, it included 998 frontiersmen. Virtually all were afoot except a dozen or so men astride horses and acting as scouts. Teams of four horses each pulled a brass six-pounder cannon and two iron four-pounders; Captain Robert George commanded the twenty-six-man gun crew. Another four-horse team pulled a supply wagon. Each company had a horse or two packed with provisions, extra munitions, kettles, axes, and other necessities. Each man was allocated a weekly ration of six quarts of corn and a gill of salt. Clark intended to supplement his provisions by pillaging the Indian corn, squash, and bean fields that were nearing harvest.

The army was split in two, with Clark commanding the first division and Logan, the second; they marched in that order with the cannons and packhorses in between. The entire column was screened by dozens of men on all sides. They filed east along the Ohio River's north shore until they reached the Little Miami River mouth, then headed up that valley. The first target was the mostly Shawnee town of Chillicothe, fifty-eight miles from the Ohio River. The expedition made slow progress with frequent stops as men widened the trail to allow passage of the wagon and cannons.

The expedition's success greatly depended on surprise. If the Indians learned of their enemy's advance, the warriors could prepare an ambush while the women, children, and old men fled to safety. Marching a thousand men on a well-traveled war trail north from the Ohio without being spotted was a long shot at best. Clark was determined to squeeze the most from those dismal odds by ordering no shots fired unless Indians were the target. Then one day, to Clark's fury, a rifle cracked. Clark ordered the shooter arrested and flogged for disobeying orders. The officer charged with punishing the miscreant requested a private word with Clark. He explained that he knew the man and could vouch for his character, and he asked for a reprieve. Clark suspended the sentence.

Indians had undoubtedly been spying on Clark's army not long after it began to gather at the Licking River mouth. They first got word of the pending campaign from a deserter. On a horse provided by Loyalist sympathizers, John Clairy galloped north from Bryan's Station on July 23. Clark's expedition later found at the Licking River mouth. He swam across the Ohio River and at some point on the trail north ran into Indians. He told them that Clark and eight hundred men would soon be upon them.[12]

As Clark's army marched within five miles of Chillicothe on the morning of August 7, scouts hurried back to report that the Indians were rapidly evacuating their town. Clark double-timed his men forward. Chillicothe was deserted and its blockhouse burned when the Kentuckians cautiously spread out and passed through. Clark ordered the houses looted and torched, and all the crops but a half dozen acres uprooted; his men would feast off that spared patch on the way back. As for loot, the pickings were fairly slim. Thanks to Clairy's warning, the Indians and a handful of British residents had either carried away or secreted in the woods nearly everything of value. The most notable cache was a three-pounder cannon and balls that artilleryman William Homan and crewmen had buried in the woods.[13]

For the night, Clark formed his men into a hollow square around the supplies and cannons. Some time that night they were pounded by a thunderstorm that "fell in torrents" leaving "the men as wet as if they had been plunged into the river." After the storm passed, Clark ordered his men to fire their weapons by company. Despite their best efforts to keep their gunpowder dry, many men discovered that the moisture had seeped in and turned their charges to gunk. They had to attach a screw to their ramrods, pull the dead charge, wipe the barrel dry, and then pour a measure of gunpowder followed by a patched ball. By morning, the men were exhausted from the miserable night, but at least their weapons were ready for battle.[14]

That same storm thwarted a planned attack by several hundred warriors led by Captain Simon Girty. The torrents of water soaked their gunpowder and slackened their bowstrings. Girty and the chiefs reluctantly agreed to return to Piqua to dry out and prepare for the pending enemy assault.[15]

The following day, Clark's army began the march to Piqua, twelve miles northwest on the Mad River, a tributary of the Little Miami River. Piqua was mostly home for the Kispoko, Mekoche, and Pekowi Shawnee bands but, like virtually all Indian towns, had a mélange of people from other tribes. Along the way, "Indian runners [were] continually before our advance guards." Clark and his officers reckoned the Indian strategy was "of leading us on to their own ground and time of action."[16]

Clark sent ahead a scout, James Guthrie, to determine whether the Indians had abandoned Piqua as well. Within a few hours, Guthrie returned with word that warriors were massed in the village and appeared determined to defend it. Clark urged his men forward. Several hundred warriors awaited Clark and his men. Most were Shawnees, with Aquitsica (Wry Neck) leading the Pekowis and Silverheels leading the Mekoches. Contingents of Wyandots, Mingos, and Delawares swelled their ranks. Buckongahelas led the Delawares; learning of the invasion, he and his men swiftly trekked down from their village thirty miles away on the Great Miami River's headwaters. The Girty brothers, Simon, James, and George, were also present. The Indians were poorly armed with few muskets and poor powder; most would fight with bows and arrows, war clubs, tomahawks, and scalping knives.[17]

Clark later reported to Jefferson that by half past two on the afternoon on August 8, "We arrived in sight of the town and posts, a plain of half a mile in width laying between us. I had an opportunity of viewing the situation and motion of the enemy near their works."[18] He quickly devised a battle plan. The path crossed from the right to the left side of the river and then ran up to the village a quarter mile away. He sent Logan in a long arc rightward through the forest around to the Shawnees' rear. As Logan's men filed off, Clark ordered the bulk of his army to cross the river and line up facing the village. With his right flank secured on the river and his left anchored by the troops of Floyd, Lynn, and Harrod, Clark signaled his men forward.

As the Kentuckians advanced, warriors scattered in patches of woods and peppered them with musket fire. Clark directed his men to rout those Indians by repeatedly flanking and driving them "from hill to hill in a circuitous direction." Some Indians slipped around to the rear of the army and opened fire. Clark detached some of his men to drive them off with rifle shots and then a charge. The firing briefly ceased as the Indians withdrew to their village. Clark "halted the troops in the woods for a few minutes, got the men in order, who had in crossing the river & running through the prairie, became disarranged." His eyes swept the village, fields, woods, and river. Before the village, the Shawnees had erected a breastwork between two huge fallen oak trees. Indians lurked there and behind nearby trees. In the village itself was a palisade with a triangular-shaped blockhouse at a corner.

Clark ordered Captain Joseph McMurtry to charge his company against that breastwork while other troops advanced on a broad front and "not suffer [the Indians] to fire twice from behind the same tree. Thus far none, as was known, were killed on either side, one white had a ball pass thro' his hat & graze the skin on the top of his head." As McMurtry led his men forward, a bullet shot off his right trigger finger, smashed his powder horn, plowed into his breastbone, and knocked him flat. Several of his men gathered around and reckoned the wound was mortal. But McMurtry revived, "inserted his thumb . . . in the wound & flirted out the ball, which had . . . flattened . . . His finger was done up with a handkerchief & then all dashed on & overtook the troops a quarter mile off."[19]

The fighting became increasingly desperate. Private Henry Wilson

being thirsty & seeing a spot where he thought might be water, & near the troops ran there but found none, he then saw three Indians dodging through the bushes—one with a cocked hat on, at whom he aimed & shot through the belly. . . . [The warrior] skulked through the bushes to a tree top, leaving his military hat where he fell. As Wilson was picking up his booty, Capt Wm McAfee came running to his aid, & both ran to the tree . . . looking for the Indian, who drew up & shot McAfee through the body less than ten feet off. A soldier now ran up, [and] when the Indian was pouring powder into his rifle without measuring it—and shot him under the arm. The other two Indians were also shot, & all scalped. McAfee lived to be carried to the mouth of the Licking on a litter, & thence by water to a friend . . . near the Falls of the Ohio, his wife was sent for & reached him two days before his death.[20]

The key Shawnee defense was the palisade's blockhouse. As some of Clark's men closed in, the stockade's gate was flung open and a swarm of

Shawnees dashed out screaming war cries and firing muskets or brandishing war clubs. Another group of Indians hiding in a nearby cornfield rose and fired. "Clark gave strict orders for the men to reserve theirs until the Indians should come close." The Kentuckians squinted down their rifle barrels and squeezed the triggers when the Shawnees were within forty paces, "which mowed them down terribly . . . checked their advancing, & the second fire caused them to retreat."[21]

Most of the Shawnee withdrew from tree to tree, firing, reloading, and war whooping. Some squeezed back into the blockhouse and shot from the loopholes. Clark had the six-pounder and two four-pounders brought up, loaded, and fired at the blockhouse. After a dozen or so rounds punched holes into the log walls, the firing from within stopped. Clark ordered his men to charge. There was no resistance; the Indians had fled out the back door.

Although the Kentuckians had routed the Indians, their victory was not decisive. Logan and his men spent the battle thrashing through woods, swamps, and rocky hills to get around the Indians and cut off their retreat, but never got there in time. Nonetheless, Clark amply praised all his men: "Nothing could excel the few regulars and Kentuckyans that composed this little army in bravery and implicit obedience to orders. Each company vying with the other, who should be the most subordinate." His only regret was not having enough provisions to march on and sack the Delaware village farther north.[22]

A personal tragedy marred Clark's victory. Through the din, a white man dressed like an Indian called on the Kentuckians to hold their fire. He was shot down as he dashed forward. As a group of frontiersmen knotted around him, he blurted out that he was Joseph Rogers, Clark's cousin; he had been captured on December 25, 1776, during the attempt to bring gunpowder to Harrodsburg, and had been with the Shawnee ever since. He gasped his desire to see Clark. The general reacted to his cousin's plight with pity and contempt rather than familial love. He "rode up, & remarked he was sorry to see him in that situation, & expressed an opinion that as he knew that the army was coming in time to have escaped & joined his countrymen, he shd have done it. He said he had no opportunity, & couldn't. He was taken to the rear & died in an hour or two after."[23]

Why did Clark react so callously to his own cousin's fate? The reports that he had heard from French traders and escaped captives was true—his cousin was a renegade and a traitor. Bombardier William Holman noted the puzzlement among the Shawnees after they returned to their devastated village and could find no sign of Rogers for whom "they harbour too good opinion of him to think he is deserted."[24] The shame of having a turncoat in the family was too much for Clark to bear, let alone admit. In a letter to his father, he articulated what would become the family's spin on that shame. He lamented "poor Joseph Rogers who lost his Life in the Moment it might have of been in his power to Render his Country great service."[25]

Piqua was littered with Indian dead and a few wounded. The Kentuckians bashed in the skulls of those who still breathed. Indian women and children were butchered along with men. A rifle ball had shattered both legs of a warrior. As the Kentuckians approached, he pulled his knife and lunged repeatedly at them until he was killed. One soldier murdered a woman by "ripping up her Belly & otherwise mangling her." Graves were dug up and the bodies scalped and mutilated. In all, the Kentuckians counted eighty-four Indian dead; most likely, other dead bodies were carried off, and some of the scores of wounded would soon die. That victory came at a high cost—the Kentuckians lost twenty-six men, and a couple score were wounded; five would later die of their wounds.[26]

As dusk approached, Clark deployed his army in a square, with half the troops on guard half the night, to be relieved by the other half until dawn. The destruction and looting resumed early the next morning. As at Chillicothe, the men plundered then burned the scores of houses and eight hundred acres of crops. Most men would return to the settlements with quite a haul of goods although they only captured about forty horses. After Chillicothe, no Indian village was closer to Kentucky and thus launched more raids and reaped more plunder than Piqua. Clark ordered his dead soldiers buried in the earthen floors of the cabins and those dwellings torched to prevent the Indians from digging up and mutilating the corpses.

Clark held a council of war to debate the next move. A majority of his officers opted for heading home. Supplies were nearly exhausted, and the corn in the fields was green, a diet more conducive to diarrhea than nutrition. The nearest Indian village was a hard two-day trek away and would likely be empty once they got there. Although Clark approved the consensus, he would later regret that decision. He learned that the Shawnees would have asked for terms had he quick-marched his army against them.[27] Indeed,

Clark would be criticized for not sending at least Logan's men in pursuit. After all, their powder horns and shot bags were full, and their ranks were not thinned by combat.

The army set off for home the next day. Discipline swiftly unraveled on the return march. The cornfields left standing could not supply the army's needs. Provisions were exhausted. The men reached the Licking River mouth on August 14. There, Clark thanked and then dismissed his troops; each company took the most direct route back to its home.

In battles fought west of the Appalachian Mountains during the Revolutionary War, none had more participants than the battle of Piqua. Clark tersely reported to Jefferson that "having done the Shawnese all the mischief in our power; after destroying the Picawey settlments, I returned." The governor fired back his congratulations along with the hope that "those Savages will be taught to fear, since they cannot be taught to keep faith."[28] Actually, the prevailing sentiment among the Shawnees and their allies would be an unquenchable desire for revenge.

However cathartic it was for those thousand Kentuckians to vent years of pent-up rage at Indian atrocities, their victory was purely tactical. They could boast of the scalps and loot they brought back, but the Indian threat remained as virulent as ever. Not only did the Shawnees immediately return to rebuild their devastated homes at Piqua and Chillicothe, but war parties soon trod the paths to the Kentucky settlement in search of vengeance. Meanwhile, delegations headed north to Detroit to council with Major Arent de Peyster and chiefs from other tribes. De Peyster dispatched horses laden with provisions to avert starvation at Piqua and Chillicothe. He promised to organize a campaign for the next summer that might well destroy the Long Knives south of the Ohio River once and for all.[29]

Spies brought back word of those councils. General Daniel Brodhead, the commander at Fort Pitt, tapped into a spy network that stretched all the way to Detroit. Sympathetic Delaware Indians and Moravian missionaries John Heckewelder and David Zeisberger played a very dangerous double game. They kept a careful count of the war parties striding past the cluster of Moravian missions of Gnadenhutten, Salem, and Schoenbrunn.[30]

Clark had his own network of Indian and white spies, mostly handled by Indian agent Major Godefroy de Linctot at Vincennes. The word that Linctot and Clark paid the sharpest attention to was a British plan to retake

Vincennes. Clark was determined to rout that attack and then launch a counterattack that would devastate the enemy all the way to Detroit. But for that, he needed an unprecedented amount of men, munitions, and provisions. He began the Sisyphean agony of amassing all that.

Meanwhile, the fort and settlement at Kentucky's western tip that Clark had founded in the spring was literally and figuratively coming apart under ever-fiercer attacks. At times, the best defense is to leave well enough alone. Fort Jefferson harmed rather than bolstered Kentucky's security. Until April 19, 1780, when the expedition disembarked at Iron Banks, the Chickasaws had been largely neutral. A few of their men, enticed by British agents with gifts and promises, had raided the Kentucky settlements. But that was contrary to and condemned by the tribal council. All that changed with the erection of Fort Jefferson and Clarksville.

The resulting war was rooted in a tragic misunderstanding. From the fort's conception, Governor Jefferson recognized that its survival would depend not only on having enough men and supplies to defend it. Diplomacy would be crucial. Jefferson sent instructions to Major Joseph Martin, one of Virginia's Indian agents, to purchase from the Indians that site "on as good terms as possible to be paid for in goods."[31] Unfortunately, Jefferson believed that the Cherokees were the rightful owners. It is not clear whether Martin actually struck a deal with the Cherokees. If so, the Cherokees would have been delighted to sell for a very good reason—that land was not theirs. In an eighteenth-century version of peddling the Brooklyn Bridge, the Cherokees would have been generously paid for territory actually owned by the Chickasaws.

Joseph Martin joined Clark's expedition as its Indian agent. His first diplomacy came not long after Clark led his men ashore. A party of Chickasaws appeared, told the Long Knives that they were trespassing, and demanded that they leave. Clark sent Martin to the Chickasaw villages down the Mississippi near present-day Memphis to purchase the site. The Chickasaw tribal council met, smoked, talked, and decided. They told a dismayed Martin that they had no intention of selling that or any other land. With as much sorrow as anger, they protested that the Long Knives had "settled a fort in our hunting ground without our leave. . . . We are a people that never forgets any kindness done us by any nation. . . . We was formerly very good friends and . . . thought we should be always so."[32] They then insisted that the invaders leave immediately. That message caught up to Clark as he was rushing to blunt the Indian and British invasion at Saint Louis and Cahokia. He defiantly ordered the fort and settlement readied for war.

War came with the summer. The Chickasaws naturally saw themselves as fighting a just war against the invaders of their homeland. Although most war parties skulked around Fort Jefferson, others raided settlements farther east. Kentucky was already fending off Indian and British attacks from across the Ohio River and from the Cherokees to the southeast. Now Chickasaw war parties were striding from the southwest to kill, capture, loot, and burn.

The first Chickasaw raids in June 1780 sought to cut off the fort by attacking supply boats on the Mississippi River and hunters in the forest. Then, on July 17, around 150 warriors assaulted the village of Clarksville, adjacent to Fort Jefferson, and killed three settlers before rifle fire from a blockhouse drove them back. Marksmen from both sides tried to pick each other off as the other warriors slaughtered livestock and tore up the cornfields. The raiders retired to their villages to rest and reequip.[33]

Captain Robert George, Fort Jefferson's commander, appealed to Clark then at the Falls for more men and supplies. Otherwise, he explained, "I cannot maintain my post with the handful of sick Men I have in Garrison. Besides the few inhabitants that are able to go out to hunt dare not as . . . the enemy . . . having been seen Sculking about since the attack."[34] Clark could only send his regrets as he had no troops or supplies to spare.

The next attack broke out on August 27, when a couple of hundred mostly Chickasaw warriors, along with Choctaw, Cherokee, and British advisors, opened fire on slaves working the fields and chased them back into Clarksville; four settlers died in that initial rush. The raiders then scattered through the woods to snipe at the fort and village. After dark, British lieutenant John Whitehead, who had come all the way from Mobile, shouted a demand that Captain George immediately surrender the fort or else suffer the full fury of an Indian assault. George retorted that he was determined to fight on. Gunfire broke out and continued sporadically throughout the night as each side's marksmen shot at the ignition flashes of their enemies. The next morning, James Colbert, a half-Scottish Chickasaw chief, approached with a white flag and asked to talk. Captain Leonard Helm strode out. Colbert repeated the terms and Helm rejected them. The men parted. A group of friendly Kaskaskia Indians allied with the Americans shot and severely wounded Colbert as he returned to the British and Indian lines. The siege persisted until the morning of August 30, when the war party departed after destroying the corn crop and slaughtering all the livestock grazing in the surrounding fields.

Although the soldiers and settlers had driven off two attacks on their community in as many months, Captain George was not confident that they could survive a third assault. Most settlers were unwilling to stick around and find out; a few days after the second attack they packed up their meager belongings and set off downriver to what they hoped was safety. Few would survive the gauntlet of Chickasaw villages not far down the Mississippi River. Under those dire circumstances, George asked Clark to consider "whether it will be most expedient to hold our Post or not."[35] Clark's answer was to hold.

The Chickasaws and their allies launched more raids in September 1780 and January 1781. The handful of remaining soldiers and settlers grew more desperate. Captain George wrote Clark of "the absolute necessity of your presence at this place we are Reduced to a Very small number at present occasioned by Famine, Desertion and Numbers daly Dying; we have but a Very Small Quantity of provision. . . . This Inhabitants is chiefly gone down the River and what there is . . . left is Very much distressed."[36]

On his way to New Orleans, Lieutenant Colonel John Montgomery stopped at Fort Jefferson and was alarmed by what he found. He wrote Virginia's governor of "the distressed situation of Fort Jefferson and the impossibility of mentaining said Post without some Speedy relief. First the Inhabitants in General are leaving the Settlement for want of Subsistance, and continually Harassed by a Unmerficul Enemy, the Loss of their Corn and Stock and we . . . Reduced for want of Funds. Secondly the certainty of our Soldiers deserting . . . for want of provisions. Thirdly Experience fully Shews me that if that late Attack had held a few days longer, all our Stores and Ammunition must fall into the hands of the Enemy." Montgomery added that "had it not been for the Assistance of Mr. Oliver Pollock . . . we must undoubtedly evacuate that Post."[37]

The issue of assistance would soon become controversial. Fort Jefferson did not escape the fog of financial impropriety. Phillip Barbour, a business associate of Oliver Pollock, happened to arrive with a boatload of goods at the fort when "it was in distress" from Chickasaw war parties and dwindling supplies. Barbour did not hesitate to take full advantage of such an ideal seller's market. In desperation, Captain George signed a promissory note for sky-high prices redeemable only in gold or silver. The note was forwarded to an undoubtedly shocked Governor Jefferson, who demanded an explanation from the region's commander. Clark fired back with what he argued was evidence that Pollock and Barbour had committed "premeditated Fraud" against Rogers, thus the note should be rejected and the bill settled only with depreciated paper money. It is unclear whether Jefferson or any of his successors followed Clark's advice for that specific transaction.[38]

As if all those problems assailing Fort Jefferson were not debilitating enough, a tug-of-war broke out over just who should command the post. Clark had left Captain George in charge. During his visit, Colonel Montgomery inspected the fort and spoke with many of the soldiers and settlers. He concluded that Captain George was unfit for the command. Before heading down the Mississippi, Montgomery sent orders to Captain John Williams at Cahokia to hurry down to Fort Jefferson and take over. Williams did so, but George adamantly refused to vacate his headquarters without a direct order from Clark himself.[39]

Although the persistent Chickasaw menace to Fort Jefferson was a definite drawback to being posted there, the officers found at least one redeeming feature. Being on the Mississippi, the garrison benefited from passing boats that carried goods and news. Even then, provisions could be short. Helm recalled "sitting by Capt Georges fire with a piece of Light wood and two ribs of an old bufloe which is all the meat We have seen these many days."[40]

Then, on New Year's Day of 1781, a seeming miracle visited Fort Jefferson. A boat appeared with "a Large [car]goe of Licours and Dry Goods which have been the saving of this Poast otherwise we could not have supported it for want of necessities." For a while, life was sweet and easy for Captain Helm, with only one crucial element missing: "I am in good health with a Bottle of Taffia at my Elbow, & my greatest want is a Woman to Crown my joys at night, as my Bottle does by day."[41]

Lacking that one vital release, Helm and his colleagues indulged all the more with the other. They were within their rights to do so—officers were entitled to two gallons of liquor a week! And that privilege was not confined to the officers. Each soldier was issued his own daily rum ration. The not-so-surprising result was that soldiering and bouts of inebriation were often inseparable, although the severity varied among commanders and posts.

The overindulgence at Fort Jefferson got so bad that reports of dereliction of duty reached Richmond. An investigation was opened and found substance in the charges. Lieutenant William Clark, the cousin of George Rogers Clark, was asked whether the officers drank and caroused as they pleased. "It was too much the case," was the lieutenant's scornful reply. "Did the Commandannt drink and carouse with the rest?" The lieutenant responded, "Yes he did at times." Yet when asked, Captain Robert George denied that any officer neglected his duty or "drank too hard to do their business generally."[42]

America's grip on Illinois was weakening to the vanishing point. In June 1780, county lieutenant John Todd sent a request to Governor Jefferson for permission to consolidate his forces into one garrison. Ten months later, Captain John Rogers reported to Jefferson that "The People of the Illinois & Fort Vincennes have been in an absolute State of Rebellion for these several months."[43]

What went wrong? Quite simply the Americans lost the war for hearts and minds. Life had indeed been far better before the American "liberation" on the night of July 4 (the most ironic date of any year), 1778. Clark had promised a future of peace, prosperity, and democracy. What the people of Illinois got instead were soaring prices, scarcer goods, intimidation, confiscations, insults, and violence. The reason for that unbridgeable chasm between the lofty promises and harsh reality was that Virginia was utterly incapable of adequately supplying those distant garrisons. Bereft of money and eventually even credit, the commanders took what they could not buy.

The depredations naturally enraged the population. Increasingly desperate, the leading citizens of Kaskaskia, Cahokia, and Vincennes sent petitions to Clark and Virginia's governor for relief. The petition from Vincennes did not mince words: "Since the arrival of the Virginia troops . . . and especially since Colonel Clark left . . . we have experienced most horrible treatment from a people who professed to be friends. . . . We have zealously furnished provisions and goods as far as was our power [which] were paid by drafts on the treasury of Virginia which remain unpaid." The plaintiffs then complained that the Virginians paid for goods with paper money whose printed value that they claimed was equal to the equivalent in coin. When the people refused to accept that script, the Virginians took "by force our property, our supplies, and even the little we had reserved to keep ourselves alive. . . . [They] slaughtered "cattle in the fields and our hogs in our yards, [took] . . . our flour from the mills and the corn in our granaries, with arms in their hands threatening all who should resist them."[44]

The Virginians' rapacity would have been outrageous in any event but was especially dishonorable given all the sacrifices and risks that the French had made for them. In a letter to Anne-Cesar, chevalier de Luzerne, France's minister to the United States, the petitioners explained why: The Virginians "came on behalf of the French and of Congress. From that time no one thought it best to resist; on the contrary, all joined them; we . . . enrolled under their colors; we helped capture the English; we restrained the Indians who wished to resist . . . we gave all for a people who claimed to be allied with France."[45]

Luzerne acted promptly on that request. He was well aware of the plight of the Illinois people under American rule since he had nurtured a spy network not only among former French subjects there as well as in Canada, but even in the United States. Among his latter agents was Brigadier General Augustin Mottin de la Balme. In early 1777, la Balme had arrived in the United States with a commission as a cavalry commander issued by Silas Deane in Paris. Congress appointed him inspector general of cavalry. In early 1780, Luzerne tapped la Balme for a vital double mission. After obtaining leave and journeying to the Ohio valley, he was to rally the French and Indians openly in a campaign against the British at Detroit, and covertly against the Americans.

La Balme arrived at Fort Pitt in May 1780. There, he met with American officials and friendly Indians and gathered supplies and men. In July, he journeyed to Kaskaskia and then Vincennes, rallying as many French and Indians as possible to his campaign. At Kaskaskia, he commiserated with both peoples for being caught between and exploited by the British and Americans. The inhabitants enthusiastically responded by recognizing him "as our protector and our supreme chief." They also massed war supplies and promised to follow him on campaign.[46]

The Wabash River Indians whom la Balme tried to rally were hardly as enthusiastic. They had many questions, of which la Balme found one especially hard to answer: "If our [French] father is allied to the Americans, why does he allow us to be in want of everything; must we die together with our wives and children while rejecting the offers which the English make to us; we do not like them; we are ready to strike, but our urgent needs will finally force us to lend an attentive ear to their proposition, if you remain obstinate in still refusing the help which is absolutely essential to us now." The Indians were completely disillusioned with the Americans: "Last year they made us a thousand promises . . . now these are not even thought of. On the one hand we are forgotten, abandoned; on the other hand we are solicited and at times threatened."[47]

Not all former French subjects rallied to la Balme. The most prominent French military leader was Daniel Maurice Godefroy de Linctot, whom Clark had commissioned a major and agent to the Illinois Indians. La Balme described Linctot as a French Canadian who had been "wandering for many years among the savages because he refused to serve under the English flag, accompanied by some thirty Indians devoted to him."[48]

La Balme clashed with each local American commander, Captain Richard Winston at Fort Clark in Kaskaskia and Captain Valentine Dalton at Fort Patrick Henry in Vincennes. Winston reported that la Balme pretended to be in the American service, but "I look upon him to be a Malcontent, most disgusted at the Virginians. Yet I must say he [has] done some good—he pacified the Indians. He was received by the Inhabitants Just as the Hebrews would receive the Masiah." Dalton was alarmed by la Balme's blatant anti-American message and tried to talk him out of his campaign.[49]

La Balme's campaign was initially a success. Journeying from Vincennes up the Wabash, he and his hundred French and several score Indians took Ouiatenon. But ultimately la Balme met with disaster. He and his followers made it as far as the Miami Indian villages on the Maumee River's headwaters. Chief Little Turtle led several hundred Miamis and some Shawnees to attack and wipe out la Balme and thirty-one of his men and to capture or rout the rest.[50]

As if la Balme's intrigues were not subversive enough to America's grip on Illinois, another threat appeared in 1780. Thomas Bentley had been Clark's best-placed spy in Illinois before the invasion, but his career was short-lived. In 1777, the British arrested him on espionage charges and conveyed him in chains to Montreal. Leading Kaskaskia residents, including the magistrate Rocheblave, wrote depositions that Bentley had first secretly met with Captain William Linn at the Ohio River mouth and later in Kaskaskia with the spies Benjamin Linn and Samuel Moore. That evidence was alarming, although ultimately tainted because Bentley's business rivals asserted it. Bentley claimed that those meetings were purely confined to business. Although the British officials lacked enough solid evidence to convict him of spying, they kept him in prison.[51]

There, Bentley remained until 1780, when he escaped and made his way to Virginia, "with a full intention to revenge myself on Gov. Hamilton," whose testimony had been instrumental in Bentley's imprisonment. Then a strange thing happened. Hamilton turned the coat of the man determined to avenge himself. Bentley "made him a tender of my services." Now a British agent, Bentley made his way back to Vincennes. There, in a letter to Clark, the double agent reported on the local conditions, asked for compensation for his past services, and offered to renew his activities.[52]

Odysseus-like, Bentley finally reached his home at Kaskaskia in August, only to find that his former life was in ruins. His wife was no Penelope; she had left him for another man, perhaps partly spurred to do so after learning of her husband's local mistress. Rivals had snatched his once-flourishing business and extensive property. He could only begin to rebuild his shattered life by ingratiating himself with whichever power dominated Illinois. The Americans had only a token presence there, a handful of officials and soldiers. A determined British campaign could retake the region. He advised just that to Canadian governor Frederick Haldimand: "If you wish to possess the Illinois & Post Vincennes you may easily accomplish it. The inhabitants discontented with the Americans will not resist regular troops." He assured the governor that "I am no enemy to my country" and "shall entertain a . . . sincere attachment . . . so long as God shall bless me with life." Fortunately for the Americans, the British did not make another attempt.

Bentley's espionage did not end at sending intelligence reports to and soliciting compensation from both the Americans and British. Richard

Winston, who had replaced John Todd as Illinois's county lieutenant, accused him of outright subversion: "Since the arrival of Cap Bentley there has been nothing but discord & disunion in the place. He has left no stone unturned to extinguish the Laws of the state and to revive the Heathen law being well accustomed to bribes & entertainments."[53]

Ironically, though Bentley would escape arrest for his spying and subversion, John Dodge, Virginia's Indian agent for Illinois, had Winston arrested on charges of "treasonable expressions Against the State." Winston was among Clark's spy ring in Illinois before Clark's invasion. Perhaps, like Bentley, Winston was hedging his bets, although not as subtly. He may also have provoked retaliation from all the enemies he had made through the zealous and greedy acts he had committed as county lieutenant; Bentley was among his enemies.[54]

After the war, Bentley applied to Virginia for compensation for his service and losses. Despite a testimony from Clark, who was unaware of Bentley's double game, he received not a penny. Such are the risks of pursuing the world's second oldest profession. And perhaps rightly so. Bentley appeared truly committed neither to the Americans nor the British; his highest loyalty was to himself.[55]

In contrast, George Rogers Clark still put his country first. For his dauntless patriotism, his victories, and his tireless efforts, his popularity remained at dizzying heights. However, he would soon be as reviled as he was now exalted.

CHAPTER 15

Fire in the Rear

The confidence the People here have in General Clarkes vigilance, his Enterprising Spirit, and other Military Virtues . . . have hardly been sufficient to Keep this County from being left entirely desolate.

Colonel John Floyd

My chain appears to have run out. I find myself enclosed with a few troops, in a trifling fort, and shortly expect the insults of those who have for several years been in continual dread of me.

George Rogers Clark

For the first time in three years, Clark headed east to Virginia in October 1780. Six weeks later, he strode into Richmond, Virginia's capital since April 18, 1780. There, he unleashed his formidable powers of persuasion to sway Governor Thomas Jefferson, the executive council, and the state assembly not just to approve but to fully fund his campaign plans for 1781.

Jefferson could not have given Clark a better Christmas gift. In a letter penned on December 25, 1780, he authorized Clark to mobilize and lead an expedition of two thousand men against Detroit by which ever route "you shall think best." His vision did not end there. As usual, Jefferson was thinking multiple moves ahead on the geopolitical chessboard. In that same letter, he first expressed his notion of an "empire of liberty" whereby the United States would conquer and transform "an extensive and fertile Country thereby converting dangerous Enemies into valuable friends."[1] Americans have been trying to reconcile the dilemma of imposing "liberty" on others at gunpoint ever since.

To facilitate Clark's campaign, the governor issued a flurry of orders to key officials over the next couple of months. Fort Pitt would be the campaign's launch site. The county lieutenants of Berkeley and Hampshire Counties were to muster 275 and 255 men there by March 1, and the county lieutenants of Fayette, Jefferson, and Lincoln Counties would each mass 500 men and 100,000 rations there by March 15. Clark's regular forces would include his Illinois regiment, two Virginia Continental army regiments commanded by Lieutenant Colonels Joseph Crockett and John Gibson, and Captain Isaac Craig's artillery company. Most supplies would be forwarded to Pittsburgh and eventually packed, along with the troops, aboard a hundred vessels. A commissary officer would journey to Baltimore and Philadelphia, purchase four tons of gunpowder, and have it transported to the Ohio River valley. Another officer would be in charge of gathering 20,000 rations of flour and salt beef. Other officers would somehow find and convey 400 camp kettles, 40 bell tents for muskets, 40 regular tents, 1,500 pounds of lead, 1,000 spades, 500 axes, 200 pickaxes, 300 packhorses, a traveling forge, ship's carpenter tools, and 4 tons of gunpowder. The artillery would include 4 six-pounders and 2 howitzers.[2]

The governor even provided Clark a successor if need be. He called on Gibson to "take any assignment which Gen Clark shall assign you. In the event of Gen Clark's death or captivity, your rank & our confidence in you, substitute you as his successor in the command; in which case you will prosecute the expedition under the instructions given to Gen Clark."[3]

Jefferson, typically, had thought of nearly everything as he carefully devised an intricate plan and timetable for Clark's campaign. Yet he left out at least one crucial element—politics. That incurable optimist, idealist, and theorist failed to account for the fatal mix of institutional frailties, rival interests, and overweening egos. An array of obstacles would prevent only a sliver of his astonishing wish list from reaching Clark, and that months behind schedule. The very forces that inspired the expedition would impede it. Exacerbating all that was a near-inevitable element of politics and power—money. Virginia's government had nothing to give but written promises to pay.

As 1781 unfolded, Clark's mission seemed progressively urgent. Although Virginians had been fighting desperately on their western frontier since 1774, their state faced a far more daunting threat as the new year dawned. Thirteen months earlier, in December 1779, the British launched a campaign to conquer the southern states. So far that campaign had been an enormous success. British troops had repeatedly routed any American forces in their way and had overrun most of Georgia, South Carolina, and North Carolina. Now, General Charles Cornwallis appeared to be readying his army for an invasion of Virginia itself. Jefferson hoped that Clark's campaign would deliver a knockout blow to British power in the Ohio valley so that Virginia could mass enough men, munitions, and provisions to stave off the worsening threat from the south.

The British realized Jefferson's fears of invasion, but much sooner and from a different direction than he expected. On the last day of 1780, the governor received word of a British flotilla of twenty-seven ships spotted sailing into Chesapeake Bay toward the James River. He promptly warned General Friedrich Wilhelm Augustus, von Steuben, the ranking Continental commander in the state; ordered the militia leaders of adjacent counties to muster one-half of their men and those from more distant counties to ready one-quarter of their men; and had supplies and documents evacuated from Richmond.[4]

Commanding the British invasion was none other than Benedict Arnold.[5] During the previous year, only luck had thwarted his plot to kidnap George Washington and surrender the fortress of West Point to the British. On September 23, 1780, pickets had captured a suspected spy in civilian dress trying to reach the British lines. He turned out to be Major John Andre, Arnold's liaison with General Henry Clinton, the British commander in North America. Learning of the capture and terrified that Andre would tell all, Arnold had himself rowed to safety on a British warship, appropriately named the *Vulture*, in the Hudson River. Washington offered Clinton a swap of Andre for Arnold. Clinton refused. Andre swung from a noose as a spy. Arnold was rewarded with a brigadier general's commission and £6,350.

Clinton was determined to reap his money's worth from Arnold. On December 20, Arnold sailed from New York in a flotilla packed with 1,600 troops, bound for Virginia. A storm scattered his ships so that only about 750 troops accompanied him when his vessels dropped anchor near Hood's Point on the evening of January 3. Nonetheless, those were formidable forces, the Queen's Rangers, with 250 infantry and 120 cavalry, 50 Hessian Jaeger riflemen, and the Eightieth Regiment of Foot.

The Queen's Rangers were among the most formidable troops in the British army.[6] As American-born Loyalists, they had an added incentive to fight as fiercely as possible and avoid capture at all costs. They were trained to fight as light infantry or cavalry, with an emphasis on dashes around the enemy's flank and long-range raids. Their commander was Lieutenant Colonel John Graves Simcoe, renowned for his daring and drive. A reputation for victory tends to fulfill itself. Standing up to British redcoats advancing with lowered bayonets was unnerving enough for American Continentals, let alone ragtag militiamen. But the sight of onrushing Queen's Rangers with their distinct uniforms of short forest green wool jackets and black leather helmets adorned with silver crescent moons was an extra spur to cut and run.

The only fortification covering the approach to Richmond was at Hood's Point, a redoubt protecting a battery of two iron twelve-pounders and a howitzer manned by seventy gunners and guards. That battery opened fire as Arnold's vessels approached. Arnold disembarked Simcoe, the Queen's Rangers, and the Eightieth's light infantry and grenadiers a mile below; those troops swiftly angled behind and captured that battery. The following morning, Arnold landed the rest of his troops at nearby Westover and swiftly marched them toward Richmond, thirty-three miles upriver.

Virginia's capital was virtually defenseless. No fortifications ringed the city, and Steuben could muster only a couple hundred each of Continentals and militiamen.[7] The Continentals were fresh recruits and so, like the militiamen, lacked discipline, arms, munitions, provisions, and morale. Steuben retained his recruits but had to send hundreds of militiamen home because they had no muskets and he had none to give them. The general tersely explained to the governor that Richmond's fall was not just inevitable, but a matter of hours. Jefferson ordered the capital evacuated of all officials, documents, and war supplies, along with Steuben and his Continental recruits. The officials and Continentals made it to safety; most of the documents and supplies did not.

Late that day, Arnold's troop marched wearily into Richmond, scattered the couple of hundred militiamen, and fanned out across the town. Arnold posted some troops on Richmond's periphery and had others secure the military warehouses and recover five four-pounder cannons that the Virginians had dumped into the river. The British loaded forty-two boats with supplies and destroyed what they could not carry away. Arnold dispatched Simcoe and his greencoats a farther seven miles to burn the cannon foundry and warehouses at Westham. Upon their return, Arnold split his command. Some troops packed aboard the supply boats and began rowing downriver. Arnold led the rest south across the James River and on to Chesterfield, where they burned a supply depot. Resuming their march, the British routed 140 militiamen astride their path at Charles City, where the flotilla was now anchored just beyond cannon shot.[8]

After the war, Clark learned that he had suffered a devastating personal loss in the bonfire at Richmond. Among the items believed to have been devoured by the flames were his wartime vouchers for $14,598 of requisitions. Without the records, he would be held personally liable for all those expenses. Thus did Benedict Arnold's raid help financially ruin George Rogers Clark for the rest of his days. Actually, the vouchers were not burned, merely misplaced. But they would not be discovered until long after Clark's death. The practical results of those missing records to Clark would not be evident for a couple of years. Now in January 1781, Clark would inflict a small sting against Arnold, and only later might reckon it a kind of vengeance in advance.[9]

Clark had already headed north to begin organizing his campaign when Arnold's troops landed downstream from Richmond. Hearing of the British invasion, Clark hurried back. By the morning of January 9, he was counseling a stunned Jefferson amid Richmond's ruins. The governor tapped Clark to act as field commander for Steuben's forces. Steuben sent Clark with three hundred militiamen and thirty horsemen down the north river road to shadow Arnold's force.[10]

By this time, the vessels of Arnold's flotilla that had been scattered by the storm had caught up. Aboard were the Loyal American and Royal Edinburgh Volunteers. Those reinforcements may have still been recovering from seasickness but at least were not footsore like the rest of Arnold's troops after their nearly seventy-mile marathon trek. On January 10, learning that

Jefferson and the rest of Virginia's government had returned to Richmond, Arnold landed Simcoe with a couple hundred men each of the Loyal Americans, Queen's Rangers, and Eightieth Foot, along with fifty jaegers at Hood's Point, with orders to surprise and destroy the American force that shadowed them. To his frustration, Simcoe could not advance with his usual speed; a heavy rain the night before had slickened the road.

Clark deployed his men just a few miles upriver at Cabin's Point and sent mounted scouts down the road. Those horsemen galloped up with word of Simcoe's advance. Clark swiftly conceived a plan. He concealed two hundred militiamen in the woods on both sides of the road. Several hundred yards eastward he posted a forty-man company whose mission was to fire a volley then flee from the enemy. It was a classic decoy and ambush strategy. Simcoe and his men, with the Loyal Americans in the lead, marched right into it.

Like hounds after hares, the British dashed after the decoys. When the road was packed with the enemy, Clark ordered his men to rise and fire. The volleys killed seventeen, wounded thirteen, and stunned the rest. But rather than retreat, Simcoe ordered his men to charge. The militiamen fled the lowered bayonets. Simcoe, in his words "seeing no probability of accomplishing the business he had ordered upon, halted till Gen. Arnold's arrival, who had followed with the main body. The troops returned to Hood's battery."[11] Clark rallied his militia and cautiously pursued the British to the flotilla, where they embarked. Arnold ordered the anchors lifted, and the expedition sailed down the James River to Portsmouth.

Jefferson sent the gratifying report to Virginia's delegation to Congress that Clark's men had inflicted thirty casualties on the British while suffering only four wounded.[12] More importantly, Clark had defeated Simcoe's attempt to surprise and destroy him. On January 14, the governor released Clark back to preparing for his expedition.[13]

Clark would have a devil of a time trying to drum up recruits for his latest campaign. Always a challenge, recruiting was now virtually impossible. Virginians saw no sense heading west to fight Indians in the Ohio valley for no pay when the British were invading their homes along the tidewater. The militia companies of Berkeley, Frederick, and Hampshire Counties flatly refused to join the expedition; only individual volunteers would be released from their duty to defend their communities. Other counties like

Greenbrier agreed to furnish men to Clark on condition that they be released from further requisitions.[14]

Jefferson tried to shame those reluctant counties into filling Clark's ranks. He expressed the "exceeding distress of mind" he experienced upon learning "that the service to which the Militias . . . have been called Westwardly is so disagreeable as to render it probable that . . . call will be very imperfectly obeyed." He presented a powerful argument for their compliance, and the equally damning consequences if they failed in their duty: "Should this expedition be discontinued, the Savages will . . . spread on our whole Western frontier." And that would only aid the British onslaught in eastern Virginia. Jefferson explained, "We are all embarked in one bottom, the Western end of which cannot swim while the Eastern sinks. . . . Nothing can keep us up but the keeping off the Indians from our Western quarter; that this cannot be done but by pushing the war into their Country; and that this cannot be attempted but with effectual aid from those three counties." He then offered a compromise—a quota of volunteers rather than the entire militia would be required. Finally, he expressed his expectation that they would fulfill their duties, but admonished them to "Be punctual in advising Genl. Clarke and myself of your progress."[15]

Jefferson was conciliatory with the more flexible Greenbrier County: "I am fully sensible of the pressure of the several calls which are made on your County for Militias and for regulars at the same time, and should not have been induced to urge the first of these at the time we did, but to counteract and prevent movements against you by the savage enemy in the West. I beg you to believe also that these calls are not made on your county alone. At present they are nearly general. . . . We have to oppose the Indians in the North West, Cornwallis in the South, and Arnold in the East." He then allowed them to postpone "raising your regular recruits till the expedition under Genl. Clarke may be supposed to have advanced so far as to leave no danger of molestation to your county from the Indians."[16]

Jefferson informed Clark of how he had handled the crisis. The diplomacy was delicate as "we were informed from various quarters that should we persist in the order it would produce open disobedience." To avoid an outright mutiny, Jefferson withdrew the order that Berkeley and Frederick Counties provide quotas of men, and instead simply called for volunteers. To make up any shortfall, he got General Steuben to assign Colonel John

Gibson's regiment of a couple hundred regulars to the expedition, "an addition of more wealth of itself perhaps than those militia." Jefferson also managed to get Captain Isaac Craig and his artillery company attached to Clark's expedition.[17]

Clark failed to recruit a single man until he reached Winchester on February 10, and the measly results there were nearly as heartbreaking. He wrote Jefferson, "I begin to fear the want of men but the Idea of a disappointment is so disagreeable to me that . . . I with Every Exertion that can be made will Carry my point I shall Certainly do it without your orders . . . the Enterprise is Countermand[ed] or a failour of supplies . . . which I hope will not be the case."[18]

As if Clark's trials with the counties were not exasperating enough, former governor Patrick Henry joined those who sought to halt his campaign in its tracks. He got the Virginia assembly to resolve that Governor Jefferson should "put a stop to the Expedition lately ordered against Detroit, and to take all necessary steps for disposing of, or applying to other uses, the stores and provisions laid in for that purpose."[19] Upon learning of that resolution, the Greenbrier County militia promptly broke from Clark's camp and headed for home.

Clark was aware of all the political forces undermining his recruiting. He vented most of his frustration not against the militia captains, but against those government officials who secretly pressured them to stay home. He was stunned that "those Gentlemen should undertake to dictate for Government or Remons[tr]ate against her orders. I wish we may not here[after] feel the fatal effects of such Conduct." He was convinced "that the Militia of those Counties would have marched with chearfullness had they not been incouraged to ye Contrary."[20]

Though Jefferson ignored Henry's resolution, he could do nothing to reverse the swelling opposition to Clark's campaign. The opponents were armed with a powerful logic. It made no sense to launch a campaign against faraway Detroit when a British army was camped in Virginia's tidewater. Seasoning those arguments was the political and personality animosity between Patrick Henry and Thomas Jefferson. Jefferson commiserated with Clark's efforts, and dismissed Henry as "all tongue without either head or heart."[21]

Jefferson eventually talked a majority in the assembly to appropriate

£75,000 to underwrite those militiamen who bothered to show up. Although that amount might appear considerable, hyperinflation had depleted Virginia's currency to near worthlessness. That sum was merely a down payment on the expedition's eventual cost. By the end of January 1781, the quartermaster had spent £500,000 and had requested another £300,000.[22]

Land was the only substantive resource that the government had to give away, and that too was an IOU. The promise the assembly made on January 2, 1781, however, would at once enormously gratify Clark and eventually enrich the nation. After years of lobbying for the idea, Jefferson finally got the assembly to approve Virginia's cession of its territorial claims north of the Ohio River to the United States with the stipulation that those lands would be settled and carved into states. A hundred and fifty thousand acres in that territory would be reserved for Clark and his men of the Illinois expedition, to be distributed among them in proportion to their respective ranks. There was a catch. The cession would be void unless the other states ratified the Articles of Confederation that established a formal American government. That inducement was a major reason for the ratification that year. But securing, surveying, and distributing what became known as the "Clark grant" would take decades to complete.[23]

However farsighted its intentions, Virginia's government unwittingly dealt a sharp blow to Kentucky's defense when it ceded the state's claim to land north of the Ohio River. Thereafter, most Virginia militiamen along with their officers saw little point in invading a region that was no longer part of their state. That became the excuse for halting a pursuit of enemy raiders on the Ohio River's south bank. The logic that Virginia's security would be enhanced by destroying the villages where those raids originated carried little weight in the calculations of the militia.

Jefferson had one more award to present. On January 22, he commissioned Clark a "brigadier general of the forces to be embodied on an expedition westward of the Ohio." Like other Virginia state commissions, Clark's would expire as soon as the mission was completed. Jefferson had tried to talk General George Washington into commissioning Clark a brigadier general in the Continental army. Washington replied that only Congress had that power.[24]

As if Clark's preparations were not tangled enough, a financial scandal flared. Major George Slaughter commanded Fort Nelson, which finally became the name for the fort at the Falls of the Ohio, and was among those whom Clark authorized to requisition supplies. Jefferson sent Clark copies of Slaughter's questionable accounts, and asked him "to have strict enquiry made (not by yourself for your time is otherwise better engaged), but by such persons of known integrity and character as you shall appoint. We do not know what to do with the bills of which Major Slaughter speaks."[25]

When confronted with the evidence against him, Slaughter pleaded his own innocence while insisting that if anyone should be suspected of fraud, it was Captain James Moore, the purchasing commissary. Slaughter hastened to add that although "I have not proved the charge against that Gentleman, I have nothing to say in justification of my own conduct more than I had put too much confidence in" those "whom I before thought were Men of the strictest Veracity and honour."[26] He also hinted that other officers elsewhere were guilty of improprieties and that Richmond should open investigations.

The scandal as much embarrassed as angered Clark. It was bad enough that Slaughter not only appeared to have cooked the books but had maligned his brothers-in-arms as the chefs. Clark had handpicked all those officers. Any corruption ultimately cast a shadow on Clark's honor. He lamented that "to be flung into my Situation by a Set of Men that are not Honoured with the Sentiments of a Soldier is truly disagreeable. I hope those Gentlemen alluded to will live to Repent of their Conduct." He assured Jefferson that all the accused "may Expect to undergo the strictest scrutiny." But he also wanted the governor to understand that "I have long Since determined to Conduct myself with a particular Regour towards every person under me." Clark quickly surmised that if anyone was guilty, it was Slaughter.[27]

Yet, having vented all that, Clark did admit that he himself was not beyond reproach. He offered both a confession and a rationale for some of his acts: "To Reflect on the steps I have been obliged to make . . . to prosecute a war for these several years there is an indignity in it that often hurt me, but a zeal that . . . Carry me to length[s] that I sometimes Regret."[28] Such is the inescapable moral dilemma of war; the higher one's rank, the more agonizing that dilemma.

A commission would later find that the evidence was not conclusive enough for formal charges against Slaughter or any other suspect. Regardless, Clark ultimately was responsible for his officer's conduct. Only Clark was authorized to buy goods on Virginia's credit. Since he could not be everywhere at once, he had shared that authority with a half dozen or so of his officers. Several of them appear to have betrayed his trust by succumbing to temptation. What seemed probable but ultimately improvable was "a Collusion and fraud betwixt the drawers and those they are made payable to; most of them are for specie when they well knew we had none amongst us, and from the largeness of the Sums, proves the transactions must have been in paper and the depreciation taken into account, when the bargains were made."[29]

An even worse scandal, this one fueled by the volatile mix of money and sex, embroiled Lieutenant Colonel John Montgomery. He appeared to have absconded to New Orleans after running up vast bills for questionable purchases and prices in which kickbacks may have figured. Montgomery had not only left behind enraged creditors but had provoked widespread condemnation or envy for "taking up with an infamous Girl, leaving his Wife & flying down the River" to refuge in the Spanish territory."[30] To extravagantly underwrite that fling, he took "large quantities of Provisions, Boats deeply laden besides five Black slaves for all which the Publick fund has suffered" for sale in New Orleans.[31]

Clark did what he could to bring the miscreant to justice. He reported to Jefferson, "I have dispatched . . . Letters to that post desiring him to Return to a trial for his Conduct and desiring no person to Credit him. . . . If he should Return by way of Richmond I hope . . . you will put him under arrest and order him to the Western Dept to answer for those accusations."[32]

Meanwhile, a swelling crowd of creditors presented payment bills with Montgomery's signature. In April, Clark received a packet from Jefferson that included a cover letter and documents. Jefferson explained that the government "had a great bundle of Draughts from Colo. [John] Montgomery. They were rejected and the holder informed that if . . . they were for articles or services really for the State, you would countersign and we pay them, according to their value at the time of drawing."[33] Clark dutifully if resentfully signed his wayward colonel's drafts as he had or would hundreds of others. Montgomery would eventually return to explain his accounts, and would escape any formal arrest or charges.[34]

Ultimately, Virginia's government would determine which bills it honored. Those holding rejected claims often vented their rage against Clark. A Pittsburgh trader fired off a letter to Clark "to Let you Know that your Bill that you Gave me on the Governor of Virginia was protested which has Ruined me and If you Do Not take Som Spedy methiod to make me hole I will take Every opertunitey in my power to Do my Self Justies."[35]

Such vicious circles of inflammatory accusations spotlighted an intractable problem of labyrinthine complexity. Who owed what to whom? That question loomed ever larger as the debt mountain of IOUs soared. Not just Clark and his own officers but hundreds of civilian and army officials had signed thousands of papers promising that the recipients would be compensated for the goods they had either enthusiastically or reluctantly parted with. Hyperinflation magnified that headache as the value of those pieces of paper plummeted. And then there was the problem that many of those who had signed notes lacked the authority to do so. Who then was liable for the loss, the signer or recipient of the paper? That national migraine would fester for generations, with only a sliver of the cases reaching a just if belated solution.

However rankling the scandals, Clark could spare little time agonizing over them. He had a campaign to muster and lead. Upon reaching Fort Pitt, Clark conferred with General Daniel Brodhead, the Western Department's commander. Brodhead promised to ensure that Clark's campaign was "properly supplied & supported" and even offered "my quarters as your Home except only for a bed which have not to give you."[36]

Brodhead's seemingly eager cooperation and hospitality was a charade. He actually intended to do what he could to thwart Clark's mission, even in defiance of orders.[37] He had received from General Washington a list of war materials and instructions to "deliver to him or his order at such time as he shall require them, all, or as many of the forgoing articles as you have in your power to furnish." It was Washington's "wish to give the enterprise every aid which our small force can afford," including Colonel Gibson's regiment and Captain Craig's artillery company. Knowing his orders would disappoint Brodhead, Washington tried to soften that blow by explaining the Continental Army's "inability . . . to undertake the reduction of Detroit." But Brodhead undoubtedly bristled when he read Washington's assertion: "I do not think the charge of the enterprise could have been committed to better hands than Col Clarke."[38]

Although Brodhead initially acknowledged receiving orders to release Gibson and his regiment to Clark, he soon found a loophole that let him squirm free. He could limit or outright negate that order if it weakened the region's defense. Using that as his excuse, Brodhead kept Gibson, his regiment, and nearly all his supplies in Pittsburgh, and ensured that Captain Craig would be unable to recruit his artillery company to full strength.[39]

Quite likely Brodhead's unwillingness to part with any significant number of troops or supplies had more to do with defending himself than the upper Ohio region. He was charged with corruption, of abusing his public powers for private gain, chiefly through land speculation. His heavy-handed confiscations alienated influential local people against him, and they complained to Congress. The colonel "has not only rendered himself universally obnoxious to the people but also to many of his officers, who have refused for these twelve months past to dine or associate with him on account of his conduct, and what was then deemed a suspicion is now rendered a fact."[40]

Brodhead hoped to trump those charges with a victorious campaign against the Indians or, ideally, Detroit itself. And for that goal, he needed all that he could command and much more. Instead, Washington recalled him to Philadelphia to face a board of inquiry. Upon leaving Pittsburgh on May 7, Brodhead turned temporary command of Fort Pitt to Gibson. Washington would formally relieve Brodhead of command on September 17, 1781.[41]

Not only Brodhead's machinations made recruiting hellish at Pittsburgh. The local Pennsylvanian authorities committed any act, fair or foul, to divert troops from Clark's campaign. A mob actually intimidated the officers of Monongahela County's militia company from conducting a draft of its members for Clark. A deal was eventually struck by which the rioters promised to serve ten months in the ranks if ever they again joined "a Riot in Suppressing a draught."[42] Gibson was "sorry to have to inform [Clark] . . . that a Set of Rascals have Begun to depreciate the Virg[inia] money now in Circulation. . . . I am afraid it will . . . retard your Proceedings." That indeed came to pass as Pennsylvanians refused to accept Clark's paper script for payment.[43]

William Croghan was then a Continental captain and nephew of renowned Indian agent and trader George Croghan, and the future spouse of Clark's sister Lucy. He sympathetically explained Clark's recruiting problems: "The reason so few went with him from this place, is owing to the dispute that subsists here between the Virginians & Pennsylvanians respecting the true bounds of the Latter. And the General being a Virginian was opposed by the most noted men here of the Pennsylvania Party."[44] Colonel John Neville, who commanded the Fourth Virginia Regiment at Fort Pitt, also commiserated with Clark. He expressed his regret that Clark "had to Deal with such a Set of Rascals as was in this Part of the Country. I mean the leading men of Washington a[nd] Westmoreland Counties Who I was informed did every thing in their power to prevent your campaign." Neville might not have been the most objective observer. He proudly proclaimed, "I shall Live and Die in the Interest of Virginia."[45] Such prevailing devotions to one's true "country" would render the United States an oxymoron for generations to come, culminating with a devastating civil war.

Gibson revealed the utterly depraved lengths to which some militiamen would go to avoid serving with Clark. He informed Jefferson "that three hundred men from the counties of Monongahela and & Ohio have crossed the river at Wheeling & are gone to cut off the Moravian Indian towns. . . . Indeed it appears . . . they have done this in order to evade going with Gen Clark." That was despicable enough. Worse was that the militia intended to attack Indians who were not only complete pacifists but who also were "always giving us intelligence of every party that came against the frontiers: & on the late expedition they furnished Col Brodhead & his party with a large quantity of provisions when they were starving."[46] The militia would miss its mark this year; the hostile Indians had forced the Moravians to abandon their three villages for the cluster of Shawnee, Delaware, and Wyandot villages in the Sandusky valley. But next year the Moravians would experience "frontier justice" when a group of them returned to their homes.

Clark reckoned that only one man could free him from that web of deceit and obstruction. On May 20, 1781, he fired off a letter to General Washington, explaining his mission and all that held him back from realizing it. First, the British invasion of Virginia forced Governor Jefferson to divert vital troops and supplies earmarked for Clark's campaign. Then Clark hurried to Pittsburgh with the understanding that General Brodhead and local authorities would furnish him troops, supplies, and transport. Instead, they did what they could to abort his campaign. He asked Washington to break the impasse and pointed out the potentially dire results if he could or would not: "If we fall through in our present plans and no expedition should take place, it is to be feared that the consequences will be fatal to the whole frontier."[47]

Washington certainly sympathized with Clark's plight. He daily experienced the same infuriating machinations from greedy merchants and politicians that literally and figuratively starved his army. Yet at his headquarters at Newburgh on the Hudson River, he found himself peering anxiously southward beyond the British army entrenched in New York City to his distant native state. First came Arnold's invasion in January, reinforced by General William Phillips's in March, and finally General George Cornwallis's in May. More than eight thousand British, German, and Loyalist troops had overrun a swath of Virginia from Portsmouth to Richmond, and seemed poised to conquer the rest of the tidewater region. America's war for independence and revolution would be won or lost on the Eastern Seaboard. Detroit was merely part of the western frontier sideshow.

The commander in chief obliquely implied as much in a letter to Congress's Board of War. Given the dire circumstances, he had done all he could for Clark: "I gave orders to Col Brodhead to deliver him a certain quantity of Artillery and Stores and to detach Captain Craig with his company of Artillery. . . . I recommended also a small detachment of Continental Troops from the 8th Pennsylvania and 9th Virginia Regiments but it was at the discretion of the Commandant and in case they could be safely spared. . . . If therefore Col Brodhead saw that the post could not be adequately defended if such a detachment of Infantry was made, he was justifiable by the spirit of my order in not sending it. . . . It is out of my power to send any reinforcement to the Westward."[48] Washington also authorized Captain Isaac Craig to recruit his artillery company to full strength.[49]

All along, Clark hung on with his usual bulldog tenacity, doing whatever he could to drum up scraps of men, munitions, and provisions in the upper Ohio region. He could have spared himself a load of frustration had he skipped the pantomime, but it was his duty to try. On June 12, he reckoned he could still bring "the Pennsylvania Gentlemen in this Quarter to tolerable terms" despite the conundrum that "the Inhabitants cry out for an expedition, but too few I doubt will turn out, afraid, I believe that they will be led on to something too desperate for their Delicate Stomachs."[50]

To force the militia to fulfill its duty, Clark had a powerful option, but one that might explode in his face. He wrote Colonel David Shepherd, whose militia refused to muster, that "I hope those that you allude to will see their folly and Honour your orders without any forcible Measures being taken—I would send you an armed force Immediately but wait a few days in hopes that your business will go on more smooth. If not it shall be done."[51] But Shepherd could not fill his quota, and Clark did not try to force the issue.

Clark did get a gratifying message from Colonel John Floyd, who commanded Jefferson County's militia. Kentucky's draft was completed: Jefferson County would supply 354 men; Lincoln County, 732 men; and Fayette County, 160 men.[52] Those 1,246 troops combined with the several hundred he brought downriver would overwhelm Detroit's defenses, if enough provisions could be massed and transported to sustain that army on its long march to the target. That, of course, was the perennial "if." Clark got word that incompetence had led to 100,000 pounds of spoiled beef in Kentucky. That was a disaster of vast proportions given the colossal loss of time and money to gather and slaughter the cattle, and then salt and barrel the beef.[53]

In the end, Pennsylvania provided just enough troops to let Clark launch his campaign. The savior was its president, Joseph Reed, who appreciated the campaign's "importance to this State, as well as Virginia." He went on to laud Clark "[in] whose abilities and good conduct we have . . . Confidence." Having said that, Reed admitted that he could not, however, "answer any demands of a pecuniary kind," given "the exhausted state of our Treasury from the great demands made upon it by the Congress, and General Washington, and other Contingencies." He assigned Colonel Archibald Lochry, who commanded the militia of Westmoreland County, Pennsylvania, which encompassed the Pittsburgh region, to Clark's expedition. He then pressured his political allies in that county to do what they could to aid Clark. On June 18, the local Committee of Safety resolved to supply Clark's campaign with three hundred men, each to be paid six pounds sterling for their service.[54]

Lochry was an enthusiastic, if ultimately inept, officer. Upon receiving his orders, he wrote Clark, "Nothing Could Give Me Greater Pleasure than assisting you in the Intended Expedition."[55] However, he faced the same obstacles to finding volunteers. His command would be undermanned and short-lived and would end tragically.

Clark thanked Reed for his efforts, then revealed some of the blatant machinations that prevented more from being done. He condemned those who "have taken Every step in their power to frustrate the design . . . at a time when their neighbors were daily massacred." He recognized that his trials were those "Every Commanding officers has Experienced." He advised Reed that those malicious acts would lessen if those who committed them "are Removed from their Respective offices."[56]

For nearly half a year, Clark endured a grueling labor to ready his campaign. During that time, he did enjoy a few fleeting moments of pleasure. In late June, Colonel Gibson invited him to a party involving "a grand Bower . . . erected in the Orchard, a Barbeque . . . and a Ball in the Evening." The occasion was to celebrate the visit of the "Gentlemen and Ladies of Stewart's Crossing." All the officers and their wives would join in the festivities. The fond memories were still warm when Gibson invited Clark to "the Celebration of the Anniversary of our Glorious Independence."[57]

Among all his regrets, one haunted Clark above all. He admitted to Jefferson that he condemned himself "for [not] undertaking the expedition against Detroit" after capturing Hamilton and Vincennes two and a half years earlier. He recalled, "I yet think had I near the number of men first proposed, should have carried it." Looking ahead, he was anything but optimistic: "I may yet make some stroke among the Indians before the close of the campaign—but at present really to be doubted. I have been at so much pains to Enable us to prosecute the first plan, that the Disappointment is doubly mortifying to me, and I feel for the dreadful consequences that will Ensue throughout the frontier if nothing is done."[58]

Clark had hoped to launch his campaign with a thousand men on June 15. By late July, he had no more than four hundred men on his rolls. He had reached a point where his men were deserting faster than he could sign up new recruits. At Carnahan's Blockhouse, eleven miles below Hannastown, Colonel Lochry had drummed up 107 volunteers. Clark sent word that he was going to embark downstream and that Lochry should finish his preparations and hurry after him. They would rendezvous at Fort Henry at Wheeling.[59]

For Kentuckians, Clark's expedition could not arrive too soon. That year they suffered a series of devastating raids. The fate of Jefferson County was typical. Colonel Floyd reported that the inhabitants were "greatly dispersed & cooped up in small Forts without any Ammunition." As of October 1781, "eighty four of the Inhabitants . . . have been killed & Captured since . . . spring & many more wounded. We are now so weakened . . . by having so many Men killed & others removing to safety . . . that when any murder is done we can not pursue the Enemy without leaving the little Garrisons quite helpless. The most distressed Widows & Orphans . . . make up a great deal of our Inhabitants." Floyd could not give an exact account of how many men were on his muster roll. He reckoned there were roughly three hundred armed men left, but "one third of these are preparing to go into the Interior parts of the State and many other would follow . . . but are unable to remove by Land having lost most of their Horses already by the Savages and the Ohio runs the wrong way." He vividly explained the nature of the enemy: "Whole families are destroyed without regard to Age or Sex. . . . Infants are torn from their Mothers Arms and their Brains dashed out against Trees. . . . Not a week Passes scarcely a day without some of our distressed inhabitants feeling the fatal effects of the infernal rage and fury those Excreable Hellhounds."[60]

Clark's campaign, or at least a portion of it, would experience similar horrors. Captain Croghan, who would have eagerly joined Clark had he not been a paroled prisoner, predicted as much. He observed Clark's preparations and departure with mounting trepidation: "From every account we have, the Indians are preparing to receive him and if they should attack him in his present situation, either by land or water, I dread the circumstances."[61]

That intelligence was spot on, lacking only the time, place, and numbers of the enemy attack. An enemy force lay in wait because some mix of loose talk and spies had carried word of Clark's campaign plan to General Henry Clinton at his New York City headquarters. Clinton relayed that intelligence to Canadian governor Frederick Haldimand, who, in turn, asked Joseph Brant to gather a war party, hurry to the Ohio valley, and destroy Clark once and for all. By mid-August, Brant, along with Alexander McKee, George Girty, and several hundred warriors, were hidden at the Miami River mouth on the Ohio River.[62]

No frontier commander during the war, including Clark, was more successful than Brant.[63] His Indian name was Thayendanegea, and he was the son of a Mohawk woman and a white trader. As the easternmost tribe of the Iroquois Confederacy, the Mohawks suffered constant pressure by the Americans for their lands. Shortly after the war erupted, Brant joined the British. In 1777, he received a captain's commission and formed a company known as "Brant's Volunteers," mostly composed of loyalists and some

Mohawks and other Iroquois. He and his men soon acquired a notorious reputation for their destructive raids that terrorized the New York frontier.

The departure of Clark's expedition from Fort Pitt hardly ended desertions; it only made slipping away more challenging. Nearly every night one or more men would disappear into the forest. That was not the only weakness. Inexplicably, the general continued on campaign a practice that should have been confined to an established fort. Each dawn the men were awakened by the roar of one of the field pieces. While that martial reveille may have roused the men's spirits, it also alerted anyone within a half dozen or so miles that a military force with artillery was in the area.

Meanwhile, Lochry and his men had set off overland from Carnahan's Blockhouse to Fort Henry, where Clark promised to await him.[64] Instead, Lochry found only a note from the impatient general urging them on. Ironically, after waiting for five days, Clark had embarked his men the day before Lochry and his men arrived. Had he waited just another twenty-four hours, the subsequent massacre would have never taken place.

Lochry scribbled a note and dispatched it with two men in a dugout canoe. He explained to Clark, "I arrived at this Post this moment. I find that there is neither Boats, provisions, or ammunition left. . . . If you send these articles mentioned and with directions where I will overtake you, I will follow. We are upwards of one hundred strong and Light Horse."[65]

Clark replied from Middle Island on August 9, "I am heartily sorry that after awaiting so long set out but a day before your arrival. . . . I am exceeding unhappy at our not joining at Wheeling, but I don't know that either of us are to blame, the militia with us continue to desert, and consequently I cannot remain long in one place otherways should be happy in forming a junction here. . . . I shall move on slowly for the reasons before recited and you use the greatest industry as you cannot possibly pass us without our knowledge. I have suffered much lately but you again encourage me."[66]

Though Lochry was able to rustle up some boats and supplies, try as he and his men might, they could not catch up to Clark. However, along the way they did pick up a number of Clark's deserters, who gave up after having depleted what was left of their provisions and courage. That extra manpower meant extra mouths to feed. Lochry's men had devoured what few supplies they had brought along.

At Camp Three Island, Clark left Major Charles Cracraft with six men and provisions to await Lochry. After conferring with Lochry, Cracraft and his men set off to catch up with Clark. Lochry rested his men for the rest of that day then early the next morning resumed their marathon downstream. Within days, they had consumed the provisions left by Cracraft. On August 16, Lochry ordered Captain William Shannon and several men to bend their backs to the oars and catch up to Clark with yet another urgent request for more supplies.[67] Adequate provisions lay far ahead if only Lochry and his men could get there before they starved. Thanks to Clark's commissary general, Joseph Lindsay, preparations for the campaign had actually unfolded more smoothly in Kentucky. Barrels of dried buffalo meat and cornmeal steadily piled up in Fort Nelson's warehouses.

Four days later, Lochry caught up with Shannon's detachment, or at least what was left of it, at the Scioto River mouth. Shannon could not have picked a more suicidal place to hunt astride the war trail leading from the cluster of villages up the Scioto River south to the Ohio River and over it to the Kentucky settlements. A war party had slaughtered most of Shannon's men and had prodded the captain himself into captivity; two men out hunting escaped the ambush.[68] A prudent commander would have already maintained the strictest vigilance, a vigilance only bolstered by the sight of the butchered bodies of Shannon's party. But Lochry was unfazed by the brutal lesson in frontier warfare he had witnessed. At odds with the most rudimentary security measures, he continued to land on the north shore to hunt, rest, and even camp.

A hundred miles downriver near the Miami River mouth, Joseph Brant and his men lay in wait for just such a reckless act. Without firing a shot, they had watched Clark's expedition row past on the night of August 18. Brant had scouts embark in a dugout and shadow that Long Knife force. Then, on August 21, Brant's men captured Cracraft and his men, who were forced to reveal that Lochry and his expedition would soon appear.

On the morning of August 24, Brant had the word spread to hold fire as Lochry and his men rowed past in midstream well beyond accurate musket fire. He dispatched scouts after Lochry. A couple of hours later, they returned with exciting news. Lochry had ordered his flotilla to disembark at a meadow eleven miles below the Miami River mouth. He did so despite the protests of Captain Thomas Stokely of the Eighth Pennsylvania Line that tarrying there would court disaster. Lochry explained that the meadow was an ideal place to graze their horses and dispatch hunters.

Brant roused his men and led them to Lochry's camp. They spread out and crept close. Suddenly, they rose, screamed war cries, opened fire, and charged, swinging musket butts, war clubs, and hatchets. They caught Lochry and his men completely by a panicked surprise. Apparently, no one resisted but either tried to surrender or flee. None escaped. The warriors killed thirty-seven soldiers and captured sixty-four. Not one of Brant's men suffered a wound or death. Lochry himself was among the dead. As he sat on a log passively awaiting his fate, a warrior strode over and bashed in his skull with a tomahawk.[69]

Satiated with their victory, Brant and his men started back with their captives on the trail up the Miami River valley. On August 27, they met Captain McKee leading three hundred Indians and Captain Andrew Thompson with a hundred Butler's Rangers. Brant split his men, with some prodding the captives to Detroit, and he and the others joined the force heading south. Together, they were strong enough to possibly destroy Clark's entire force. Upon reaching the shore opposite the Kentucky River mouth on September 5, Brant sent a war party toward the Falls of the Ohio. On September 9, Brant's men returned with two prisoners who confessed that Clark had abandoned his campaign plan for that year. The leaders held a council but could not forge a consensus. Most reasoned that with dwindling supplies and Clark no longer posing a threat, they should call off their own campaign. Lochry's defeat left Brant and his men eager for more. As a result, most Indians dispersed to their homes while Brant led his war party into Kentucky, where they reaped a bloody toll in scalps, plunder, and captives.[70]

The word that Clark had given up any notion of attacking north of the Ohio River that year was true. Lochry's defeat had wiped out a fifth of Clarks' command. That loss fired Clark with a fierce desire to reap vengeance. Yet he could only set forth if the militia companies joined him. But the captains, led by Benjamin Logan of Lincoln County and John Todd of Fayette County, flatly refused to leave the settlements unprotected for a campaign north of the Ohio River that year. They instead insisted that forts be erected at the Kentucky River mouth and across from the Miami River mouth to seal off those war paths leading to Kentucky's heartland. They did, however, call for a campaign up the Miami River next year.[71] The refusal of the militia captains to join him deeply disheartened Clark. All that he had worked for was unraveling. He might even have to abandon Vincennes because of a lack of men to adequately defend it. His dream of one day capturing Detroit seemed nothing but a chimera.

Clark had failed to realize another of his ambitions earlier that summer. After a couple months of hard labor rowing up the Mississippi River from New Orleans, Lieutenant Colonel John Montgomery and his escort stepped ashore at Fort Jefferson on May 1, 1781. He "found the Troops in a very low and Starving Condition." It took more than a month to fulfill his order to evacuate Fort Jefferson, a duty completed on June 8, 1781. By early August, the colonel and his command disembarked from their flotilla at the Falls of the Ohio. Montgomery found the conditions at Fort Nelson to be just as wretched, with "not a Mouthfull for the Troops to eat nor money to purchase it with, & . . . the Credit of Government is wore thread bare."[72]

With each new enemy raid, Clark and his fellow Kentuckians were harshly reminded of their failure to destroy that distant nest of exhortations and rewards at Detroit for war parties stalking the Kentucky frontier. The latest came in mid-September. Clark and Captain Floyd learned that Indians were harassing Squire Boone's settlement at Clear Creek. To the rescue, Clark hastened twenty-four horsemen under Lieutenant Thomas Ravenscroft, while Floyd sent eight men under Lieutenant James Welsh. Those relief parties reached the settlement, but the lieutenant found it so exposed to attack that they talked the inhabitants into abandoning it. Three people stayed behind, Boone who was injured, one of his sons, and a widow who refused to leave. The militia escorted the settlers along the trail toward Linn Station. Along the way, Indians butchered a dozen stragglers. Learning of those killings, Floyd galloped back with twenty-seven horsemen. Near Long Run, they spotted several Indians rooting through belongings abandoned by the settlers. Spotting the horsemen, the Indians fired and ran. Although some of the men warned Floyd not to pursue them, he ordered a charge. Scores of other warriors scattered in the woods, converged on the road, and opened fire. The Indians picked off eighteen Kentuckians. A bullet clipped Floyd's foot, but he and nine other men broke loose and fled. Upon learning of the defeat, Clark mobilized and dispatched over three hundred men to clear that trail, bury the dead, and rescue any survivors all the way to Squire Boone's Station. Astonishingly, Boone, his son, and the widow were still alive. The Indians burned his station shortly after they left with the rescue party.[73]

The year's brutal succession of political and military defeats rendered Clark darkly pessimistic about the future. He wrote Governor Thomas Nelson, who had taken over from Jefferson in June 1781, "Our possession in . . . Illinois and Kentucky have been the salvation of the interior frontiers since the commencement of the war." But, Clark observed, now Virginia's security was threatened by "the evacuation of Fort Jefferson for the want of supplies, and our few troops drawn from the Illinois, except St. Vincennes. . . . Two thirds of those formerly in our interest have already taken the hatchet this fall." Clark feared that next year an overwhelming horde of Indians and British would descend on Kentucky "if no army moves early in the spring from [Fort Nelson] . . . or Pittsburg." Clark concluded, "My chain appears to have run out. I find myself enclosed with a few troops, in a trifling fort, and shortly expect the insults of those who have for several years been in continual dread of me."[74]

Then the latest bookkeeping scandal erupted again. Word arrived that Virginia's assembly had condemned the "waste and misapplication of public property" by "certain officers and others in the western country." Clark took the criticism personally. He fired off a letter to Virginia's latest governor, Benjamin Harrison, who took over from Nelson in October, arguing that only by resigning could he keep his character "unimpeached."[75]

With words carefully calibrated at once to soothe and shame, Harrison refused that and a second resignation letter from Clark. "It is a matter of great Surprise to us," the governor wrote, "that we could not conceive how General Clarke could take that resolution as aimed at him whose Character has ever stood unimpeached. You must be sensible that great Abuses have been committed and that it was necessary for the Assembly to correct them and to bring the Offenders to Justice. . . . A resignation at this time would be extremely injurious to the State in as much as it would throw the whole back Country into Confusion and perhaps occasion its Loss the thought of which I am confident induce you if you have not done it to lay aside your Resentment."[76]

Some of Clark's gloom was dispelled by electrifying news that reached the Kentucky settlements late that year. On October 19, 1781, General

George Cornwallis surrendered his army of 7,500 men at Yorktown, Virginia, to a combined American and French army of 20,000 troops commanded by General George Washington and seconded by General Jean Baptiste Rochambeau. General Henry Clinton, the commander in chief of His Majesty's forces in North America, promptly declared a cease-fire. A peace treaty ending the war and acknowledging American independence was just a matter of time. But would even that bring peace to Kentucky?

CHAPTER 16

The Bloodiest Year

A report much to his prejudice prevails here of his being addicted to liquor as to be incapable of Attending to his Duty.

Benjamin Harrison

I am greatly embarrassed & grieved for the loss of our Friends & so many brave Men. . . . Dear Genl when shall we have it in our power to retaliate? Shall we ever?

John Floyd

I am (unsolicited) Raised by my Cuntry to an Exalated Station with all the powers necessary to Support me in the Rank I now bear but how long I shall be able to Claim a Continuation of the Lawrels I have already won is quite uncertain. One unlucky stroke may Reduce me in the Eyes of the world. Virtue is lost.

George Rogers Clark

For Virginia's governor and most assemblymen, after Cornwallis's surrender at Yorktown on October 17, 1781, independence and peace were only a matter of time. They swiftly acted on that belief.[1] The assembly hammered the last nail in the coffin of Clark's dream of attacking Detroit when, on December 11, it passed a "Plan for Kentucky Defense" resolving that "the proposed expedition against Detroit ought not for the present to be attempted." Governor Benjamin Harrison followed that up on December 20, by ordering Clark and all forces in Kentucky to stand down: "An offensive war cannot at this Time be carried on. We must therefore turn our Attention to defensive measures and make use of every means in our power that this be done in the most effectual manner." Clark was immediately to notify all militia officers of the policy. Of Clark's 304 regular troops, 100 would be deployed at Fort Nelson, and 68 each at forts to be built at the mouths of the Kentucky and Licking Rivers and at Limestone Creek.

Related strategic and financial imperatives justified that policy of bolstering Kentucky's defenses and hunkering down within them. Richmond could not have afforded a Detroit expedition even if the war on the Eastern Seaboard persisted. Virginia's government, like those of the other dozen states and Congress, was bankrupt. To Clark, Harrison explained that overwhelming reality: "The deranged Situation of the Finances of the State, and the reduced values of the paper Currency made this Step necessary. . . . You will very probably ask how the Business required to be done can be carried on without Money. The answer is indeed difficult. We have nothing to depend on for the present but the virtue of the people."[2]

The campaign's cancellation did not leave only Clark feeling bitter and betrayed. Harrison mulled a barrage of protests from frontiersmen who demanded a knockout blow against the enemy who for a half dozen years had devastated their lives. In February 1782, the governor replied by explaining that reconciliation with the Indians strengthened and vengeance weakened frontier security. He urged "the citizens on our frontier to use every means in their power for preserving a good understanding with the savage tribes, and to strike no blow until compelled by necessity."[3]

Clark scoffed at the notion. He explained to Harrison that the British and Indians did not suffer the constraints of bankruptcy, morality, or even Cornwallis's surrender. Spies had revealed to Clark that Detroit governor Arent de Peyster had "collected Chiefs of the different hostile Tribes of Indians and instructed them not to disturb the Frontiers, and particularly Kentucky until towards Spring . . . by which Conduct the Country wou'd be off their Guard, that the whole would . . . lay the whole Country waste."[4]

And that slaughter indeed nearly happened. As the year unfolded, the

234 GEORGE ROGERS CLARK

governor's message must have dumbfounded and enraged any Ohio valley pioneers familiar with it. Death and destruction plagued the region from spring as de Peyster exhorted, equipped, and dispatched one war party after another against the Kentucky and Pennsylvania frontiers. From January through March, forty-seven Kentucky settlers were killed or captured. That was just the prelude. War parties attacked Stroud's Station and Estill's Station in April, and McAfee's Station in May. At Estill's Station, the Indians tried to provoke the defenders to come out and fight by scalping alive a captive girl. That worked. A dozen enraged frontiersmen charged from the fort and were wiped out.

The Indians and British had an edge beyond simply His Majesty's implacable will and generosity. Colonel John Floyd explained, "[The] Enemy have all the advantages of a heavy Current from high up the Miamis to the very place of their destination. They can float from the Mouth of that River to the Falls in less than thirty hours."[5] They could then load their plunder on captured horses and carry it back to their towns.

At first, most Kentuckians vented their blame and rage for the atrocities on Richmond's cancellation of Clark's expedition. Many people expressed apocalypse fears and secession fantasies. Floyd warned that with "the immediate danger in which every one conceives his own Family, the Authority of Militia Officers at such a distance from Government growing every day weaker & weaker, and the new invented idea of a Separate State, calculated on purpose for disaffection & an Evasion of duty . . . seems to threaten us on all sides with Anarchy, Confusion, & I may add Destruction."[6]

To his credit, Harrison did what he could to bolster Kentucky's defenses, mostly by expediting the transfer of cannons at Fort Pitt downriver to Kentucky. But the assembly had tied his hands "on the subject of offensive operations in your quarter," at least for the time being. As for the future, who knew? Although "the Assembly have interdicted . . . [an] Injunction of silence to me . . . they meet early in May, when it is probable they will again take up the subject."[7]

Until November 1782, Clark was a bystander in that year's fighting. At first, few people criticized him for heading east to Richmond or holing up at Fort Nelson rather than fighting Indians. The image of Clark as Kentucky's heroic leader persisted. Floyd informed Jefferson that only two forces kept the Kentucky settlements alive. One was the faith most settlers had in

Clark, and the other was their inability to flee to safety east of the Appalachian mountains: "The confidence the People here have in General Clarkes
vigilance, his Enterprising Spirit, and other Military Virtues together with
their inability to remove, have hardly been sufficient to Keep this County
from being left entirely desolate."[8] That was a wonderful tribute. But that
exultant view would soon change radically.

A policy of Virginia's governor and assembly played a powerful role in
transforming Clark from a hero into a villain in the eyes of most folks. They
heaped yet more burdens upon his already-crushing labors by ordering him
to build forts at the mouths of the Kentucky and Licking Rivers and Limestone Creek. Each fort was to be garrisoned with sixty-eight men and have
two row galleys to patrol that stretch of the Ohio River. Just where could he
get the money, men, and material to do all that? Clark reckoned the only
sensible thing to do was to lock eyes and minds with the politicians, explain
the frontier realities, and plead for more resources.

Clark's latest journey to the east occurred in May. He arrived at Richmond in rags, making him appear more a poverty-stricken beggar than
a victorious general, although he was certainly more than a bit of both. He
appealed to Governor Harrison "to grant me a small sum of money on Acc.
I can assure you Sr that I am exceedingly destresse'd for the want of necessary cloathing &c and don't know of any channel thro which I could procure any—Except that of the Executive. The State I believe will fall consid-
erably in my debt, any supplies that your Excellency favour me with might
be deducted out of my Accounts."[9] It is unknown whether the governor
helped clothe the general, but it would have been astonishing from both an
official and personal level had he not.

What the governor and assembly did not do was grant him enough
money to fulfill the mission they assigned him. Clark would be widely and
unfairly condemned for their failure. Without money, he could only build
those forts and galleys with supposedly free militia labor. But the militia
refused Clark's summons. Colonels John Todd and Benjamin Logan, the
respective commanders for Fayette and Lincoln Counties, complained that
Clark's demand for labor was "oppressive upon the Militia," that lacked the
proper tools and anyway was busy with the harvest.[10]

Yet, starting the previous year, Clark's growing chorus of critics had
claimed that his lack of will rather than money was the decisive reason. To

Governor Nelson, Colonel Todd had complained that Clark had no desire to build any of those forts because his beloved Fort Nelson and the surrounding region was, "as he always expressed it, the Key of the Country." Clark and the militia colonels heatedly exchanged their views during a meeting at Louisville in early September 1781. The result was a deadlock. No important projects were agreed upon let alone implemented. Clearly, the militia was hurting for armed men. All three Kentucky counties had only 760 militiamen on their muster rolls.[11]

Clark did assign men to construct a row galley, christened the *Miami*, at Louisville. When the *Miami* was launched in the spring of 1782, the vessel was seventy-three feet long and twenty feet wide, sat a half dozen feet deep in water, and had forty-six oars each drawn by two men. Each member of the 102-man crew was armed. There were four cannons—a 6-pounder, a 4-pounder, and two 2-pounders.[12]

Clark assigned Captain Robert George to command the *Miami*. George was a fine leader, but nothing he did could overcome the *Miami*'s deficiencies—the craft was awkward to maneuver, its crew was unreliable, and it failed to intercept any war parties. The crew's morale was dismal. George reported, "There has been nothing but murmouring and grumbling on their part; first they insisted on being allowed double Rations of Flour—this was granted them—then they must be allowed to march on the shore and not work on the boat—that was granted them. . . . At last this morning they have determined to go off at all Events, altho their Tour is no out this seven days."[13] In all, the galley was a waste of scarce resources that would have been much better invested elsewhere along the frontier. Recognizing that the *Miami* was an extravagant folly, Kentuckians tended to blame Clark rather than Virginia's assembly.

Meanwhile, aside from his two-month lobbying trip to Richmond, Clark spent most of that year at Fort Nelson struggling to keep his men from deserting and to scrape up enough provisions and pay for them. The conditions were abysmal, occasionally lightened by rays of very bleak humor. One day Clark sent a courier, a man named Burk, with dispatches to Vincennes. As he saw him off, Clark cautioned Burk to avoid prairies, where Indians could spot and kill him. The courier reached Vincennes without incident and then hurried back. Overconfident, he rode through rather than skirted a prairie. Three lurking Indians opened fire but missed. Rather than flee, Burk charged and shot, killed, and scalped all three. Upon returning to Fort Nelson, he immediately reported to Colonel Clark and handed over the letters.

As Clark poured rum for the courier and himself, he asked, "Well Burk, did you see any Indians?"

"Yes, three."

"Well, what did you do with them?"

"Well, by J-a-s, I surrounded them, and killed all three."

"Oh no, Burk, you could not have done that."

"Well, your honor, count these," Burk replied as he proudly displayed his grisly trophies.[14]

The year 1782 would exceed all others in bloodshed and sheer viciousness in the Ohio valley. In March, Colonel David Williamson led three hundred Pennsylvania militiamen from Fort Pitt to the Moravian Indian village of Gnadenhutten midway up the Muskingum River valley. Although the mostly Delaware converts were pacifists and kept a strict neutrality, their ministers John Heckewelder and John Zeisberger actually spied for the Americans and sent back numerous warnings of war parties striding toward the upper Ohio valley frontier. When Williamson and his men failed to find any hostile Indians in the area, nearly all of them vented years of pent-up rage against Indians on the pacifists. Major William Croghan was among the few disgusted by the subsequent massacre: "The Pennsylvania militia formed an expedition against the Indians . . . but instead of going against the enemies of the country, they turned their thoughts on robbing, plundering, murdering . . . our well known friends, the Moravian Indians, all of whom . . . after living with them apparently in a friendly manner for three days . . . men, women & children, in all ninety-three, tomahawked, scalped, & burned, except one boy, who after being scalped made his escape to the Delaware Indians (relations of the Moravians) who have ever since been exceeding cruel to all prisoners they have taken."[15]

The Indians would soon avenge the Gnadenhutten massacre. In late May, Colonel William Crawford and Colonel Williamson led 480 militiamen from Fort Pitt across 150 miles of wilderness to the Sandusky River valley with its cluster of hostile Wyandot, Shawnee, Mingo, and Delaware villages. On June 4, an overwhelming number of warriors from those tribes attacked the invaders as they neared the valley. The fighting lasted two days before the Americans broke and fled, leaving a couple score dead and captured behind. As irony would have it, Williamson, who had gleefully ordered the Gnadenhutten massacre, reached safety. Nearly all those who surrendered were fiendishly tortured to death, including Crawford. One survivor recalled how Crawford begged British Indian agent Simon Girty to put him out of his misery: "The traitor, Simon Girty, was standing by; the Colonel cried out to him, 'No mercy—only shoot me,' to which his reply was, 'Crawford I have no gun,' with a laugh, 'how can you expect any other [treatment] . . . in retaliation for the Moravians that were murdered last spring?"[16]

The Indians followed up that victory with the latest series of raids against the upper Ohio and Kentucky settlements. The largest and most destructive war party numbered over three hundred Indians, mostly Shawnees with a handful of Wyandots, led by Alexander McKee, William Caldwell, and the Girty brothers, Simon, George, and James. Just before dawn on August 16, 1782, they crept up to Bryan's Station.[17] Alert sentinels spotted the enemy lurking in the woods and quietly passed the word. The defenders faced a quandary. The fort's well was dry. Without water, they would soon have to give up. But the Indians would surely attack any armed party that ventured out to the nearby creek. So the women agreed to pretend that they were unaware of the danger and to go out with their buckets to draw water. The Americans gambled that the British and Indians would remain hidden in hope that the community's men would soon amble out to their crops and pastures.

The gamble worked. In twos and threes, the women strolled out to the spring, filled their buckets, then returned to the fort, all the while trying to act as nonchalant as possible. The British and Indians realized that they had been fooled only when the fort's men did not head out to the fields after breakfast. They opened fire on the defenders and demanded surrender. The siege continued through that day, night, and early the next morning.

Upon learning of Bryan's Station's plight, Colonels John Todd and Benjamin Logan gathered four hundred men from the other settlements and hurried to the rescue. After scouts brought word of that large approaching force, the British and Indian leaders deemed it prudent to break off the siege and withdraw to safety across the Ohio River. Logan and his men trailed the raiders north and, on August 19, caught up at the Blue Licks crossing of the Licking River. Through the woods and meadows beyond the river, Logan's party spotted the enemy column disappearing over a large hill. The militia leaders debated what to do. Most, including Daniel Boone, urged caution. But pride, the false version, led to a disaster.[18]

Captain Hugh McGary, as hotheaded as he was dim-witted, shouted words designed to goad the proud frontiersmen to throw caution to the wind: "Delay is dartardly! Let all who are not cowards follow me, and I will show them the Indians."[19] That outburst left "the principal officers . . . confused . . . each afraid to speak Candidly for fear of being Suspected of Timidity." Spurred by that challenge to their manhood, "the whole Moved forward apparently without order."[20] The Kentuckians surged into an ambush. The Indians killed seventy-seven of them and routed the rest; John Todd and Daniel Boone's son Israel were among the dead. The bodies strewn around Blue Licks had no sooner begun to swell and stink in the torrid summer heat when the finger pointing began. Ironically, the worst villain targeted for the Blue Licks debacle was nowhere near the battle. And that was the point.

Criticism of George Rogers Clark soared with the Blue Licks debacle and that year's other devastating attacks. For years, settlers had complained that Fort Nelson was situated on a secondary war path that had been effectively blocked when Vincennes was captured. The worst threat of attack came down the Miami, Little Miami, and Scioto River valleys to the Kentucky settlements. The confluence of the Licking River and Limestone Creek with the Ohio River were clearly the logical sites for forts. But Clark was attached to Fort Nelson and angrily dismissed any suggestions that he abandon that site and relocate where his men might actually intercept war parties.

As a result, Kentucky's defense was grossly and tragically skewed. Daniel Boone never forgave Clark for his strategic priorities and especially for being at Fort Nelson during the battles of Bryan's Station and Blue Licks. That was bad enough, but, Boone claimed, "our Men are often call'd to the falls to Guard them."[21] Benjamin Logan protested Clark's orders "to send the men to the falls of the Ohio in order to build a strong Garrison and a new Galley thus by weakening One end to strengthen another the upper part of the country was left entirely exposed & the enemy intercepting our designs brought the intended expedition against the Frontiers of Fayette. . . . The immense expences incurred by the State in the western country . . . is enough to prevent the Government from giving us any farther aid." Nine surviving Fayette County militia officers protested to Harrison that "Our Militia are called on to do Duty in a manner that has a tendency to protect Jefferson County, or Rather Louisville, a Town without Inhabitants [and] a fort situated in such a Manner that the Enemy coming with a design to Lay waste our Country would scarcely come within one Hundreds miles of it, [leaving] our own Frontiers, open & unguarded. . . . we beg the plan of building Garrison at the Mouth of Lime stone & another at the mouth of Licking . . . exactly in the Enemys principal crossing places."[22] At least one critic attacked Clark for more than misplaced strategic priorities. Arthur Campbell whispered that Clark "has lost the confidence of the people, and it is said become a sot; perhaps something worse."[23] What that "something worse" was can only be vividly imagined, and that surely was Campbell's intent.

Governor Benjamin Harrison could not help but concur with the barrage of criticisms. He offered a similar reply to each protest letter that he received. The Blue Licks tragedy most likely would have been averted but for "Clark's conduct in not erecting strong forts at the mouth of the Kentucky river and at the mouth of Licking and Limestone creeks and garrisoning them with sixty eight men each as he was order'd to do in December. . . . The Executive saw the importance of these posts for the protection of the Country and gave Orders accordingly, and I had not the least suspicion that they were not obey'd till the receipt of your letter." The reports of Clark's alcoholism and hints of even grosser offenses deeply disturbed Harrison. Yet only the British and Indians would benefit should a scandal erupt over the character of one of America's most valiant and victorious war leaders. To those Kentucky leaders who the governor asked to investigate the allegations, he advised discretion: "A report much to his prejudice prevail here of his being so addicted to liquor as to be incapable of Attending to his Duty, by which the public Interest suffers much. I must beg the favor of you Gentlemen to inquire into this in a private Way and let me know your sentiments, his being a Military Man makes it improper to have a public inquiry by those who are not so." Harrison explained his distaste at the whole business and having to use intermediaries to investigate. "The great distance," however, "leaves me no other Way of coming at a knowledge of his Conduct."[24]

Not everyone joined the mob scapegoating Clark. Captain Joseph Crockett, who commanded the regular company at Fort Nelson, wrote Harrison, "I cannot think he is deserving censure." Indeed, Clark "strain'd every nerve in his power to raise a sufficient number to penetrate into the heart of the Enemy's Country, and was assisted by a small number of good men to complete his Laudable design." But Crockett did pointedly insist that he would only address Clark's "military character," leaving unsaid and thus darkly veiled any discussion of Clark's private behavior.[25]

No one typically defended Clark more eloquently and profoundly than Thomas Jefferson, Virginia's former governor, who had endured charges of cowardice and ineptness for his handling of the British invasion of Virginia. Jefferson reassured Clark that "Your services to your country have . . . made due impression on every mind." He then pointed out that all eminent men attract enemies consumed with jealousy. Had Clark "meant to escape malice you should have confined yourself within the sleepy line of regular duty. When you transgressed this and enterprized deeds which will hand down your name with honour to future times, you made yourself a mark for malice & envy to shoot at." He dismissed Clark's critics as mostly "being all tongue without either head or heart."[26]

Clark found the barrage of attacks on his honor as painful as they were predictable. He had prophesized the chance of just such an onslaught a year earlier in a letter to his brother Jonathan, who had been paroled after being captured at Charleston. After congratulating Jonathan for his release, he waxed philosophic about the fleeting and related natures of pleasure, happiness, virtue, and esteem. His own fate might model his thoughts: "I am (unsolicited) Raised by my Cuntry to an Exalated Station with all the powers necessary to Support me in the Rank I now bear but how long I shall be able to Claim a Continuation of the Lawrels I have already won is quite uncertain. One unlucky stroke may Reduce me in the Eyes of the world. Virtue is lost."[27]

The criticism of Clark's performance as the commander of Kentucky's defense was new. Those charges were painful enough but burned all the more coming atop chronic money problems and the opening of his account books to investigators. So far no one had directly tarred him with accusations of financial chicanery. Yet the finger pointing at some of his hand-picked officers inevitably reflected badly on Clark himself.

The troubling financial questions could not escape the reality that the war somehow had to be paid for even if the fighting was drawing to a close, at least on the Atlantic Seaboard. Claims for payment, at times seemingly padded, continued to pile up at the state governments and Congress. In April 1782, Congress's War Office condemned the "exorbitant expenditures in the western country," which had "arisen from the licentious practices and abuse of power exercised by the commanding officers of separate posts, under the mistaken idea that their quality of commandant entitled them to order and dispose of the stores at their posts as they should think best." As the lower Ohio valley's ranking officer, Clark was instructed to "issue the most pointed instruction to restrain any such unwarrantable claims, and to put it out of the power of the commanding officer to draw a single article, but what by a previous estimate of your own, you may think necessary for the maintenance of the post."[28] That order would have angered any field commander, especially one as quick-tempered as Clark. Congress had trapped him in a classic Catch-22. To fulfill that order would gridlock all operations. He would have to scrutinize and either approve or reject every decision, however minute, at every post over a vast region. But if he failed to do so, he would be liable for the malfeasance of any of his commanders.

Clark was well aware of the mounting criticism, and it sharply stung his pride. But perhaps nothing affected him more than a haunting appeal from Colonel John Floyd: "I am greatly embarrassed & grieved for the loss of our Friends & so many brave Men. . . . Dear Genl when shall we have it in our power to retaliate? Shall we ever?"[29] Clark could only redeem his reputation and self-esteem with a crushing campaign against the Indians. He hoped to coordinate his campaign with one that General William Irvine at Fort Pitt was rumored to be organizing. He wrote Irvine to learn "the time you march and what is your object: If you will be so good as to favour me with such intelligence it may be much to the publick interest; as it will be in our power to make a diversion much in favour of yours."[30]

Clark's message boosted Irvine's rock-bottom spirits. The Indians were not just devastating the Kentucky frontier. After defeating Crawford's expedition, war parties had trod southeastward to raid settlements in the upper Ohio region. Like Clark, Irvine lacked the resources vital to repel let alone crush that assault. Now, he had the hope that if they "could concert measures . . . to strike different towns at the same time, the probability of success will be greater." Among all the obstacles to realizing that plan or any other during that era, one was especially daunting. To Governor Harrison, Irvine confessed, "I am not without my fears. You know that the militia are as brave as regulars, yet it is impossible to bring them to act with necessary promptitude or exactness indispensable in war."[31]

To be a frontier commander was to mire in near constant futility, exacerbated by gut-wrenching report after report of Indian atrocities with fleeting and usually illusory opportunities to retaliate. How many times had hopes soared on the wings of an ambitious campaign plan, only to plummet when it proved impossible to enact? Thus was restraint rather than enthusiasm the only sensible reaction to any ambitious military proposal. So Irvine did not share with Clark the enthusiasm he expressed to Governor Harrison. Instead, his initial response to Clark's message was brief and vague. Everything depended on Richmond. Irvine would embrace the plan only if the governor and assembly supported it with the resources vital to realizing it. Harrison agreed to do so and sent word to Kentucky's militia leaders that he had authorized Clark to muster them.[32]

Clark smoldered with rage at being scapegoated for the Blue Licks debacle. Like a threatened turtle, he had reacted by withdrawing into his shell. Tightlipped and scowling, he threw himself into organizing his campaign. He had no choice but to correspond with and eventually command many of his leading accusers. But he drew the line with Governor Harrison of all people. Rather than defend him, the governor had joined his chorus of critics. Among all his critics' lashes, the governor's betrayal appears to have inflicted the deepest and most festering wound. Clark's only way to retaliate against Harrison was simply to ignore him, at least for a while.

That silence provoked a scolding by the governor: "No official account from you of the situation of the part of the Country committed to your care has reached me for several months for which I am at a loss to assign a reason. Government can never be administer'd properly unless the Officers of it are regular in their correspondence, punctual in their execution of orders, and particular in their descriptions of the Wants and distresses of their departments." He then went on to blast Clark for not obeying his December 1781 orders to build those three forts on the Ohio River. Had Clark done so, that "would have been a great curb on the Indians, the country might from these posts have been alarm'd at the approach of an Enemy, and with the assistance of the garrisons better enabled to repel their attacks." He ended his letter by announcing his dispatch of commissioners into the region to investigate "all the Accounts of your military expenditure . . . and when this is done I shall expect your attendance here for a final settlement of them."[33]

As irony would have it, a day after Harrison fired off that blistering letter, Clark lifted pen and wrote the governor. Why then? Perhaps Clark's passions had cooled to the point where he felt he could defend himself rationally. He grounded his case on the argument that he was allocated barely enough men and material to strengthen Fort Nelson and had nothing to spare for any other tasks. However, that bolstering of Fort Nelson's defenses had "sav'd the western country" by forcing the Indians to lose hope of taking it and dividing their forces between raids on Kentucky and Wheeling. Without the "Extreamly Reprihensible" conduct of the officers at Blue Licks, "the country would have sustained little damage."[34]

Clark would be even more explicit in defending himself and blaming others in a letter penned after his triumphant return from that year's Indian campaign. First, he explained that he had "always made a point to inform the Government of every Circumstance I thought necessary for them to know except the importance of it was too trifling a consequence to be at the expense of any express." He then again blamed his inability to build the three forts on the government's failure to send him enough men and material to do so. The failure of the militia to fulfill its duty vigorously to patrol permitted Captain Bird's expedition to appear before Martin's Station without being spotted. The militia leaders' "Mad pursuit" and "Shamefull neglect" to attack without proper reconnaissance led to the Blue Licks catastrophe. He then castigated his critics' "true character" and power to warp the governor's mind against him. He warned the governor that "as long as you Conutenace those . . . kind of people you encourage Enimies to the state and keep part of your government in Confution." Finally, he assured Harrison that he remained steadfast in the "Zeal I have for the publick interest."[35]

Clark meanwhile mobilized 1,106 men at the Licking River mouth by November 2. He was forced to underwrite his campaign by selling 3,500 acres for 70,000 pounds of flour. Among the commanders were Daniel Boone, Benjamin Logan, and John Floyd, while Simon Kenton was the chief scout.

Over the next two days, Clark ferried his men and supplies across the Ohio River, and then led his army up the Little Miami River valley.[36]

Clark organized an order of march designed to spring any ambushes before them.[37] Four parallel parties of twenty-five men each spearheaded the expedition, with two on either side of the trail. Should any of those patrols encounter a small group of Indians, they should pin them down with rifle fire while the others raced to cut off and destroy them. Following two hundred yards behind those four advanced patrols on the trail itself would be a fifty-man company, and then a hundred yards behind them would be the main column, paralleled a hundred yards by fifty-man companies. The packhorses and cannons would be protected in the middle of the main column. Finally, a fifty-man company would serve as a rear guard.

Clark issued equally strict orders about the fate of prisoners and plunder.[38] As for prisoners, none were to be executed without authorization. Three powerful reasons lay behind that policy. First, if the Indians learned of the executions, they would retaliate by killing their own prisoners. Second, any prisoners could be valuable sources of intelligence. Finally, they could be exchanged for captive Americans. Then there was the question of plunder. Clark warned his soldiers that unauthorized looting would be severely punished. Any potential loot should be delivered to the quartermaster, who would divide it proportionally among all according to rank.

Chillicothe was still an abandoned charred ruin from Clark's campaign two years earlier. As the men neared the site, Clark issued strict orders for "no firing on any Account Except on an Enimy" and that they should spare any captured Indians to prevent "the immediate Masseerce of all our Citizens that are in the hands of the Enimy and Also deprive us of the advantage of Exchanging for our own people."[39] They encountered no enemy there.

Clark deployed his men in the same formation as they approached Willstown, named after Shawnee chief Captain Will, on a side trail to Piqua. Among Clark's guides was John Sovereigns, who had been a captive there for four years. He led them to the ford beside the village. Only a score or so Indians lived at Willstown, and they fled at the approach of the Long Knives. Although the warriors escaped, Clark's men ran down and rounded up several women and children. Within hours "their Towns was laid in ashes and everything . . . destroy'd except such articles most usefull to the Troop."[40]

Those who fled apparently hid in the woods near their homes and did not hurry to Piqua with word of Clark's expedition. Astonishingly, Piqua's people were unaware of the enemy's approach until the Long Knives appeared at the town's edge. But once the alarm was shouted, nearly everyone fled, and once again Clark and his men captured only a few stragglers and occupied a deserted town. Clark dispatched Benjamin Logan and his men to the Frenchman Louis Lorimier's trading post a few miles up the trail. After looting the store, the men burned the cabin to the ground.

Clark and his army camped for four days at Piqua, hoping to draw the Shawnees into a decisive battle. But the Shawnees were too few and poorly armed for that. All they could do was slip close and snipe at sentinels or hurl insults in broken English in hopes of provoking a sortie into an ambush. The ruse nearly worked. About a hundred mounted Kentuckians chased a group of thirty warriors and scattered them but then beat a hasty retreat from a barrage of musket balls and arrows fired from cover.

The men undoubtedly cheered Clark's order on November 15 that the time had come to head home. The campaign had been a success. Although the Kentuckians killed just ten Indians, they did destroy the towns and food supplies that would sustain those Indians for the winter. Hundreds of refugees would shelter in other villages or Detroit, thus spreading the burden. The Kentuckians had suffered only three dead and several wounded. Among the plunder from Willstown, Piqua, and Lorimier's post were goods that had previously been looted from the Kentucky settlements. Upon returning to the settlements, the companies auctioned off some of the excess goods to underwrite part of the campaign's costs.

Clark reckoned that the tribes might be ready for peace. He assigned James McCulloch the mission of escorting back to the Shawnee villages a dozen or so Indian prisoners in exchange for white captives. While he was there, McCulloch was to council with the chiefs and determine whether they were interested in peace and, if so, on what terms. The chiefs rejected Clark's initiative.

Clark and his men hoped that Irvine's campaign had inflicted just as much devastation along its path. They would be disappointed to learn that Irvine had led his men no farther than Fort McIntosh, west of Fort Pitt, when he received orders from Congress to withdraw. The reason behind that order was electrifying. Irvine wrote Clark that "General Washington had been assured by the British . . . that all the Savages were called in from the frontiers, and were not to commit any farther depredations upon the inhabitants."[41]

Clark must have returned from campaign bone weary but satisfied that he had redeemed a measure of his reputation. He soon opened a letter from Virginia's governor that upset any peace of mind. Harrison attacked Clark "for undertaking an expedition . . . without consulting me. I have reason to apprehend it will rather prolong than soften the Indian war, and my advice from the Northward tell me that the English have called in all their parties, and mean no more to act on the offensive."[42]

A month later, the general received a stunningly contradictory message from the governor. Harrison had received highly favorable accounts of the campaign not just from Clark but, more importantly, from many of the same influential frontier leaders who had earlier blistered him behind his back. Without explaining or apologizing for his earlier condemnation, Harrison now congratulated Clark "on the Success of your expedition against the Indians, the officers and men under your command deserve the highest praise from their Country. . . . The blow was well timed, and if it had been seconded by Gen. Irvine would perhaps have quieted the Indians for some Time. . . . your Expedition will be attended with good Consequences: it will teach the Indians to dread us, and convince them that we will not tamely submit to their depredations. It has ever been in my Opinion the attacking them in their own Country was the only way to keep them quiet, and save expense."[43]

Was Harrison completely oblivious to what he had written Clark just a month earlier? Did he believe Clark had not received that letter or had forgotten its damning content? Certainly, the governor's ability to harshly condemn Clark in one letter and warmly praise him in the next for the same acts raises troubling questions about Harrison's own character. Regardless, Clark could take some solace that the barrage of criticism appeared to have peaked and subsided. Yet he could not help but wonder what would spark the next round.

CHAPTER 17

Peace

I feel myself called in the most forcible Manner to return you my Thanks and those of my council for the very great and singular services you have rendered your Country, in wrestling so great and valuable a Territory out of the hands of the British Enemy, repelling the attacks of their Savage Allies, and carrying on a successful war in the Heart of their Country.

Governor Benjamin Harrison

No reward for past services could be as satisfactory to me as that of the gratitude of my country.

George Rogers Clark

Except what the state owes me I am not worth a Spanish dollar.

George Rogers Clark

Thirteen months after Yorktown, a dream team of American diplomats—Benjamin Franklin, John Jay, and John Adams—negotiated a peace treaty with their British counterparts. Under the preliminary articles of peace of the Treaty of Paris, signed on November 30, 1782, Britain recognized an independent United States bound by East Florida; West Florida at the 31st parallel; the center of the Mississippi River to its source; a line through the center of Lakes Superior, Huron, Erie, and Ontario; the 45th parallel to the watershed of the Saint Croix River; and down the center of that river to the Atlantic Ocean. In addition, the Americans could continue to fish in the Newfoundland Banks; creditors on both sides would be free to pursue their debtors; Congress would encourage the states to compensate Loyalists for their losses; and the Mississippi River would be forever free for the navigation of Americans and Britons alike. Finally, a "perpetual peace" would reign between the United States and Britain, and, to that end, hostilities would cease, all prisoners would be released, and all British forces would be withdrawn from American territory "with all convenient speed" without taking or destroying property and with the return of all documents and other property previously confiscated.

It took another ten months before the envoys signed the definitive Treaty of Paris on September 3, 1783. The terms were the same with only the wording slightly altered. The delay was largely due to the "no separate peace" clause of America's alliance with France. That was overcome only when Britain signed preliminary articles of peace with France and Spain on January 20, 1783, bringing a formal cease-fire on all fronts on what had become a global war. The ratified copies of the Treaty of Paris between the United States and Britain were not formally exchanged until January 14, 1784.

Like all patriotic Americans, Clark celebrated the peace and independence granted by the Treaty of Paris. But he would soon discover that the treaty harbored ambiguous and outright contradictory tenets that would complicate his own life and that of American diplomacy for decades to come.

Peace came last to the Kentucky frontier and proved to be fleeting. Ingrained hatreds and habits died hard. The butchering persisted long after the guns had fallen silent along the Eastern Seaboard. The bloody struggle for the Ohio valley did not end with news of the Treaty of Paris, but merely recessed for a few years before flaring up anew. A series of wars and tense truces would sputter on for generations, ending only after the Black Hawk War and the expulsion of the last defiant Indian bands east of the Mississippi far west of that river in the 1830s. And all those tragedies were largely

provoked by American land hunger, racism, and the refusal to honor treaties signed with the Indians. Yet there were other causes as well.

Through 1815, British imperialism played a vital role in the Indian wars
by seeking to uphold Britain's domination of the region's fur trade, protect
their Indian customers against American rivals for markets and lands, and
create an Indian buffer state in the Northwest Territory. To those ends, the
British held their forts on American territory until 1796, and the allegiance
of most Indians until 1815. Trade stayed with the flag. British merchants
enjoyed a decisive advantage over their American rivals. George Washington vividly explained how the "Bribery and every address which British art
could dictate have been practiced to soothe [the Indians], to estrange them
and to secure their trade."[1]

At the Sandusky River villages, Indian superintendent Guy Johnson
declared victory along with the war's end. He reassured the crowd, "The
King still considers you his faithful allies as his children and will continue to
promote your happiness by his protection." That promising message was
belied when he explained a key element of the peace treaty. "The Great
Father" across the sea had conceded to the United States all lands west to
the Mississippi, north to the Great Lakes, and south to the Spanish territory. That meant the British would have to withdraw from all their forts
south of the Great Lakes.[2] That announcement enraged the chiefs. Clearly,
the Long Knives rather than the redcoats had won the war. And now the
"Great Father" was abandoning his children. How could the Indian peoples
defend their lands without British arms, munitions, and troops?

The collective rage among the tribes was so intense that Canadian
governor Frederick Haldimand feared an Indian revolt similar to what had
erupted in 1763. To forestall that, he had word spread among the tribes
that he would delay the withdrawal from the forts for as long as possible.
That expedient designed to appease enflamed Indian passions would persist
for another thirteen years. Whitehall soon embraced Haldimand's policy by
falsely claiming that the Americans had not fulfilled their treaty duties on
debts and compensation.

It did not take long for the Americans to comprehend just how determined the British were to hang on to their forts and thus their influence and
trade with the northwest tribes. Shortly after receiving word of the Treaty
of Paris, General George Washington dispatched Major General Friedrich

von Steuben to Quebec to arrange the transfer of the forts to the United States. Haldimand curtly rejected any notion of letting American officials inspect let alone possess the forts. Steuben vainly protested that the Treaty of Paris required the complete British evacuation of those posts. And that was the end of the matter for the time being. For Congress, the states, and the American people, peace was too precious and those forts too trivial to fight over.[3]

Like most frontiersmen, Clark was at first skeptical that a treaty signed by diplomats on the Atlantic's far side would end the bloodshed west of the Allegheny Mountains. But when no Indian war parties appeared south of the Ohio in the spring of 1783, he cautiously hoped that "the agreeable news with Britain" would "greatly alter the face of affairs in the back country."[4] While the American frontier's relentless advance was the underlying cause of every Indian war, the capacity of tribes to fight back depended on their ability to secure enough arms and munitions from foreign powers. Peace might well prevail if the British henceforth restrained rather than encouraged the Indians to war against the Americans. If true, that posed a vital question for Clark. He was now thirty years old. He had spent a decade fighting on the frontier. What was he going to do with the rest of his life? How could any path other than war satisfy Clark who naturally craved adventure, command, and power?

Clark was then saddled with the command of Fort Nelson, where he presided over an ever-dwindling body of men who either deserted or disappeared as soon as their enlistments were up. Few could blame them. The garrison was malnourished, sickly, and demoralized. The script they received was all but worthless while the prices of goods soared. As for provisions, there was no salt meat let alone fresh meat, and the flour was disappearing fast. During dry spells, the fort's well was little more than a mud seep fouled with the runoff of excrement and offal from the parade ground. North of the river, Indians often lurked in the woods and preyed on soldiers who ventured there to supplement their meager diets through hunting or fishing. But the Grim Reaper at Fort Nelson mostly swung the scythe of diseases like dysentery and typhoid.[5]

Impotent to alleviate such wretched conditions, many a man in charge might find fleeting escape by tipping a jug. Even under the best circumstances, Clark needed no urging. The sordid spectacle of their commander in his cups worsened the misery of the soldiers, especially the officers who worked alongside him.[6] In February 1783, the officers indirectly staged what is now known as an intervention. But the dismal conditions they vented their desperation and rage against were not those of Clark but of the fort he commanded.

Major George Walls presented to Clark a report written and signed by the subordinate officers. Clark agreed to forward the report to Governor Harrison along with his own brief cover letter. They hoped that the report would shock the government into providing some relief. The report vividly described a garrison on the verge of collapse:

> There is not above one third of the men necessary for its defense, and in a short time the unavoidable casualties will reduce the number to not more than twenty or thirty men. That there is not more than three months Flower [sic] in store, not one pound of meat, and no possibility of procuring a sufficiency by the usual methods of hunting. That there is not a sufficiency of lead to defend the Garrison twenty hours in case of an assault. Some parts of the Fortifications going to wreck, and not men to make necessary repairs. also that the men appear to be on the Verge of Mutiny in consequence of having served so long without receiving pay & other necessaries, and no prospect of an alteration for the better.[7]

Clark shrugged off his officers' hopes that their report would jolt Richmond into action. For a half dozen years, he had pleaded for aid from well-meaning but bankrupt, overwhelmed, and distant authorities back east, and got but a sliver of what he had needed. Yet, if the governor, council, and assembly were far away and distracted by an array of pressing issues, an arm of Virginia's government was close at hand.

No postwar question was more pressing for Congress and every one of the states than who owed what to whom. To help answer that question for Virginia, Governor Benjamin Harrison dispatched to Kentucky a four-man commission made up of William Fleming, Caleb Wallace, Thomas Marshall, and Samuel McDowell. The men arrived in Kentucky in November 1782, when Clark was on his latest campaign north of the Ohio River.

News of the commission's arrival sparked a flood of petition claims for compensation. It also provoked fear in many a military or civilian official. Sorting out the financial mess would likely expose corruption among some of those who had been appointed or elected to positions of public trust. As the commissioners methodically amassed evidence and pointed fingers, Clark read pressing letters from his officers like Richard Winston, John Dodge, and others who had been accused of pocketing public funds and other abuses of power. They asked him to intercede on their behalf with the commissioners. There was little that Clark could do. He too was under investigation.[8]

As the region's commander, Clark was the commissioners' number one suspect. James Monroe, then a Virginia official, informed Clark of just what lay ahead. The "little appearance of order or economy" in Clark's records raised suspicions of corruption and fraud. They would look into whether Clark had "engag'd in private speculations" and "further that you drink to excess."[9]

Clark reckoned he could divert their aim to what he believed was the worst problem. He fired off a letter in which he identified "the want of Aids from Government, hath in great measure, been the occasion of reducing this Department to a defenseless state . . . this Country . . . surrounded by numerous Savage Tribes, inflamed from . . . the prospect of British reward. The Credit of our State sunk, not a Shilling of money, not a ration to be procured any other way than by voluntary advances from a few individuals. The Illinois Settlements like to be lost to the State through inattention that will nearly double the Enemy."[10] He then ticked off a list of the men, material, and money needed to arrest and ideally reverse Kentucky's descent into anarchy, violence, and ultimate extinction.

The commissioners did act on Clark's plea. They wrote Harrison, warning him that Kentucky "will be entirely lost to this State without some speedy coercive steps are taken."[11] But while the commissioners could explain such harsh realities, they were powerless to act against them. Their mandate was to root out and persecute corruption, and that itself was proving to be an impossible mission. Those accused of corruption denied all wrongdoing while indignantly pointing to others. The paper trail was loaded with false leads and dead ends. Many documents had disappeared through neglect, disaster, or design if they ever existed. The exact meaning of many existing documents was ambiguous or outright unintelligible.

Eventually, the commissioners summoned Clark to explain his wartime expenses. Clark had a lot of explaining to do. He was directly or indirectly responsible for the lion's share of what may have appeared to be deliberate frauds but were actually honest mistakes. He was a warrior, not a bookkeeper, and his accounts were a mess. His records were sketchy at best, and many had been captured, soaked, or misplaced. Few account books survived, and many of the numerous scraps of paper were little more than the scribblings of illegible dates, requisitions, and expenses. Like most theater commanders, he had signed his share of promissory notes and handed out bundles of Virginia and Continental currencies with plummeting values. By one estimate, inflation skyrocketed 4,000 percent in a mere two and a half years from September 1, 1777, to March 18, 1780![12] The biggest expense was the Illinois campaign. When all the claims and receipts were calculated, they amounted to Clark's direct credit of $146,000 from Virginia, along with the signature of him and his officers for additional costs of $533,939 and £583,036. But that figure is but a shadow of the final tally for all the expenditures he authorized, a mind-boggling $2,201,392. The actual value of that amount is impossible to determine since nearly all of it was issued in Virginia's steadily depreciating credit and currency.[13]

Although Clark directly accounted for the bulk of the debts piled up on the Kentucky frontier, he had authorized officers with autonomous commands like Colonel John Montgomery and Captain Robert George to run up their own expenses. Captains Joseph Lindsay and William Shannon had served as commissaries and had signed many a voucher in Clark's name. Lindsay would have borne the brunt of the investigation had he not been killed at the battle of Blue Licks.

Whatever other feelings that investigation provoked in Clark, he only publicly expressed his enthusiasm for the chance to clear his name. He wrote the commissioners, "I have long most ardently wished for" their investigation and promised "nothing in my power shall be wanting to facilitate the business."[14] His worries were confined to the behavior of his subordinates. To the relief of all who had made requisitions, the commissioners found no evidence of malfeasance for Clark or his subordinates that was compelling enough for indictments.[15] Yet that finding did not deter the creditors.

Clark had his own grievances. Virginia owed him four years of back pay, and he had often paid for the demands of war out of his own pocket. To his relief, the commissioners did grant him that, certifying that he had received no pay since January 2, 1778. Virginia owed him a grand total £3,397/16s/5 ½d, including £1,092/10s for back wages, and £2,305/6s/5 ½d for flour and wages he had underwritten at Fort Nelson.[16] Eventually, the state would reimburse a portion of that debt.

Clark suffered the loss of not only his money but—far more troubling to such a proud man—his reputation. In a letter to his brother Jonathan, he revealed how "painful" such accusation of malfeasance was considering all the "Exertions I have us'd to save the public monies."[17] He could not always stifle his rage against those whose accusations sullied his character. When Angus Cameron, a merchant, questioned some of his dealings, Clark "put his hand on his sword and observed his reputation was sacred & he would put any man to Death who would attempt to injure him in that way."[18]

The last thing Clark wanted was to spend much of his life's remainder battling creditors. But that was his fate. In 1782, he got a harbinger of what lay ahead when Eli Cleveland filed suit against him for failing to pay for the whiskey he requisitioned for his 1780 expedition against Chillicothe and Piqua. When presented with the suit, Clark explained that he had given Cleveland a state voucher for the requisition, and thus Virginia was liable. He bluntly refused to "give security for my appearance in court and you can put me in jail if you want to and feel able."[19] Although that suit would be dismissed, a flood of others would follow, many with more traction.

The largest claim came from Oliver Pollock, the American agent in New Orleans, who had sent convoys of boats crammed with vital supplies up the Mississippi River to Clark and other frontier commanders. With the war all but over, Pollock returned to the United States in 1782. For months, he lingered in Richmond, seeking payments for fistfuls of vouchers that tallied $139,739. Clark was among Pollock's worst debtors. On July 24, 1782, Pollock wrote Clark, "My fortune which was respective when you Sir by your address found the way to draw it from me is now exhausted & annihilated and I would be content were it not worse. . . . I have Extended my Credit for the Service of Virginia and borrowed for the same purpose 100,000 Dollars from different people at New Orleans and now Sir when I appeared here with my accounts in hopes of finding Government disposed to pay, and to pay me with gratitude assurances of which I have had from you, I find they are as destitute of instruction as of the means of paying me."[20]

That letter eventually caught up to Clark. He replied that he greatly appreciated all that Pollock had accomplished and sympathized with his plight. Yet Clark himself was broke and could do nothing to alleviate Pollock's debts: "Except what the state owes me I am not worth a Spanish dollar." Thus, Pollock would have to join all those "Many whom I know have advanced all they had on the faith of government." Those claims were the source of "all the uneasiness I have suffer'd."[21]

The revolutionaries who had signed the Declaration of Independence did so on behalf of all American patriots. With time, many of those who either fought, bought, or negotiated for American independence would ruefully recall the Declaration's last line by which "we mutually pledge to each other our lives, our fortunes, and our sacred honor." George Rogers Clark and Oliver Pollock were among those whose fortunes were lost and honor was questioned in that great cause.

Faced with intractable problems with his debts, duties, and psyche, Clark did not simply drown his sorrows in alcohol. Drunk or sober, Clark's family was dear to him and often in his thoughts. For a dozen years, the Clark brothers had scattered, first with the frontier's opportunities and then with the war's demands. Throughout that time, Clark dreamed of the day when they would be reunited, ideally to clear virgin land in the Ohio valley. He had fallen in love with the region at first sight and ever since had evaluated the lands he traversed for the richness of the soil, the purity of the water, and the access to current or future markets.

Enormous opportunities to get land and make money beckoned in postwar Kentucky. But those opportunities would dwindle fast as more people crowded into the territory. The key was to get to Kentucky and stake a claim as the Indian danger diminished but the terror they provoked lingered. Hoping to hurry along his family, Clark pointedly explained, "All persons that incline to Come to the Cuntrey my [may] Move amediately as it will then be out of the power of the Enemy to distress us much." He then announced that he had bought some land for their father "in Case he moved ameadiately as it was in the Hart of the Settlement knowing that it would Continue to Raise in value I have some prospect of future happiness in living near Each other. I can supply you with Lands if you Settle on the

Ohio as fortune seems to determine that I posses an unprecedented Quantity of the finest Lands in the Western World."[22]

Clark hoped they would enjoy that bounty together. But he scribbled that letter on the eve of his November 1782 campaign. He had an uneasy feeling about this one: "I can prejudge that I have this Campaign to Incounter greater dangers than I have heretofore there is no knowledge the fate of war if I Fall I hope you will not suffer any part of my property to fall into the Hands of those that have no right to it you will find it very Considerable give half to my father and keep the other yourself."[23] He survived that military campaign as he had and would all others without a scratch. But ahead lay fierce battles over land that would be fought with all means fair and foul just shy of brutal violence.

Official acknowledgement of the debt Virginia owed Clark was only half the struggle. Somehow, he had to collect what he was owed from a bankrupt state treasury. For the time, what Clark received, like everyone else with claims against Virginia, was a promise. Clark and veterans of his Illinois legion could split among them 150,000 acres north of the Falls of the Ohio, with the shares determined by rank.

Not all land was created equal. Clark was determined that any grant he received would be rich in soil, water, timber, and game. To that end, he organized with his officers a company in February 1783 that would stake out and secure title to the richest lands available. Clark and four of his officers would act as the company's board of directors while Walker Daniel would serve as their land agent. Their survey of their 150,000 allocated acres revealed many "mountains Knobs or Hills, which shall be unfit for cultivation." In their petition to Richmond in May 1783, they asked that those lands be excluded from the grant and that they only receive "valuable lands."[24]

That claim joined a mounting pile with hundreds of others and would take years to process. Meanwhile, Governor Harrison sought to alleviate one festering problem. He tried to sooth Clark's feelings battered by Virginia's inability to supply his needs and recent tendency to scapegoat him for its own shortcomings. On April 9, 1783, he wrote that he was "fully impress'd with the Services you have render'd your Country on many Ocassions, and have often lamented that the Situation of the State should be such as to put it out of my Power to enable you to gain fresh Laurels; that you have some enemies is certain, and that they have misrepresented you is as certain, but their representations have never had sufficient weight to injure you materially with the Executive. . . . I shall be glad to see you as soon as your Affairs will permit you to come to Richmond."[25]

Clark eagerly took him up on the invitation. In the early summer of 1783, he was in Virginia's capital lobbying the government for the relief of his forces and sharing his thoughts on how to prevent another round of war with the Indians. He got more than he bargained for. With the war over, his services were no longer needed. On July 2, 1783, Governor Harrison officially released Clark from the military in a letter replete with eloquent words of gratitude: "But before I take leave of you I feel myself called on in the most forcible Manner to return you my Thanks and those of my council for the very great and singular services you have rendered your Country, in wrestling so great and valuable a Territory out of the hands of the British Enemy, repelling the attacks of their Savage Allies and carrying on a successful war in the Heart of their Country, this Tribute of Praise and Thanks so justly due I am happy to communicate to you as the united Voice of the Executive."[26] In reply, Clark expressed his heartfelt feeling that "no reward for past services could be so satisfactory to me, as that of the gratitude of my country."[27]

Clark spent the rest of 1783 relaxing at his family's home in Caroline County. At some point, four of the five Clark brothers-in-arms were together, swapping tales, laughter, and tears over many a tankard of spirits. In order of rank, George Rogers was first as a brigadier general; Jonathan was then a lieutenant colonel who would later rise to general. Edmund and John were lieutenants. Captain Richard was still in Kentucky. Jonathan had been among 5,611 troops that General Benjamin Lincoln surrendered to General Henry Clinton at Charleston on May 12, 1780, and eventually paroled. And then, hovering nearby in adulation and envy was the youngest brother who would eventually surpass all of them in fame—William was then thirteen years old, imbibing deeply the intoxicating glories and boisterous manly company of his older brothers.

CHAPTER 18

Distant Horizons

How would you like to lead such a party?

Thomas Jefferson

George Rogers Clark received possibly the most intriguing offer of his life in the last month of 1783. With American independence won, Clark was one of countless patriots struggling to find an outlet for his energies and dreams. Another of those men was Thomas Jefferson. Clark and Jefferson had forged a powerful wartime partnership from 1779 to 1781, when Jefferson was Virginia's governor. That relationship disappeared after Jefferson retired to Monticello and devoted himself to tending his plantation. But in late 1782, they renewed their ties through the first of a series of letters.

At first glance, that relationship between a hotheaded adventurer and a buttoned-down intellectual may seem surprising. Perhaps each was attracted to those dimensions of the other lacking in himself. Far more important was what united them. They shared a fascination for the West and the natural world. Jefferson was especially eager to learn what Clark had found during his visits to Big Bone Lick, in northern Kentucky, littered with the fossils of ancient animals. His interests that he asked Clark to explore were typically encyclopedic, including "any observations of your own on the subject of the big bones . . . animals, vegetables, minerals, or other curious things, notes as to the Indians, information on the country between the Mississippi & waters of the South Sea [Pacific Ocean]" and anything else that "strike your mind as worthy of being communicated." Clark promised to bring back some specimens from a future visit to that enigmatic site and share any worthy observations on that array of other subjects.[1]

The zinger came with Jefferson's December 1783 letter.[2] He was alarmed to learn that Whitehall was mulling an expedition to explore the territory between the Mississippi River and the Pacific Ocean. Though the British "pretend it is only to promote knowledge, I am afraid they have thought of colonizing into that quarter." Jefferson was determined to beat the British to the punch on both counts. For that goal, of the handful of men that he was confident could do so, one transcended the others in daring and fortitude. Jefferson came straight to that point, asking Clark, "How would you like to lead such a party?"

The offer was an electrifying jolt out of the blue. How could any man of adventure and ambition turn it down? But Clark did just that, although he cited a want of money rather than enthusiasm as the deciding factor: "Your proposition respecting a tour to the west . . . of the Continent would be Extremely agreeable to me could I afford it." While he agreed that such an expedition was "what I think we ought to do," he worried that "Large Parties will never answer the purpose. They will alarm the Indian Nations they pass through." It would be better to dispatch "three or four young Men well qualified for the task" who "might perhaps compleat your wishes at a Trifling Expense" for a journey that might well last four or five years. Yet Clark had no intention of being among those young men. A dozen years of relentless frontier war had satiated his craving for adventure, at least for the time being. He would devote himself "to the lucrative policy of the world."[3]

Clark's decision is certainly understandable. Two related reasons bolstered that shift in his primary drive from exploring wilderness to making money. First, he reasoned that neither the bankrupt Virginian or American governments could afford such an undertaking. His years of mostly fruitless struggles to extract crucial resources from both had left him bitter and exhausted. The last thing he wanted was to renew those Sisyphean labors. Then there was his immediate duty to secure for his men and himself the promised bounty lands in the Ohio valley. Twenty years later, his feelings must have been bittersweet as his kid brother William jointly led Jefferson's

Corps of Discovery to the Pacific Ocean and back, thus achieving immortality as half of Lewis and Clark.

Clark returned to the Ohio valley in 1784, this time as a surveyor and diplomat rather than soldier. In December, he convened his Illinois regiment association that he had organized the previous February to survey and distribute the 150,000 acres of lands promised by Virginia to its veterans on January 2, 1781.[4] On February 9, 1784, he received his official appointment from Virginia to be one of two surveyors for the lands earmarked for all of Kentucky's veterans; William Croghan was the other. Each could hire up to four assistants and would be paid three shillings for each thousand acres he surveyed. On March 4, 1784, Congress tapped Clark to be one of the peace commissioners to the Ohio valley Indians. It was Jefferson who informed him of his appointment and implored him to accept. He grounded his appeal both in Clark's sense of duty and desire for fame. Clark was the man for that mission "because you can render essential service in it, & it will bring you forward on the Continental stage."[5]

An implacable conflict of interest entangled those two duties—land claims north of the Ohio River undermined peace with the Indians. Though Clark accepted both appointments, he soon revealed his preference. After arriving at Louisville on April 11, he spent a month organizing a surveying party. By May, he and his men were deployed in the region straddling the Ohio valley near Louisville, and he had dispatched a surveyor named Clay Green to stake out 74,000 acres below the mouth of the Tennessee River that he had acquired.

Clark and his associates finished their survey of the Illinois—known as Clark's Grant—and formally petitioned Virginia's government to transfer the land to them. By the time Richmond received that claim, it was no longer in a position to honor it. On March 1, 1784, Virginia's government officially ceded to Congress land claims north of the Ohio River. It did so as part of a sweeping deal between those six states with western land claims and the seven without. The deal initially had been cut in February 1779, when Maryland was the only state that had not ratified the Articles of Confederation, America's first constitution. That holdout's delegates explained that Maryland's government would ratify the articles only if those states with claims ceded them to the United States, which in turn would distribute tracts of those lands as bounties for soldiers and sell them to settlers for revenues. The deadlock persisted until September 6, 1780, when Congress officially adopted Maryland's condition. One by one, those states with claims gave them to the United States. In 1786, Connecticut would be the last to do so. Until then, the question of just how that land would be distributed was in abeyance.

The deal may have benefitted the nation but was a terrible setback for Clark and his Illinois regiment veterans. They would now have to lobby Congress to process their claim. That process would get sidelined by Congress's priority to keep peace with the Indians.

To supplement his surveying work, Clark formed a partnership with Dr. Alexander Skinner and John Saunders for "procuring beef, bear meat, bear's oil and venison hams, and curing them in a proper manner for keeping sound & fie for use, during the Winter and Spring." They divided the duties. Saunders would find an able assistant and "use every possible means to secure the said meat, &c. by pitching on a good hunting grounds, and being assiduous & industrious." Skinner would handle the curing, warehousing, and marketing. Clark would provide overall management. The plan made sense on paper, but there was a crucial problem. Game was increasingly scarce across the region as the swelling number of settlers shot it or scared it off. By December 5, 1785, the partners had dried only three thousand pounds of meat. They appear to have dissolved their company shortly thereafter.[6]

Of the tens of thousands of acres that Clark surveyed on both sides of the Ohio River, two patches were especially dear to him. One was a homestead for the Clark family. In the spring of 1784, he acquired a 256-acre tract 3 miles southeast of Louisville on the South Fork of Beargrass Creek. He and his slaves cleared the land and began erecting a house for the family that would be called Mulberry Hill. It took a while before the family reached its new home. That fall the Clarks awaited the death of brother John, who, on October 29, 1783, finally succumbed to a lingering illness he had contracted as a war prisoner. He was buried on November 2. The following day most of the Clark family—the parents, Lucy, Elizabeth, Frances, and William—packed their wagon, hitched up the team, and headed west, bound for Louisville, Kentucky. Jonathan would stay behind with his wife and young daughter. The journey lasted four months. Finding the Monongahela River low and icy, they decided to winter at Redstone Landing, upstream from Pittsburgh. They rode the swift late winter flood waters down to Louisville, arriving in March 1784.

Mulberry Hill was nearly finished as they moved in. John Clark bought the house and the surrounding 256 acres on August 29, 1785.[7] The two-story cabin was forty by twenty feet, with two windows flanking the front door on the first floor and three windows on the second floor. A stone fireplace and chimney rose on each side. The kitchen was in a detached cabin. Slave cabins and eventually a gristmill and sawmill were erected. There was a whiskey still in one of the outbuildings. Like most plantations, Mulberry Hill produced three crops, tobacco for cash, and corn and wheat for food; it also had various fruit trees.

As he helped develop Mulberry Hill, Clark had far more ambitious plans for another, much larger expanse of land. He set aside 1,000 acres of the 150,000 acres allocated to him and his veterans for a settlement named Clarksville at the lower end of the Falls of the Ohio. He laid out the town's street grid, sold off lots, and eventually had his slaves build him a small cabin, sawmill, and gristmill. By 1785, Clarksville had the grand total of twenty-three inhabitants. Clark proudly chaired a "convention" that drew up laws and regulations "to maintain peace and tranquility among the People." His cousin William Clark was appointed the judge, and one John Jackson was named the sheriff.[8]

Clarksville, however, was born in controversy. The general had jumped the gun. He had not received official approval to settle the land from Congress, which now owned the Northwest Territory beyond the Ohio River. Congress feared that Clarksville would provoke an Indian war and called on Governor Harrison to restrain Virginia's impetuous son. Harrison rebuked Clark for the "cruelty in the proceedings which was never expected from" him "as he must [have] known it would involve us in a most bloody and expensive war, which we are at this time not in any degree able to support. True it is the act vests the Lands in the Trustees for the use of you and your corps but" now only Congress can dispose of those lands. "I request of you Sir to reflect on what you have done and the distress you will bring on your country. . . . I am persuaded you will immediately recall the settlers and wait for a more favorable opportunity to carry your intentions into execution."[9]

Harrison put teeth into that "request" by suspending the survey of lands north of the Ohio for three years. The delay atop Congress's refusal to recognize Clarksville stifled its development. Clark bitterly added that complication to a growing list of grievances against the governments of the United States and Virginia. His alienation would fester to the point where he involved himself in plots that the government would actually condemn as seditious.

Most of his town's settlers lingered even though officially they were deemed squatters. The population dropped to seventeen in 1787. Clarksville stirred mixed feelings in General Richard Butler, who served with Clark on the Indian peace commission—he loved the site and despised the inhabitants. Though he found "the country and river beautiful beyond description," he was appalled by the callousness of "the most vulgar people I have seen" who "diverted themselves at cards (a very favorite amusement here) while their ears were assailed with the cries" of people whose boat had wrecked at the Falls. He was no more enthralled across the river at Louisville, where "we found the people engaged in selling and buying lots in the back streets. . . . There are several good log houses . . . but the extravagance in wages, and laziness of the tradesmen keep little doing but card playing, drinking, and other vices."[10]

The wheeling and dealing in Louisville was typical of most of Kentucky, whose land sales and titles were tangled in worsening legal and political knots. No professional services were in greater demand than surveyors and lawyers. The land rush persisted. By 1784, Kentucky's population had swelled to 56,000 people, many with overlapping land titles.[11] Justices of the peace also increasingly worked overtime. Though the war was officially over, violence persisted in the Ohio valley. An Illinois petition for relief cited several related reasons, including "want of Order and good Government. . . . Many ill-disposed Persons have taken Refuge in the Country. . . . The Population is daily increasing. . . . Their property is invaded and arrested by them by the Hands of daring Intruders."[12] With the threat of Indian attacks eclipsed and the profusion of conflicting land claims, the settlers turned on each other, often violently.

Yet islands of progress appeared amid all the upheaval stirred by greed, aggression, and vengeance. In 1780, Governor Jefferson had talked Virginia's assembly into passing a farsighted bill. The government would donate eight thousand acres of land confiscated from Loyalists to Kentucky to support higher education there. George Rogers Clark was among twenty trustees named when Transylvania College was chartered in 1783. That was a wonderful tribute to Clark, who as a boy was an indifferent student during his brief schooling, but who with time had become an avid scholar of human and natural history. Transylvania College opened in Lexington in February 1785 as America's first institution of higher education west of the Appalachians, and remains a well-respected school today.

Louisville itself was in transition from a crude frontier and garrison hamlet into an orderly and prosperous town. Major Erkuries Beatty recalled a memorable evening that he spent with Clark and other dignitaries in 1786. They first enjoyed "a very elegant dinner," after which they strolled to the dance school. There, they enjoyed a performance by a dozen girls, "some of whom had made considerable improvement in that polite accomplishment and indeed were middling neatly dressed, considering the distance from where luxuries are to be bought and the expense attending the purchase of them here."[13]

Looming over Kentucky for the foreseeable future was the Indian threat. Richmond tried to dissipate that threat by inviting the Northwest tribes to a peace conference at the Falls of the Ohio in May 1784. Little came of the initiative. Major Arent de Peyster at Detroit and other British agents wielded bribes and warnings to convince nearly all chiefs to stay away. Those who did show up did not tarry. The Americans lacked enough goods with which to buy a truce let alone a peace. That weakness inspired progressively more war parties to raid south of the Ohio River in search of scalps, loot, and captives.

Late in 1784, word reached the Ohio valley of the Treaty of Fort Stanwix, signed by the Iroquois with congressional commissioners on October 22.[14] As with previous treaties, the Iroquois received huge amounts of gifts for giving away title to distant lands that they did not really own. The Ohio valley Indians were outraged when they learned how much of their land the Iroquois had surrendered. Over the decades, the Ohio valley tribes had suffered much from their grudging acceptance of the Iroquois claim to hold suzerainty over them by dint of ancient wars and deals. Under the Fort Stanwix Treaty, a line was drawn down the Cuyahoga River to its headwaters, then west to the Miami River headwaters, then down the Miami to the Ohio River, and down the Ohio to the Mississippi River. The Americans would own all land east and south of that line; the Indians, everything north and west of it.

Congress was eager to get the Ohio valley tribes to ratify the Fort Stanwix Treaty by signing a similar treaty. In January 1785, it called on the tribes to send delegations to Fort McIntosh, at the mouth of Beaver Creek on the Ohio River thirty miles downstream from Pittsburgh, and commissioned George Rogers Clark, Arthur Lee, and Richard Butler as the diplomats to the conference. The three were a distinguished and effective mix. Butler had spent several years of his early manhood trading on the Pennsylvania frontier, where he learned to speak Shawnee and Delaware, and had served with distinction throughout the war for independence. Arthur Lee, the brother of Richard Henry Lee and Francis Lightfoot Lee, was a veteran diplomat, having served on missions to France, Spain, and Prussia. Butler and Lee, along with Oliver Wolcott, had negotiated the Treaty of Fort Stanwix with the Iroquois.

Most Ohio valley Indians were dead set to contain the Americans south of the Ohio River and east of the Allegheny River. Those most fiercely opposed to any further cessions stayed away from the peace talks. Though most Shawnees and all Miamis were absent, Clark and his fellow commissioners did greet delegations of Delawares, Wyandots, Ojibwas, Ottawas, and a small contingent of Shawnees. After negotiations opened on January 8, it took two weeks of bribes and bullying of the Indian delegates by the commissioners before a treaty was signed on January 21, 1785. To the rage of those who had spurned the talks, the Fort McIntosh Treaty essentially confirmed the Fort Stanwix Treaty's vast concessions. The hostile Shawnees, Miamis, and factions of other tribes not only refused to recognize the treaty but vowed to kill any Americans they found anywhere north of the Ohio River.[15]

Squatters did not just face threats from war parties. On September 22, 1783, Congress issued a resolution forbidding any settlements on unceded Indian lands. Colonel Josiah Harmar, who commanded American forces in the Ohio valley, had the unenviable duty of enforcing that resolution, the Treaty of Fort McIntosh, and other treaties. He dispatched troops to evict squatters and burn their cabins.

Clark and his veterans despaired of ever receiving the lands promised them by Virginia and Congress. Then they got a glimmer of hope after learning that on May 20, 1785, Congress passed the first law governing the surveying and sale of Northwest Territory lands. Inspired by the report of a committee chaired by Thomas Jefferson, the law would divide those lands into townships of six square miles that in turn would be divided into thirty-six one-square-mile sections. One section in each township would be devoted to public schools. Land would be auctioned off with a minimal price of a dollar an acre. Of course, that law applied only to lands ceded by the Indians to the United States. And so far those lands were far east of the 150,000-acre Clark Grant at the Falls of the Ohio.

The Stanwix and McIntosh treaties were worthless unless all the powerful tribes accepted them. Congress tried again to talk the Shawnees, Miamis, and other holdouts into accepting the cession. On April 18, 1785, Clark and Butler were reappointed as commissioners, while Samuel Parsons replaced Arthur Lee. Parsons was a distinguished general but had spent little time on the frontier let alone with Indians.

Two fascinating journals provide insights into this time of Clark's life.[16] Richard Butler provides an insider's view of the months of diplomacy leading up to the conference and the subsequent negotiations. Ensign Ebenezer Denny reveals how officers and enlisted men saw the proceedings.

The twelve-boat flotilla bearing Butler, Parsons, and Major Walter Finney; two companies of regulars; and tons of provisions and Indian gifts disembarked at the confluence of the Miami and Ohio Rivers on October 22. Clark soon joined them by canoe from the Falls. The first step was to choose an appropriate site for a fort. The others agreed to Clark's suggestion that high ground a mile downstream of the Miami River was the best choice. Possibly more than practicalities lurked behind that choice. Just an hour's paddle downriver, Joseph Brant and his warriors had killed or captured a hundred of Clark's men commanded by Colonel Lochry in 1781. Perhaps in a deep emotional sense, Clark was trying to retake that ground. But in clearing the forest and building a fort there, the expedition was violating both the government's orders and the Forts Stanwix and McIntosh treaties. The commissioner's instructions had explicitly ordered them to build a fort above the Miami River mouth to assert a right to land ceded by the treaties. The conference began brazenly on the wrong legal foot.

The officers set the men to work constructing what would be called Fort Finney. Four twenty-four-by-eighteen-feet two-story blockhouses anchored corners of a palisade a hundred feet on each side. The troops erected a magazine and storehouse inside the fort and a twenty-by-sixty-feet council house within gunshot beyond. The commissioners and troops lived in wedge tents pitched within the fort.

Meanwhile, the commissioners sent out runners to call the Ohio valley tribes to the council. It would take three long, mostly tedious, dreary months before enough Shawnees and other Indians showed up for the conference to begin. The weather worsened with days of rain, hail, and snow becoming more frequent. The troops were frequently drunk from rum sold to them by sutlers who charged sky-high prices. A number of troops deserted, some on stolen horses.

The commissioners tried to break the tedium by hunting, fishing, and making excursions to Big Bone Lick—where they dug up fossilized bones of mastodons—and to the Falls of the Ohio. Tensions rose among them. Butler lamented, "Although there is several gentlemen at this place, yet converse soon runs out for want of the pleasure of variety, which naturally arises from a diverse company of ladies and gentlemen, which is always a fund of pleasure and useful knowledge which fills up the blanks of life." He dismissed Parsons as "very illy informed and has no manner of personal knowledge, and frequently traps with question in the most abrupt and impolite manner."[17]

As for Clark, Butler found "a mysterious something in his conduct, which I cannot comprehend, or am I certain he can comprehend in himself, as I cannot remember a single proposition of his which has not been neither agreed to or himself convinced of its being improper, but he is very modest and makes but few."[18] That portrait of a subdued Clark clashes with the assertive, commanding figure recalled by most of his contemporaries. Butler seems to have intimidated Clark as much as Clark mystified Butler. Unlike Clark, who spoke no foreign languages, Butler was proficient in Shawnee and Delaware. Butler had fought with General George Washington in major battles on the Eastern Seaboard. He was well educated, articulate, and highly intelligent. Though he was short and stout, he shared Clark's intense energy. He was genial and good-hearted but could be unsparing of those whose performance or character faltered. As the senior officer, he would preside over the conference, with Clark and Parsons playing supporting roles.

Indian delegations began showing up in late December and trickled in over the next couple of months. Half King and Crane led in groups of

Wyandots; and Buckongehelas, Big Cat, Council Door, and White Eyes brought groups of Delawares. Buckongehelas's meeting with Clark was dramatic. The chief was "esteemed as one of the greatest warriors now among all the Indians. After he had seated himself he discovered General Clark, and knowing him to be a great warrior, rose and saluted him very significantly—instead of taking hold of each other's hands, they gripped nearly at the shoulder, and shook the left hand underneath the right arms."[19]

But most Wyandots and Delawares had already made peace with the Long Knives. It was the still-hostile Shawnees that the commissioners most anxiously awaited. Finally, on January 14, 1786, a Shawnee procession of about 150 men and 80 women danced into Fort Finney, led by Moluntha, their "oldest chief." Butler described him as carrying "a small drum on which he beats time and sings; two young warriors, who dance well, carry each the stem of a pipe painted and decorated with many feathers of the bald eagle and wampum. These are joined in the dance by several other young men. . . . The whole of the party painted and dressed in the most elegant manner. . . . These are followed by the chief warrior . . . and the warriors armed; then come the head woman . . . in front of all the women and children. . . . They sung for some time" until the chief uttered a cry and all stood in silence. The chief issued another command, and all the warriors cocked their muskets and fired skyward.[20]

The conference opened on January 19. The number of Indians present was 448, including 318 Shawnees, 83 Wyandots, and 47 Delawares. Buckongehelas sought to establish a spirit of amity and reconciliation by declaring "to the Great Spirit . . . thanks for the preservation of his own and Gen. Clarke's life through the war, and for putting it once more in their power to see each other . . . that he is determined to support" peace "with all his endeavor."[21]

Although the Delaware and Wyandot chiefs acquiesced, the Shawnees remained defiant. They rejected the vast surrender of Indian lands embedded in the Forts Stanwix and McIntosh treaties, and resented the transfer of sovereignty from the "Great Father" in London to the new one in Philadelphia. It took two weeks to win them over. The days passed with long, eloquent speeches, angry retorts, and persistent tension, and the nights with dances and feasts.

Finally, with great reluctance, the Shawnees agreed to a treaty. But a crisis erupted on January 30, when the commissioners presented a list of principles upon which to ground the deal. The Indians murmured approval of those that called for peace, inviolable boundaries, friendship, justice, and sovereignty, but the Shawnees erupted in protest at the requirement that they hand over five hostages to ensure that they lived up to their promises. A chief angrily denounced the Americans for having grown "proud because you have thrown down the King of England." He then asserted, "God gave us this country, we do not understand measuring out the lands, it is all ours. . . . We have never given hostages and we will not comply with this demand." He then flung a mixed black and white wampum belt on the table before the commissioners. The choice for them was clear—either rescind the demand for hostages or prepare for war.[22]

Butler heatedly replied, "Have you forgotten your breach of treaties in the beginning of the late war? Do you think we have forgot the burning of our towns, the murder and captivity of our people in consequence of your perfidy, or have you forgotten them? It rests with you, the destruction of your women and children, or their future happiness depends on your present choice. Peace or war is in your power: make your choice like men." At the end of his speech, Butler threw black and white wampum belts on the table.[23]

Until then, Clark managed to mask whatever anger and trepidation he was feeling as if he were watching a play. Suddenly, he rose and "with his cane, pushed" the belts onto the floor, rose, stepped over them, and then ground them beneath his heel. Locking eyes with the Shawnee chiefs, he declared his intention to give them provisions for their journey home and at least eight days to prepare before he followed and destroyed them. "It rests now with you; the destruction of your women and children, or their future happiness, depends on your present choice. Peace or war is in your power; make your choice like men and judge for yourselves."[24] The council broke up chaotically, with each delegation hurrying to its camp, seizing arms, and preparing for a possible battle.

Fortunately, cooler heads prevailed. The Delaware acted as go-betweens and talked the Shawnees into standing down. The council convened the next morning. As he entered, Shawnee chief Moluntha bore the white wampum belt of peace. The Treaty of Fort Finney was signed later that day, February 1, 1786. This latest treaty merely reconfirmed what the

peace chiefs had previously ceded under the Stanwix and McIntosh treaties. The signature of Moluntha and a few other chiefs represented only
themselves and their followers. Most Shawnees condemned their act. The
Fort Finney treaty no more brought peace than its predecessors had. General Josiah Harmar spoke for all knowledgeable observers when he stated,
"All these treaties will be ineffectual. Possessing the British posts ought to be
first grand object, then a treaty at Detroit will answer all purposes. The
United States will never have either dignity or consequences among the Indians until this is affected."[25] In that, of course, Harmar was merely echo-
ing Clark's fruitless exhortations over the previous decade.

War belts circulated among the tribes. Enraged Indians attacked surveyors and settlers who dared venture north of the Ohio River. Warriors lurked
in the woods near Fort Finney and sniped at anyone foolish enough to expose
himself. Ever more war parties crossed the Ohio River and raided deep into
Kentucky, killing scores of people and running off hundreds of horses.

The most vulnerable American community was at Vincennes. That
town was no longer the welcoming allied community that Clark and his
men had enjoyed when they captured Hamilton there seven years earlier.
The population was split between the majority of largely French and Indian
older inhabitants, a small group of British traders, and a swelling number of
American newcomers. In late March 1786, Clark received a plea for help
from the Americans who wrote, "This place that once trembled at your
victorious army and these savages overawed by your Superior power is
now entirely anarchical, and We shuder at the daily expectation of horrid
murthers, and probably total depopulation of the Americans by imperious
savages. . . . Knowing you to be a friend to the distressed, and possess'd of
humanity we therefore earnestly look to you for assistance."[26]

How had relations reached that point? The old-timers soon despised the
newcomers for being greedy and aggressive, for squeezing established merchants from the market and established landowners from their land. The
British fed those resentments with bribes and arms. Animosities worsened
into hatreds. A group of Indians attacked some Americans and wounded
two. The Americans retaliated by murdering an Indian. The local Indians
appealed to their brothers up the Wabash valley to help them wipe out the
hated Americans in their midst. Colonel Jean Legras, the local magistrate,
tried to evict the troublemakers by requiring everyone without a permit to

be in the territory to leave. The Americans erected a stockade and swore they would die fighting to defend their "right" to stay. Happy to oblige that vow, several hundred Indians descended the Wabash to destroy the Americans. Legras sent messengers to them with an appeal that they turn back. Undeterred, the Indians barged into Vincennes and besieged the fort. Most French kept to their homes, although a few aided the Indians. Legras was able to arrange a truce. The Indians withdrew after slaughtering the livestock and looting the homes of the Americans.[27]

Meanwhile, Clark mustered and sent 130 frontiersmen to the rescue, although he did not join them. They never reached Vincennes. Along the way, they attacked a friendly village of Piankeshaws and killed six and wounded seven, while suffering a man killed and four wounded. Despite their light losses, the Kentuckians lost courage and returned to Louisville.[28]

Clark also appealed to Governor Patrick Henry and Congress for help in crushing the Indian threat in the Ohio valley. He explained to Henry, "If Detroit was in our possession it might in a great measure silence the Indians; but nothing will effectively do it but dissolution, and all humanity shewn them by us is imputed to timidity. Great expenditures and numbers of lives might be saved by now reducing them to obedience, which they so richly deserve."[29]

Governor Henry likely shrugged off Clark's insistence that driving the Indians from their lands and the British from Detroit would end frontier violence. That was a utopian vision, at least for the short term. The United States lacked the power to realize that for the foreseeable future. He harbored no illusion over the true cause of the latest round of murders. Three years earlier he had written, "With too much Truth . . . our own people are the aggressors. . . . The character of such Americans as usually frequent the Indian Borders . . . necessarily produces contention." For Henry, the only long-term solution to that conundrum was to appoint Indian agents with the power to keep the Americans from Indian lands and to placate the Indians with gifts.[30] Regardless, the governor was willing to authorize a campaign against the Indians. Yet, with his own state's treasury typically bare, he appealed to Congress for help. Although Congress was even more financially bankrupt than Virginia, a majority of congressmen agreed to do what they could. On July 3, 1786, Charles Thomson, a congressional secretary, informed Henry that Congress was sending two infantry companies to Louisville, where they would unite with whatever militia the governor mustered against the Indians. Henry sent word to the county lieutenants of Kentucky to gather their men at the Falls of the Ohio.[31]

Major Walter Finney arrived with two understrength companies on August 16. His orders were to abandon the fort named in his honor near the Miami River mouth and to erect a new fort on the Ohio's north shore across from Louisville. That fort would first be called Fort Finney and then Fort Steuben. Yet, contrary to the promise of Congress, he had no orders to join an expedition against the Indians, so he did not.

Who would lead that campaign? For most Kentucky military leaders meeting at Lexington in July, one man topped the list of candidates. Captain John May expressed the popular view: "General Clark is the properest person to take command here . . . and should an expedition be carried on against the Indians I think his name alone would be worth half a regiment." May did note that the choice was not universal, that some believed that he was "not being capable of attending to business," an apparent reference to Clark's addiction to alcohol and faltering health. May reassured Governor Henry that "I have been with him frequently and find him as capable of Business as ever."[32]

Weeks passed with no word from the governor over who should command the campaign. On August 2, Kentucky's militia officers met at Harrodsburg and, led by Colonel Benjamin Logan, publicly issued a resolution that "an Expedition against the Waubauch & other inimical Indians is at this time Justifiable" and called for "George Rogers Clark" to "have the Command & Direction of the Army" whose ranks could be filled "by Impressment if necessary."[33] They called on all militia companies west of the Licking River to muster for that campaign.

Clark reluctantly agreed to head the campaign and called for the companies to gather at Clarksville by the first of September. His reluctance was understandable. The campaign would receive no help from either Virginia or Congress. Virginia had officially ceded its claims to territory north of the Ohio River to the United States government on March 1, 1784. Henceforth, it would be the duty of Congress to smite any enemies in what was being called the Northwest Territory. But Congress was bankrupt and could give nothing but encouragement.

The campaign would have to be completely financed and provisioned by the companies themselves. Overseeing that thankless labor fell mostly on the shoulders of John May, the commissary, and Christopher Greenup, the quartermaster. Each company was required to collect fifty days' worth of supplies, with one packhorse for every four men. A mere 1,200 men, or less than half of the 2,500 expected, showed up at Clarksville by September 10, 1786. Those militia companies that did not appear sent word that they were required only to serve in their state and thus would not set foot across the Ohio River. Clark condemned that excuse and sent Colonel Logan to round them up. It would take too long to bring them to Clarksville, so Clark authorized Logan to gather them at Limestone and lead them against the Shawnees in the upper Miami River, while he headed with his army against the Miami villages on the upper Wabash River.

The excuse that militia companies did not have to serve north of the river since it was no longer part of Virginia proved to be infectious. Hundreds of those camped at Clarksville eventually went home. Only 790 armed men, including about 500 mounted volunteers, finally agreed to follow Clark north against the enemy on September 17.

Then a bitter debate erupted over which path to take. While Clark wanted to head straight for the hostile villages, most of the officers demanded that they angle northwest to Vincennes and then follow the Wabash River valley to the enemy. Logistics lay in the heart of the dispute. Clark insisted that horses could carry all they needed overland. The dissidents countered that boats could carry far more supplies to within striking distance of the villages. Each method had its shortcomings since each depended on a critical resource—fodder for the horses and water for the boats. Clark finally yielded. He would soon regret doing so. It only took eight days for him and his men to march the 130-mile trail from Clarksville to Vincennes. But there they had to wait a couple of weeks for the boats to catch up. It had been an unusually dry summer, and water levels had dropped to near bottom. Then they discovered that the water from leaky boats and a couple of hard rains had seeped into poorly constructed barrels and had ruined critical supplies of cornmeal and salted pork. The men began stealing chickens, cattle, and anything else edible from the local people. John May, the quartermaster, quit in disgust. To worsen matters, more men deserted.

Vincennes teetered on the brink of civil war when Clark and his army arrived. That overwhelming military presence quelled those inclined to violence on both sides for the time being. But the American community pleaded with Clark to act decisively on their behalf. That put Clark in an awkward position. He needed the French and Indians to support his campaign up the Wabash and would alienate them if he openly sided with the Americans. Atop that, Colonel Legras, who headed the French community, was an old friend and brother-in-arms. Yet if Clark spurned the American appeal, he would not only alienate them but would provoke criticism across the frontier for betraying his own countrymen. He finally decided to set aside that issue until the campaign was over.

Clark led his force up the Wabash valley. The army was only a few days on the trail when a crisis erupted. As they neared the Vermillion River mouth, cries of "who's for home?" resounded among the Lincoln County militia. After conferring with their men, the Lincoln County officers announced that they were heading back. Clark tried to sway them by promising that if they went "with me two days march . . . if I don't furnish you with as much provisions as you want, I will return with you." But they hooted at him and strode off.[34] Clark called a council of war among his remaining officers. They reluctantly agreed that the force was now too depleted to continue. That decision may have averted a catastrophic defeat. They later learned that an ambush awaited them at Pine Creek a few days march farther up the trail. Once they returned to Vincennes, Clark dismissed all but 150 of his troops, whom he quartered in Fort Patrick Henry.

George Rogers Clark's last campaign was plagued by desertion, dissent, mutiny, and a humiliating withdrawal without firing a shot against the enemy. He tried to save face by having Vincennes's French leaders spread the word that they had restrained him and his men from attacking and devastating the upper Wabash Indians. That probably did not fool many Indians.

Clark himself may have been the ultimate source of his campaign's failure. It is hard to command anything, especially respect, when one is inebriated. A merchant named Robard revealed, "I had business with the General while there [Vincennes] and he was drunk chief of the time and not capable of business."[35]

The ignominious end to Clark's last campaign was exaggerated by how well Logan's went. His campaign against the Shawnees on the upper Great

Miami River and Mad River was as successful as Clark's was a failure. His men destroyed a cluster of seven villages and 15,000 bushels of corn, killed 10 warriors, and took 34 prisoners, including Moluntha, the war chief. The Kentuckians might have used Moluntha as an instrument for peace. Alas, Hugh McGary, who was responsible for the Blue Licks debacle, sought a scapegoat for his own criminal ineptness. He asked Moluntha if he had fought at Blue Licks. When the chief indicated that he had, McGary buried his hatchet in Moluntha's skull.

The glaring disparity in the results of the two campaigns hammered additional spikes into the coffin of Clark's reputation. His enemies seized the opportunity to renew their attacks that he was nothing more than a bumbling drunkard unfit for any public office, especially a military command. Colonel Levi Todd was among those who asked that Governor Henry investigate officially why Clark's campaign had failed. Todd cautioned that any inquiry be made "by some judicious and discerning men of the district, not officers of that army." Future failures might be avoided by exposing to public condemnation "men who officiate without merit."[36]

While Clark escaped an official investigation, he was powerless against his enemies' attacks. As for the hostile Indians, without an army, Clark now only had the power to talk. Had all gone well, a diplomatic victory would have capped a military victory. That was no longer possible. All Clark could do was send out friendly Indians with appeals to the hostile chiefs to join him in peace negotiations at Clarksville on November 20. Those envoys would encounter nearly universal disdain for their message. The chiefs had no incentive to negotiate if their enemy was bereft of the power to crush or corrupt. And besides that, the Indians were losing their respect and fear for the once seemingly invincible George Rogers Clark.

In any event, Clark was spared the humiliation of holding a peace conference that was contemptuously spurned by the invited chiefs. A far worse humiliation trumped that one. Clark fled Vincennes for refuge with his family at Mulberry Hill, but, like an ever-lengthening shadow, a scandal he had tried to leave behind trailed him home.

CHAPTER 19

Conspiracies

Neither property nor Character is safe in a government as weak and unsettled as the United States, and this, in short, has induced me to put in practice what I have for so great a time contemplated, to offer myself to His Majesty the King of Spain.

George Rogers Clark

To save congress from a rupture with Spain on our account, we must first expatriate our selves and become French citizens. This is our intention.

George Rogers Clark

For nearly fifteen years, from the mid-1780s through the late 1790s, George Rogers Clark engaged in a series of conspiracies with the governments of first Spain and then France. Although each plot was unique, three characteristics underlay his role in them. One was his ambition to grab land, riches, and power in parts of the Mississippi valley. Another was the ease with which he was prepared not just to immigrate to a foreign land but actually to renounce his own American citizenship. Finally and most astonishing of all was Clark's determination to defy and at times even betray the United States government.

What explains Clark's not just willingness but eagerness to turn coat? It certainly reveals the depths of his bitterness that his countrymen had failed to appreciate and compensate him for his sacrifices during the war for independence. It also reflects the view among westerners that the United States had abandoned the West, and so the West owed nothing to the United States. That revolution in sentiments among westerners was a long time coming.

During the American War of Independence, the United States and Spain were unofficial, but no less effective, allies against Britain, especially in the Mississippi valley. Spain made genuine sacrifices of money and material aid for the fledgling United States. Governor Bernardo de Galvez at New Orleans and Lieutenant Governor Fernando de Leyba at Saint Louis worked closely with Americans in the region to advance their common interest in defeating Britain. The most dramatic manifestation of that relationship occurred in May 1780, when Governor De Leyba and General Clark repelled British offensives on opposite sides of the Mississippi River.

Yet, unlike its wartime relationship with France, America's relationship with Spain would never be official. Madrid and Paris signed a treaty of alliance on April 12, 1779, and Charles III issued a war declaration against Britain on June 17, 1779. Congress dispatched John Jay to the Spanish court to secure recognition of the United States, an alliance, and a list of other goals. Jay spent more than two frustrating years at Madrid, from April 1780 to June 1782, without ever being officially received by Spain's government. At most, foreign minister José Moñino y Redondo, Conde de Floridablanca met unofficially with him, only to inform him politely that the United States would not receive recognition, an alliance, a loan, free trade, or navigation on the Mississippi River through Spanish territory. He then patiently listened to Jay's attempts to change his mind on each of those points. As for navigation on the Mississippi River, Jay would later explain, "The Americans, almost to a man, believed that God Almighty had made that river a highway for the people of the upper country to go to the sea . . . and that the [western] inhabitants would not readily be convinced of the justice of being obliged, either to live without foreign commodities, and lose the surplus of their productions, or be obliged to transport both over rugged mountains and through an immense wilderness . . . when they daily saw a fine river flowing before their doors."[1] Floridablanca and his colleagues were unmoved by variations on these views and appeals on related issues in the decades to come.

Fear explains the Spaniards' reluctance. Even at the height of its unofficial alliance with the United States against Britain, Madrid never lost sight of the likelihood that today's friend would sooner or later become an enemy. Americans were overrunning the territory east of the Mississippi River. By 1783, America's roughly 85,000 settlers west of the Appalachians were more numerous than Spain's subjects in the Mississippi Valley. Eventually, those Americans would cross the Mississippi River and spread across Spain's Louisiana Territory. To counter that threat, Madrid adopted a policy of containing the United States geographically and economically. During the war, Governor Galvez's brilliant series of campaigns that captured West Florida from Britain also effectively sealed off the Gulf of Mexico from the United States. Peace then dissolved the mutual interest of the United States and Spain. Yesterday's ally was now and would be for the foreseeable future a clear and ever-worsening danger to the Spanish empire.

The Spaniards expressed two key elements of that policy in 1784. On March 12, Charles III decreed that henceforth the Mississippi River would be shut to Americans. That decree reversed a policy by which Spain allowed British subjects free navigation down the Mississippi after 1763. The decree was published in the United States in July 1784. The Spaniards would strictly enforce that decree by confiscating American cargos and imprisoning any Americans who entered Louisiana. Madrid also announced that West Florida's northern border ran eastward from the confluence of the Yazoo River with the Mississippi, at roughly the 32nd parallel, 28 degrees. That indeed was the boundary of West Florida fixed in a 1763 treaty by which Spain ceded that territory to Britain. That boundary, however, contradicted the 31st parallel boundary ceded by the British to the Americans in the 1783 Treaty of Paris.

Spain's policies appeared solidly grounded in international law. Every sovereign state had the right to set the terms by which foreigners entered and remained in its territory, and could outright deny any entry. Yet, although West Florida's more northern boundary was well documented, the Americans would eventually find legal cracks and political gaps to wiggle through. They would point to the fact that Madrid neither immediately protested the 31st parallel line when the Treaty of Paris was published nor tried to define West Florida's northern boundary in its peace treaty with Britain. Indeed, the Spaniards would remain silent on that issue until the Americans tried to negotiate a trade treaty with them in 1783. The Americans would argue that Spain's silence implied consent until Charles III changed his mind. As for the issues of trade and navigation on the Mississippi, Madrid's keep-out policy came at a high price. For decades, the relations between the United States and Spain became so acrimonious that those nations teetered on the brink of war with each other.

Spain's policies directly threatened American national security by loosening the new nation's grip on its western territory. Governor Patrick Henry warned that the closure of the Mississippi River would "crush all our hopes of prosperity for the western country."[2] The longer the United States took to open that waterway, the greater the sentiment among westerners to break away and form their own country or join the Spanish empire. To avert that potential catastrophe, Congress sought a diplomatic solution. It authorized Secretary of State John Jay to negotiate a treaty that ensured free trade and navigation of the Mississippi, and a southern boundary as close to the Gulf of Mexico as possible. On July 26, 1786, Jay began haggling with Diego de Gardoqui, Spain's minister to the United States. Gardoqui was unyielding. In despair, Jay asked Congress on August 3 to approve a deal whereby the United States gave up navigation on the Mississippi River below Natchez for thirty years in return for trade with Spain.

Word of Jay's proposal delighted northeasterners and enraged westerners. Though Congress rejected Jay's proposal, the political damage had been done. Westerners now vented their anger against the easterners who would quite literally sell them out. Prominent westerners argued that they should declare independence for their own sovereign country between the Mississippi River and Appalachian Mountains. If they did so, they could negotiate directly with the Spanish. Some went so far as to suggest that western interests would be best served by being part of the Spanish empire. A few secretly conspired for that end.

The Spanish authorities were happy to encourage those sentiments. They insisted that they would never open the Mississippi River to navigation and their empire to trade as long as the westerners remained part of the United States. However, Madrid would embrace the westerners if they declared independence or, better yet, outright joined the Spanish empire.

Gardoqui was the chief instigator and paymaster for most of the plots among westerners for either option. Before he left the United States in October 1789, he had entangled a dozen or so of the most prominent western leaders in a web of treasonous plots. Indeed, the list of Spain's American secret agents reads like a who's who of western leaders. George Rogers Clark is merely the best known, alongside James Wilkinson, John Sevier, James Robertson, George Morgan, William Blount, Friedrich von Steuben, and the lesser known John Rogers, James O'Fallon, James White, and Thomas Green.

None among the men was a worse traitor than James Wilkinson.[3] Although much less known than Benedict Arnold, Wilkinson inflicted incalculably more damage to American national security. While Arnold's plot to sell out George Washington and West Point to the British was thwarted, Wilkinson's machinations insidiously undermined American interests for decades. He amply deserves his reputation for being the Judas of early American history. Wilkinson sold out as early as August 1787, shortly after arriving at New Orleans with a boatload of smoked ham and tobacco. The Spanish officials did not confiscate that cargo and toss Wilkinson and his hired men into prison. Instead, the glib-tongued Wilkinson talked Governor Esteban Miro into giving him special business privileges at New Orleans and an annual payment in return for spying against the United States. Agent Number Thirteen would be on Spain's payroll for the next two decades. During that time, he rose to command the American army and to govern the Louisiana Territory!

Wilkinson's successful journey to New Orleans shifted the thinking of Clark and many other western leaders from conquering to collaborating with the Spanish. That was quite a flip-flop. For several years, Clark had been obsessed with destroying Spain's empire in the Mississippi valley. Clark took his first aggressive step against Spain in autumn 1786, during his sojourn at Vincennes. The act he committed seemed routine enough at the time but would haunt him for years. He ordered the confiscation of a boatload of goods owned by three Spaniards. He did so for three reasons. The legal justification was that the owners lacked the proper papers. The practical reason was that Clark needed those supplies for his campaign. Finally, there was the emotional satisfaction of retaliating in kind for an act that the Spanish government regularly committed against American merchants trying to descend the Mississippi River to Louisiana and West Florida.[4]

The immediate headache for Clark was a lawsuit by the victims of that confiscation. That lawsuit's legal shadow was troubling enough, but rumors swirled that Clark was plotting a "confiscation" immeasurably grander than that against the hapless Spanish merchants.[5] An anonymous letter "from a gentleman in Kentucky to a friend in Philadelphia" was published in Richmond in December 1786. The writer charged Clark with "playing Hell. He is raising a regiment of his own and has 40 men stationed at [Vincennes] Clarke is eternally drunk, and yet full of design. I told him he would be hanged. He laughed and said he could take refuge among the Indians. A stroke is meditated against St. Louis and Natchez."[6]

That and similar charges from other publicly unidentified sources so alarmed Virginia's government and Congress that both opened investigations. In February 1787, Virginia's Board of Commissioners issued a report that condemned Clark for raising troops and massing supplies without authorization. As a result, on February 28, 1787, Governor Edmund Randolph declared, "The Attorney General has been instructed to take every step allowed by law, for bringing to punishment all persons who may be culpable."[7] The subsequent findings, however, were hardly objective. For "evidence," the committee simply shifted through the same anonymous, inflammatory, and unsubstantiated accusations from the "gentleman in Kentucky" and his coterie that Richmond had accepted.

Not surprisingly, Congress came to the same conclusion about Clark as Virginia. Congress acted decisively on those findings on April 24, 1787. Secretary of State John Jay formally apologized to the Spanish government and promised to thwart any expeditions against its empire. Secretary of War Henry Knox issued orders to Colonel Josiah Harmar, who commanded American forces in the Ohio valley, to muster his troops "for dispossessing a body of men who had, in a lawless and unauthorized manner, taken possession of Post Vincennes in defiance of the proclamation and authority of the United States."[8]

In mid-June, Harmar set off with several companies of soldiers downstream from Fort Harmar at the Muskingum River mouth. He must have had very mixed feelings about his mission. He had gotten to know Clark at the Fort McIntosh conference and likely respected his military and diplomatic prowess. He would not relish crossing swords with such a formidable opponent as well as a fellow American. But neither Clark nor his supposed army awaited Harmar and his troops when they arrived at Vincennes on July 17. Clark had long before dispersed his command and returned to his family at Mulberry Hill outside of Louisville. There, he eventually got word that Congress had quietly dropped its charges against him. Nonetheless, the government's accusations and Harmar's campaign deeply hurt his feelings and reputation; his subsequent bitterness would eat away at him to his dying days.

Publicly, Clark struggled to keep up a façade of stoic indifference. To Governor Edmund Randolph, he acknowledged suffering "many malignant pen's flaying." Yet, though one "might reasonably Suppose that of course I must be unhappy the Reverse hath taken place Contious of having done every thing in the powers of a person under my Circumstances not only for the defense of the Country but to Save Every Expence possible I can with pleasure Veew Countres flourishing I have Stained with the Blood of its Enimies."[9]

Who among Clark's many enemies spearheaded that smear campaign? The most likely suspect for that "gentleman from Kentucky" was James Wilkinson. He later boasted to Spanish officials that he "was the first and principal factor who destroyed the undertaking Brigadier Clark was meditating."[10] If so, then Wilkinson was shamelessly projecting his own nefarious schemes onto Clark. Why would he do that?

James Wilkinson had arrived in Kentucky in 1784 with the overweening ambition to rise to the pinnacle of economic and political power by any possible means. He saw Clark as among his chief rivals in that quest. In accusing Clark with such righteous indignation, Wilkinson at once elevated himself and buried his rival in the public mind. Clark was an easy mark—hot-tempered, frequently drunk, and, some whispered, guilty of even more sordid private vices. Yet, however tarnished, Clark was still a hero. And Wilkinson was anything but a hero. Wilkinson's duties during America's war for independence were largely confined to serving as a staff or supply officer. In the latter post, he enriched himself through corruption: skimming money from budgets, black-marketing "surplus" materials, and palming kickbacks from contractors. Although formal charges were never brought against him, he resigned under a very dark cloud in 1781. Like countless other Americans, Wilkinson turned his back on his troubles and headed west to renew his life. Alas, the only things new about his life would be the setting and scale of his crimes. Special talents and luck let him get away with grand theft and treason for decades. The key to Wilkinson's success was his mastery of that very American art of peddling a carefully contrived image to mask an insipid or, in his case, treacherous character. Countless people fell for it.

Meanwhile, Clark was in desperate need of hard cash to keep the swelling ranks of his creditors, including Virginia's government, at bay. Governor Randolph requested that Clark provide him with all documents that could help resolve the conflicting accusations, denials, and claims over who owed what to whom. Clark's reply at once defended himself and attacked those who accused him of corruption. He lamented, "What mischief false informers, envious and malicious persons have in their power to do in this country." He insisted that he had "done everything . . . not only for the defense of the country, but to save every expense possible."[11]

The only potential source of money for Clark was his land claims. Yet he was trapped in the dilemma of being at once land-rich, cash-poor, and increasingly deeper in debt. He vented that frustration in a letter to his brother Jonathan: while "the family . . . are well . . . as for my Self I don't find times so agreeable. . . . Great possessions of Lands without any Means of getting Money I find is not the plan I shall sell out as fast as I can except particular tracts."[12] The trouble was finding ready buyers with cash on the barrelhead. The alternative was to sell land to buy land. But that only made sense if the new acquisitions were unburdened by conflicting claims unlike the old. Kentucky's lands had long since lost their legal virginity, and that newly acquired territory north of the Ohio River was already getting entangled with overlapping claims. But the empire next door had a sparse population and an orderly system of land grants.

With the spirit of "if you can't beat them, join them," Clark submitted to Spain's government a petition to found a settlement west of the Mississippi River across from the Yazoo River mouth. Spanish officials rejected his terms by which he would have served as governor assisted by an elected council, while the settlers would have freely practiced their Protestant faith. To sweeten the deal, Clark made an extraordinary offer. In a March 1788 letter to Diego de Gardoqui, Spain's minister to the United States, he renounced America for Spain: "Neither property nor Character is safe in a government as weak and unsettled as the United States, and this, in short, has induced me to put in practice what I have for so great a time contemplated, to offer myself to His Majesty the King of Spain with a numerous colony of desireable subjects."[13]

Spain's prompt rejection of Clark's petition is hardly surprising. His proposal seems Quixotic given the notoriety for his filibuster plot atop robbing the three Spanish merchants at Vincennes. Did he really believe that the Spanish had such short memories, empty archives, lack of informants, and innocent minds? Was Clark serious about becoming a law-abiding Spanish subject or was it simply a ploy to penetrate a government that he hoped eventually to overthrow? That is now impossible to determine. What is clear is his indignation at suffering rejection. He angrily wrote Louisiana governor Esteban Miro, "I have given my time, my property, and every exertion of my faculties to promote the interests of the Spanish monarchy. By this conduct I have hazarded the indignation of the American union."[14]

After Spain's rejection of his plans for a colony, Clark left his family at Mulberry Hill and settled in a small cabin at his Clarksville settlement just below the Falls of the Ohio. His unbroken string of humiliations, failures, and scandals deeply depressed him. From a young age, he had been a hard drinker but was usually able to keep his vice within bounds, however pliable. He had most enjoyed tipping a jug with boisterous male companions as they swapped tales, feats of strength, and bawdy humor. Now he abandoned all restraint to drown his sorrow and rage with whiskey. His companions dwindled, repelled by his bitter rants and depleted prowess. Although his binges increasingly may have been solo, all too many of them remained pathetically public. Major Erkuries Beatty recorded in 1787, "Saw Genl Clark, who is still more of a sot than ever, not company scarce for a beast; his character which once was so great, is now entirely gone with the people in this country. . . . I think the man ruined in character as in property."[15]

Clark's depression was so smothering that he might well have stepped into the abyss had he known what lay ahead. At age thirty-four, he was already years beyond his life's greatest glory, and he would never again lead men against an enemy. Instead, all that stretched before him was an unrelenting gauntlet of creditors and critics, of lawsuits and slander, of filibuster plots equal parts bumbling and treasonous, and of drunken binges and decaying health until eternity finally swallowed him.

As Clark conspired first against and then with the Spanish empire, the American Revolution entered a new stage. The new nation was trapped in a vicious cycle in which a weak government and economy dragged each other down. The Articles of Confederation established not a government but a committee of thirteen squabbling sovereign states. Those states and Congress were all mired deeply in debts racked up during the war for independence. Most people had emerged from that war poorer than they had entered it, and countless were completely ruined. Skyrocketing inflation stifled potential buyers and makers of goods from acting, thus stalling the economy. As usual, a few made out like bandits. Speculators made and lost immense fortunes trading the worthless script, that era's equivalent of derivatives and credit default swaps. And the result was just as disastrous for America and most of its people.

A few farsighted men like George Washington, Alexander Hamilton, and James Madison recognized that only a muscular, problem-solving national government could break that vicious cycle and usher the United States into a virtuous cycle of political stability, economic prosperity, and national security. To create just such a government, these leaders organized a meeting of like-minded men at Philadelphia in May 1787. Over the next four long hot summer months, as many as fifty-five delegates attended part or all of the debates over how to realize that vision. The Constitution that they crafted and presented to the states for ratification in September was rooted in a series of ideals, innovations, and compromises. The framers sought inspiration from both classical and modern political philosophers. Much more importantly, they drew from the practical institutions, experiences, and experiments of each of the thirteen colonies that had emerged in the New World over the preceding century and a half. In eighty-five essays that became known as the Federalist Papers, Hamilton, Madison, and Jay explained just what the framers had constructed, why they had done so, and how the new system was supposed to work.

Nine of the thirteen states had to ratify the Constitution before it could take effect; New Hampshire became number nine in June 1788. The framers then got busy fleshing out the blueprint of government into actual institutions. Each state held the different elections for the House of Representatives, Senate, and president. On April 23, 1789, George Washington took the oath as America's first president under the new system. Congress convened, organized into committees, and passed laws creating cabinet positions, the federal court system, and what became the Constitution's first ten amendments, known as the Bill of Rights. One of the many deals struck was for New York to serve as the nation's capital for a year and a half until it moved to Philadelphia in 1790, where it would sit for a decade before being transferred to its permanent home in Washington City.

Not everyone was pleased with the new government. Those who preferred either the old confederation of sovereign states or a weak national government were first known as the Anti-Federalists. They would soon call themselves the Republicans in opposition to the Federalists who championed the Constitution.

Clark played no part in the transformation of the United States into "a more perfect union." That is not surprising. Philadelphia was far beyond the Appalachian Mountains. Clark shared a western fatalism toward what the eastern elite did unless it directly affected him. Forming a new government was a role for farsighted statesmen, philosophers, and politicians. A warrior like Clark would have been decidedly out of place in the proceedings. None of his surviving letters reveal even a flicker of interest in those revolutionary events. Of course, that does not mean he was indifferent. Perhaps his views were lost or never recorded. Regardless, the same silence is true for dramatic political changes in his own backyard.

As early as 1783, Danville became Kentucky's unofficial capital when the district court was set up there. In September 1786, the first of a series of conventions there among Kentucky's political elite would lead to statehood a half dozen years later. Clark played no role in that progress. He may have wanted to, but early on his nemesis, James Wilkinson, ensured that Kentucky's leaders shut Clark out of the proceedings. Kentucky finally achieved statehood on June 1, 1792.

Kentucky statehood pleased Clark. He certainly marveled at all the changes he had witnessed and helped spur since he first reached Kentucky's heartland in 1774. In just a generation, the population had soared from a couple score of white hunters and surveyors to 73,677 people, of whom 12,430 were slaves. That transformation, however, exacerbated long-standing problems, especially the snarl of conflicting land claims. Elbow room was ever harder to find. Yet for the venturesome, there was still plenty of land beyond Kentucky.

To assuage his own hunger for land, Clark once again eyed the Spanish territory. In 1790, he became an agent for the South Carolina Yazoo Company, one of three enterprises that had staked overlapping claims to vast swaths of the region surrounding the confluence of the Yazoo and Mississippi Rivers. Clark's initial role was to drum up settlers for that colony. Then word arrived that Spanish governor Esteban Miro had rejected the company's application. That did not faze Clark, James O'Fallon, the company's field chief, and the other partners; they were determined to steal what they could not legally take. To that end, by May 1791, Clark was to muster 750 men, descend the Mississippi River, and fortify Walnut Hills, the present site of Vicksburg, Mississippi. Using Mulberry Hill as his headquarters, Clark immersed himself in all the familiar frustrations of organizing a campaign.

James O'Fallon was among that era's more notorious flimflam artists. Indeed, he resembled James Wilkinson in an array of unsavory ways. It was a toss-up over who was more narcissistic, mendacious, loquacious, treacherous, and shrewd. Wilkinson was projecting when he dismissed O'Fallon as "a vain blockhead."[16] Born in Ireland, O'Fallon first fancied becoming a priest until a visit to Rome disabused him of that notion. Instead, he studied medicine at the University of Edinburgh before immigrating to the colonies in 1774. He joined the patriots during the war and served as a doctor, soldier, and pamphleteer. At the war's end, he journeyed to Charleston, South Carolina, where, with his carpetbag figuratively in hand, he was determined to reap a fortune from the postwar chaos. He soon acquired a reputation for shady business deals, though he never faced any formal criminal charges. His mission for the South Carolina Yazoo Company was to circulate through the Ohio and Cumberland valleys in search of more men, money, and material. He got plenty of promises for all three, though little actually materialized after his charm wore off.

Yet it was not O'Fallon's flawed character that doomed the Yazoo plot. Rumors of that pending filibuster expedition led by Clark reached Spain's envoys at Philadelphia, Josef de Jaudenes and Josef de Viar, who lodged a formal protest with the Washington administration. The president declared illegal any such filibuster scheme and warned that any conspirators would be arrested and prosecuted. With the plot blunted, O'Fallon fled to Clark's side at Mulberry Hill.

President Washington's firm stand against the Yazoo plot and other filibuster plots obscured the reality that he, his cabinet, and most Americans hoped eventually and peacefully to acquire adjacent parts of Spain's empire. Secretary of State Thomas Jefferson best articulated that long-term policy when he asserted, "Our citizens have a right to go where they please. I wish a hundred thousand of our inhabitants would accept the invitation." Hard-nosed calculations of American national interests rather than lofty sentiments lay behind that view: "It will be the means of delivering to us peaceably what may otherwise cost us a war."[17] Plots like those of Clark could enhance American power if they were deftly manipulated. Jefferson instructed William Carmichael, America's minister at Madrid, to warn Spain's government that "More than half the territory of the United States is on that [Mississippi] river. Two hundred thousand of our citizens are settled on them, of whom forty thousand bear arms. These have no other outlet for their tobacco, rice, corn, hemp, lumber, house timber, ship timber." Jefferson informed Carmichael that he should free Madrid of any delusion that the United States would not go to war for those western interests to "preserve them in our union."[18]

Although O'Fallon failed to get rich with the Yazoo plot, he emerged from it with something that he appears to have found priceless, at least initially. It was through his scheming with Clark that he met, fell in love with, and wed Frances, affectionately known as Fanny, the baby of the Clark siblings, in February of 1791. Tragically, the honeymoon did not last long. At first, Clark embraced his brother-in-law and within a few years was doting over two nephews, John Julius and Benjamin. But eventually, Fanny fled to her family after O'Fallon abused her. An enraged Clark tracked O'Fallon down and beat him to a bloody pulp with his cane, all the while shouting that he was "a Rogue, Rascal, and Villain."[19]

As Clark's Yazoo scheme emerged, peaked, and collapsed, the latest Indian war erupted and raged in the Ohio valley. That war came despite the best intentions of the national government to prevent it. Congress's policy toward the Indians contained a fatal contradiction—it simultaneously sought both peace and land. George Washington expressed the prevailing view: "The Indians will ever retreat as our Settlements advance upon them and they will ever be ready to sell as we are to buy. That is the cheapest as well the least distressing way of dealing with them."[20]

Buying off Indians was certainly far cheaper than fighting them. Yet two troubling problems haunted that policy. History belied the assumption that the Indians would be willing to sell out. In the past, they had done so only after being defeated in war. Then there was Congress, which, as usual, had no money to buy land, fund an army, or, if need be, fight an Indian war. Nonetheless, it was with visions of peace and justice that Congress designed the Northwest Ordinance, which became law on July 13, 1787. That law would eventually guide the transformation of the Northwest Territory into five states. That process of state building was designed to be increasingly democratic. At first, the territory would be run by a governor and judges appointed by Congress, although the settlers could elect a non-voting representative to Congress. When the population of a region within the Northwest Territory exceeded 50,000, the people could apply for statehood. Other progressive measures included a ban on slavery and the setting aside of land to establish and maintain public schools. The Northwest Ordinance was just as progressive in governing relations with the original inhabitants: "The utmost good faith shall always be observed toward the Indians," and "their lands and property shall never be taken from them without their consent; and in their property, rights, and liberty, they never shall be invaded or disturbed upon, unless in just and lawful wars authorized by Congress; but laws founded in justice and humanity shall from time to time be made for preventing wrongs being done to them, and for preserving peace and friendship with them."

The letter and spirit of the Northwest Ordinance guided Governor Arthur St. Clair and Colonel Josiah Harmar as they desperately tried to keep the peace by negotiating two more treaties with delegations of tribes from across the region at Fort Harmar in December 1788 and January 1789. In return for generous handouts of gifts, those tribes' chiefs simply reconfirmed the previous treaties of Stanwix, McIntosh, and Finney that ceded the territory east and south of a zigzag line along the Cuyahoga River to its headwaters, then west to the Miami River's headwaters, and down it to the Ohio

River. And, once again, most Shawnees and Miamis not only rejected that cession but stepped up their attacks against whites on both sides of the Ohio River.

When asked how he would quell those hostile tribes, Clark fired back a response: "Excell them if possible, in their own policy, treat them with indifference, make war on them, prosecute it with all the vigor and devastation possible, mention nothing of peace to them, and you would soon have them suing for mercy. Turn the scale upon them and oblige them to give up a part of their country to pay for the expense of the war. . . . All other policy in the Indian department except something similar to this, is the result of the want of judgment or information."[21]

Although Clark's plan was eventually implemented, he played no role in the subsequent war and peace.[22] He would be only a distant and frustrated observer. He was enraged first at the incompetence of General Josiah Harmar in October 1790, and then at that of General Arthur St. Clair in November 1791, who led their troops into devastating defeats by the Shawnees and Miamis. Harmar and St. Clair respectively lost over two hundred and nine hundred men. Those debacles resulted not from any one cause but from many. The army was mired in a vicious cycle of ever more deficient money, men, supplies, training, and morale. Underlying all that was criminally inept generalship.

A competent general could break that vicious cycle by systematically and simultaneously confronting and overcoming all those interrelated problems. Great leaders are above all great psychologists. Knowing what motivates men, they manipulate those emotions and drives into an overwhelming force for victory. Success breeds success. Someone with a reputation for victory inspires others to make sacrifices so they can claim a share in his future glories. Politicians are more inclined to scrape up the money vital for underwriting an army's payroll, housing, provisions, munitions, and transport if it is led by a victorious general. Officers lead from the front rather than prod from the rear. Soldiers are more willing to submit to the dictates of their superiors in camp, march, and battle. The enemy is fearful, cautious, and inclined to flight rather than fight. And, once the army marches, the general devises the strategy and tactics necessary to trap and destroy the enemy.

Few matched and none exceeded that art of command more than George Rogers Clark. The devastating defeats of first Harmar then St. Clair fueled growing talk that only Clark was capable of defeating the Indians. Jonathan Clark jubilantly related that shift in public opinion to his brother: "I am told your Kentucky enemies are done yelping. Some of them I understand begin to fondle . . . you." That, in turn, had encouraged Clark's "friends . . . to talk very bold and loud—some begin to inquire how you came to be left in the manner you were on your last expedition, and whether some of those who were at the head of those who came off, were not afraid you would actually and in earnest carry them where there were Indians— and others think you are not an improper person to be sent on the present expedition and I have lately heard that there are those who have become bold enough to say you ought to command it; these things must give you pleasure, after the evils that have been attempted to be done you."[23]

Clark certainly fantasized that the people and government would turn to him as their savior. In September 1791, even before St. Clair's campaign had reached its horrifying climax, Clark confided to his brother Edmund, "I am convinced that they will continue to spend their blood and treasure until myself or some person with similar abilities should undertake to put an end to the horrid Indian war that rages." He vented his frustration again in his reply to Jonathan's letter: "It is a pity that the blood and treasure of the people should be so lavished, when one campaign properly directed, would put an end to the war." Yet Clark knew that, despite Jonathan's optimistic views, his enemies would kill any chance of that happening. His wrath for them remained undiminished: "I stood in the way of the whole of them. I dispise them and pity the publick."[24]

In the end, the glory of victory over the Indians fell on the capable shoulders of General Anthony Wayne. He methodically recruited and trained an army, then led it north to build a chain of forts increasingly closer to the clusters of Indian villages in the upper Wabash and Maumee River valleys. Though his army defeated the Shawnees, Miamis, and contingents from other regional tribes at the battle of Fallen Timbers on August 20, 1794, it took another year before a treaty was negotiated. Under the Treaty of Green- ville signed on August 3, 1795, the Indians accepted a boundary line modi- fied from previous treaties. This line slanted from Fort McIntosh on the Ohio River across Ohio and then, at the present-day Indiana line, sharply cut down to the Ohio River to include a thin slice of southeastern Indiana.

Once again, that Indian cession did not include the 150,000 acres promised by Virginia to Clark and his veterans.

In the summer of 1789, Clark acted on a request that would provide him sporadic relief from an array of torments. He opened a letter from John Brown, Kentucky's representative to Congress, asking a favor initiated by Representative James Madison and supported by their colleagues "that you will favor the World with a Narrative of your campaigns in the Western Country." That memoir would be of practical as well as scholarly value. The Northwest Territory was being opened to settlers and its lands sold to pay off the national debt. But Indian villages and British forts still dotted that land, impeded American settlement, and threatened another frontier war. Clark's observations would be enormously helpful to those military officers and Indian agents responsible for securing the territory. To that end, he was encouraged to be "minute in the details of the Causes & Effects, of Views and Measures, of occurances & transactions during those success-ful campaigns." Should Clark feel inadequate in providing a polished man-uscript, Brown assured the general of Madison's willingness to "carefully attend to the arrangement & style so as to usher it into the world in a Dress suitable to the importance of the subject."[25]

Clark's initial reaction to the letter was typical of how he treated any message from a government official—he cast it aside with red-faced loath-ing. And there the letter sat gathering dust for a month before he reread it, this time with a mind in which curiosity and gratitude had largely diluted battered feelings and false pride. In his reply, Clark explained that to com-ply with that request would mean "destroying a resolution that I have long concluded on, that of burying the rise and progress of the War in this quar-ter in oblivion." He then admitted that reconstructing such a memoir would be tough since the "great part of the most material papers are either lost or made use of as waste paper." Embittered by the ingratitude of the govern-ment and settlers for his sacrifices for them, Clark had "frequently destroyed papers that were of such a nature that the reading of them would cool the spark that still remained, and tend to aggravate the crime of the people." Yet he was confident enough material survived from which to construct "a true narrative." He promised to "immediately set about this business, and as soon as finished, enclose them to you, probably in four or five months." He hoped that the process of writing his memoir would be cathartic, so that "I might again reconcile myself to live in a country that I was always fond of and with people whose prosperity I have, until lately, studied with delight."[26]

The project took longer than Clark anticipated. He wrote to old comrades-in-arms to see if they had any documents, letters, or other writings that they could copy and send him. To his surprise, as Clark progressed his attitude flipped from dread to joy, and regret to confidence: "The more I enter this business, the better I am pleased at the undertaking, and . . . experience the same feeling that actuated me at the time. . . . I believe that through myself every thing past, relative to this country, will be known."[27]

Thomas Jefferson was serving as minister to France when he learned that Clark had agreed to write his memoir. Jefferson brightened in anticipation of that crucial manuscript but grew frustrated when it did not appear. In March 1791, Jefferson asked if it were "not possible . . . to bring Genl. Clark forward?" Clark's accounts "will be valuable morsels of history, and will justify to the world those who have told them how great he was." Although he was well aware of Clark's weaknesses and all the disturbing rumors swirling about him, Jefferson never lost complete faith in the man. He explained, "I know the greatness of his mind, and am the more mortified at the cause which obscures it. Had not this unhappily taken place, there was nothing he might not have hoped: could it be surmounted, his lost ground might yet be recovered. No man alive rated him higher than I did and would again, were he to become again what I knew him."[28]

Jefferson's assessment of Clark, like all others that survive, alludes rather than reveals. Just what was "that cause" that had "unhappily taken place" that stripped him of the power to realize "the greatness of his mind"? It seems to point not to Clark's chronic and worsening state of debt, drunkenness, and ill humor, but to one damning incident. The mystery of what happened will never be revealed. What is certain is that inner demons plagued Clark and prevented him from fulfilling his vast potential. Those demons were deeply rooted in chemistry and unresolved conflicts in his psyche and genes.

Jefferson's letter's recipient was Judge Harry Innes, one of Clark's few remaining friends. Himself an often shrewd appraiser of character, Jefferson quite likely wanted Innes to share that letter with Clark, which is what

Innes did. Two months later, Innes replied with the welcome news that Clark "is writing the History of his Expedition and will complete the work in the course of this summer." He related, "I took the liberty of showing him your letter from a hope that it might cause him to reflect upon his present folly. He was perfectly sober, was agitated by the contents, observed it was friendly, and shed tears."[29]

Unfortunately, Clark was not moved to the point of seeking the wrenching reforms that might have led to his redemption. Nonetheless, at times he could be an entertaining companion. John Pope, who wrote *A Tour through the Western and Southern Territories*, recalled his visit with Clark: "Arrive at his house under an apprehension that he had forgotten me. He immediately recognized me and, without ceremony, entered into a familiar though desultory conversation, in which I was highly pleased with . . . his wit, the genuine offspring of his native genius. On serious and important occasions, he displays a profundity of judgment aided by reflection and matured by experience."[30]

Clark finished his memoir sometime in 1791. An unsolved mystery followed. If he informed those who had urged him to write his memoirs that he had done so, no existing letters allude to that event. Regardless, there was no follow up. None of his backers—Brown, Innes, Madison, or Jefferson—took possession of the manuscript and had it edited for publication. Instead, Clark packed his manuscript away where it rested in obscurity until historian Lyman Draper got his hands on it decades later. Milos Milton Quaife, who followed Draper as head of the Wisconsin Historical Society, edited Clark's memoir and arranged for Lakeside Press of Chicago to publish it in 1920. Quaife's edition is certainly easier reading than the original, with its crude grammar and spelling, but Clark's intelligence, energy, and character animate either version. How accurate is Clark's memoir? Like virtually anyone writing his own life's story, Clark tends to take the lion's share of credit for his triumphs and spread blame for his defeats. Looking back, he tends to ascribe foresight and planning to actions that at the time may have been shaped more by improvisation and luck. Although he consulted as many primary documents as he could get his hands on, there are the inevitable discrepancies in different accounts by participants in the same events. So, like any memoir, Clark's must be read with caution. Nonetheless, his narrative is generally as accurate as it is vividly written.

Writing his memoir provided an emotional anchor within Clark's turbulent mind that let him mull other ideas and embark on other projects. For instance, after having considered the question for a couple of decades, he was now confident enough to enter the debate on the origins of the Indian mounds. He shared his view in a carefully crafted letter to Matthew Cary, who directed the American Museum in Philadelphia. His first step was to establish his credentials among those learned eastern men with their college degrees and contrary views. What elevated Clark above the armchair theorists was field experience: "I don't suppose there is a person living that knows the Geography and Natural History of the Back cuntrey better if so well as I do myself, it hath been my study for many years." He then offered his explanation. Most people assumed that the Indians were too primitive to have constructed such monumental works. Clark disagreed and cited tribal traditions that attributed those mounds to their ancestors. He was far ahead of his time in putting credence in how the Indians saw themselves and their past: "This is their Tradition and I see no good reason why it should not be received as good History, at least as good as [a] great part of ours."[31] Though he changed few minds then, scholars would eventually validate his views.

During the same time that he was writing his memoir, Clark devised a riverboat with a special propulsion system, although animated by human muscle rather than steam. In January 1790, he shared that idea with John Brown, Kentucky's congressional representative. His letter showed that he was still a master of psychology. He designed his opening line at once to preempt any automatic rejection, stimulate curiosity, and celebrate a revolutionary idea by admitting that some might "smile . . . as it may appear to border a little on the marvelous, when I inform you of an invention that will give a new turn to the face of things throughout the western country." He then presented the expertise behind his invention. Years of study had made him the "master of the mechanical powers" that he then applied to a practical problem. The result was "an actual device that could be installed in any sized boat and propel it easily upstream." He "had the machine actually on a small scale and proved every conjecture beyond a doubt. It moves any number of oars you choose to apply, with more regularity and dispatch than men can possibly do." Although Brown encouraged him to submit a formal patent application to Congress, Clark never got around to doing so.[32]

Somehow, the man of a near constant whirl of action in his twenties had in his early thirties metamorphosed into the late eighteenth-century version of a couch potato. He was content to talk rather than act, tinker rather than invent, rant rather than crusade. He admitted as much to his brother Jonathan in 1791. He was leading a peaceful if humdrum existence: "For several years I have lived quite retired reading hunting fishing and fowling hath been my genl amusement and corresponding with a few close friends in different parts of the continent and attention to my private business without concerning myself with that of the Publick, in any point of view."[33] Soon, a painful rejection followed by a chance to revive his faded glory would goad him from his early retirement.

Clark's ambitions suffered a major setback in May 1792. His brother Jonathan reported that Virginia's government had rejected his petition for compensation for his wartime expenses. Although Jonathan promised to appeal that decision, the harsh news provoked Clark's latest rage: "I have given the United States half the territory they possess, and for them to suffer me to remain in poverty, in consequence of it, will not rebound much to their honor thereafter. If I meet with another rebuff I must rest contented with it, be industrious, and look out further for my future bread." That rebuff came in November 1792, when Jonathan admitted that he had "not been able to bring on your memorial, and begin to fear I shall not have it in my power to do anything for you in this assembly."[34]

At some point, Clark's storm abated as he suddenly realized where he just might get his "future bread." From 1789 through 1793, as he had conspired, dabbled in various projects, ranted, drank to excess, and procrastinated writing his memoir, the French Revolution had erupted and surged through several extraordinary stages. That revolution had many related causes. The most pressing was financial. In one of history's more glaring ironies, the French Revolution occurred after the absolute monarchy bankrupted itself aiding the American Revolution. Louis XVI summoned the Estates General, a representative body that had last met in 1614, to convene at Versailles in May 1789 and rubber-stamp tax raises to service France's soaring debt. Thereafter, a series of inept acts by the king and his ministers emboldened liberals in the Estates General and radical mobs in Paris to rebel. On July 14, the mob stormed the Bastille fortress, a symbol of royal oppression and repository for a large arsenal. On July 17, liberals declared a national assembly and began to transform France into a constitutional monarchy. On August 26, the National Assembly issued its Declaration of the Rights of Man and of the Citizen, inspired by America's Declaration of Independence.

So far, the revolution had achieved stunning liberal reforms with relatively little bloodshed. The Marquis de Lafayette and Thomas Paine were among the leaders. But having overthrown the royalist absolutists, the liberals found themselves in a tug-of-war with radicals who demanded the monarchy's abolition. In June 1791, the radicals got the upper hand after the failed attempt of the king and his family to flee into exile. The radicals purged the liberals from power and executed Louis XVI on January 21, 1792. On April 20, 1792, France declared war on Austria. Soon, Prussia and several smaller principalities joined Austria against France. Those who hoped that coalition would crush the revolution suffered a setback with the battle of Valmy, on September 21, 1792, when a French army routed the invaders.

Virtually all Americans had initially acclaimed the French Revolution. They remained grateful for the enormous sacrifices of treasury and blood that France had made for their own revolution and were happy that America's liberal ideals had inspired France's revolution. But informed Americans observed with growing alarm that nation's worsening convulsions, violence, and radicalism. By late 1792, when word of Valmy reached the United States, Americans were split over whether to support or condemn that revolution.

George Rogers Clark was among those who cheered France's revolution and victories. His reasons were practical rather than philosophical or sentimental. He reckoned that sooner or later, republican France would go to war against royalist Spain. And when that happened, with the maxim "the enemy of my enemy is my friend," France would become the ally of every American westerner. If the United States government was too weak in cash, arms, and will to force Spain to open the Mississippi River to free navigation and trade, then westerners would ally with France to those ends.

Clark dreamed of spearheading that alliance of American frontiersmen and French troops to conquer Spain's holdings in the lower Mississippi valley. Clark and James O'Fallon concocted the scheme on Christmas of 1792. O'Fallon wrote up a plan and sent it to his friend Thomas Paine in Paris, who promptly shared it with key leaders. The timing was fortuitous. France's hard-pressed government mulled that offer around the time it declared war against Spain on March 7, 1793. Fighting a war against Spain alone would have been challenging enough, but Paris had declared war earlier that year on February 1 against Britain and the Netherlands, thus pushing those countries into alliance with Austria, Prussia, and a host of smaller realms against France. With nearly all of Europe united against them, the French were in desperate need of allies wherever they could find them. The notion of Clark leading the campaign certainly excited interest. His reputation in faraway Paris was removed from the familiarity that led to contempt among many people closer to home. Most of France's elite still marveled at Clark's feats during the war for independence

Clark received an unofficial, indirect reply to his proposal in the spring of 1793. Paine wrote O'Fallon that the French government had enthusiastically embraced the plan and would soon send Clark a major general's commission and full authorization to mount his campaign. Paine asked to be kept informed "of every intelligence and write often." Clark and his coterie were to work closely with Edmond Genet, who would soon arrive in Philadelphia to serve as France's minister to the United States. Paine described Genet as "my sincere friend and yr. Name is already made known to him by me. . . . The rulers of this Republic hold him in very high estimation."[35]

Clark was eager to get Genet committed to his proposed campaign as soon as he reached Philadelphia. He sent Genet an astonishing letter on February 5, 1793, that deftly played on the ideals, egos, and ambitions of Genet and his fellow revolutionary leaders.[36] Much like an Indian warrior trying to inspire followers for a war party, Clark first recited his litany of war coups: "I took the Illinois & Post St. Vincennes from the Britons, saved St. Louis and the rest of Louisiana for the Spaniards from that nation— humbled the whole Northern & Southern tribes of Indians (those in particular who are now so hostile & triumphant) to the very dust, preserved Kentucky, Cumberland, and the whole territory north of the Ohio to the United States, and protected the western frontier of Virginia & Pennsylvania from British & Indian depredations." In case his reader might imagine otherwise, he insisted, "These are not exaggerations." That done, Clark explained just how he could advance French national interests. He noted that the "contest" pitting the French Republic "against almost all the Despots of Europe is among the most awful, interesting, and solemn, in all its consequences, that has ever arisen in the world. . . . The whole human race are deeply interested." To that great cause, he was now devoting himself. His contribution would be to inflict a mighty blow against Spain by conquering "the whole of Louisiana for France—If further aided, I would capture Pensacola." For that, "All we immediately want is money to procure provisions and ammunition for the conquest of St. Louis or upper Louisiana." After that step, Clark insisted, the conquest "would pay for itself."

There was one essential delicate diplomatic issue, the maintenance of America's then unofficial but soon declared neutrality. Clark explained, "To save congress from a rupture with Spain on our account, we must first expatriate our selves and become French citizens. This is our intention." But for Clark, that switch in allegiance was no mere marriage of convenience. He was embittered that "my country has proved notoriously ungrateful for my Services . . . [and] this in my very prime of life, to have neglected me. . . . On receiving a reply of approbation from you, I shall instantly have myself expatriated. . . . I thirst for the opportunity."

Clark's willingness to renounce his loyalty to the land of his birth and swear an oath to another country, alien in language and culture, may surprise many people today. It is hard for most contemporary Americans to understand that the identity of most Americans then was primarily rooted in their state or region rather than their nation. And Clark was alienated from both Virginia and the United States. He no longer felt loyal to a state and nation that he felt had grossly betrayed him.

Edmond Genet created quite a stir when he stepped ashore at Charleston, South Carolina, on April 9, 1793. He had been heading to Philadelphia, but his ship was blown off course. That turned out to be a blessing for his mission, at least in the short run. His exuberant personality and worldliness won over the local elite. Soon, Genet and the French counsel, Michel-Ange de Mangourit, were signing letters of marque to commission privateers against British and Spanish shipping, and drumming up recruits for a filibuster expedition against East Florida. Genet then proceeded by carriage to Philadelphia, where he would replace Jean-Baptiste Ternant as France's minister to the United States. That twenty-eight-day journey was a triumphant parade for both those who fervently supported the French Revolution and those who just wanted a bit of novelty to briefly illuminate their monotonous lives. All that adulation irreparably inebriated Genet, and he would commit follies that got himself and many others, including Clark, in hot water.

Meanwhile, George Washington and his administration had been debating American policy toward revolutionary France and the war raging across much of Europe. The cabinet, like the country, was split between the Federalists led by Treasury Secretary Alexander Hamilton, who favored neutrality, and the Republicans led by Secretary of State Thomas Jefferson, who advocated helping France by all measures short of war. Hamilton's arguments prevailed. On April 22, 1793, President Washington issued a proclamation of American neutrality.

Genet shrugged off Washington's proclamation. After reaching Philadelphia on May 6, he devoted himself to reversing that policy by every possible means. As he had in Charleston, he organized privateering expeditions in defiant violation of American neutrality. If that move was not provocative enough, Genet threw his support behind one American political party against the other. The French Revolution exacerbated the already-bitter differences between Federalists and Republicans. While Republicans embraced the French Revolution's ideals, Federalists were horrified at its worsening carnage. To advance his plans, Genet embraced the Republicans against the Federalists. In July 1793, he and leading Republicans in Philadelphia formed a Democratic Society, inspired in style and substance by the radical Jacobin Clubs of France. They fired off letters to Republican leaders across the country, explaining their new organization and encouraging those local leaders to establish their own branches. Their hope was to form a grassroots, nationwide political party that would undermine and eventually supplant Federalist rule.

By the summer's end, Democratic Societies had sprouted in a score of towns across the United States, including Lexington, Paris, and Georgetown in Kentucky. Members of Kentucky's clubs included such leaders of government and society as Kentucky Secretary of State James Brown (Senator John Brown's brother), Attorney General John Breckinridge, and *Kentucky Gazette* Editor John Bradford. The enthusiasm among Kentuckians for the Democratic Societies was fueled more by a hatred of Spain than by a love of France's revolution. Spain's closure of the Mississippi River strangled the Ohio valley's economic dynamism and potential. Prominent westerners were loudly calling for the federal government to open that river by any means possible, including war if need be. A convention of Kentuckians met at Lexington in May 1793 and sent a thirteen-clause petition to the federal government for relief of various problems. Among their demands was that "Spain should be compelled immediately to acknowledge our right or that an end be put to all negotiations on that subject." A petition called on George Washington to determine "of the Spanish King whether he will acknowledge the right of citizens of the United States, to the free and uninterrupted navigation of the river Mississippi."[37] The Washington administration's inability to do so provoked an angry reaction among westerners.

Genet dispatched five agents to Kentucky to rally those western sentiments into an army that Clark would lead against the Spanish empire. Heading that team was Andre Michaux, an acclaimed botanist. Botany was certainly an excellent espionage cover, given its excuses for observation and interviews with locals. But Michaux had other qualities that made him a good case officer including an easy ability to befriend, size up, and manipulate others. The only flaw with Michaux's mission was that it was anything but secret. Genet and his agents spoke frankly of their intentions. That at once encouraged sympathizers to open their doors and wallets to the cause and prompted the Washington administration to do what it could to thwart it.

Michaux embarked on his "botanical" mission with letters of introduction from both Genet and Jefferson to Governor Isaac Shelby, George Rogers Clark, and other leading Kentuckians, most of whom were Democratic Society members.[38] The roles of Clark and Shelby complemented each other. Shelby, who had been a brilliant frontier leader during the war and had risen high in the Kentucky branch of Jefferson's budding Republican Party, would rally men and money for Clark, while providing political cover.

Clark welcomed Michaux to Mulberry Hill on September 17. At some point during what was surely an intense discussion, Michaux presented Clark his commission as a "major general of the Independent and Revolutionary Legion of the Mississippi," along with blank officers' commissions for him to fill out, sign, and present to those worthy of the rank. Clark must have received the title and commissions with mixed emotions. Without the coin to back them up, they would be nothing more than fancy pieces of paper. Money was the bottom line of any enterprise, especially a military campaign. With Clark's encouragement, Michaux and the four other agents spent considerable time in Lexington and other Kentucky towns trying to drum up investors.[39] More Kentuckians gleefully joined the plot. Yet as they pooled their resources and boasted of all the adventures and riches that lay westward, far beyond the eastern horizon, the federal government was mobilizing forces that would throttle that campaign in its cradle.

Within the Washington administration, the plot's most prominent and secret American supporter had reluctantly switched sides. Thomas Jefferson had initially embraced Genet's efforts as a way at once to bolster the French Revolution and undermine the British empire and other monarchies. But Genet's defiance of common political sense and American law had gotten so outrageous that he finally alienated his greatest supporter. Jefferson explained to James Madison, "I saw the necessity of quitting a wreck which could not but sink all who would cling to it."[40] The far less politically savvy Clark would go down with the ship.

Jefferson told Genet, "Enticing officers and soldiers from Kentucky to go against Spain was really putting a halter about their necks, for they would assuredly be hung, if the commd. Hostilities agt. a nation at peace with the U.S." He then added, "Except for that I did not care what insurrections should be excited in Louisiana."[41] Genet interpreted that as a wink and a nod rather than condemnation. The fervor and pace of his efforts did not slacken.

Rumors of Clark's expedition reached the ears of Josef de Jaudenes and Josef de Viar, Spain's envoys to the United States. In August, they raised with Jefferson their expectation that the Washington administration would be good to its word and prevent American citizens "from sharing in any hostilities by land or sea against the subjects of Spain or its dominions."[42] Jefferson could only assure them that the Washington administration remained committed to its neutrality policy.

Although rumors of Clark's plot had circulated for months, it was not until August 1793 that the president amassed enough hard intelligence to become genuinely alarmed. Washington convened his cabinet, presented the evidence, and asked members' advice on how to respond. A consensus swiftly formed that the administration had to mobilize all appropriate authorities to thwart that plot. It fell to Jefferson to convey that policy to Governor Shelby: "I have it . . . in charge from the President to desire you to . . . take those legal measures . . . necessary to prevent any such enterprise."[43] A follow-up letter from Arthur St. Clair, the Northwest Territory's governor, was more explicit about the plot that Shelby was asked to thwart: "General Clark has received a commission from the government of France, and is about to raise a body of men in Kentucky to attack the Spanish settlements upon the Mississippi." St. Clair issued a proclamation at Marietta, Ohio, on December 7, 1793, that required the region's inhabitants "to observe a strict neutrality towards Spain" Anyone informed with a campaign against Spain would be "prosecuted and punished with the utmost rigor of the law."[44]

As one of the plot's ringleaders, Shelby obviously was not surprised at the allegations. He was being asked to stop a campaign that he was helping to lead, a conflict of interest if there ever was one. In a carefully crafted reply, Shelby grounded his refusal to act in the highest constitutional principles and rights: "If it is lawful for any one citizen of the state to leave it, it is equally so for any number of them to do it. It is also lawful for them to carry with them any quantity of provisions, arms and ammunition; and if the act is lawful in itself, there is nothing but the particular intentions with which it is done that can possibly make it unlawful; but I know of no law which inflicts a punishment on intention." He made no secret of which side he supported. He was firmly against the Spanish king "who openly withholds from us an invaluable right and who secretly instigates against us a most savage and cruel enemy."[45] Thus did Shelby explain that he was bound by the Constitution not to act unless Clark broke the law. Until then, Clark and his followers could freely exercise their rights of assembly, speech, and press. Meanwhile, the Democratic Society of Lexington, chaired by John Breckinridge, defiantly issued a proclamation on December 13, 1793, that condemned Spain for closing the Mississippi and repressing its population, and called on all patriots to aid any efforts to join any campaign that would liberate those waters and peoples.

The Washington administration's warning that anyone involved in a filibuster against Spain would be prosecuted did not intimidate Clark. So far he had done nothing beyond talking up the campaign to his close friends. Then came the Democratic Society's endorsement followed by the publication of Shelby's rejection of the official requests to suppress his plan. After that, he threw all his still formidable energies into turning his latest dream into a reality. Here was perhaps his last chance to redeem himself in the eyes of the world and his own tormented mind. He made that intention

clear in a letter to Genet, in which he declared, "I will surmount every obstacle and pave my way to Glory, which is my object."[46]

Clark's first step was to get his old comrades-in-arms to help him organize and lead the campaign. Among the first to enlist were Colonels Benjamin Logan and John Montgomery. Logan wrote, "I have once more offered
my feeble aid knowing you are honoured with a commission from the Minister of France and is to be at the head of the business undertaken." Montgomery was just as eager to follow Clark: "I had the honor of converging
with you . . . on the subject—whereas I expressed a willingness to embark
into the business with you and was happy enough to have your promise of
favour. . . . I have collected the sentiments of a number of the principal inhabitants of this country . . . and find that it will be in my power to raise
Several Hundred . . . in a very short period of time. . . . There are several
old Veteran Officers residing in my part of the country that are very willing
to serve in your command under me."[47]

The next step was far tougher. Somehow, Clark had to fill the ranks
with hundreds of recruits. He had lost none of his mastery of psychology in
knowing how to appeal to the spectrum of possible motives a man might
harbor to set aside his family and livelihood and march off for all the depri-
vations, drudgery, and dangers of war. Yet now the challenge was greater
because the nation was at peace and the proposed act was illegal. He could
certainly tap the regional outrage provoked by Spain's closing of the Mississippi River. Atop that was the classic pitch to young men, bursting with
hormone-fueled excitement for adventures of all kinds.

Clark openly advertised for recruits in newspapers like the *Kentucky Gazette* and *Cincinnati Centinel of the Northwest Territory*. In February 1794, he
bought space in the *Gazette*, in which he declared himself as a "Major General in the armies of France, and Commander in Chief of the French Revolutionary Legions on the Mississippi River." He then called for volunteers to
join him in "the reduction of the Spanish posts on the Mississippi, for opening trade of the said river, & giving freedom to all its inhabitants." Each
recruit would be entitled either to a dollar a day or one thousand acres of
acres of land for each of up to three years they served. And then there was
the promise that all "lawful plunder" would "be equally divided agreeable
to the custom of War."[48]

Leaders and followers, of course, were not enough. They had to be paid, armed, fed, and transported. And all that was extremely expensive. Michaux and his agents had little money to spare. Once again, Clark had to dig deep into his own pocket and rely on his credit to underwrite his campaign. He scrapped up $4,680 by selling off some of his land claims and borrowing money with the promise that the campaign would reap a fortune in spoils. With that, he began amassing provisions and munitions.

Although Governor Shelby and most Kentuckians would stymie any federal efforts to thwart his preparations, Clark was still careful not to be too provocative. He explained to Genet, "I must be very circumspect while in this country and guard against doing anything that would injure the United States or giving offense to their Govt but in a few days after seting sail we shall be out of their Government I shall then be at liberty to give full scope to the authority of the Commission you did me the Homour to send."[49]

The only easy part of a campaign for Clark was planning its strategy. Clark's first target would be New Madrid on the Mississippi River close to the Ohio River mouth. Capturing that town would sever upper Louisiana's communications with New Orleans. He would then point his men north to take first Saint Genevieve, then Saint Louis. After securing that region, he and his men would descend the Mississippi to conquer the lower Mississippi valley.

After that, Clark intended to rest on his laurels. His retirement plans included exile from his native land—he "would sail to France after the expedition."[50] In that, Clark would not be alone. At least one of his cabal would join him. Federal policies had so enraged Benjamin Logan that he had "taken my leave of appointments in this state or the United States and do presume that I am at liberty to go to any foreign country I please and intend to do so."[51] It is amusing to imagine how those hardened frontiersmen would have fared in a world as alien as revolutionary Paris. The language barrier would have been formidable enough. But as bewildering would have been all the intricacies of French culture and trying to exist within a densely populated, poverty-stricken, volatile city like Paris.

But a glorious retirement in France, like the rest of the elaborate plot, proved to be nothing more than a dream. By the spring of 1794, Clark was forced to shelve the plan. On March 6, 1794, Jean Antoine Joseph Fauchet, who had replaced Genet as minister, publicly declared that France would not support any filibusters against Spain and was revoking any commissions that had been issued to that end. President Washington then pronounced on

March 24 a sweeping declaration that identified and condemned the armed force organized for "invading and plundering the territory of a nation at peace with the United States." He ordered General Anthony Wayne to "establish a strong military post at Fort Massac on the Ohio, and prevent by force, if necessary, the descent of any hostile party down that river."[52]

After learning of Fauchet's decree but before hearing of Washington's, Clark fired off a desperate letter to Genet. Clark was ready to launch his campaign, having "Set eavery wheele in motion in This Quarter . . . and upwards of two thousand men have been waiting with impatience to penetrate into that Country." Then came word of Fauchet's decree "which hath inflamd the minds of a great number of people." Clark begged Genet to "use eavry means in your power to have the expenses we have been at Refunded." Otherwise, the loss of those who had financially backed the campaign would be "Suffisiant to Rune me, and hurt many others."[53] The only thing Genet was now capable of saving was his own life. The revolutionary regime had sternly recalled him to Paris, most likely to face a guillotine's blade. When Genet asked for asylum, President Washington graciously extended it to the man who had been a painful political thorn in his side ever since he had arrived in the United States.

Fauchet's official cancellation at once financially ruined Clark and let him off a moral hook. The French Revolution was self-destructing with the Terror. From September 1793 through July 1794, the radical Jacobins formed a dictatorship and murdered thousands of people in the name of revolutionary purity and power. Clark was well aware of the Jacobin's mass atrocities. In addition to newspaper accounts, he received a letter from Andre Michaux describing those horrors. Though Clark undoubtedly seethed with impatience, it was a good time to lie low.[54]

Eventually, the moderates overthrew the Jacobins and sent their leaders to the guillotine. Clark learned of the revolution's latest twist in a November 1794 letter from Samuel Fulton, one of his most trusted coconspirators: "Thare has [been] a verry great Change in the affares of the nation For the better Since the execution of Roberspiere and his party, the Gulletines have Dissappeard and a greater Degree of tranquility prevailing over the nation than Has been since the revolution." With Clark's go-ahead, Fulton would sail to France and lobby the government to "Renew the expedition."[55] Clark promptly dispatched Fulton with a letter for France's new rulers. To them, he explained that "the peculiar situation of Kentucky is such that their only natural door to Foreign Commerce is the Mississippi, they despair of ever getting it opened through the mediation of the present American ministry." He promised that he could raise "men in great numbers" that are "ready to come forward when called for."[56]

What Fulton found in Paris appeared promising. In February 1795, he wrote Clark that "the full navigation of the Mississippi will be obtained either by Sword or by Treaty, but I believe by the former. . . . If the Expedition be renewed I shall amediately Set out for Kentucky."[57] But frustration soon trampled that initial hope. No money or agents arrived at Clarksville from Paris. Clark did eventually receive another French general's commission, issued on May 26, 1797, but the latest demoted him from a major to brigadier general. Regardless, he viewed the commission as nothing more than an empty honor.

The lack of French support was just as well. Earlier that year in April, Clark had missed a chance to repolish his military credentials with the French. Pierre Auguste Adet, France's minister to the United States, had dispatched General Henri Victor Collot on an intelligence mission to the Ohio and Mississippi valleys. Collot called on Clark at Louisville but hurried on when he found that once-great warrior in "a drunken stupor."[58]

The final nails in the coffin of Clark's plan were driven in 1795 and 1796. On July 22, 1795, France and Spain signed a peace treaty. Upon learning of the truce, Clark angrily wrote the French government that had they not replaced Genet, "those cuntries [Louisiana and the Floridas] would have long since been in possession of the Republick."[59] On August 5, 1796, France and Spain became formal allies. All that, of course, should have killed Clark's scheme of spearheading a French-backed expedition against Spain's Mississippi valley empire. But the most powerful blow to those westerners who sought to conquer Louisiana occurred on April 26, 1796, when the United States and Spain exchanged ratifications of the Treaty of San Lorenzo. The deal that Thomas Pinckney had signed on October 24, 1795, let Americans navigate the Mississippi River in Spanish territory and deposit goods at New Orleans for three years; Americans could continue to deposit goods at New Orleans after three years if no other place was mutually acceptable. The boundary between the United States and West Florida ran along the 31st parallel between the Mississippi and Perdido Rivers.

All that effectively rendered moot the concrete complaints of westerners against the governments of Spain and the United States. But Clark and his coterie would not let that reality dissolve their obsession. Their rage persisted void of all reason. Then other events made that obsession not just Quixotic but downright treasonous.

Ever since war had erupted in Europe in April 1792, the United States had struggled to stay neutral and enrich itself by trading with all sides. But that was increasingly difficult as the two greatest and now enemy naval powers, Britain and France, ordered their warships to seize neutral vessels sailing to the other's ports. Hundreds of American merchant ships and their cargos were confiscated, and their crews imprisoned. British captures of American ships lessened somewhat after John Jay negotiated a treaty with the British on November 19, 1794, and the Senate ratified it on June 24, 1795. But the French interpreted Jay's Treaty as forming an alliance between the United States and Britain. That excuse and their need to gather any supplies from any sources, led the French government, now known as the Directory, to decree an all-out war on neutral shipping on July 2, 1796.

In hope of negotiating a treaty with France, President John Adams sent John Marshall, Elbridge Gerry, and Charles Pinckney to Paris. But foreign minister Charles Maurice de Talleyrand-Perigord refused to negotiate unless he and his underlings received a huge bribe. The indignant Americans reported Talleyrand's attempted shakedown, which became publicly known as the XYZ Affair for the letters that were substituted for the would-be bribers' names. The subsequent public outrage, French refusal to talk, and continued confiscations presented Adams with only one realistic option. On March 19, 1797, he made the first of a series of requests to Congress for a massive naval buildup and the dispatch of frigates to protect American merchants and attack any predators. Because the president did not directly ask Congress for a war declaration and the fighting was confined to the sea, the subsequent naval hostilities with France became known as the Quasi-War.

Even then, Clark clung to his dream despite the overwhelming evidence that it was nothing more than a chimera. In June 1798, he instructed Fulton "to assure the Directory of my inalterable attachment to the cause of France . . . and I eagerly await . . . instruction." He bitterly complained that he had supported France for five years without receiving a penny of compensation.[60] What primarily kept that flickering vision alive was Clark's need to redeem himself, bolstered by friends like Samuel Fulton or John Brown who continued to act as if the plan remained viable. And then there were others outside Clark's coterie that took his plan seriously. In 1797, Canada's governor general offered to underwrite Clark's assault on Spain's North American empire. To that, Clark "refused, for you know that I detest despots in general, and the English in particular."[61]

Clark's lobbying for a filibuster expedition attracted attention not only in Paris but also in Philadelphia, the nation's capital. Clark was in Philadelphia in the summer of 1798, and the timing could not have been worse. The United States was at war with the country with which Clark had not only conspired but pledged allegiance.

It was subversives like Clark who inspired President Adams to get Congress to pass the Alien and Sedition Acts. The Alien and Naturalization Act of June 18 and the Alien Enemy Act of July 6, 1798, collectively empowered federal officials to arrest and expel any foreigners who threatened national security and extended the time for foreigners to become citizens from five to fourteen years. The Sedition Act of July 14, 1798, empowered federal officials to arrest not just anyone "suspected of treasonable and secret inclinations," but even those critical of those in power. The Sedition Act was the most blatant attempt to throttle the rights of freedom of the press, speech, and assembly before the McCarthy era.

The Adams administration viewed George Rogers Clark as a clear and present danger to the nation's security and wielded the Sedition Act's full powers to eliminate that threat. Clark was stunned to receive from the federal government a stark, uncompromising choice—either he could give his "resignation to the counsel general of France or . . . retire from the United States."[62] Angrily swearing to pursue the latter, Clark hurried from Philadelphia to Louisville. He wrote John Brown that he intended to accept the Spanish government's offer of exile in Saint Louis "for a friend and ally of France." There, he would "cooperate with the commandant . . . to thwart all hostile attempts that our common enemy can make against the Spanish establishments on the Mississippi River."[63] That was an extraordinary flip-flop from all his years of scheming to conquer that very realm!

So far those were just desperate sentiments. But a nasty surprise awaited him at Louisville: "The president of the United States gave an order to have me arrested. But the detachment he sent to take me was attacked and disarmed by a certain number of men, volunteers, that my old comrades could assemble."[64] That intervention only bought Clark crucial time. Once the federal authorities learned that their initial arresting force was rebuffed, they would most likely send a far larger one.

Clark hastily gathered some belongings and fled to Saint Louis, ironically among the first places he intended to capture in his conquest of the Spanish territory. Indeed, he now had the excuse to conduct a full reconnaissance of that still potential target. In an intelligence report to Paris, he had, after "carefully observing the means of defense, and number of inhabitants and troops, of Upper Louisiana," concluded that "this country has no means of resisting an invasion. Neither the soldiers nor inhabitants are attached to Spain. In case of a rupture with the United States, Louisiana must be easy prey." He encouraged France to take over Louisiana and entice the Americans west of the Appalachian Mountains, presumably with offers of free trade and navigation on the Mississippi River. If so, Clark predicted that those westerners "would end their attachment to the federal government" and join the French empire. He urged the French government to act fast. Otherwise, "within nine or more months this country will be conquered by the United States or England." He ended his letter with a bitter note: "In submitting these remarks to the Directory, I would like you to explain to them that for five years I have received nothing, and that I am obliged to make continual sacrifices."[65] In all, Clark's conspiracy foreshadowed Aaron Burr's far more advanced and dangerous version a decade later. Like Burr, while Clark evaded conviction for treason, his reputation would never recover.[66]

The Adams administration's blatant violations of the Constitution provoked a political backlash against not just the Alien and Sedition Acts but also the Federalist Party that would bring Thomas Jefferson and the Republican Party to power in 1801. Jefferson and James Madison spearheaded the assault against those laws. They respectively ghostwrote the radical Virginia and Kentucky Resolutions of November 13 and December 24, 1799, in which they declared the Constitution nothing more than a compact among sovereign states that could nullify any federal laws or even secede if they wished. That move pressured Adams to back off on his political purge.

Adams's restraint came as an enormous relief to Clark and countless other "suspects." It was now unlikely that they would join the ranks of the score or so already arrested and convicted under the Sedition Act. That might have been the time for Clark to return from exile. But long before that, he had quietly slipped back into the United States and joined his family at Mulberry Hill. Tragic personal news rather than defiance of the government had brought him home.

CHAPTER 20

Final Reckonings

I have given the United States half the territory they possess, and for them to suffer me to remain in poverty, the consequences of it, will not rebound much to their honor.

George Rogers Clark

The father of the Western Country is no more!

Judge John Rowan

C lark's exile in Saint Louis was brief. He likely returned to Louisville in the spring of 1799. It was a sorrow-filled homecoming. Clark's mother had passed away on December 24, 1798. He was with his father when he died on July 29, 1799.

The family patriarch had amassed quite an estate during his lifetime and distributed it generously after his death. Each son or son-in-law except George Rogers received at least a thousand acres of land in Kentucky, Virginia, Indiana, or Ohio. In addition, twenty-three slaves were distributed among the siblings. To William, he left Mulberry Hill, its surrounding acres, slaves, including York—who had been William's childhood playmate and who would later travel with him on his expedition to the Pacific Ocean—and the Indiana lands that George Rogers had put in his name.

Well aware of all the creditors lined up to snatch whatever wealth they could from George Rogers, his father left him only four slaves.[1]

The youngest son, William, inherited the most for two reason—he was the most dutiful of the boys and had dedicated himself to managing the family's business affairs.[2] Indeed, George Rogers became ever closer and more reliant on William, who had resigned from the army in July 1796, after a four-year stint in which he rose to lieutenant. For the next seven years, the brothers worked together on various business schemes. William became Clark's front man, staving and occasionally paying off creditors and lawsuits and swapping land claims, crops, merchandise, and slaves in pursuit of usually elusive profits. To those ends, he embarked on numerous journeys throughout the Ohio and Mississippi River valleys, and back east to Philadelphia, Richmond, and Washington.[3] Atop those onerous burdens was the added psychic weight of weathering Clark's drunken binges and venomous rants. Yet William endured, bound by genuine affection, familial duty, and awe at his older brother's military exploits. Awe is among the more powerful social cements. Living in a legend's shadow can be addicting and, like all addictions, degrading.

William certainly had little to brag about in measuring his military service to that of his older brother. Though he was mustered to serve in two militia campaigns against the Indians north of the Ohio in 1789 and 1791, he apparently did not come under fire. He then received a commission in the regular army in which he chiefly acted as a recruiting and logistics officer. The highlight of his early army career was serving under General Anthony Wayne during the campaign against the Indians that culminated with the battle of Fallen Timbers on August 20, 1794. Ironically, as an officer he fell under the charismatic spell of General James Wilkinson, who had secretly spearheaded the character assassination of his older brother. The most notable event during William's four years in the army would not be apparent until July 1803. In May 1795, he met and became close friends with ensign Meriwether Lewis, who was four years his junior.

Though diminished, the surviving Clark siblings reunited in July 1802, when Jonathan and his family arrived and began building a home at Trough Spring, just east of Mulberry Hill. Everyone now lived in close proximity. Fanny had a home in Louisville. Ann lived on a farm on Harrod's Creek. William and Edmund lived at Mulberry Hill. Eight miles east of Louisville, Lucy and William Croghan lived in a brick version of Mulberry Hill that they dubbed Locust Grove; Clark would spend his last nine years there.

That tight cluster of family homesteads loosened a bit in early 1803. William joined George Rogers at Clarksville in an attempt to help him breathe life into that village and namesake. To finance their venture, William sold Mulberry Hill to Jonathan and his mill to Edmund. The brothers had their slaves build a cabin for them at Point of Rocks, later called Clark's Point, on Clarksville's outskirts, just below the Falls of the Ohio. It was a beautiful and soothing setting overlooking the churning white water and the steadily expanding town of Louisville at the head of the Falls.

Clark kept up a sporadic correspondence with Jefferson. In 1802, he informed his old mentor that he had "long since laid aside all Idea of Public affairs by bad fortune and ill health. I have become incapable of persuing those enterprising & active persuites which I have been fond of from my youth." Instead, he was passing the torch for potential great achievements to his youngest brother William, who was "well qualified for any business." He asked the president to "confer on him any post of Honor and profit" which would be of "Service to your administration."[4] Jefferson would soon find a very special duty for William Clark.

William Clark's role in life took a stunning turn when he opened a letter dated July 17, 1803, from Meriwether Lewis asking him to join an expedition authorized by President Jefferson for "exploreing the interior of the continent of North America." William leapt at the opportunity. The following day he wrote a letter to Lewis gratefully accepting the offer.[5] That exciting news must have stirred Clark's memory of Jefferson's request for him to lead just such an expedition twenty years earlier. What bittersweet feelings must have surged through Clark as he mulled how different his life would have been had he embarked on that adventure.

The Lewis and Clark Corps of Discovery Expedition began literally before his eyes. On October 15, 1803, Lewis and his crew ground their keelboat to shore at the Louisville landing, where his old friend William awaited his arrival. It is possible that George Rogers was with William that day. If not, he first met Lewis the next day after the expedition shot the Falls and tied up at Clarksville. The brothers likely had slaves bring food and libations to the men as they set up camp. One can imagine Clark strolling through the camp or leaning on his cane as he chatted with the soldiers sprawled around their fires. Later, Lewis and the Clark brothers most likely retired to the cabin where their animated talk over cups of whiskey stretched late into the night. At dawn as the crew pushed the keelboat off for the main current, did Clark's eyes well with tears as he waved and watched intently as his kid brother and Lewis disappeared downriver into history?

Throughout his epic journey, thoughts of his family and bouts of home-sickness tugged at William Clark. The expedition passed its second winter at the Mandan village near where the middle Missouri River's eastward flow angles sharply southeast. In April 1805, Clark, Lewis, thirty-two men, and one Indian woman and her child headed upstream in pirogues while a score of men poled the keelboat down the Missouri. The keelboat's cargo included wooden boxes carefully packed with artifacts collected over their grueling journey upriver. Most of those boxes were bound for President Jefferson at Washington City, but en route in June 1805 three would be diverted to the Clark family at Louisville. Imagine the Clark family's excite-ment as they pried open those boxes and passed around a white buffalo robe, antelope and big horn sheep horns, a stuffed prairie dog, a Mandan woman's dress and moccasins, and other marvels.[6] They would not hear again from William until October 1806.

The Clarks were among the first people east of Saint Louis to learn of the expedition's triumphant return. William penned them a long account of their journey on September 23, 1806, not long after arriving at Saint Louis. He ended his letter with the promise "I Shall shortly be with you."[7] He soon kept that promise. After discharging most of their men and repacking their artifacts, Clark, Lewis, and a few men headed east. The joyful reunion be-tween William and his family took place at the home of Lucy and William Croghan at Locust Grove on November 8, 1806. In Washington City, Presi-dent Jefferson was among countless other people who eagerly awaited the return of the intrepid explorers. Lewis left with the main party a couple of days later, but William stayed until mid-December.

The expedition's whirlwind visit briefly infused Clark with excitement. Quite likely those feelings dissipated just as quickly, and Clark was left to fume in his own straight-jacketed life. How did George Rogers Clark fill the empty time of his remaining years? It seems that his most unsullied joy was reading. By the time of his death, he had amassed a library of several score books. He still liked toying with notions in his mind. His most ambitious project was to build a mile-and-a-half canal around the Falls of the Ohio. He rounded up some partners to form a company and buy a strip of land for the canal. But the project eventually died because they could muster only a fraction of the estimated $150,000 cost. Had that project been realized, it would have at once enriched its investors and the region.[8] Try as he might, Clark could not develop his hamlet. Clarksville competed for business and settlers with Jeffersonville two miles upstream at the top of the Falls.

Clark petitioned Congress for a land grant in 1805. He crafted his pitch to provoke the lawmakers' admiration for his accomplishments and sacrifices, and pity for the depths to which he had fallen. He began by explaining that his petition was a last resort. He had not submitted one years earlier for two reasons. He did not want to divert Congress's time from more pressing concerns, and his financial prospects then appeared to make a government land grant unnecessary. But now, he explained, "those prospects are vanished." He recalled, "I engaged in the Revolution with all the Ardour that Youth could possess. My Zeal and Ambition rose with my success . . . at the hazard of my life and fortune. At the most gloomy period of the War, when a Ration could not be purchased on Public Credit I . . . gave my Bonds, Mortgaged my Lands for supplies, Paid strict attention to every department, flattered the friendly and confused the hostile tribes . . . baffled my internal enemies (the most dangerous of the whole to Public interests), and carried my Point. Thus at the end of the War I had the pleasure of seeing my Country Secure." But then the bill came due, and he faced "a prospect of future indigence . . . for the payment of those debts," the result of which was "a shattered fortune." He concluded, "I see no other resource remaining, but to make application to my Country for redress."[9]Although Clark got Kentucky Senator John Breckinridge to spearhead his petition, the Committee on Public Lands rejected it.

That latest rejection accelerated Clark's decline. He drew deeper into himself. His once irrepressible energy and boisterous camaraderie withered. He penned fewer letters and eventually stopped writing one once close friend after another. Samuel Fulton complained that over "eighteen months I have written you near twenty letters . . . without being able to obtain a single answer."[10] In company, he was increasingly tight-mouthed, ill-tempered, and inebriated. He frequently vented his spleen at having sacrificed so much and being rewarded so little from his country.

William was in Louisville and Clarksville in the late summer of 1807 and lingered until early 1808, when he departed for Virginia and his bride-to-be, Julia Hancock. During his sojourn, he struggled to sell off his lots and bring some order to his older brother's affairs. The highlight was an excursion upriver to Big Bone Lick, where the brothers excavated mastodon bones for Jefferson. Tension marred the thrill of discovery. William wrote Jonathan that brother George Rogers was again drinking to excess and "has given me Some uneaseness but he appears to be more thoughtful to-day." His wayward brother was often in William's thoughts even as he immersed himself in his duties as a husband, father, and Indian superintendent at Saint Louis. He mentioned to Jonathan that he had sold off some of his Clarksville lots to "leave a little money" in George Rogers's "hands to purchase a little Coffee & Sugar," and intended to continue serving as one of Clarksville's trustees. He would periodically pay off back taxes that he or Clark owed on his various properties that were mostly undeveloped. The brothers preferred to sell off that land, but there were no takers. During a trip back east in 1810, William unsuccessfully lobbied in both Washington and Richmond for a pension for his brother.[11]

If Clark was now but a shadow of his former heroic self, he was still a celebrity, however notorious. Curiosity seekers showed up at his doorstep to shake hands, take advantage of his hospitality, and then carry away anecdotes that may or may not have reflected the prejudices or hopes with which they arrived. Not just the morbidly curious showed up at Clarksville and from June 1809 at Locust Grove. Some were or would-be celebrities in their own right. Naturalists like John Audubon, Alexander Wilson, and Andre Michaux, and the historian Henry Rowe Schoolcraft sought out Clark for his insights into their fields.

At times, fleeting moments of lucidity and charisma broke through the drunken self-pity. Josiah Espy, who was traveling through the region in 1805, described Clark as "frail and rather helpless, but there are the remains of great dignity and manliness in his countenance, person, and deportment." Espy related a melancholy glimpse of "seeing this celebrated warrior at his lonely cottage seated on Clark's Point. This point is situated at the . . . end of the Falls . . . commanding a full and delightful view. . . . The general has not taken much pains to improve . . . this beautiful spot, but it is capable of being made one of the handsomest seats in the world."[12]

Pleasant company with George Rogers Clark was increasingly rare during the last decade or so of his life. He could spend hours sullenly nursing his grievances until something sparked an eruption into red-faced curses. The related effects of excessive drinking, ill health, and sloth had prematurely aged him and transformed his once-muscular body to corpulence. William admitted sorrowfully that his brother "has given up more to that vice, which has been so injurious to him, than ever."[13]

Yet Clark had a much kinder, gentler side. During these years, he became especially close to his nephew, John O'Fallon. He seems to have doted on the lad as the son he never had. In one letter, O'Fallon thanked his uncle for a horse he had given him and in another related his diligence at boarding school. Years later, O'Fallon recalled a modest, generous Clark, who "rarely, if ever, spoke of himself or achievements," and exemplified "unselfishness," being "always willing to divide all he possessed with a friend or with those he imagined in need."[14]

A letter from his brother-in-law Owen Gwathmey reveals both a glimpse of Clark's life at that time and his family's depth of love and concern for him: "When I saw you at the Spring the other day, you told me you were busily engaged in finishing your house. That is well enough, but I shd feel better satisfied if you would come & spend the Winter with me. Every thing that is in my power to make your situation comfortable shall be done & think you had better come."[15]

His health took a nosedive in 1809. That year, he suffered a stroke that paralyzed his right side and slurred his speech. Not long after that, his debilitation combined with inebriation to topple him into the fireplace where his leg was severely burned. Gangrene set in and began to spread. Dr. Richard Ferguson gave Clark the grim news that he had to choose between losing his leg or his life.[16] For the operation and months of recovery, Clark stayed with his sister Fanny, who had married the wealthy merchant Dennis Fitzhugh, at their home at the corner of Fifth and Main Streets in Louisville.

Clark arranged a going-away ceremony for his leg, which was amputated on March 25. He asked a family friend, Captain George Rogers Clark Floyd, the local militia commander, to have the "drummer and fifer to come and play." What followed was a poignant tribute to a once-great and now fallen warrior: "Floyd then took the hint and had all the men placed around the house with two drums and two fifes and played for about two hours and his leg was taken off in the meantime." Clark was said to have drummed his fingers in time with the songs and "was effected more by the music than the pain." The musicians returned that evening "and played for about an hour, and then at ten at night four elegant violins two drums and two fifes marched around the house for about an hour playing elegant marches."[17]

Learning of his brother's terrible accident, William Clark was relieved that he was "mending fast" but wondered, "What will he do and where will he live, will he return to the point of rocks do you know? pore fellow I wish it was more in my power to assist him than it is."[18] The assessment of Clark's health that reached William was correct, and he would soon have his other questions answered. Surprisingly, over the following weeks, Clark remained "in high spirits and the wound healed up." But Clark was no longer able to care for himself, even with the aid of three slaves. After spending several months recovering at his sister Fanny's home in Louisville, he moved in with his sister Lucy and her family at Locust Grove, where he would spend the rest of his life.

Lucy Clark and William Croghan had married at Mulberry Hill in 1789 and the following year had begun building Locust Grove on a lovely site about eight miles east of Louisville and half a mile south of the Ohio River. The bond between General Clark and Major Croghan was deep. Croghan was a Revolutionary War veteran, had served as a surveyor with Clark after the war, and was the nephew of George Croghan, the legendary Indian trader and agent.[19]

Clark would suffer no lack of help or company at Locust Grove. William and Lucy had eight children, thirty-three slaves, and two white servants. The slaves worked a prosperous plantation that eventually expanded to 693 acres. Croghan supplemented his income from harvesting crops like tobacco and corn with a ferry across the Ohio River. He was rich enough to send his sons to colleges back east.[20]

Clark still had a cadre of faithful supporters. Francis Vigo, who had provided crucial aid in rallying the inhabitants behind Clark during his Illinois campaign, expressed his "lament that the meritorious services of the best patriots of those days were too easily forgotten . . . by my adopted country with ingratitude." But Vigo was heartened to witness Jefferson County's Fourth of July celebration for 1811 pay a special tribute to Clark. In reply,

Clark expressed his "affection & esteem" for Vigo "as Companions amidst the din of war & those struggles, when the indefatigable exertion of every muscle and nerve was demanded." He then lauded Vigo for "your inestimable conduct" to "your adopted Country." He ended his letter, though, by darkly lamenting that "providence" had "cut asunder" his "life's tenderest string" to happiness; for that fate, he could submit "with manly patience."[21]

Perhaps no one beyond his immediate family meant more to Clark than Thomas Jefferson. Toward the end of his presidency, Jefferson penned an affectionate and wistful letter to Clark that may have briefly sweetened some of his bitterness. Jefferson assured him "that time has not lessened my friendship for you. We are both now grown old, you have been enjoying in retirement the recollection of the services you have rendered your country and I am about to retire without an equal consciousness that I have not occupied places in which others could have done more good; but in all places & times I shall wish you every happiness and salute you with great friendship and esteem."[22]

With a statement of support from Dr. Ferguson, Clark applied for a disability pension from Virginia in December 1809. More than two years passed with no word from Richmond. Clark had long ago given up any hope when someone unexpectedly came to his rescue. In January 1812, during a trip through the Ohio valley, General Charles Mercer stopped for a visit with Clark and was appalled by what he saw. Upon returning to Richmond, he devoted himself to "preparing, presenting, and urging the passage of" a bill that would award Clark an annual pension of four hundred dollars and a ceremonial sword. The turning point came with Mercer's impassioned speech explaining to a new generation of Virginian leaders Clark's brilliant feats and sacrifices.

Governor James Barbour had Mercer deliver to Clark the sword and a letter extolling his services. There are several conflicting accounts of just how Clark reacted to the honor. The most gracious and eloquent reply attributed to him reads, "When Virginia needed a sword I gave her one. I am too old and infirm to ever use a sword again but I am glad my old mother state has not entirely forgotten me, and I thank you for your kindness and friendly words." But by several accounts, Clark was anything but grateful. To Mercer he is said to have bitterly remarked, "Young man, when Virginia needed a sword, I found her one. Now I need bread." He also reportedly quipped, hopefully out of Mercer's hearing, "Damn the sword, I have had enough of that, a purse well filled would have done me more service." In a letter to the government, he vented the irony that "You now vote me a sword, when time and misfortune have rendered me unable to wield it."[23] Clark may have later softened. He had Croghan reply on his behalf to a letter from Governor Barbour extolling his accomplishments. Given Clark's resentment, it is not hard to read a tinge of sarcasm in his expression of gratitude. Clark found "this letter of yours . . . Flattering indeed . . . that his Exertions when doing his Duty should meet the approbation of so Respectable a body of his fellow Citizens as your Excellency and the General Assembly of Virginia."[24]

Clark suffered a second stroke in February 1813, with noticeable damage to his body and mind. A family member lamented, "For many years before his death . . . his bodily infirmities had been so great, and bore so heavily on his mind, and had so impaired his faculties as to render him almost a child. His afflictions also rendered him incapable of moving about. . . . His speech also became much impaired, so much so that his most familiar friends could scarcely . . . understand him."[25]

Yet at times his mind cleared and let him make lucid observations about the world. In 1814, he offered a political insight in response to word of Napoleon's first exile: "As to Bonaparte we may truly say 'How are the mighty fallen.' On the reception of the news of his having abdicated the Throne, To an impartial person, it would have been a source of Laughter to have viewed the . . . [reactions] of the different Persons. Some elated beyond expression, others truly depressed. Thus You see that notwithstanding we are all members of the same Community, Our principle of action is different, our view & wishes are never in unison."[26] And in reflecting on the grand glories and follies of Napoleon's adventures, Clark may have seen similarities with his own life.

Somehow, despite his punishing physical and emotional life, Clark endured year after year. During that time, he "suffered greatly from depression of spirits" and was often little more than "an animated clod." His ravaged mind and eyesight forced him to give up reading. Several times he was taken for treatment to Spa Springs at nearby Jeffersonville, Indiana. There were fleeting periods where somehow his mind rallied. He was taken to a meeting of the Board of Commissioners of the Illinois Land Grant on

February 1, 1813, although he may not have understood most of the proceedings.[27]

Clark's bitterness lingered to his dying breath. A year before he died, an anonymous tribute appeared explaining the reasons for Clark's apparent ingratitude: "Instead of paying the debt which the state . . . owed him with interest . . . that body voted him a sword and prospective pension. . . . They owed him a debt of more than 25 years, the annual interest of which doubled the sum of four hundred dollars. After degrading him from high service to which his services, virtues, and talents placed him, they voted him the paltry sum of four hundred dollars per annum . . . and a sword, when time and misfortune had deprived him of the power of wielding it in his country's cause."[28]

Clark had dictated a will on November 5, 1815. He had little to leave behind. He had long since sold off his slaves and most of his land, and had handed over his pension to Croghan. He shared his remaining land and personal property with his brother William, brothers-in-law William Croghan, Dennis Fitzhugh, and Owen Gwathmey, and nephews John and Benjamin O'Fallon.

Creditors hounded him to the very last and stymied his ability to invest what little money he had. The lion's share of those bills and creditors, and all the accompanying stress and foregone opportunities, were grounded in his inability to prove that his IOUs were legitimate wartime expenses. That lack of documents was a moral as well as financial cloud that darkened his life. Tragically, that cloud did not dissipate until long after he was buried. Clark's reputation got a boost when a clerk found his lost vouchers misfiled in Virginia's state archives. Eventually, the government reimbursed the Clark family through his sister Lucy and her husband William Croghan for $25,000.

A stroke killed George Rogers Clark on February 13, 1818. Appropriate last words were attributed to him: "Come on my brave boys! St. Vin."[29] Two days later, he was buried in the family cemetery at Locust Grove. Despite a snowstorm, Clark's funeral was attended "by a large assemblage of persons."[30]

Although he was only sixty-five years old, Clark was a wreck. Given his array of worsening and related physical, mental, and emotional sicknesses, it is astonishing that he survived as long as he did. His passage was probably an immense relief to himself and all those who had struggled to care for him in his last years. Yet love is what kept him alive year after tormented year. Ultimately, nothing mattered more to him than expressing and receiving the love of "those so dear to me."[31] At times, he was a challenge to be with. His rants drove away many of his admirers. But his family and a coterie of friends remained devoted to him throughout his life and to the ends of theirs.

What did George Rogers Clark contribute to American history? Judge John Rowan asserted the popular view in the opening line of his obituary of Clark: "The father of the Western Country is no more!"[32] Whether that sobriquet is hyperbole or fact has been hotly debated ever since.

At the time, Virginia's leaders certainly believed that Clark's tireless exertions were crucial to retaining the Ohio valley. Governor Jefferson noted that at the very least, Clark's conquest of Illinois would not just delay Indian attacks against the frontier, but would "have an important bearing ultimately in Establishing our North Western Boundary."[33] Governor Harrison expressed to Clark "my Thanks and those of my Council for the very great and singular services you have rendered you Country, in wrestling so great and valuable territory out of the Hands of the British Enemy, repelling the attacks of their Savage Allies and carrying on successful war in the Heart of their Country."[34] George Morgan, America's Indian agent to the Ohio valley, was especially farsighted in envisioning the fate of those western lands. In December 1780, he expressed his hope that "the Affairs of the Illinois can be placed on proper Footing. All the Country West of Allegany Mountains will probably be put under Direction of the United States, & Virginia limited to the Waters which fall into the Atlantic. . . . In this Case several New States will be established, independent tho United with our present Confederacy of Thirteen."[35] And Clark's own officers recognized the importance of their efforts on the future territory of the United States. In a plea for more troops, John Todd tried to impress on Colonel William Fleming the region's strategic worth: "Are you, pray Sir, or not raising an army for the Mississippi? If Government is not active in it already, the Back Country will be lost. . . . If the possession of the Ohio Waters are of any service to the united States it is time to enter the List & dispute the Domination of the Mississippi—the sooner the better."[36]

Most nineteenth- and early twentieth-century historians echoed those views. Reuben Thwaites argued that "throughout the protracted negotiations Jay and Franklin persisted in demanding the country which Clark had so gallantly won and was still holding." For John Bakeless, without "George Rogers Clark, a vast expanse of America today would, almost certainly, have been something very different from what it is today—probably British, just possibly Spanish. . . . By his middle twenties, George Rogers Clark had saved the 'back country' for America." More recent historians tend to dilute or outright deny those claims. Randolph Downes pointed out that "few 'conquests' have been followed by such a sudden and complete disappearance of the power of the 'conquerors' and of any respect of them among the 'conquered.'"[37]

So which side is correct? However dramatic Clark's campaigns were, their relative importance to the outcome of America's war for independence should not be exaggerated.[38] The war was won at Concord, Philadelphia, Bunker Hill, Trenton, Saratoga, Yorktown, and Paris, not on the western frontier.

As for Paris, how much did Clark's takeover of Illinois shape America's diplomatic strategy? Benjamin Franklin and his colleagues had only sketchy reports of the seesaw war on those distant Ohio and Mississippi frontiers.[39] Indeed, the very ignorance of the American envoys enabled them to make straight-faced claims to the entire Northwest and beyond when no American settlements existed north of the Ohio River and only a handful of civilians and soldiers clung to posts at Kaskaskia, Cahokia, and Vincennes amid an increasingly hostile population. A glance at a map reveals that Cahokia and Vincennes were less than a hundred miles up the Mississippi and Wabash Rivers, respectively, making up a tiny portion of the vast Northwest Territory eventually secured by the Treaty of Paris. Franklin initially sought far more. All of Canada topped his list of "advisable" goals that he presented to his British counterpart on July 10, 1782. That advisable goal, however, was primarily a bargaining chip in return for British concessions on "necessary" interests. Fulfilling the promises of land north of the Ohio River that Congress and several states had made to potential recruits was probably far more important in motivating the envoys' position than the tenuous American hold of a few villages on the fringe of that vast territory.

Though the British refused to render Canada, they did agree to setting the Mississippi River and the Great Lakes as America's western and northwestern boundaries. This was despite the hard fact that Clark and his colleagues never came close to planting the flag on the Great Lakes. The reason England conceded is simple. The king and his ministers were willing to cede that expanse of earth because they were ignorant of its true economic and strategic value, and thus deemed it far less important than issues concerning trade, fisheries, debts, compensation for Loyalists, and, above all, the soaring national debt and opposition to an unwinnable and widening war. The low priority that Whitehall attached to the territory between the Great Lakes and Ohio River is revealed by how quickly the British gave up their original demand for that region. In doing so, they literally sold out that region's Indians tribes, whose warriors they had spent a fortune arming, supplying, and leading against the American frontier during the war.[40]

Thus, those boundaries came not so much from the efforts of American arms, but from combined American diplomatic chutzpah and British indifference and exhaustion. The Americans in Paris won an empire of which American soldiers and civilians occupied only a tiny portion. In doing so, they fulfilled the goals and logic of the congressional instructions issued to them on October 17, 1780. The United States would ground its claim to that territory on Clark's campaign that had "by the success of their arms, obtained possession of all the important posts and settlements on the Illinois and Wabash, rescued the inhabitants from British domination and established civil government in its proper form over them."[41]

If Clark's Illinois campaign was the triumph of symbolism over substance in winning the Northwest, all of his efforts clearly disrupted the ability of the Indians and British to destroy the clusters of settlements in central Kentucky and Tennessee. Had they fallen and America's frontier been punched back east of the Appalachians, that might well have been the boundary imposed on the United States, and, if so, the subsequent history of not just America but the entire world would have been radically different.

Of course, not only Clark but other intrepid frontier leaders and their followers saved those settlements from extinction. Yet no man did more than he did. He was a master of military and diplomatic strategy and tactics. Certainly Clark alone envisioned and realized the Illinois campaign. His midwinter march from Kaskaskia to Vincennes and the complex strategy he wielded to intimate Hamilton into surrender was truly epic and deserves every accolade lavished upon it. And to achieve that took extraordinary reserves of imagination, will, charisma, and courage.

Clark was as adept a diplomat as he was a commander. He mastered most of the nuances of Indian diplomacy. As such, he simply adapted his own understanding of, and thus ability to manipulate, human nature to the distinctions of Indian culture. Power was the bottom line of diplomacy. Peace was rooted in strength. Indians yielded to the strong and trampled the weak. For Clark, the Indian wars were provoked not from American imperialism and greed, but from American disunity and kindness: "It is notorious that those tribes that have been for the greatest length of time acquainted with us firmly believe that their can make war or peace with us at their pleasure. And that we would at all times gladly Embrace the offer of any terms with them. . . . Every kind of lenity Shewn them by us is Imputed to timidity, and until this Idea is destroyed, a war will be the consequence of the least Supposed affront they Receive from us, which . . . the young warriors will often wish for and promote in order to have the Opportunity to show their Valour [and] are also excited by the prospect of . . . plunder."[42]

Yet Clark's Indian diplomacy had its limits. He spoke no Indian language and had never lived among them. Thus, he undoubtedly missed plenty of subtleties that otherwise would have strengthened his diplomatic hand. At least one prominent historian argues that racism also flawed Clark's diplomacy. Professor Richard White, usually a meticulous historian, issued the blanket condemnation that "George Rogers Clark hated Indians."[43]

There is certainly no question that Clark warred fiercely against the Indians. He led two campaigns that reached Indian villages, routed the defenders, and burned their homes and crops. That was the nature of frontier warfare. Yet he did commit a more controversial act. During the siege of Vincennes, he not only ordered but may actually have helped carry out the execution without trial of five warriors who were captured returning with scalps from a raid on Kentucky. A desire for justice and vengeance partly motivated that act. But far more important was the desire to intimidate into surrender the "Hair-buyer," Henry Hamilton, who commanded the fort before which the executions took place. That tactic worked. Hamilton gave up within an hour of witnessing the grisly scene. Then there is the chilling vow that Hamilton claimed that Clark made to him, that he would "see the whole race of Indians extirpated, that for his part he would never spare Man women or child of them on whom he could lay his hands."[44] If Clark actually uttered this, it was likely intended to chill into deterrence

Hamilton and any other redcoat leaders, who themselves had unleashed, supplied, and at times led an Indian war without mercy against the American frontier. Clark certainly never acted on that vow on any of his campaigns. Indeed, he called on his men to save rather than summarily kill any Indians who surrendered.[45] He did so for inseparable practical and moral reasons. Captives could be swapped for whites held by Indians. Likewise, the Indians would surely retaliate should Clark's men execute any warriors who surrendered.

Actually, Clark had decidedly mixed feelings about Indians. On the one hand, he respected most of the Indian leaders he encountered either in diplomacy or war. On the other hand, as a man of his times he shared the nearly universal attitude that Indians were a savage, inferior race that was doomed to extinction or assimilation; if so, then a Darwinian morality along with self-interest justified the conquest of their lands.[46]

Clark's fame as a warrior and notoriety for self-destructiveness obscures an essential point—he could build as well as destroy. He founded two enduring settlements, Louisville, that eventually developed into a bustling city, and Clarksville, the first American town in Indiana. He was a key player in getting the Virginia government to recognize Kentucky as a county. He proved to be an able administer of Kaskaskia.

Yet, despite all his accomplishments, George Rogers Clark suffered a deep character flaw that eventually transformed his life from triumph to tragedy. Alcoholism afflicted him from his early twenties and worsened with time. Without that debilitating addiction, nothing would have restrained him from achieving great feats after the war, perhaps culminating with leading Jefferson's Corps of Discovery to the Pacific Ocean and back.

Like everyone, George Rogers Clark was complex, yet more so than most. He was afflicted by inner demons that exacerbated his alcoholism. We can never know just what fueled his rage. For instance, countless other patriots sacrificed their fortunes and health for the cause with little or no compensation after independence was won. While anger and disillusionment were natural reactions, whose bitterness equaled Clark's red-faced vitriol? Throughout his life, he needed someone or something against which to vent a rage whose source was much deeper than that current enemy.

Fortunately, love diluted some of Clark's rage and kept him from destroying himself even earlier than he did. Clark deeply loved his family. Few lines in the hundreds of surviving family letters and other documents are devoted to their personal affairs. However, those that do reveal close and affectionate bonds. A November 1781 letter from elder brother Jonathan to George Rogers mentions the momentous event of Cornwallis's surrender of his army at Yorktown in a line, then devotes entire paragraphs to news of the family and friends: "Your letter to the old Gentleman [their father] gave him and the family much pleasure [and] they all desire you to accept of their love affection well wishes." Father "says he has nothing material to inform you of, except he and the family are all very well, and . . . you will excuse his not writing to you" since he was no longer capable of doing so.[47]

If love is defined as a deep, persistent, emotional attachment to someone or something, then there are many kinds of love. The most powerful love of Clark was for father figures. In the dozen or so surviving letters concerning family affairs, he refers most frequently to his father, rarely to his siblings, and almost never to his mother, although his parents lived until he was in his late forties and died within a year of each other. Although Clark lived in an age of patriarchy and patronage, his need for paternal recognition was as much emotional as practical.

Clark best revealed that side of himself in a letter to George Mason, who served with Thomas Jefferson and George Wythe on Virginia's executive council that, along with Governor Patrick Henry, approved his Illinois expedition. Clark and Mason appear to have forged a powerful son-father type relationship during the two months Clark spent in Williamsburg presenting his case for the campaign. His opening lines in a seventy-five-page account of the expedition hunger not just for Mason's approval but for his guidance and even reproach: "Continue to favour me with your valuable Lessons. Continue your Repremands as though I was your Son: when suspicious, think not that promotion or confer'd Honour will occation any unnecessary pride in me. You have infus'd too many of your Valuable precepts in me to be guilty of the like, or to shew any indifference to those that ought to be dear to me. It is with pleasure that I obey in transmitting to you a short sketch of my enterprise."[48]

What explains such a hunger for paternal guidance in such an otherwise fiercely independent young man? Was Clark's own father among those who responded to his son's achievements with criticism or indifference rather than praise or encouragement? Or was John Clark actually supportive but far away, thus forcing an emotionally dependent son to seek a substitute? The Clark siblings all served in the military. Doubtless there was an undercurrent of rivalry beneath the fraternal love and support. Was the father controlling or nurturing? Did he play his sons off against each other or exhort them to love one another? Unfortunately, the surviving documents offer no answers to these questions. All that can be said is that Clark attached himself to a few older men characterized by wisdom, learning, eloquence, and power, who encouraged him in his great ambitions.

If those relationships filled a void in Clark's life, another type remained empty throughout his life—those with women. What is definitively known is that Clark, like another legendary frontiersman, Meriwether Lewis, never married. The handful of secondhand references to romance in his life are shrouded in haze and refer to only one woman. As has been seen, Teresa was not Governor Fernando de Leyba's sister as legend would have it, but was likely a friend and perhaps even a servant of his family. Clark met Teresa during his 1778 Illinois campaign when he journeyed to Saint Louis to solicit Spanish aid. Long after Clark died, a niece related the story that he "promised to marry her at the close of the war, but in consequence of the Government refusing to sell all of his property, he thought it was not honorable in him to marry a lady educated as she was and accustomed to all the luxuries of wealth, without having any means of supporting her."[49]

Clark's huge debts were not the only obstacle to a relationship between them. He was an unrefined, boisterous, overbearing frontiersman, Protestant, and American. Teresa was refined, aristocratic, Catholic, and Spanish. Even if there was a mutual attraction, they could express it with little more than flirtatious glances and gestures since apparently neither was fluent in the other's language. But those chasms, while daunting, would not have been unbridgeable had Clark's love for her been genuine.

If that attraction ever did exist, why would Teresa have been the unrequited love of his life? Perhaps because it had so little chance of success. He seems to have loved the idea of loving her more than he actually loved her. That idea could serve as a convenient excuse whenever irritating questions arose over why he had never married or pursued any other woman in his life. He could then sigh and mutter allusions to that distant Spanish beauty who had broken his heart. His niece recalled his "reflections on her appeared to distress him very much; I have often seen him shed tears."[50]

Clark's disinterest in women suggests two other possibilities—either he had no interest in sex or had an orientation that could not be expressed openly at that time. If the latter were true, then it would certainly explain the ultimate source of his rage. In all surviving documents, there is only one possible allusion to that, a 1781 letter from one of his officers reporting that Clark "has lost the confidence of the people and is said become a sot; perhaps something worse."[51] So, while one must raise such questions, the only responsible answer is that the truth has been lost to time. And if genetics is decisive in shaping one's sexuality, then George Rogers was not the only Clark male with little apparent interest in women. Only Jonathan and William married and had children. John and Richard died unmarried in their twenties. Edmund, like George Rogers, remained a bachelor until his death at an advanced age. All four sisters, however, did marry and bear children.

John O'Fallon, Clark's favorite nephew, offers the only direct account of what Clark was like around women. The trouble is that his observations date to his boyhood and teenage years when Clark was in his forties and fifties, he did not write them down until three decades after Clark died, and what he says raises more questions than he answers. Clark "appeared to avoid female society, courting, or much familiarity with the young of both sexes." The presence of young women "caused him to withdraw from the room," an act O'Fallon could anticipate by "by the condition of his countenance and motions of his fingers." O'Fallon attributed Clark's extreme nervous and bashful reaction to women to his having been "at an early age . . . disappointed in love."[52] The biggest mystery of Clark's life will most likely never be solved.

Like any other time and place, the prevailing values of late eighteenth-century America determined just how much and in what ways a person could express his or her genuine self. Virtue and honor were the early American republic's most important values. They were certainly the most powerful guides for how Clark struggled to live both his public and private lives. In that revealing letter to Mason, Clark explained how honor and virtue shaped his reaction to opportunities for public office. Fame brought him "a friend in many Gentlemen of note that offered [th]eir interest in me in case I should offer at any Post. Many was supris'd that I would not solicit for some Birth. I must confess that I think myself often to blame for not making use of Interest for my promotion but to merit it first is such a fixed principal with me that I never could, and I hope never shall ask for a Post of Honour, as I think the Publick ought to be the best Judge whether a Person deserves it or not. If he did he would certainly be Rewarded according to the Virtue they had."[53] Here, Clark is doing nothing extraordinary. Politicians of that era climbed the ladder of political power by feigning disinterest while remaining constantly in the public eye as exemplars of republican virtue.

Clark explored the dynamic relationship between public and private virtue in a letter to Jonathan. He lamented what appeared to be the government's loss of virtue. Yet he was philosophical about that loss since he could find "that Valuable principal only survive in a few." He then suggested that perhaps the nascent republic had not completely lost its way. After all, the government had continued "to Confer Honour on me greater than I could have expected." And that "enlivens my ambition to perform services adequate to them." Clark's "Greatest happiness will . . . be to find" virtue "shine forth in our Family with double luster. Merit is not generally Rewarded by a Government that is lost its Virtue." He lauded his brother "to hear of your being universally esteemed in the Continental Army which is Justly due to [your] Virtue. Courage and fortitude will always command it in the Breasts of those whose Interest is only Valuable to us."[54]

Thomas Jefferson ranked among the virtuous few that Clark deemed worthy of the public's trust. And Jefferson felt the same about Clark even if he was well aware that alcoholism was his Achilles' heel. For decades, Jefferson supported Clark no matter how far he sank in drink, debt, and despondency. Their mutual admiration began in December 1777, when Clark was in Williamsburg lobbying for his Illinois campaign. They shared a fascination with the natural world and a vision of American expansion. Indeed, it was with Clark that Jefferson first shared his notion of an American "empire of liberty" spreading steadily across the continent. Each was also attracted to those qualities in the other that he lacked in himself. Jefferson was an armchair adventurer who lived vicariously through the courageous deeds of others, especially Clark. Clark, in turn, deeply respected Jefferson's erudition, knowledge, and gravitas. Nine years separated their ages. That difference was another force that drew them closer. In Clark, Jefferson filled a need for younger protégées to nurture. In Jefferson, Clark found an older mentor who unconditionally backed him. Together, they represented the yin and yang or archetypes of early American history.

Symbols, however, do not necessarily reflect genuine achievements. Today, Thomas Jefferson rightfully remains firmly seated with a score or so others in the pantheon of American history. In stark contrast, George Rogers Clark squandered whatever potential he had to join their ranks. As in a Greek tragedy, Clark's deep character flaws not only destroyed his ability to make truly enduring contributions to America's development but eventually drove him to outright betray his country. While Clark's treasonous plots in the 1780s and 1790s are terrible blots on his life, his flaws rendered them pathetic rather than villainous.

How Clark should chiefly be recalled is for what he did during a few intense years in his twenties. His grueling midwinter march at the head of 130 men to Vincennes, where they forced "Hair-buyer" Hamilton and his troops to surrender, is the stuff of legend. But that was just the most dramatic of Clark's stunning military and diplomatic feats during that all-too-fleeting time. By any measure, those adventures were like something from an epic Greek heroic myth rather than a tragedy.

Napoleon once warned that it was but a step from the sublime to the ridiculous. That same step separates triumph from tragedy. Few people more vividly personify that fate than George Rogers Clark.

Notes

Abbreviations

CP James Alton James, ed. *George Rogers Clark Papers*, vols. 1 and 2
CVSP Calendar of Virginia State Papers
DAR K. G. Davies, ed. *Documents of the American Revolution, 1770–1783*
DM Draper Manuscripts
GP Thomas Gage Papers
JCC Worthington C. Ford et al., eds. *Journals of the Continental Congress*
JP Julian Boyd, ed. *The Papers of Thomas Jefferson*
KR Clarence W. Alvord, ed. *Kaskaskia Records, 1778–1790*
MHS Missouri Historical Society
MP Robert Rutland, ed. *The Papers of George Mason, 1725–1792*
MPHC Michigan Pioneer Historical Collection

Introduction

Epigraph 1. George Rogers Clark to George Mason, November 19, 1779, MP, 2:583.
Epigraph 2. George Rogers Clark to Patrick Henry, February 3, 1779, CP, 1:98–99.
1. Arthur Campbell to William Davies, October 3, 1782, CP, 2:122.
2. For the leading biographies, see Bakeless, *Background to Glory*; James, *Life of George Rogers Clark*; and Bodley, *George Rogers Clark*.

For more limited accounts of Clark, see English, *Conquest of the Country*; Lockridge, *George Rogers Clark*; Thomas, *Hero of Vincennes*; Palmer, *Clark of the Ohio*; Havighurst, *George Rogers Clark*; and Schrodt, *George Rogers Clark*.

3. For leading books that explore the northwestern frontier during the late colonial and early republic eras, see Slotkin, *Regeneration through Violence*; White, *Middle Ground*; Calloway, *Crown and Calumet*; Calloway, *American Revolution in Indian Country*; Hinderaker, *Elusive Empires*; Perkins, *Border Life*; Hurt, *Ohio Frontier*; Hammon and Taylor, *Virginia's Western War*; Nester, *Frontier War for American Independence*; Griffin, *American Leviathan*; and Silver, *Our Savage Neighbors*.

1. Nature and Nurture

Epigraph 1. Dorman, "Descendants of General Jonathan Clark"; Bakeless, *Background to Glory*, 15.
Epigraph 2. Lyman Draper Memorandum, DM, 10J162.
1. Lyman Draper Memorandum on Clark Ancestry and Childhood, DM, 7J147; Dorman, "Descendants of General Jonathan Clark"; Bakeless, *Background to Glory*, 15.
2. Lyman Draper Memorandum, DM, 7J137–41, 143–52.
3. Ibid.
4. Ibid., 7J148.
5. Quotes from Lyman Draper Memorandum, DM, 7J105–203; 10J162. See also Diana Gwathmey Bullit interview, DM, 10J176A.

2. The Surveyor

Epigraph 1. Dunmore to Dartmouth, December 24, 1774, in Thwaites and Kellogg, *Documentary History of Dunmore's War*, 371.
Epigraph 2. Rev. David Jones Journal, 1772, in Cist, *Cincinnati Miscellany*, 1:245.
1. Bakeless, *Background to Glory*, 22.
2. For the most extensive overview of the reasons for, campaigns of, and results of the French and Indian War, see Nester, *Great Frontier War*; and Nester, *First Global War*.
3. Nester, *"Haughty Conquerors."*
4. For the two best biographies, see Faragher, *Daniel Boone*; and Morgan, *Boone*.
5. Dunmore to Dartmouth, December 24, 1774, in Thwaites and Kellogg, *Documentary History of Dunmore's War*, 371.
6. John Floyd to William Preston, April 26, 1774; anonymous letter from Carlisle, July 4, 1774; and Dunmore to Dartmouth, December 24, 1774, in Thwaites and Kellogg, *Dunmore's War*, 7–9; 66–68; 387–95.
7. Rev. David Jones Journal, 1772, in Cist, *Cincinnati Miscellany*, 1:245.
8. For the broader context of this horrifying crime, see Nester, *"Haughty Conquerors,"* chapter 6.
9. Cresswell, *Journal of Nicholas Cresswell*, 30.

10. John B. Roy to Jonathan Clark, March 22, 1772, DM, 1L8; Bakeless, *Background to Glory*, 23.

11. George Rogers Clark to Jonathan Clark, January 9, 1773, CP, 1:2.

12. Ibid.

13. Bakeless, *Background to Glory*, 23.

3. Lord Dunmore's War

Epigraph. Henry Hamilton to General Guy Carleton, November 30, 1775, DM, 45J101.

1. Ibid.

2. Unfortunately, there is no good book on Dunmore's War. For an overview, see Nester, *Frontier War for American Independence*; for insights into the frontier mentality that provoked such wars, see Slotkin, *Regeneration through Violence*.

3. George Rogers Clark to Samuel Brown, June 17, 1798, CP, 1:5.

4. Ibid., 1:6.

5. Ibid.

6. Ibid.

7. Ibid., 1:7–8.

8. Ibid., 1:8

9. Reminiscences of Henry Jolly; Michael Cresap; Bazaleel Wells; and Michael Myers, in Thwaites and Kellogg, *Dunmore's War*, 9–14; 14; 14–15; 15–19.

10. Dunmore commission of George Rogers Clark, May 2, 1774, in Seineke, *George Rogers Clark Adventure*, 150–51.

11. Circular letter of Dunmore, June 10, 1774; Dunmore to John Connolly, June 20, 1774; William Christian to William Preston, June 22, 1774; William Russell to William Preston; and William Preston to William Christian, in Thwaites and Kellogg, *Dunmore's War*, 33–35; 37–38; 42–46; 49–51; 52–55.

12. John Floyd to William Preston, August 28, 1774; and Daniel Smith to William Preston, in Thwaites and Kellogg, *Dunmore's War*, 167–68; 248–49.

13. For an excellent discussion of the role of Daniel Boone and other frontier heroes in American culture, see Slotkin, *Regeneration through Violence*.

14. Angus MacDonald to John Connolly, August [n.d.], 1774, in Thwaites and Kellogg, *Dunmore's War*, 151–54.

15. Dunmore to Andrew Lewis, July 12 and 24, 1774, in Thwaites and Kellogg, *Dunmore's War*, 86–87, 97–98.

16. William Christian to William Preston, September 7, 1774, in Thwaites and Kellogg, *Dunmore's War*, 186, 185–88.

17. William Fleming to Adam Stephen, October 8, 1774; William Fleming to his wife, October 13, 1774; William Fleming to William Bowyer, [October 13, 1774];

William Ingles to William Preston, October 14, 1774; William Christian to William Preston, October 15, 1774; John Floyd to William Preston, October 16, 1774; and Isaac Shelby to John Shelby, October 16, 1774, in Thwaites and Kellogg, *Dunmore's War*, 236–38; 253–54; 254–57; 257–59; 261–66; 266–69; 269–77.

18. William Preston to Patrick Henry October 31, 1774, in Thwaites and Kellogg, *Dunmore's War*, 293.

19. John Floyd to William Preston, October 16, 1774, in Thwaites and Kellogg, *Dunmore's War*, 268–69.

20. Fleming Orderly Book, October 12, 1774, in Thwaites and Kellogg, *Dunmore's War*, 344, 346–47.

21. Council between Lord Dunmore and the Indians, in Craig, *Olden Time*, 2:32.

22. For the best overall analysis of these cycles of frontier war, trade, and migration, see White, *Middle Ground*.

23. Cornstalk speech, November 7, 1776, in George Morgan Letterbook.

24. Dunmore to Dartmouth, December 24, 1774, in Thwaites and Kellogg, *Dunmore's War*, 371, 368–95.

25. George Rogers Clark to Jonathan Clark, December 18, 1774, CP, 2:3.

26. George Rogers Clark to Jonathan Clark, April 1, 1775, CP, 1:9.

4. The Dark and Bloody Ground

Epigraph. George Rogers Clark to Jonathan Clark, July 6, 1775, CP, 1: 9–10.

1. For an fascinating account of that journey and the American frontier, see Cresswell, *Journal of Nicholas Cresswell*, 52. The three weeks that Cresswell and Clark passed together are recorded from page 52 to 57.

2. George Rogers Clark to Jonathan Clark, July 6, 1775, CP, 1: 9–10.

3. Ibid., 1:11.

4. Nathaniel Henderson deposition, October 27, 1778, CVSP, 1:305–307.

5. Samuel Wilson deposition, April 15, 1777, CVSP, 1:283.

5. Rebellion

Epigraph 1. Declaration of Independence.
Epigraph 2. Clark, *Conquest of the Illinois*, 13.

1. Cresswell, *Journal of Nicholas Cresswell*, xii, 26.

2. Treaty with the Western Indians, September 12 to October 21, 1775, in Thwaites and Kellogg, *Revolution on the Upper Ohio*, 25–34, 67–71, 73–127.

3. Treaty with the Western Indians, 96, 95, 99.

4. Extracts of a letter published after Connolly's capture, November 25, 1775, in Seineke, *George Rogers Clark Adventure*, 163.

5. George Rogers Clark to Jonathan Clark, February 6, 1776, in English, *Conquest*, 1:68.

6. John Floyd deposition, October 28, 1778, CVSP, 1:309.

7. Clark, *Conquest of the Illinois*, 4–5.

8. Petitions from the Inhabitants of Kentucky, June 15, 1776, and June 20, 1775, in Seineke, *George Rogers Clark Adventure*, 180–81, 181–83.

9. Cayton, *Frontier Indiana*, 82.

10. Clark, *Conquest of the Illinois*, 6.

11. Ibid., 7.

12. Ibid.

13. Ibid., 8.

14. Ibid., 10.

15. Ibid., 12.

16. Clark, *Conquest of the Illinois*, 13.

17. Powder Granted for the Defense of Kentucky, August 23, 1776, CP, 1:18–19.

18. Clark diary, December 24, 1776, to March 31, 1777, in English, *Conquest*, 1:579–83.

19. Patrick Henry to Bernardo de Galvez, October 18, 1777 (two letters), in Henry, *Patrick Henry*, 3:105–106.

6. Promotion

Epigraph. Clark, *Conquest of the Illinois*, 21.

1. Thomas Gage to Guy Carleton, April 21, 1775, GP, vol. 121.

2. Dartmouth to Guy Johnson, July 5 and July 24, 1775, DAR, 11:55–56; Thomas Gage to Dartmouth, June 12, 1775, DAR, 9:168–71.

3. Edward Abbott to Guy Carleton, June 8, 1778, CP, 1:46–47.

4. Germain to Guy Carleton, March 26, 1777, MPHC, 9:347.

5. Guy Carleton to Henry Hamilton, October 6, 1776, and March 14, 1778, in Seineke, *George Rogers Clark Adventure*, 188, 231.

6. Henry Hamilton to Lord Dartmouth, August 29 to September 2, 1772, MPHC, 10:264–70.

7. Hamilton's letter has been lost, but his words are quoted in Germain to Guy Carleton, March 26, 1777, MPHC, 9:346–48.

8. Hamilton Report of Indian Council at Detroit, June 17–30, 1777, in Thwaites and Kellogg, *Frontier Defense*, 13, 12.

9. Ibid., 12–14; and Hamilton Proclamation, June 24, 1777, in Thwaites and Kellogg, *Frontier Defense*, 14.

10. Henry Hamilton to Guy Carleton, [July 1777], MPHC, 9:440–42.

11. John Bowman to Edward Hand, December 12, 1777, in Thwaites and Kellogg, *Frontier Defense*, 182–83.

12. Clark, *Conquest of the Illinois*, 20.

13. Ibid., 21.

14. Clark diary, August 5, 1777, in English, *Conquest*, 1:580–81.

15. Joseph Bogey to Mann Butler and Daniel Henry, DM, 8J28; 8J110–15; Bakeless, *Background to Glory*, 50.

16. Thomas Bentley to Daniel Murray, August 1, 1777; Defense of Thomas Bentley, August 1, 1777; Report of Henry Hamilton, August 15, 1777; Court of Enquiry, September 11, 1777; Petition of Thomas Bentley, October 6, 1777; Joseph Bowman to Richard Lernoult, March 20, 1779; and Father Gibault to Richard Lernoult, [n.d.], KR, 8–12; 12–16; 16–17; 18–40; 41–42; 73–74; 74.

17. George Morgan to Richard Winston, July 6, 1776; Daniel Murray to Thomas Bentley, May 25, 1777; and Registration, November 5, 1777, KR, 1–3; 6–8; 43–44; Patrick Henry to George Morgan, March 12, 1777; George Morgan and John Neville to Patrick Henry, April 1, 1777, in Henry, *Patrick Henry Papers*, 46–47.

18. Petition to Guy Carleton, April 30, 1777, in Seineke, *George Rogers Clark Adventure*, 197–99.

19. Richard McCarty to John Askin, June 7, 1778; and Arent de Peyster to Frederick Haldimand, August 15, 1777, KR, 44–45; 45–46. See also Thomas Bentley to Daniel Murray, August 1, 1777; Defense of Thomas Bentley, August 1, 1777; Report of Henry Hamilton, August 15, 1777; and Rocheblave and other testimonies, Court of Inquiry, September 11, 1777, KR, 8–12; 12–16; 17–18; 18–40.

20. Daniel Murray to Thomas Bentley, May 25, 1777, KR, 6–8.

21. The details of Clark's journey are gleaned from Clark's diary, CP, 1:23–28.

7. The Bloodless Conquest

Epigraph 1. George Wythe, George Mason, and Thomas Jefferson to George Rogers Clark, January 3, 1778, JP, 2:132–33.

Epigraph 2. Clark, *Conquest of the Illinois*, 34.

1. Unless otherwise indicated, the details from this chapter come either from Clark, *Conquest of the Illinois* or George Rogers Clark to George Mason, November 19, 1779, MP, and usually supplement details from other sources.

2. George Rogers Clark to George Mason, November 19, 1778, MP, 2:555.

3. For an undated but likely version of the plan Clark presented, see Clark to [Patrick Henry], December 10, 1777, CP, 1:30–32.

4. George Rogers Clark to George Mason, November 19, 1779, MP, 2:555.

5. Ibid., 2:556.

6. Ibid., 1:39.

7. Ibid., 1:38.

8. George Wythe, George Mason, and Thomas Jefferson to George Rogers Clark, January 3, 1778, JP, 2:132–33.

9. Secret Instructions to Clark, January 2, 1778, CP, 1:34.

10. Public Instructions to Clark, January 2, 1778, CP, 1:36.

11. Clark, *Conquest of the Illinois*, 24–25.

12. James Willing to Frederick Haldimand, July 6 and November 11, 1772, and January 3 and April 10, 1773, in Seineke, *George Rogers Clark Adventure*, 126–27, 128, 128–29, 129; Oliver Pollock to Frederick Haldimand, December 1, 1772, in Seineke, *George Rogers Clark Adventure*, 134–35.

13. Robertson, "Tories or Patriots?" 445–62.

14. James Willing to Edward Hand, January 7, 1778; Patrick Henry to Edward Hand, January 15, 1778; and Edward Hand to Horatio Gates, in Thwaites and Kellogg, *Frontier Defense*, 198–99; 199; 278–29.

15. George Rogers Clark to William Harrod, March 15, 1778, in Thwaites and Kellogg, *Frontier Defense*, 226–27.

16. George Rogers Clark to George Mason, November 19, 1779, MP, 2:556–57. See also George Rogers Clark to William Harrod, April 12, 1778, in Thwaites and Kellogg, *Frontier Defense*, 263–64.

17. William Smith to George Rogers Clark, March 7, 1778; William Smith to George Rogers Clark; and George Rogers Clark to Edward Hand, April 17, 1778, and March 29, 1778, CP, 1:40; 42; 44.

18. Patrick Henry to Edward Hand, January 2, 1778; and Edward Hand to David Shepherd, March 22, 1778, CP, 1:36–37; 41; Edward Hand to Horatio Gates, February 12, 1778, in Thwaites and Kellogg, *Frontier Defense*, 202–203.

19. Clark, *Conquest of the Illinois*, 35; Holm, "Supply Issues," 169–72.

20. Clark, *Conquest of the Illinois*, 28–29.

21. Ibid., 32–33

22. Ibid., 33.

23. Ibid., 34.

24. Ibid.

25. Ibid., 38.

26. Ibid., 39.

27. John Campbell to George Rogers Clark, June 8, 1777, CP, 1:45.

28. Guy Carleton to Rocheblave, October 28, 1776, in Seineke, *George Rogers Clark Adventure*, 191.

29. Daniel Murray to Guy Carleton, March 31, 1777; and Thomas Bentley to Daniel Murray, August 1, 1777, KR, 4–6; 8–12.

30. George Rogers Clark to George Mason, November 19, 1779, MP, 2:558–59.

31. Ibid., 2:588.

32. Fernando de Leyba to Bernardo de Galvez, July 11, 1778, in Seineke, *George Rogers Clark Adventure*, 263.

33. George Rogers Clark to George Mason, November 19, 1779, MP, 2:559.

34. Clark, *Conquest of the Illinois*, 41.

35. Fernando de Leyba to Bernardo de Galvez, July 11, 1778, 263.

8. War of Words

Epigraph 1. Fernando de Leyba to Patrick Henry, April 23, 1779, in Kinnaird, "Clark-Leyba Papers," 107.

Epigraph 2. Bakeless, *Background to Glory*, 98.

1. Unless otherwise indicated, the details from this chapter come either from Clark, *Conquest of the Illinois* or George Rogers Clark to George Mason, November 19, 1779, MP, 2:560.

2. Clark, *Conquest of the Illinois*, 46.

3. Ibid.

4. George Rogers Clark to George Mason, November 19, 1779, MP, 2:560.

5. Clark, *Conquest of the Illinois*, 47–48.

6. Fernando de Leyba to Bernardo de Galvez, July 11, 1778, in Seineke, *George Rogers Clark Adventure*, 263.

7. Henry Hamilton to Guy Carleton, April 25, 1778, in Thwaites and Kellogg, *Frontier Defense*, 281.

8. Edward Abbott to Guy Carleton, May 26, 1777, and April 25, 1778, in Seineke, *George Rogers Clark Adventure*, 203, 237.

9. George Rogers Clark to the Inhabitants of Vincennes, July [13], 1778, CP, 1:50–53.

10. Gabriel Cerré to George Rogers Clark, July 11, 1778, CP, 1:48.

11. Clark, *Conquest of the Illinois*, 56.

12. Gabriel Cerré to George Rogers Clark, July 11 and July 25, 1778, DM, 48J24–25.

13. Bakeless, *Background to Glory*, 98.

14. Clark, *Conquest of the Illinois*, 69–70.

15. Ibid., 71–74.

16. George Rogers Clark to George Mason, November 19, 1779, MP, 2:564.

17. Clark, *Conquest of the Illinois*, 80.

18. Ibid.

19. George Rogers Clark to the Chief of the Winnebago, August 22, 1778, CP, 1:65.

20. George Rogers Clark to George Mason, MP, 2:564–65.

21. Clark, *Conquest of the Illinois*, 84.

22. Ibid., 85.

23. See Nester, *"Haughty Conquerors."*

24. Clark, *Conquest of the Illinois*, 92.

25. Ibid., 92–93.

26. Ibid., 94–95.

27. Ibid., 95–96.

28. Ibid., 86–90; George Rogers Clark to George Mason, November 18, 1778, CP, 1:223.

29. For a typical treaty, see Clark's Proclamation to the Fox Indians, August 28, 1778, CP, 66–67.

30. Fernando de Leyba to George Rogers Clark, July 8, 1778, in Kinnaird, "Clark-Leyba Papers," 94, 92–112.

31. Fernando de Leyba to George Rogers Clark, July 21, 1779, in Kinnaird, "Clark-Leyba Papers," 98.

32. Fernando de Leyba to Bernardo de Galvez, November 16, 1778, in Kinnaird, "Clark-Leyba Papers," 101.

33. Fernando de Leyba to Patrick Henry, April 23, 1779, in Kinnaird, "Clark-Leyba Papers," 107.

34. George Rogers Clark to George Mason, November 19, 1778, MP, 2:567.

35. Fernando de Leyba to Bernardo de Galvez, November 16, 1778, in Kinnaird, "Clark-Leyba Papers," 102.

36. Carstens, "Making of a Myth," 60–79.

37. George Rogers Clark to Fernando de Leyba, October 26, 1778, and January 23 and March 1, 1779, in Kinnaird, "Clark-Leyba Papers," 100, 105–106.

38. John Todd to George Rogers Clark, October 3, 1779, KR, 128.

39. Carstens, "Making of a Myth," 64–65.

40. Fernando de Leyba to Bernardo de Galvez, October 18, 1779, in Kinnaird, "Clark-Leyba Papers," 111–12.

41. Ibid.

42. Clark, *Conquest of the Illinois*, 65.

43. George Rogers Clark to George Mason, November 19, 1778, CP, 1:223.

44. Ibid.

45. Ibid., 2:467.

46. Ibid.

47. Bakeless, *Background to Glory*, 107.

9. Counterpunch

Epigraph. George Rogers Clark to Patrick Henry, February 3, 1779, CP, 1:98–99.

1. Oath of Inhabitants of Vincennes, July 20, 1778, CP, 1:56–59.

2. Henry Hamilton to Frederick Haldimand, October 14, 1778; and Certificate of Captain Leonard Helm to Chief Tobacco, August 7, 1778, in Seineke, *George Rogers Clark Adventure*, 327; 268–69.

3. Oliver Pollock to Bernardo Galvez, May 2, 1778, in Seineke, *George Rogers Clark Adventure*, 238–39.

4. George Morgan to Bernardo de Galvez, April 26, 1778; and George Morgan to Francisco Cruzat, April 26, 1778, in Thwaites and Kellogg, *Frontier Defense*, 290–93.

5. Rocheblave to Edward Abbot, June 20, 1778; Rocheblave to Guy Carleton, July 4, 1778; Bernardo de Galvez to Don Carlos de Granpre, February 22 and March 1, 4, and 7, 1778; and Bernardo de Galvez to Don Diego Navarro, March 11, 1778, in Seineke, *George Rogers Clark Adventure*, 256–57; 257–58; 227–29; 229–31.

6. Board of War to Bernardo de Galvez, October 10, 1778, in Seineke, *George Rogers Clark Adventure*, 294.

7. Patrick Henry to Bernardo de Galvez, January 14, 1778, in Seineke, *George Rogers Clark Adventure*, 216–18.

8. Bernardo de Galvez to Patrick Henry, May 6 and September–November [n.d.], 1778, in Seineke, *George Rogers Clark Adventure*, 240–41, 301–303.

9. For an excellent overview, see Caughey, *Bernardo de Galvez in Louisiana*.

10. Robert George to Bernardo de Galvez, August 14, 1778; and Passport for Colonel David Rogers, February 8, 1779, in Seineke, *George Rogers Clark Adventure*, 272; 303–304.

11. George Rogers Clark to Oliver Pollock, July 18, 1778, August 6, 1778, CP, 1:55, 64–65.

12. Clark, *Conquest of the Illinois*, 54–55.

13. Judgment by G. R. Clark in Civil Case between Hanson and Decosta, October 22, 1778; and Decision by G. R. Clark on Antoine Bienvenu Petition, November 11, 1778, in Seineke, *George Rogers Clark Adventure*, 295–96; 299–300.

14. Patrick Henry to George Rogers Clark, December 12, 1778, in Henry, *Patrick Henry*, 3:211, 209–12

15. William Beckley interview, August 1858, DM, 8J8.

16. Clark, *Conquest of the Illinois*, 102.

17. Petition of the Inhabitants, December 29, 1778, in Seineke, *George Rogers Clark Adventure*, 306.

18. Proclamation by Clark, December 24, 1778, CP, 1:93, 91–95.

19. Bogert, "Clark, the Slave Trade, and the Illinois Regiment," 134–47.

20. Petition to Governor Galvez, [n.d.], 1780, McDermott, *Spanish in the Mississippi Valley*, 370.

21. Barnhart, *Henry Hamilton and George Rogers Clark* (hereafter *Hamilton and Clark*); Report by Lieutenant-Governor Henry Hamilton, on his Proceedings from November 1776 to June 1781, CP, 1:174–207. Hamilton's unpublished autobiography is at Harvard University's Houghton Library.

22. Barnhart, *Hamilton and Clark*, 11–12; Bass, *Green Dragoon*, 9.

23. Henry Hamilton to Guy Carleton, January 15, 1779; and Henry Hamilton to Frederick Haldimand, September 22, 1778, MPHC, 9:431–33; 477–82.

24. Henry Hamilton to Guy Carleton, January 15, 1779; and Henry Hamilton to Frederick Haldimand, September 22, 1778, MPHC, 9:431, 477, 465; Filson, *Discovery, Settlement, and Present State of Kentucky*, 64.

25. Unless otherwise noted, the quotations and information for the expedition were gleaned from Barnhart, *Hamilton and Clark*.

26. Henry Hamilton to Germain [n.d.], CP, 1:330–31; Henry Hamilton to Guy Carleton, August 8, 11, 1778, in Seineke, *George Rogers Clark Adventure*, 269–71.

27. Frederick Haldimand to Henry Hamilton, August 6, 1778, MPHC, 9:399–400.

28. Explained in Frederick Haldimand to George Germain, October 25, 1778, MPHC, 9:402–404.

29. Henry Hamilton to Frederick Haldimand, September 22, 1778, in Seineke, *George Rogers Clark Adventure*, 309.

30. Report by Lieutenant-Governor Henry Hamilton, CP, 1:179, 180.

31. Barnhart, *Hamilton and Clark*, 130.

32. Ibid., 110.

33. Ibid.

34. Ibid., 128.

35. Ibid., 122.

36. Ibid., 146.

37. Leonard Helm to George Rogers Clark, December 17, 1778, CP, 1:89–90.

38. Barnhart, *Hamilton and Clark*, 148; Evans, *Detroit to Fort Sackville*, 112–13.

39. Barnhart, *Hamilton and Clark*, 153.

40. Lieutenant-Governor Hamilton to the People of Illinois, December 28, 1778, CP, 1:96, 95–97.

41. Henry Hamilton to Bernardo de Galvez, January 13, 1779, in Kinnaird, "Clark-Leyba Papers," 103–104.

42. Report by Lieutenant-Governor Henry Hamilton, CP, 1:183.

43. Barnhart, *Hamilton and Clark*, 156.

44. George Rogers Clark to George Mason, November 19, 1779, MP, 2:570–71.

45. Clark, *Conquest of the Illinois*, 106–107.

46. George Rogers Clark to George Mason, November 19, 1779, MP, 2:574.

47. Clark, *Conquest of the Illinois*, 108, 111–12.

48. Ibid., 112; George Rogers Clark to George Mason, November 19, 1779, MP, 2:574.

49. George Rogers Clark to Patrick Henry, February 3, 1779, CP, 1:98–99.

10. Purgatory

Epigraph. Clark, *Conquest of the Illinois*, 119–20.

1. Clark, *Conquest of the Illinois*, 113.

2. George Rogers Clark to George Mason, November 19, 1779, MP, 2:575.

3. George Rogers Clark to John Rogers, February 5, 1779, in Seineke, *George Rogers Clark Adventure*, 349.

4. George Rogers Clark to John Rogers, February 3, 1779, CP, 1:100.

5. Bakeless, *Background to Glory*, 150.

6. Clark, *Conquest of the Illinois*, 117.

7. English, *Conquest*, 520–21.

8. Clark, *Conquest of the Illinois*, 119–20.

9. Bowman's Journal, February 19 and 20, 1779, CP, 1:158.

10. Unless otherwise noted, the following quotations are from Bowman's Journal.

11. Clark, *Conquest of the Illinois*, 124.

12. Ibid., 126.

13. Ibid., 128.

11. Caging the Hair Buyer

Epigraph 1. Barnhart, *Hamilton and Clark*, 178.
Epigraph 2. George Rogers Clark, February 24, 1779.

1. Clark, *Conquest of the Illinois*, 129.

2. Ibid., 128.

3. Ibid., 130.

4. Ibid.

5. Ibid., 131.

6. Ibid., 132–33.

7. George Rogers Clark to George Mason, November 19, 1779, MP, 2:577.

8. Frank Doughman (chief ranger, George Rogers Clark National Historical Park), interview by author, May 25, 2010.

9. George Rogers Clark to George Mason, November 19, 1779, MP, 2:577.

10. Clark, *Conquest of the Illinois*, 133–34.

11. Barnhart, *Hamilton and Clark*, 178.

12. Ibid., 187.

13. Report by Lieutenant-Governor Henry Hamilton, CP, 1:186.

14. Clark, *Conquest of the Illinois*, 138.

15. Ibid., 137.

16. Barnhart, *Hamilton and Clark*, 179.

17. Ibid., 182.

18. Clark, *Conquest of the Illinois*, 141–42.

19. Garrison at Vincennes, February 24, 1779, CP, 1:110–11; Barnhart, *Hamilton and Clark*, 180.

20. Bowman's Journal, CP, 8:160.

21. Clark, *Conquest of the Illinois*, 143.

22. Barnhart, *Hamilton and Clark*, 180.

23. Ibid., 181.

24. George Rogers Clark to George Mason, February 19, 1779, MP, 2:579.

25. Ibid.

26. Barnhart, *Hamilton and Clark*, 182–83; Schieffelin Deposition, in Seineke, *George Rogers Clark Adventure*, 546.

27. Barnhart, *Hamilton and Clark*, 182; Schieffelin Deposition, 546.

28. Schieffelin Deposition, 546–47.

29. Ibid., 546.

30. Barnhart, *Hamilton and Clark*, 183.

31. Ibid.

32. The following dialogue weaves elements from the Clark and Hamilton accounts (Barnhart, *Hamilton and Clark*; Clark, *Conquest of the Illinois*; and Clark to Mason).

33. Report by Lieutenant-Governor Henry Hamilton, CP, 1:191.

34. Schieffelin Deposition, 546.

35. Report by Lieutenant-Governor Henry Hamilton, CP, 1:194.

36. Bowman's Journal, February 17, 1779, CP, 1:163.

37. George Rogers Clark to Patrick Henry, April 29, 1779, JP, 2:257.

38. Ibid., 2:258.

39. Inventory at Fort Patrick Henry, March 9, 1779, in Seineke, *George Rogers Clark Adventure*, 358–60.

40. Barnhart, *Hamilton and Clark*, 189; Report by Lieutenant-Governor Henry Hamilton, CP, 1:195.

41. Barnhart, *Hamilton and Clark*, 189; Clark, *Conquest of the Illinois*, 150.

42. Prisoners of War, March 9, 1779; and Prisoners who took the Oath, March 9, 1779, CP, 1:112; 111.

43. Report by Lieutenant-Governor Henry Hamilton, CP, 1:197.

44. Indictment of Lieutenant-Colonel Henry Hamilton, June 16, 1778, CP, 1:337–40.

45. Report by Lieutenant-Governor Henry Hamilton, CP, 1:175.

46. William Phillips to Thomas Jefferson, July 5, 1779, JP, 3:25–28.

47. Thomas Jefferson to Guy Carleton, July 22, 1779, CP, 1:347–52.

48. Thomas Jefferson to George Washington, July 17, 1779, JP, 3:40–41.

49. George Washington to Thomas Jefferson, July 10 and August 6, 1779, JP, 3:30–31, 61.

50. Barnhart, *Hamilton and Clark*, 90–92; Rocheblave to Frederick Haldimand, September 9, 1780, KR, 173–80.

12. Crossroads

Epigraph 1. Clark, *Conquest of the Illinois*, 167.

Epigraph 2. Ibid., 170.

1. George Rogers Clark to Patrick Henry, March 10, 1779, CP, 1:305.

2. George Rogers Clark to Patrick Henry, April 29, 1779, JP, 2:258.

3. George Rogers Clark to Richard Lernoult, March 16, 1779, CP, 1:306–307.

4. General Return of the Inhabitants of Detroit, September 22, 1773, MPHC, 9:649; Hamilton to Haldimand, August 29, 1776, MPHC, 10:267.

5. Richard Lernoult to Mason Bolton, March 26, 1779, CP, 1:325.

6. Ibid., 1:308.

7. Frederick Haldimand to Henry Clinton, August 29, 1779, in Kellogg, *Frontier Retreat*, 50.

8. Clark, *Conquest of the Illinois*, 163–64.

9. George Rogers Clark to George Mason, November 19, 1779, MP, 2:583.

10. Clark, *Conquest of the Illinois*, 161–64.

11. Patrick Henry to George Rogers Clark, December 15, 1778 (two letters), in Henry, *Patrick Henry Papers*, 3:60–64; George Rogers Clark to George Mason, November 19, 1779, MP, 2:585.

12. Instruction to George Rogers Clark from the Virginia Council, December 12, 1778, CP, 1:78–82.

13. Clark, *Conquest of the Illinois*, 167.

14. Ibid., 167–68.

15. Ibid., 168.

16. George Rogers Clark to George Mason, November 19, 1779, CP, 2:585.

17. Address of Clark to the People of Kaskaskia, May 12, 1779, CP, 1:320–21.

18. Patrick Henry to John Todd, December 12, 1778, CVSP, 1:312–14.

19. Address of Clark to the People of Kaskaskia, May 12, 1779, CP, 1:320–21

20. John Todd speech, May 12, 1779, KR, 84.

21. Thomas Jefferson to [John Todd], January 28, 1780, KR, 143.

22. Protest Concerning Notes of Exchange by Joseph Perrault, June 24, 1779; Gabriel Cerre to George Rogers Clark, July 12, 1779; and Protest of Inhabitants to Magistrates, December 8, 1779, KR, 98–101; 102–103; 136–42.

23. Magistrates to John Todd, May 21, 1779, KR, 88–89.

24. John Williams to George Rogers Clark, September 25, 1779, KR, 123.

25. John Montgomery to George Rogers Clark, November 15, 1779, KR, 133.

26. Becker, "Currency"; George Rogers Clark to Oliver Pollock, June 12, 1779, CP, 1:331.

27. Oliver Pollock to Patrick Henry, July 17, 1779, DM, 49J60.

28. Patrick Henry to George Rogers Clark, December 12 (two letters), and December 16, 1778, CP, 1:75–76, 77–78, 88–89.

29. George Rogers Clark to Patrick Henry, March 9, 1779, CP, 1:303–304.

30. For a very revealing letter of that trade relationship and the reputation of Spanish horses, see George Morgan to Richard Winston, July 6, 1776, KR, 1–3.

31. For a detailed account of the campaign, see Nester, *Frontier War for American Independence*, 251–68.

32. George Washington to Daniel Brodhead, October 18, 1779, in Kellogg, *Frontier Retreat*, 101.

33. Troops under Clark at Kaskaskia, May 21 and June 2, 1779; and Joseph Bowman to George Rogers Clark, June 3, 1779, CP, 1:323; 326; 327.

34. Proclamation about Spanish Deserters, June 19, 1779, CP, 1:343.

35. Draper narrative of the Rogers Expedition; Basil Brown deposition and narrative; and George Rogers Clark to [n.n.] October 9, 1779, in Kellogg, *Frontier Retreat*, 79–88; 88–93; 93–94. John Campbell to Richard Lernoult, October 23, 1779; and Arent de Peyster to Frederick Haldimand, November 1, 1779, in Seineke, *George Rogers Clark Adventure*, 404–405; 405–406.

36. George Rogers Clark to William Fleming, October 22, 1779, in Kellogg, *Frontier Retreat*, 104–105.

37. George Rogers Clark to George Mason, November 19, 1779, MP, 2:586–87.

38. John Bowman to George Rogers Clark, June 13, 1779, DM, 49J52.

39. George Rogers Clark to George Mason, November 19, 1779, MP, 2:585.

40. Clark, *Conquest of the Illinois*, 170. See also George Rogers Clark to George Mason, November 19, 1779, MP, 2:581.

41. George Rogers Clark to his Officers, August 5, 1779, in Seineke, *George Rogers Clark Adventure*, 392–93.

42. Young, *Westward into Kentucky*, 55.

43. Young, *Westward into Kentucky*, 56.

44. Bakeless, *Background to Glory*, 235.

45. Leonard Helm to George Rogers Clark, May 9, 1779, CP, 1:316–17.

46. Bakeless, *Background to Glory*, 241.

47. George Rogers Clark to his father, John Clark, June 15, 1779, CP, 1:335–36.

48. Ibid., 326.

49. John Page to George Rogers Clark, September 4, 1779, in English, *Conquest*, 2:875.

50. Colonel George and John Croghan interview, November 8, 1844, DM, 10J204.

13. Forting Up

Epigraph. Thomas Jefferson to George Rogers Clark, January 1, 1780, JP, 3:259.

1. George Rogers Clark to George Mason, November 19, 1779, MP, 2:587.

2. "Estimated Population of American Colonies," University of California at Davis, http://web.viu.ca/davies/H320/population.colonies.htm.

3. Quoted in Hammon and Taylor, *Virginia's Western War*, 117–18.

4. "Colonel William Fleming's Journal of Travels in Kentucky, 1779–1780," in Mereness, *Travels*, 630.

5. For a typical uncovering and suppression of a plot, see William Preston to

Thomas Jefferson, March [n.d.], 1780; William Preston to James Byrne, July 5, 1780; and William Preston to Isaac Taylor, July 12, 1780, in Kellogg, *Frontier Retreat*, 143–45; 211–13; 215–16.

6. For the quotes, see George Rogers Clark to John Clark, August 23, 1780, CP, 1:453.

7. Daniel Brodhead to George Rogers Clark, April 4 and May 20, 1780, CP, 1:408–409, 419–20; Daniel Brodhead to George Washington, April 24, 1780, in Kellogg, *Frontier Retreat*, 173.

8. Thomas Jefferson to George Washington, February 10, 1778, in Kellogg, *Frontier Retreat*, 133–34.

9. George Rogers Clark to Thomas Jefferson, September 23, 1779, JP, 3:88.

10. Thomas Jefferson to [John Todd], January 28, 1780, KR, 143.

11. Thomas Jefferson to George Rogers Clark, January 1, 1780, JP, 3:259.

12. Ibid.

13. Thomas Jefferson to George Rogers Clark, January 29, 1780, JP, 3:276.

14. Thomas Jefferson to George Rogers Clark, March 19, 1780, JP, 3:317.

15. Thomas Jefferson to George Rogers Clark, January 29, 1780, JP, 3:276.

16. George Rogers Clark to Thomas Jefferson, September 23, 1779, JP, 3:88; George Rogers Clark to Silas Martin, September 30, 1779, CP, 1:368–69.

17. George Rogers Clark to John Todd, March 1780, CP, 1:410–12.

18. Conditions in Kentucky, Boonesborough, March 10, 1780; Petition from the Inhabitants of Boonesborough, March 10, 1780; and Petition from Bryan's Station, March 13, 1780, CP, 1:396–98; 398–400; 401–402.

19. Grant of Land to Clark, January 29, 1780; and Registration of Grant of Land to Clark, January 29, 1780, CP, 1:393; 393–94.

20. Carstens, "George Rogers Clark's Fort Jefferson," 259–84; Carstens, *Personnel of George Rogers Clark's Fort Jefferson*.

21. Patrick Sinclair to Frederick Haldimand, May 29, 1780, in English, *Conquest*, 2:677–79; Frederick Haldimand to Arent de Peyster, February 12, 1779, in Seineke, *George Rogers Clark Adventure*, 421.

22. Frederick Haldimand to Henry Clinton, January [n.d.], 1780, in Kellogg, *Frontier Retreat*, 122–23.

23. Arent de Peyster to Frederick Haldimand, June 27, 1779, in Seineke, *George Rogers Clark Adventure*, 387.

24. For the best overview of the campaign as historiography and narrative, see Gilman, "L'Annee du Coup."

25. Patrick Sinclair to Frederick Haldimand, May 29, 1780, in English, *Conquest*, 2:677–79.

26. John Montgomery to George Rogers Clark, May 15, 1780; and John Rogers to George Rogers Clark, May 15, 1780, in Seineke, *George Rogers Clark Adventure*, 433–34; 434.

27. Bradford, *Voice of the Frontier*, 32.

28. George Rogers Clark to Oliver Pollock, May 11, 1780, in Seineke, *George Rogers Clark Adventure*, 432. For the best analysis, see Quaife, "When Detroit Invaded Kentucky," 53–67.

29. Unless otherwise noted, the information for the defense of Saint Louis comes from McDermott, "The Myth of the Imbecile Governor," 336–37, 314–88; and McDermott, "The Battle of St. Louis," 131–51.

30. Patrick Sinclair to Frederick Haldimand, July 8, 1780, in English, *Conquest*, 2:679–80.

31. Fernando de Leyba to Bernardo de Galvez, October 18, 1779, in Kinnaird, "Clark-Leyba Papers," 111–12.

32. For the John Murphy stories, see Bakeless, *Background to Glory*, 249–50.

33. William Shannon to George Rogers Clark, May 25, 1780, in Seineke, *George Rogers Clark Adventure*, 439.

14. The Village Burner

Epigraph. Thomas Jefferson to George Rogers Clark, January 1, 1780, JP, 3:259.

1. Bradford, *Historical Notes on Kentucky*, 75, 77–78; Arent de Peyster to Frederick Haldimand, May 8, 1780, MPHC, 10:396; DePeyster to Mason Bolton, May 16, 1780, MPHC, 19:519; Henry Bird to Arent DePeyster, June 3, 1780, MPHC, 19:527–29; Coleman, *British Invasion of Kentucky*.

2. John Bowman to Daniel Brodhead, May 27, 1780; Arthur Campbell to William Preston; David Zeisberger to Daniel Brodhead, June 12, 1780; and Killbuck and the Delaware Council to Daniel Brodhead, July 19, 1780, in Kellogg, *Frontier Retreat*, 184–86; 192; 193; 217–20.

3. Harrison, *George Rogers Clark and the War*, 73–74.

4. For an excellent analysis, see West, "Clark's 1780 Shawnee Expedition," 176–97.

5. John Bradford account, "Notes on Kentucky, [n.d.]," in West, *Clark's Shawnee Campaign*, 15.

6. Proposed Grant of Land to Clark, June 30, 1780, CP, 1:428.

7. Account of the Campaign against the Shawnee Indians by Henry Wilson, [n.d.], CP, 1:478.

8. West, "Clark's 1780 Shawnee Expedition," 181.

9. Account of the Campaign against the Shawnee Indians, 477–78.

10. Ibid.

11. Ibid., 480.

12. Intelligence from John Clairy, August 5, 1780, in West, *Clark's Shawnee Campaign*, 8.

13. William Homan to Henry Bird, August 15, 1780, in West, *Clark's Shawnee Campaign*, 9.

14. John Bradford account, 16.

15. Ibid., 17.

16. West, "Clark's 1780 Shawnee Expedition," 182.

17. Ibid., 183–84.

18. George Rogers Clark to Thomas Jefferson August 22, 1780, JP, 3:560.

19. Account of the Campaign against the Shawnee Indians, 480.

20. Ibid., 480–81.

21. Ibid., 481–82.

22. George Rogers Clark to Thomas Jefferson, August 22, 1780, JP, 3:561.

23. Account of the Campaign against the Shawnee Indians, 482.

24. William Holman to Henry Bird, August 15, 1780, in West, *Clark's Shawnee Campaign*, 9.

25. George Rogers Clark to John Clark, August 22, 1780, in West, *Clark's Shawnee Campaign*, 14.

26. William Holman to Henry Bird, August 15, 1780, 9; West, "Clark's 1780 Shawnee Expedition," 190–91.

27. Account of the Campaign against the Shawnee Indians, 483.

28. George Rogers Clark to Thomas Jefferson, August 22, 1780; and Thomas Jefferson to George Rogers Clark, September 29, 1780, JP, 3:561; 670.

29. Speech of the Delaware and Shawnee to Major DePeyster, August 22, 1780, in West, *Clark's Shawnee Campaign*, 12.

30. For a typical intelligence report, see John Heckewelder to Daniel Brodhead, August 9, 1779, in Kellogg, *Frontier Retreat*, 45–46.

31. Thomas Jefferson to Joseph Martin, January 24, 1780, CP, 1:385.

32. Message from the Chickasaw, July 9, 1782, CP, 2:72.

33. John Rogers to George Rogers Clark, July 22, 1780; and Robert George to George Rogers Clark, July 31, 1780, in Seineke, *George Rogers Clark Adventure*, 445–46; 448–49.

34. Robert George to George Rogers Clark, July 31, 1780, 448–49.

35. Robert George to George Rogers Clark, September 2, 1780, in Seineke, *George Rogers Clark Adventure*, 459.

36. Robert George to George Rogers Clark, October 28, 1780, CP, 1:461–62. For conditions at Fort Jefferson, see also Thomas Wilson to George Rogers Clark, February 15,1780; Robert George to George Rogers Clark, July 31, 1780; and Robert George to John Montgomery, September 9, 1780, MHS.

37. John Montgomery to Thomas Jefferson, January 8, 1781, JP, 4:319–21.

38. George Rogers Clark to Thomas Nelson, October 6, 1781, CP, 2:4–5.

39. John William to George Rogers Clark, October 28, 1780, CP, 1:463.

40. Leonard Helm to George Slaughter, October 29, 1780, CP, 1:466.

41. Bakeless, *Background to Glory*, 255.

42. Robert George testimony, [n.d.], 1781, CVSP, 3:842.

43. John Todd to Thomas Jefferson, June 2, 1780; Thomas Jefferson to the Speaker of the House of Delegates, June 14, 1780; and John Rogers to Thomas Jefferson, 29, 1781, CP, 1:422–23; 427–28; 546.

44. Petition of the Inhabitants of Vincennes to the Governor of Virginia, June 30, 1780, CP, 1:430–32. See also Petition to Clark from Cahokia, April 11, 1780, CP, 1:430–32, 410–12; and Magistrates to Captain Rogers, November 18, 1780; Petition from Kaskaskia to Virginia's governor [n.d.]; and Memorial of the Inhabitants of Illinois to the Commissioners of Virginia, March 1, 1783, KR, 207–209; 233–40; 329–44.

45. Memorial of the Inhabitants of Vincennes to the French Minister, Luzerne, August 22, 1780, CP, 1:443–44.

46. Silas Deane to President of Congress, October 17, 1776, in Seineke, *George Rogers Clark Adventure*, 189–90; Address of Colonel de la Balme, September 17, 1780, KR, 181–89. Quote from Inhabitants of Kaskaskia to De La Balme, September 29, 1780, KR, 189–92. See also Goods Furnished De La Balme, October 2, 1780, KR, 193–94.

47. De la Balme to Luzerne, June 27, 1780, KR, 163–68.

48. Ibid.

49. Richard Winston to John Todd, October 24, 1780; and Valentine Dalton to George Rogers Clark, July 29, 1780, in Seineke, *George Rogers Clark Adventure*, 464; 447.

50. Francisco Cruzat to Bernardo de Galvez, November 21, 1780, in Seineke, *George Rogers Clark Adventure*, 467–68.

51. Daniel Murray to Thomas Bentley, May 25, 1777; Thomas Bentley to Daniel Murray, August 1, 1777; Defense of Thomas Bentley, August 1, 1777; Report of Henry Hamilton, August 15, 1777; Court of Enquiry, September 11, 1777; Petition of Thomas Bentley, October 6, 1777; Joseph Bowman to Richard Lernoult, March 20, 1779; and Father Gibault to Richard Lernoult, [n.d.], KR, 6–8; 8–12; 12–16; 16–17; 18–40; 41–42; 73–74; 74; Frederick Haldimand to Henry Hamilton, August 26, 1778, in Seineke, *George Rogers Clark Adventure*, 276.

52. Thomas Bentley to Arent de Peyster, July 28, 1780; and Thomas Bentley to George Rogers Clark, July 20, 1780, KR, 168–69; 169–71.

53. Richard Winston to John Todd, October 17, 1780, KR, 196. For insights into how Bentley stirred up trouble, see Thomas Bentley to my Enemies, September 5, 1780, KR, 202–205.

54. John Dodge Arrest of Richard Winston, April 29, 1782; and Certificate of Richard Winston concerning Bentley, March 9, 1781, KR, 272–74; 227–28.

55. Thomas Bentley to Frederick Haldimand, August 12, 1780, KR, 171–72.

15. Fire in the Rear

Epigraph 1. John Floyd to Thomas Jefferson, April 16, 1781, JP, 5:467.

Epigraph 2. George Rogers Clark to Thomas Nelson, October 1, 1781, CP, 1:606.

1. Thomas Jefferson to George Rogers Clark, December 25, 1780, JP, 4:237.

2. Ibid., 233–38.

3. Thomas Jefferson to John Gibson, February 13, 1781, in Kellogg, *Frontier Retreat*, 331.

4. Thomas Jefferson to Frederick von Steuben, December 31, 1780; Thomas Jefferson to the County Lieutenants, January 2, 1781; and Thomas Jefferson to Thomas Nelson, January 2, 1781, JP, 4:254; 294–95; 297.

5. For an excellent account of Arnold's treason plot, and an outstanding biography, see Randall, *Benedict Arnold*.

6. For a vivid firsthand account, see Simcoe, *Queen's Rangers*.

7. For an account of Steuben's defense and a fine biography, see Lockhart, *Drillmaster of Valley Forge*, 229–57.

8. Thomas Jefferson to George Washington, January 10, 1781, JP, 4:333–35.

9. Swem, "Lost Vouchers," 424; Meeker, "Original Vouchers," 87–93.

10. Holm, "Clark's Ambush," 198–213; Thomas Jefferson to Frederick von Steuben, January 9, 1781, JP, 4:326; Frederick von Steuben to Thomas Jefferson, January 7, 1781, CVSP, 1:420–21.

11. Simcoe, *Queen's Rangers*, 164.

12. Thomas Jefferson to Virginia delegates in Congress, January 18, 1781, JP, 4:398–400.

13. Thomas Jefferson to George Rogers Clark, January 13, 1781, JP, 4:348.

14. From the Officers of the Berkeley County Militia to Thomas Jefferson, January 25, 1781; From the Officers of the Green County Militia to Thomas Jefferson, January 29, 1781; Thomas Jefferson to the County Lieutenants of Berkeley and Frederick, February 16, 1781; and Thomas Jefferson to the County Lieutenant of Hampshire, JP, 4:451–52; 469; 627–98; 629.

15. Thomas Jefferson to the Country Lieutenants of Berkeley and Frederick, 628.

16. Thomas Jefferson to the Officers of the Greenbrier County Militia, February 17, 1781, JP, 4:641.

17. Thomas Jefferson to John Gibson, February 13, 1781; and Thomas Jefferson to George Rogers Clark, February 13, 1781, JP, 4:598–99; 597–88.

18. George Rogers Clark to Thomas Jefferson, February 10, 1781, JP, 4:574–75.

19. For an account of Patrick Henry's censure of Thomas Jefferson in the Assembly on June 22, 1781, see Henry, *Patrick Henry*, 2:134–54.

20. George Rogers Clark to Thomas Jefferson, January 18, 1781, JP, 4:394.

21. Thomas Jefferson to George Rogers Clark, November 26, 1782, JP, 6:204–205.

22. R. Madison to Thomas Jefferson, January 23, 1781, CVSP, 1:455.

23. Enclosure House of Delegates, January 2, 1781, JP, 4:386–88.

24. Thomas Jefferson to George Rogers Clark, January 22, 1781, JP, 4:424.

25. Thomas Jefferson to George Rogers Clark, February 19, 1718, JP, 4:653. See also the accusation against Slaughter by William Shannon to George Rogers Clark, May 21, 1781, KR, 248–49.

26. George Slaughter to Thomas Jefferson, April 13, 1781, JP, 5:439.

27. George Rogers Clark to Thomas Jefferson, March 27, 1781, JP, 5:252–53.

28. Ibid.

29. Benjamin Harrison to William Fleming, January 29, 1782, CP, 2:33.

30. John Todd to Thomas Jefferson, January 24, 1782, CP, 2:31.

31. Richard Winston to John Todd, October 17, 1780; and Richard Winston to Officers Commanding at Louisville, October 24, 1780, KR, 196; 197.

32. George Rogers Clark to Thomas Jefferson, March 27, 1781, CP, 1:517.

33. Thomas Jefferson to George Rogers Clark, April 20, 1781, JP, 5:503.

34. George Rogers Clark to Thomas Jefferson, June 10, 1781, CP, 1:563–64.

35. John Gibson to George Rogers Clark, March 5, 1782, CP, 2:40.

36. Daniel Brodhead to George Rogers Clark, February 23, 1781, CP, 2:509. See also Daniel Brodhead to Thomas Jefferson, January 17, 1781; and Daniel Brodhead to George Washington, March 27, 1781, in Kellogg, *Frontier Retreat*, 317–18; 352–53.

37. Daniel Brodhead to Richard Peters, January 22, 1781, in Kellogg, *Frontier Retreat*, 324–25.

38. George Washington to Daniel Brodhead, December 29, 1780, in Kellogg, *Frontier Retreat*, 311–13; see also George Washington to Daniel Brodhead, April 16, 1781, in Kellogg, *Frontier Retreat*, 383–84.

39. John Gibson to George Rogers Clark, May 6, 1781, CP, 1:547–48; George Rogers Clark to Board of War, April 2, 1781; and Isaac Craig to George Rogers Clark, April 15, 1781, in Kellogg, *Frontier Retreat*, 370–71; 382–83.

40. Alexander Fowler to Joseph Reed, March 29, 1781, in Kellogg, *Frontier Retreat*, 357, 356–60. See also "Memorial of the Pittsburgh Inhabitants," [n.d.]; Petition of Pittsburgh Inhabitants, [n.d.]; and Joseph Reed to Samuel Huntington, April 18, 1781, in Kellogg, *Frontier Retreat*, 360–63; 363–70; 387–88.

41. George Washington to Daniel Brodhead, May 5, 1781, in Kellogg, *Frontier Retreat*, 385–96.

42. George Rogers Clark to the Inhabitants of Monongahela County, June 18, 1781; and Agreement of the Part of Some of the Inhabitants of Monongahela County to Submit to Future Military Orders, June 19, 1781, CP, 1:567; 568.

43. John Gibson to George Rogers Clark, May 30, 1781, June 5, CP, 1:559–60; 561.

44. William Croghan to Colonel Davies, August 18, 1781, CP, 1:589.

45. John Neville to George Rogers Clark, April 14, 1782, CP, 2:57–58.

46. John Gibson to Thomas Jefferson, May 30, 1781, in Kellogg, *Frontier Retreat*, 399–400.

47. George Rogers Clark to George Washington, May 20, 1781 CP, 1:551–52.

48. George Washington to Board of War, June 8, 1781, CP, 1:562–53.

49. George Washington to Isaac Craig, April 25, 1781, in Kellogg, *Frontier Retreat*, 390–91.

50. George Rogers Clark to William Fleming, 12, 1781, CP, 1:565.

51. George Rogers Clark to David Shepherd, July 8, 1781, in Kellogg, *Frontier Retreat*, 416.

52. John Floyd to George Rogers Clark, May 22, 1781, CP, 1:558.

53. George Rogers Clark to Thomas Jefferson, May 23, 1781, CP, 1:558.

54. Joseph Reed to George Rogers Clark, May 15, 1781; and Plan of Defense of a Committee of Westmoreland County, June 18, 1781, CP, 1:550; 566–67. See also George Rogers Clark to the Officers of Pennsylvania and Virginia, June 23, 1781, CP, 1:569–70.

55. Archibald Lochry to George Rogers Clark, May 11, 1781, CP, 1:549. See also Archibald Lochry to George Rogers Clark, June 9 and July 3, 17, and 22, 1781, MHS.

56. George Rogers Clark to Joseph Reed, August 4, 1781, CP, 1:579–80.

57. John Gibson to George Rogers Clark, June 26, July 2, 1781, CP, 1:570, 571

58. George Rogers Clark to Thomas Jefferson, August 4, 1781, CVSP, 2:294–95.

59. George Rogers Clark to Thomas Jefferson, August 4, 1781; and Return of Infantry under Colonel Joseph Crockett, August 28, 1781, CP, 1:577–79; 594.

60. Quotes from John Floyd to Thomas Jefferson, October 6, 1781, CP, 2:2. See also John Floyd to Thomas Jefferson, April 16, 1781, JP, 5:467.

61. William Croghan to William Davies, August 18, 1781, CVSP, 2:346.

62. John Montgomery to Virginia Governor, August 10, 1781, CVSP, 2:313–14.

63. For an outstanding biography, see Kelsay, *Joseph Brant*.

64. Lt. Isaac Anderson diary, DM, 13J52; English, *Conquest*, 2:725–27.

65. Pershing, "The Lost Battalion," 44–51.

66. George Rogers Clark to Archibald Lochry, August 9, 1781, CP, 1:583. See also Maurer, "British Version of Lochry's Defeat," 216, 215–230.

67. George Rogers Clark Efforts to Assist Archibald Lochry, August 10, 1781, CP, 1:584.

68. Lt. Isaac Anderson diary, DM, 13J52, 56, 57; 16J62; English, *Conquest*, 2:725–27.

69. Thompson to Arent de Peyster, September 26, 1781; and Alexander McKee to Arent de Peyster, September 26, 1781, MPHC, 10:515–16; 516–17.

70. Thompson to de Peyster, September 26, 1781; and McKee to de Peyster, September 26, 1781, in Haldimand Papers, MHPC, 10:515–16; 516–17.

71. John Todd to Clark, September 6, 1781; and Proceedings of a Council of the Kentucky Officers, September 7, 1781, CP, 1:599–600; 601–603.

72. John Montgomery to Thomas Nelson, August 10, 1781, CP, 1:585–86.

73. John Floyd to George Rogers Clark, September 14, 1781, CP, 1:604; Isaiah and Moses Brown interview, DM, 19CJ 95–96, 36–37; Sam Murphy interview, DM, 3CJ40–45.

74. George Rogers Clark to Thomas Nelson, October 1, 1781, CP, 1:606.

75. Clark's words are referred to in the reply by Benjamin Harrison to George Rogers Clark, December 20, 1781, CP, 2:21.

76. Benjamin Harrison to George Rogers Clark, December 20, 1781, CP, 2:21.

16. The Bloodiest Year

Epigraph 1. Benjamin Harrison to William Fleming, October 16, 1782, CP, 2:132.
Epigraph 2. John Floyd to George Rogers Clark, August 31, 1782, CP, 2:106.

1. Plan for Kentucky Defense, December 11, 1781, Journal of Virginia House of Delegates; and Benjamin Harrison to George Rogers Clark, December 20, 1781, CP, 2:15–17; 19–21.

2. Benjamin Harrison to George Rogers Clark, December 20, 1781, CP, 2:21.

3. Benjamin Harrison address, February [n.d.], 1782, DM, 32J64.

4. George Rogers Clark to Benjamin Harrison, March 5, 1782, CP, 2:4.

5. John Floyd to John May, April 8, 1782, CP, 2:55.

6. Ibid., 54. For muted criticism of the government, see also John Evans to Benjamin Harrison, March 9, 1782, CP, 2:46.

7. Benjamin Harrison to George Rogers Clark, March 25, 1782, CP, 2:50.

8. John Floyd to Thomas Jefferson, April 16, 1781, JP, 5:467.

9. George Rogers Clark to Benjamin Harrison, May 1782, CP, 19:235

10. John Todd and Benjamin Logan to George Rogers Clark, October 13, 1781, CP, 2:5–6.

11. John Todd to Thomas Nelson, October 21, 1781, CP, 2:8–10.

12. "William Whitley Narrative."

13. Robert George to John Todd, July 19, 1782, CP, 2:79.

14. James Galloway interview, September 1846, DM, 8J304.

15. William Croghan to William Davies, July 6, 1782, CP, 2:71–73. For in-depth analyses, see Silver, *Our Savage Neighbors*, 265–76.

16. John Hardin to William Davies, July 28,1782, CP, 2:80.

17. "Attack on Bryan's Station," in Cist, *Cincinnati Miscellany*, 1:236–39.

18. Benjamin Logan to George Rogers Clark, August 30, September 7, 1782, MHS.

19. "Battle of Blue Licks," in Cist, *Cincinnati Miscellany*, 2:92.

20. Battle of Blue Licks, Major Madison's Account, September 3, 1782, CP, 2:92.

21. Daniel Boone to Benjamin Harrison, August 30, 1782, CP, 2:98.

22. Benjamin Logan to Benjamin Harrison, August 31, 1782; and Fayette Officers to Benjamin Harrison, CP, 2:102–103; 113–14.

23. Arthur Campbell to William Davies, October 3, 1782, CP, 2:122.

24. Benjamin Harrison to Benjamin Logan, October 14, 1782; Benjamin Harrison to William Fleming, October 16, 1782; and Benjamin Harrison to Joseph Crockett, October 16, 1782, CP, 2:126; 132; 133.

25. Joseph Crockett to Benjamin Harrison, October 24, 1782, CP, 2:142.

26. Thomas Jefferson to George Rogers Clark, November 26, 1782, CP, 2:155–56.

27. George Rogers Clark to Jonathan Clark, April 19, 1781, CP, 1:534.

28. William Davies to George Rogers Clark, April 10, 1782, CP, 1:57.

29. John Floyd to George Rogers Clark, August 31, 1782, CP, 2:106.

30. George Rogers Clark to William Irvine, August 10, 1782, CP, 2:87.

31. William Irvine to Benjamin Harrison, September 3, 1782, CP, 2:110–11.

32. William Irvine to George Rogers Clark, September 9, 1782; and Benjamin Harrison to militia captains, October 10, 1782, CP, 2:111; 132.

33. Benjamin Harrison to George Rogers Clark, October 17, 1782, CP, 2:133–35.

34. George Rogers Clark to Benjamin Harrison, October 18, 1782, CP, 2:135.

35. George Rogers Clark to Benjamin Harrison, November 30, 1782, CP, 2:161–63.

36. For accounts of the campaign, see George Rogers Clark to Benjamin Harrison, November 27, 1782; and John Crittenden to William Davies, November 29, 1782, CP, 2:157; 158; and Harding, *George Rogers Clark and his Men*, 158–97.

37. Clark's Plan of Campaign for 1782, CP, 2:150–51.

38. General Orders, November 9, 1782, CP, 2:151.

39. General Orders, November 9, 1782, CP, 19:152–53. See also Clark's Plan of Campaign for 1782, CP, 19:150–51.

40. John McClasland interview, DM, 8J121–28.

41. William Irvine to George Rogers Clark, November 7, 1782, CP, 2:149.

42. Benjamin Harrison to George Rogers Clark, December 19, 1783, CP, 2:170–71.

43. Benjamin Harrison to George Rogers Clark, January 13, 1783, CP, 2:181–82.

17. Peace

Epigraph 1. Benjamin Harrison to George Rogers Clark, July 2, 1783, CP, 2:245–46.

Epigraph 2. George Rogers Clark to Benjamin Harrison, July 2, 1783, CP, 2:246.

Epigraph 3. George Rogers Clark to Oliver Pollock, October 25, 1782, CP, 2:144.

1. George Washington to Jacob Reed, November 3, 1784, in Abbot and Twohig, *Papers of George Washington*, 2:120–21

2. Guy Johnson, Transaction with Indians at Sandusky, September 8, 1783, MPHC, 20:174–82.

3. George Washington to Frederick Haldimand, July 12, 1783; Frederick Haldimand to Frederick Von Steuben, August 12, 1783; Frederick Von Steuben to Frederick Haldimand, August 17, 1783; and Frederick Haldimand to George Washington, August 11, 1783, MPHC, 20:141; 167–68; 168; 165.

4. George Rogers Clark to Benjamin Harrison, October 1, 1781, CVSP, 3:351.

5. Conditions in Kentucky, Six Fort Nelson officers, February 18, 1783, CP, 2:203.

6. William Clark to George Rogers Clark, April 15,1783, MHS.

7. George Walls to George Rogers Clark, February 11, 1783, CP, 2:201–202. See also George Rogers Clark to Benjamin Harrison, February 23, 1783; and Conditions in Kentucky, Six Fort Nelson officers, February 18, 1783, CP, 202; 203.

8. John Dodge to George Rogers Clark, March 3, 1783; and Richard Winston and others to George Rogers Clark, March 30, 1783, KR, 345–46; 346; John McDowell to George Rogers Clark, November 14, 1782; Western Commissioners to George Rogers Clark, November 14, 1782; and William Fleming to George Rogers Clark, December 18, 1782, MHS.

9. James Monroe to George Rogers Clark, January 5, 1782, CP, 2:178–80.

10. George Rogers Clark to the Western Commissioners, February 25, 1783, CP, 2:203–206.

11. Commissioners to Benjamin Harrison, March 9, 1783, CP, 2:216.

12. John Calvert to George Rogers Clark, January 11, 1782, MHS.

13. Holm, "Supply Issues," 149, 151.

14. George Rogers Clark to the Western Commissioners, December 15, 1782, CP, 2:167.

15. Commissioners to Benjamin Harrison, February 17, 1783; Commissioners to Benjamin Harrison, April 14, 1783; Journal of Western Commissioners, November 1, 1782–July 1, 1783; and Virginia Accounts, July 1, 1783 CP, 2:197–200; 224–25; 290–402; 402–12.

16. Journal of Western Commissioners, November 1, 1782 to July 1, 1783, CP, 2:390, 290–401; Commissioner Report of Money Owed George Rogers Clark, June 28,1783, MHS.

17. George Rogers Clark to Jonathan Clark, February 18, 1782, CP, 2:xxxv.

18. Deposition of John May before the Board of Commissioners, February 3, 1783, CP, 2:192.

19. Reuben Durrett anecdote, June 17, 1883 DM, 2J92. See also Walker Daniel to George Rogers Clark, September 15, 1783, CP, 2:246–48.

20. Oliver Pollock to George Rogers Clark, July 24, 1782, CP, 2:144.

21. George Rogers Clark to Oliver Pollock, October 25, 1782, CP, 2:144.

22. George Rogers Clark to Jonathan Clark, February 16, 1782, CP, 2:39–40.

23. Ibid.

24. Officers of the Illinois Regiment to the General Assembly of Virginia, May 21, 1783, CP, 2:233–35.

25. Benjamin Harrison to George Rogers Clark, April 9, 1783, CP, 2:224.

26. Benjamin Harrison to George Rogers Clark, July 2, 1783, CP, 2:245–46.

27. George Rogers Clark to Benjamin Harrison, July 2, 1783, CP 2:246.

18. Distant Horizons

Epigraph. Thomas Jefferson to George Rogers Clark, December 4, 1783, JP, 6:371.

1. Thomas Jefferson to George Rogers Clark, November 26, 1782, CP, 2:155.

2. Thomas Jefferson to George Rogers Clark, December 4, 1783, JP, 6:371.

3. George Rogers Clark to Thomas Jefferson, February 8, 1784, in Jackson, *Letters of the Lewis and Clark Expedition*, 2:655–66.

4. Clark Appointed Principal Surveyor of Bounty Lands, December 17, 1783; and Records of the Proceedings of the Illinois Officers Respecting a Grant of Lands, February 1, 1784; CP, 2:251–52; 413–15.

5. Thomas Jefferson to George Rogers Clark, March [n.d.] 1784, JP, 7:8–9.

6. Bakeless, *Background to Glory*, 313–14; Articles of Agreement, October 18, 1784, in English, *Conquest*, 2:925–26.

7. Kinkead, "How the Parents of George Rogers Clark Came to Kentucky," 1–4.

8. George Rogers Clark description of land at and near Clarksville, [n.d.] 1784, MHS; "The Clarksville Conventions," 691–93.

9. Benjamin Harrison to George Rogers Clark, August 17, 1784, DM, 53J14.

10. Gen. Butler Journal, in Craig, *Olden Time*, 2:493, 484, 496.

11. Hammon and Taylor, *Virginia's Western War*, 186, 253.

12. Memorial of Francois Carbonneaux to Congress, December 8, 1784, KR, 369.

13. "Diary of Erkuries Beatty," 241.

14. Treaty of Fort Stanwix, Commissioner's accounts, September 23 to October 21, 1784, CP, 2:404–27.

15. Arthur Lee Journal, November 24 to December 29, 1784, in Craig *Olden Time*, 2:334–44.

16. Gen. Butler Journal, 2:433–64, 481–531; Denny, *Military Journal*.

17. Gen. Butler Journal, 2:511, 484.

18. Ibid., 2:489.

19. Denny, *Military Journal*, 70–71.

20. Gen. Butler Journal, 2:512–13.

21. Ibid., 2:531, 517.

22. Ibid., 2:522.

23. Ibid., 2:523–24.

24. Denny *Military Journal*, 73.

25. Josiah Harmar to Thomas Mifflin, June 25, 1785, in Denny, *Military Journal*, 214.

26. Vincennes petition to George Rogers Clark, March 6, 1786, DM, 53J23.

27. Jean Legras to George Rogers Clark, May 15, 1786, MHS.

28. John May to Patrick Henry, July 14, 1786, in Henry, *Patrick Henry*, 3:369–70.

29. George Rogers Clark to Patrick Henry, May 1786, CVSP, 4:122.

30. Patrick Henry to Virginia Delegates in Congress, July 5, 1783, in Henry, *Patrick Henry*, 3:365, 362–68.

31. Patrick Henry to Richard Henry Lee, President of Congress, May 16 1786; Charles Thomson to Patrick Henry, July 3, 1783; and Patrick Henry to Josiah Harmar, July 12, 1786, in Henry, *Patrick Henry*, 3:353–54; 361–62; 368.

32. John May to Patrick Henry, July 14, 1786, in Henry, *Patrick Henry*, 3:369–70.

33. Resolution of the officers of the Kentucky, signed by Benjamin Logan, August 2, 1786, DM, 53J42.

34. Levi Todd to Patrick Henry, November 20, 1786, in Henry, *Patrick Henry*, 3:381.

35. Robard, Clark's 1787 Campaign, DM, 11J79.

36. Levi Todd to Patrick Henry, November 20, 1786, in Henry, *Patrick Henry*, 3:381.

19. Conspiracies

Epigraph 1. George Rogers Clark to Diego Gardoqui, March 15, 1788, DM, 33J120.

Epigraph 2. George Rogers Clark to Provisionary Executive Council, February 5, 1793, DM, 55J1.

1. John Jay to Diego Gardoqui, September 3, 1780, in Johnston, *Correspondence and Public Papers of John Jay*, 1:394–95.

2. Patrick Henry to Joseph Martin, October 4, 1786, in Henry, *Patrick Henry*, 374–77.

3. For the best biography on Wilkinson, see Linklater, *Artist in Treason*.

4. Clark to Citizens of Vincennes, October 1786, DM, 52J53.

5. Court proceeding, October 18, 1786, DM, 53J53; William Clark to Edmund Clark, DM, 2L45; Jonathan Clark to George Rogers Clark, July 17, 1801, DM, 55J53.

6. Anonymous Gentleman from Kentucky to a friend in Philadelphia, December 1786, CVSP, 4:202.

7. Protest Against Clark, [n.d.] 1787, JCC 32:189–99; Board Findings, February 28, 1787, DM, 53J63; Edmund Randolph proclamation, February 28, 1787, DM, 53J65.

8. Congress Resolution, April 24, 1787; and Henry Knox Report, April 19, 1787, JCC, 37:231; 222.

9. George Rogers Clark to Beverly Randolph, October 8, 1787, CVSP, 4:347.

10. Bakeless, *Background to Glory*, 335.

11. George Rogers Clark to Edmund Randolph, October 3, 1787, DM 12S161–63.

12. George Rogers Clark to Jonathan Clark, April 20, 1788, DM, 33J139 (1).

13. George Rogers Clark to Gardoqui, March 15, 1788, DM, 33J120.

14. George Rogers Clark to Esteban Miro, September 17, 1789, quoted in James, *Life of George Rogers Clark*, 401.

15. Major Erkuries Beatty journal, April 19, 1787, DM, 33J86.

16. Whitaker, *Spanish-American Frontier*, 129–33.

17. Thomas Jefferson to George Washington, April 2, 1791, in Ford, *Writings of Jefferson*, 5:316.

18. Thomas Jefferson to William Carmichael, August 22, 1790, in Ford, *Writings of Jefferson*, 5:225.

19. James O'Fallon to Fanny Clark O'Fallon, November 23, 1793, DM, 2M47. See also James O'Fallon prenuptial agreement, February 21, 1791, MHS.

20. George Washington to James Duane, September 7, 1783, in Fitzpatrick, *Writings of Washington*, 8:480–84.

21. George Rogers Clark to John Brown, August 20, 1789, CP, 1:626.

22. For the best history, see Sword, *President Washington's Indian War*; for a fascinating participant's account, see Denny, *Military Journal*.

23. Jonathan Clark to George Rogers Clark, April 8, 1792, DM, 53J92.

24. George Rogers Clark to Edmund Clark, September 2, 1791, DM, 34J7; George Rogers Clark to Jonathan Clark, [n.d.], in English, *Conquest*, 2:788.

25. John Brown to George Rogers Clark, July 5, 1789, CP, 1:620.

26. George Rogers Clark to John Brown, August 20, 1789, CP, 1:621–22. The entry is dated January, but a subsequent letter from Brown clearly identified the month as August.

27. George Rogers Clark to John Brown, July 15, 1790, CP, 1:621–22. See also George Rogers Clark to John Brown, July 29, 1790; and John Brown to George Rogers Clark, April 27, 1790, CP, 1:622–23; 23.

28. Thomas Jefferson to Harry Innes, March 7, 1791, JP, 19:521–22.

29. Harry Innes to Thomas Jefferson, 1791 JP, 20:480–81.

30. Pope, *Tour through the Western and Southern Territories*, 19.

31. George Rogers Clark to Matthew Carey, [n.d.], DM, 53J81. See also Thomas and Conner, "George Rogers Clark," 210.

32. George Rogers Clark to John Brown, January 30, DM, 27CC39. See also George Rogers Clark to John Brown, July 15, 1790; and John Brown to George Rogers Clark, April 27, 1790, DM, 27CC40; 53J88.

33. George Rogers Clark to Edmund Clark, September 2, 1791, DM, 34J7.

34. George Rogers Clark to Jonathan Clark, May 11, 1792, in English, *Conquest*, 2:788–90; Jonathan Clark to George Rogers Clark, November 1, 1792, DM, 53J94.

35. Thomas Paine to James O'Fallon, February 17, 1793, DM, 12J60. See also the unsigned letter to general [Clark], February [n.d.], 1793, DM, 12J59. The original letter from James O'Fallon to Thomas Paine has been lost, but its content can be inferred from the reply.

36. George Rogers Clark to Provisionary Executive Council, February 5, 1793, DM, 55J1.

37. From Citizens West of the Allegheny Mountains, May 24, 1793, in Abbot and Twohig, *Papers of George Washington*, 14:655–57.

38. Thomas Jefferson to Andre Michaux, April 30, 1793, JP, 25:624–26.

39. George Rogers Clark to Andre Michaux, October 10, 1793, DM, 11J205; Andre Michaux to George Rogers Clark, October 7, 1793, DM, 55J4; Andre Michaux to George Rogers Clark, October 10, 1793, DM, 55J5.

40. Thomas Jefferson to James Madison, August 11, 1793, JP, 26:651–53.

41. Anas, July 5, 1793, JP, 26:437–39.

42. For background, see Josef de Jaudenes and Josef de Viar to Thomas Jefferson, June 18, 1793; and Thomas Jefferson to Josef de Jaudenes and Josef de Viar, July 11, 1793, JP, 26:313–15; 473. For the quote, see Josef de Jaudenes and Josef de Viar to Thomas Jefferson, August 27, 1793, JP, 26: 771–73.

43. Thomas Jefferson to Isaac Shelby, August 29, 1793, JP, 26:785.

44. Arthur St. Clair to Isaac Shelby, November 7, 1793, quoted in Henderson, "Isaac Shelby and the Genet Mission," 455.

45. Isaac Shelby to Thomas Jefferson, October 5, 1793, JP, 27:196.

46. George Rogers Clark to Edmond Genet, October 3, 1793, DM, 11J202.

47. Benjamin Logan to George Rogers Clark, December 31, 1793, DM, 55J9; John Montgomery to George Rogers Clark, October 26, 1793, DM, 55J6.

48. Carstens, "George Rogers Clark and the French Conspiracy," 241.

49. George Rogers Clark to Edmond Genet, October 3, 1793, DM, 11J202.

50. Ibid.

51. Benjamin Logan to George Rogers Clark, December 31, 1793, DM, 55J9.

52. Jean Antoine Joseph Fauchet Declaration, *Philadelphia General Advertiser*, March 7, 1794; George Washington proclamation, March 24, 1794, in Abbot and Twohig, *Papers of George Washington*, 15:446–47.

53. George Rogers Clark to Edmund Genet, March [n.d.], 1794, reprinted in *American Historical Review* 18, no. 4 (July 1913): 781–82.

54. Andre Michaux to George Rogers Clark, December 27, 1793, DM, 55J8.

55. Samuel Fulton to George Rogers Clark, November 10, 1794, DM, 55J23; see also Samuel Fulton to George Rogers Clark, February 18, 1795, DM, 55J27.

56. George Rogers Clark to Committee of Public Safety, November 2, 1794, DM, 55J33.

57. Samuel Fulton to George Rogers Clark, February 18, 1795, DM, 55J27.

58. Collot, *Journey in North America*, 1:214–17.

59. George Rogers Clark to the Committee of Public Safety.

60. George Rogers Clark to Samuel Fulton, June 3, 1798, in James, *Life of George Rogers Clark*, 511–13.

61. George Rogers Clark to Samuel Fulton, March [n.d.], 1797, in James, *Life of George Rogers Clark*, 510.

62. George Rogers Clark to Samuel Fulton, June 3, 1798.

63. Ibid., 512.

64. George Rogers Clark to [Samuel Fulton], September 10, 1798, in James, *Life of George Rogers Clark*, 513.

65. Ibid.

66. For the best Burr biography and account of Burr's plot, see Isenberg, *Fallen Founder*.

20. Final Reckonings

Epigraph 1. George Rogers Clark to Jonathan Clark, May 11, 1792, in English, *Conquest,* 2:788–90.

Epigraph 2. Judge John Rowan obituary of George Rogers Clark, DM, 55J85.

1. John Clark will, July 24, 1799; and Codicil to the above Will, July 26, 1799, in English, *Conquest,* 1:46–50; 50–51. Hudson, "Slavery in Early Louisville," 277.

2. The information in the following biographical sketch comes from Jones, *William Clark and the Shaping of the West.*

3. For insights in the relationship and holdings, see George Rogers Clark sale of land to William Clark, August 10,1797; William Clark property, July 5, 1802; and George Rogers Clark to William Clark, April 11, 1803, in MHS.

4. George Rogers Clark to Thomas Jefferson, December 12, 1802, in Jackson, *Letters of the Lewis and Clark Expedition,* 1:7.

5. Meriwether Lewis to William Clark, June 19, 1803; William Clark to Meriwether Lewis, July 18, 1803, in Jackson, *Letters of the Lewis and Clark Expedition.*

6. William Clark to Jonathan Clark, April [n.d.], 1805, in Holmberg, *Dear Brother,* 84–86.

7. William Clark to Jonathan Clark, September 23, 1806, in Holmberg, *Dear Brother,* 101–106. For Holmberg's discussion of the debate over whether the letter was penned to George Rogers or Jonathan, see 106–107.

8. *Kentucky Argus,* Canal Project, November 1819, DM, 35J10.

9. George Rogers Clark to Congress, October 29, 1805, DM, 54J50.

10. Samuel Fulton to George Rogers Clark, December 27, 1802, DM, 55J54.

11. William Clark to Jonathan Clark, September 9, 1807; November 22/24, 1808; August 26, 1809; January 12, 1810; December 14, 1810; August 30, 1811, in Holmberg, *Dear Brother,* 126, 171, 209, 234, 251–52, 262.

12. Espy, *Memorandums of a Tour,* 12–14.

13. George Rogers Clark Lawsuit, 1799, DM, 34J88, 92; CP, 8:625. For medicines and treatments, see Richard Ferguson to George Rogers Clark, May 20, 1808, MHS.

14. John O'Fallon to George Rogers Clark, November 18, 1808, DM, 55J64; and February 9, 1809, DM, 55J65.

15. Owen Gwathmey to George Rogers Clark, July 31, 1808, DM, 55J63.

16. William Croghan to James Barbour, December 15, 1812, DM, 55J82.

17. George Rogers Clark Sullivan to John O'Fallon, April 24, 1809, in English, *Conquest,* 2:870.

18. William Clark to Jonathan Clark, May 28, 1809, in Holmberg, *Dear Brother,* 201.

19. Thomas, "William Croghan, Sr."

20. Bryant, *Croghans of Locust Grove.*

21. Francis Vigo to George Rogers Clark, July 15, 1811; and George Rogers Clark to Francis Vigo, August 1, 1811, DM, 44J19–20.

22. Thomas Jefferson to George Rogers Clark, December 19, 1807, in Lipscomb, *Writings of Thomas Jefferson*, 11:406.

23. James, *Life of George Rogers Clark*, 470–71; Bakeless, *Background to Glory*, 354–55; English, *Conquest*, 871–84.

24. William Croghan to James Barbour, December 15, 1812, in English, *Conquest*, 2:882–83.

25. English, *Conquest*, 892.

26. George Rogers Clark to William Clark, July 30, 1814, DM, 44J55–56.

27. For Clark's last years, see John Croghan to William Croghan, October 20, 1810; David Todd interview, February 10, 1848; William Gwathmey interview, January 23, 1847; Samuel Gwathmey interview, February 10, 1848; and Sarah Gamble to Lyman Draper, June 3, 1889, DM, 12J21; 10J181; 10J355; 10J214; 44J36 (1).

28. Anonymous, *Louisville Correspondent*, January 27 1817.

29. Eloise DeKautsow to J. B. Gwathmey, August 5, 1848, DM, 10J169.

30. *Western Courier*, February 21, 1818.

31. George Rogers Clark to William Clark, July 30, 1814, DM, 44J55–56.

32. Judge John Rowan obituary of George Rogers Clark, DM, 55J85.

33. Thomas Jefferson to George Rogers Clark, March or April 1777, JP 2:246.

34. Benjamin Harrison to George Rogers Clark, July 2, 1783, CP, 2:245–46.

35. George Morgan to John Dodge, December 1, 1780, KR, 210.

36. John Todd to William Fleming, August 18, 1779, KR, 109.

37. Thwaites, *How George Rogers Clark Won the Northwest*, 71; Bakeless, *Background to Glory*, 19; Downes, *Council Fires on the Upper Ohio*, 229.

38. For an excellent overview, see Smith, "Old Northwest and the Peace Negotiations," 92–105. See also Philbrick, *Rise of the West*, 75; and Sosin, *Revolutionary Frontier*, 117.

39. Petre Serge to Benjamin Franklin, July 6, 1779, reprinted in Carey, "Franklin Is Informed," 375–78.

40. For the best overview and analysis, see Nester, *Frontier War for American Independence*.

41. Congress to Peace Commissioners, October 17, 1780, *American State Papers: Foreign Relations* 6:868.

42. George Rogers Clark to Benjamin Harrison, May 22, 1783, CP, 2:236.

43. White, *Middle Ground*, 368.

44. Barnhart, *Hamilton and Clark*, 189.

45. General Orders, George Rogers Clark, November 9, 1782, CP, 1:151.

46. For the best accounts of the frontier mentality toward the Indians, see Slotkin, *Regeneration through Violence*; and Silver, *Our Savage Neighbors*.

47. Jonathan Clark to George Rogers Clark, November 8, 1781, CP, 2:12–13.

48. George Rogers Clark to George Mason, November 19, 1779, MP, 2:555.

49. Quoted in Carstens, "Making of a Myth," 60–79.

50. Quoted in Carstens, "Making of a Myth."

51. Arthur Campbell to William Davies, October 3, 1782, CP, 2:122.

52. John O'Fallon to Lyman Draper, January 18, 1847, DM, J3410, 8–12.

53. George Rogers Clark to George Mason, November 19, 1779, MP, 2:555–56.

54. George Rogers Clark to Jonathan Clark, January 16, 1780, CP, 1:381–82.

Bibliography

Archival Sources

Calendar of Virginia State Papers. Virginia Historical Society, Richmond.

Draper Manuscripts. Wisconsin Historical Society, Madison.

Thomas Gage Papers. American Series. William Clements Library, University of Michigan.

Michigan Pioneer and Historical Collections. Michigan State University Library.

Missouri Historical Society, Saint Louis.

Books and Articles

Abbot, W. W., and Dorothy Twohig, eds. *The Papers of George Washington: Confederation Series.* 16 vols. Charlottesville: University of Virginia Press, 1992.

Alvord, Clarence W., ed. *Kaskaskia Records, 1778–1790.* Springfield: Illinois State Historical Library, 1909.

Bakeless, John. *Background to Glory: The Life of George Rogers Clark.* Lincoln: University of Nebraska Press, 1992.

Barnhart, John D., ed. *Henry Hamilton and George Rogers Clark in the American Revolution, with the Unpublished Journal of Lieut. Gov. Henry Hamilton.* Crawfordsville, Ind.: R.E. Banta, 1951.

Bass, Robert D. *The Green Dragoon: The Lives of Banastre Tarleton and Mary Robinson.* Orangeburg, S.C.: Sandlapper Publishing, 2003.

Becker, Robert. "Currency, Taxation, and Finance, 1775–1787." In *The Blackwell Encyclopedia of the American Revolution*, edited by Jack Greene and J. R. Pole, 362–73. Cambridge, Mass.: Blackwell, 1994.

Bodley, Temple. *George Rogers Clark: His Life and Public Service*. Boston: Houghton Mifflin, 1926.

Bogert, Pen. "Clark, the Slave Trade, and the Illinois Regiment." In *The Life of George Rogers Clark, 1752–1818: Triumphs and Tragedies*, edited by Kenneth C. Carstens and Nancy Carstens, 137–47. Westport, Conn.: Praeger, 2004.

Bradford, John. *Historical Notes on Kentucky*. Compiled by G. W. Stipp. San Francisco: Grabhorn Press, 1932.

———. *The Voice of the Frontier: John Bradford's Notes on Kentucky*. Edited by Thomas D. Clark. Lexington: University Press of Kentucky, 1993.

Bryant, Gwynne, ed. *The Croghans of Locust Grove*. Louisville: Division of Historic Homes Foundation, 1988.

Calloway, Colin G. *The American Revolution in Indian Country: Crisis and Diversity in Native American Communities*. New York: Cambridge University Press, 1995.

———. *Crown and Calumet: British-Indian Relations, 1783–1815*. Norman: University of Oklahoma Press, 1987.

Carey, Lewis. "Franklin Is Informed of Clark's Activities in the Old Northwest." *Mississippi Valley Historical Review* 21, no. 3 (December 1941): 375–78.

Carstens, Kenneth. "George Rogers Clark's Fort Jefferson, 1780–1781." *FCHQ* 71, no. 3 (July 1997): 259–84.

———. *The Personnel of George Rogers Clark's Fort Jefferson and the Civilian Community of Clarksville, Kentucky, 1780–1781*. Bowie, Md.: Heritage Books, 1999.

Carstens, Nancy. "George Rogers Clark and the French Conspiracy, 1793–1801." In *The Life of George Rogers Clark, 1752–1818: Triumphs and Tragedies*, edited by Kenneth C. Carstens and Nancy Carstens, 137–47. Westport, Conn.: Praeger, 2004.

———. "The Making of a Myth: George Rogers Clark and Teresa de Leyba." In *The Life of George Rogers Clark, 1752–1818, Triumphs and Tragedies*, edited by Kenneth Carstens and Nancy Carstens, 60–79. Westport, Conn.: Praeger, 2004.

Caughey, John Walton. *Bernardo de Galvez in Louisiana, 1766–1783*. Gretna, La.: Pelican, 1998.

Cayton, Andrew R. L. *Frontier Indiana*. Bloomington: Indiana University Press, 1996.

Cist, Charles. *The Cincinnati Miscellany*. 2 vols. New York: Arno Press, 1971.

Clark, George Rogers. *The Conquest of the Illinois*. Edited by Milo Milton Quaife. Carbondale: Southern Illinois University Press, 2001.

———. *George Rogers Clark Papers, 1771–1781*. Vol. 1. Edited by James Alton James. Springfield: Illinois State Historical Library, 1912.

———. *George Rogers Clark Papers, 1781–1784*. Vol. 2. Edited by James Alton James. Springfield: Illinois State Historical Library, 1926.

Clark, George Rogers, to Edmund Genet, March [n.d.], 1794. Reprinted in *American Historical Review* 18, no. 4 (July 1913): 780–83.

"The Clarksville Conventions, 1785, 1787." *American Historical Review* 2, no. 4 (July 1897): 691–93.

Coleman, J. Winston. *The British Invasion of Kentucky.* Lexington, Ky.: Winburn Press, 1951.

Collot, George Henri Victor. *A Journey in North America.* 2 vols. New York: AMS Press, 1974.

Continental Congress. *Journals of the Continental Congress, 1774–1789.* Edited by Worthington C. Ford et al. 34 vols. Washington D.C.: Government Printing Office, 1848–53.

Craig, Neville, ed. *The Olden Time.* 2 vols. Cincinnati: Robert Clarke, 1876.

Cresswell, Nicholas. *A Man Apart: The Journal of Nicholas Cresswell, 1774–1781,* ed. Harold Gill and George Curtis. New York: Lexington Books, 2009.

Davies, K. G., ed. *Documents of the American Revolution, 1770–1783.* 21 vols. Shannon: Irish University Press, 1972–82.

Denny, Ebenezer. *The Military Journal of Ebenezer Denny.* Philadelphia: J. B. Lippincott, 1859.

"Diary of Erkuries Beatty, 1786." *Magazine of American History* 1, no. 1 (1877): 175–79, 253–63, 309–15, 380–86, 432–38.

Dorman, John Frederick. "Descendants of General Jonathan Clark, Jefferson County, Kentucky, 1750–1811." *FCHQ* 23, no. 1 (January 1949): 25–33.

Downes, Randolph. *Council Fires on the Upper Ohio: A Narrative of Indian Affairs in the Upper Ohio Valley until 1795.* Pittsburgh: University of Pittsburgh Press, 1940.

English, William H. *The Conquest of the Country Northwest of the Ohio River, 1778–1783, and Life of Gen. George Rogers Clark.* 2 vols. Indianapolis: Bowen-Merrill, 1896.

Espy, Josiah. *Memorandums of a Tour Made by Josiah Espy in the States of Ohio and Kentucky and Indiana Territory in 1805.* Cincinnati: Robert Clarke, 1870.

Evans, William A., ed. *Detroit to Fort Sackville, 1778–1779: The Journal of Normand MacLeod.* Detroit: Wayne State University Press, 1978.

Faragher, John Mack. *Daniel Boone: The Life and Legend of an American Pioneer.* New York: Henry Holt, 1992.

Filson, John. *The Discovery, Settlement, and Present State of Kentucky.* New York: Corinth Books, 1962.

Fitzpatrick, John C., ed. *The Writings of George Washington.* 39 vols. Washington, D.C.: Government Printing Office, 1931–44.

Ford, Paul Leicester, ed. *The Writings of Thomas Jefferson.* 10 vols. New York: G. P. Putnam's Sons, 1892–99.

Gilman, Carolyn. "L'année du Coup: The Battle of St. Louis, 1780." *Missouri Historical Review* 103, no. 3:133–47; no. 4:195–211.

Griffin, Patrick. *American Leviathan: Empire, Nation, and Revolutionary Frontier.* New York: Hill and Wang, 2007.

Hammon, Neal O., and Richard Taylor. *Virginia's Western War, 1775–1786*. Mechanics-burg, Pa.: Stackpole Books, 2004.

Harding, Magery Heberling, ed. *George Rogers Clark and his Men: Military Records, 1778–1784*. Frankfort: Kentucky Historical Society, 1981.

Harrison, Lowell H. *George Rogers Clark and the War in the West*. Lexington: University Press of Kentucky, 1976.

Havighurst, Walter. *George Rogers Clark: Soldier in the West*. New York: McGraw Hill, 1952.

Henderson, Archibald. "Isaac Shelby and the Genet Mission." *Mississippi Valley Historical Review* 6, no.4 (March 1920): 451–69.

Henry, Patrick. *The Patrick Henry Papers*. Compiled by Stanislaus Vincent Henkels. New York: Samuel T. Freeman, 1910.

Henry, William Wirt. *Patrick Henry: Life, Correspondence and Speeches*. 3 vols. New York: B. Franklin, 1969.

Hinderaker, Eric. *Elusive Empires: Constructing Colonialism in the Ohio Valley, 1673–1800*. New York: Cambridge University Press, 1997.

Holm, Gregory F. "Clark's Ambush of Benedict at Hood's Point." In *The Life of George Rogers Clark, 1752–1818: Triumphs and Tragedies*, edited by Kenneth C. Carstens and Nancy Carstens, 198–213. Westport, Conn.: Praeger, 2004.

———. "Supply Issues of the Illinois Regiment under George Rogers Clark." In *The Life of George Rogers Clark, 1752–1818: Triumphs and Tragedies*, edited by Kenneth C. Cartsens and Nancy Carstens, 148–75. Westport, Conn.: Praeger, 2004.

Holmberg, James J., ed. *Dear Brother: Letters of William Clark to William Clark*. New Haven, Conn.: Yale University press, 2002.

Hudson, J. Blaine. "Slavery in Early Louisville and Jefferson County, Kentucky, 1780–1812." *FCHQ* 73, no. 3 (July 1999): 249–83.

Hurt, R. Douglas. *The Ohio Frontier: Crucible of the Old Northwest, 1720–1830*. Blooming-ton: University of Indiana Press, 1998.

Isenberg, Nancy. *Fallen Founder: The Life of Aaron Burr*. New York: Viking, 2007.

Jackson, Donald, ed. *Letters of the Lewis and Clark Expedition, with Related Documents, 1783–1854*. 2 vols. Urbana: University of Illinois, 1978.

James, James Alton. *The Life of George Rogers Clark*. Chicago: University of Chicago Press, 1928.

Jefferson, Thomas. *The Papers of Thomas Jefferson*. 38 vols. Edited by Julian Boyd. Prince-ton, N.J.: Princeton University Press, 1950–.

———. *The Writings of Thomas Jefferson*. 20 vols. Edited by Andrew A. Lipscomb and Albert Ellery Bergh. Washington D.C.: Thomas Jefferson Memorial Associa-tion, 1903.

Johnston, Henry, ed. *The Correspondence and Public Papers of John Jay*. 4 vols. New York: G. P. Putnam's Sons, 1891.

Jones, Landon Y. *William Clark and the Shaping of the West*. New York: Hill and Wang, 2004.

Kellogg, Louise Phelps, ed. *Frontier Retreat on the Upper Ohio, 1779–1781*. Madison: Wisconsin Historical Society, 1917.

Kelsay, Isabel Thompson. *Joseph Brant, 1743–1807: Man of Two Worlds*. Syracuse, N.Y.: Syracuse University Press, 1984.

Kinkead, Ludie J. "How the Parents of George Rogers Clark Came to Kentucky in 1784–85," *FCHQ* 3, no.1 (October 1928): 1–4.

Kinnaird, Lawrence, ed. "The Clark-Leyba Papers." *American Historical Review* 41, no. 1 (October 1935): 92–112.

Linklater, Andro. *An Artist in Treason: The Extraordinary Double Life of General James Wilkinson*. New York: Walker, 2009.

Lockhart, Paul. *The Drillmaster of Valley Forge: The Baron de Steuben and the Making of the American Army*. New York: HarperCollins, 2008.

Lockridge, Ross F. *George Rogers Clark: Pioneer Hero of the Old Northwest*. Chicago: World Book Company, 1927.

Mason, George. *The Papers of George Mason, 1725–1792*. 3 vols. Edited by Robert Rutland. Chapel Hill: University of North Carolina Press, 1970.

Maurer, C. J. "The British Version of Lochry's Defeat." *Bulletin of Historical and Philosophical Society of Ohio* 10 (July 1952): 215–30.

McDermott, John Francis. "The Battle of St. Louis, 26 May, 1780." *Bulletin of the Missouri Historical Society* 16, no. 3 (1980): 131–51.

———. "The Myth of the Imbecile Governor: Captain Leyba and the Defense of St. Louis in 1780." In *The Spanish in the Mississippi Valley, 1762–1804*. Chicago: University of Illinois Press, 1974.

———. *The Spanish in the Mississippi Valley, 1762–1804*. Chicago: University of Illinois Press, 1974.

Meeker, Mary Jane. "The Original Vouchers in the George Rogers Clark Bicentennial Exhibition." *Indiana Historical Bulletin* 53, no. 6 (June 1976): 87–93.

Mereness, Newton, ed. Mereness's *Travels in the American Colonies*. Carlisle, Mass.: Applewood Books, 2007.

Morgan. George. George Morgan Letterbook. Carnegie Library of Pittsburgh.

Morgan, Robert. *Boone: A Biography* Chapel Hill, N.C.: Algonquin Books, 2008.

Nester, William. *The First Global War: Britain, France, and the Fate of North America, 1756–1775*. Westport, Conn.: Praeger, 2000.

———. *The Frontier War for American Independence*. Mechanicsburg, Pa.: Stackpole Books, 2004.

———. *The Great Frontier War: Britain, France, and the Imperial Struggle for North America, 1607–1755*. Westport, Conn.: Praeger, 2000.

———. *"Haughty Conquerors": Amherst and the Great Indian Uprising of 1763*. Westport, Conn.: Praeger, 2000.

Palmer, Frederick. *Clark of the Ohio: A Life of George Rogers Clark*. New York: Dodd, Mead, 1929.

Perkins, Elizabeth. *Border Life: Experience and Memory in the Revolutionary Ohio Valley.* Chapel Hill: University of North Carolina Press, 1998.

Pershing, Edgar J. "The Lost Battalion of the Revolutionary War." *National Genealogical Society Quarterly* 16, no. 3 (1928): 44–51.

Philbrick, Francis S. *The Rise of the West, 1754–1830.* New York: Harper and Row, 1965.

Pope, John. *A Tour through the Western and Southern Territories of the United States of North-America.* New York: Charles L. Woodward, 1888.

Quaife, Milo M. "When Detroit Invaded Kentucky." *FCHQ* 1, no. 2 (January 1927): 53–67.

Randall, Willard Sterne. *Benedict Arnold: Patriot and Traitor.* New York: Dorset Press, 1990.

Robertson, Henry O. "Tories or Patriots? The Mississippi River Planters during the American Revolution." *Louisiana History: The Journal of the Louisiana Historical Association* 40, no. 4 (Autumn 1999): 445–62.

Schrodt, Philip. *George Rogers Clark: Frontier Revolutionary.* Bloomington: Buffalo Wallow Press, 1976.

Seineke, Kathrine Wagner. *The George Rogers Clark Adventure in the Illinois.* Madison: University of Wisconsin, 1981.

Silver, Peter. *Our Savage Neighbors: How Indian War Transformed Early America.* New York: W. W. Norton, 2008.

Simcoe, John. *Queen's Rangers: John Simcoe and His Rangers During the Revolutionary War for America.* London: Leonaur Books, 2007.

Slotkin, Richard. *Regeneration through Violence: The Mythology of the American Frontier, 1600–1860.* New York: Harper Perennial, 1973.

Smith, Dwight L. "The Old Northwest and the Peace Negotiations." In *The French, the Indians, and George Rogers Clark in the Illinois Country: Proceedings of an Indiana American Revolution Bicentennial Symposium,* 92–105. Indianapolis: Indiana Historical Society, 1977.

Sosin, Jack M. *The Revolutionary Frontier, 1763–1783.* New York: Holt, Reinhart, and Winston, 1967.

Swem, E. G. "The Lost Vouchers of George Rogers Clarke [sic]." *Virginia Journal of Education* 22 (1927): 24–30.

Sword, Wiley. *President Washington's Indian War: The Struggle for the Old Northwest, 1790–1795.* Norman: University of Oklahoma Press, 1985.

Thomas, Lowell. *The Hero of Vincennes: The Story of George Rogers Clark.* Boston: Riverside Press, 1929.

Thomas, Samuel W. "William Croghan, Sr. (1752–1822): A Pioneer Gentleman." *FCHQ* 43, no. 1 (January 1969): 30–61.

Thomas, Samuel W., and Eugene H. Conner. "George Rogers Clark (1752–1818): National Scientist and Historian." *FCHQ* 41, no. 3 (July 1967): 202–26.

Thwaites, Reuben Gold. *How George Rogers Clark Won the Northwest.* Chicago: A. C. Mc-Clug, 1918.

Thwaites, Reuben Gold, and Louise Phelps Kellogg, eds. *Documentary History of Dunmore's War, 1774.* Madison: Wisconsin Historical Society, 1905.

——, eds. *Frontier Defense on the Upper Ohio, 1777–1778.* Westminster, Md.: Heritage Books, 2009.

——, eds. *The Revolution on the Upper Ohio, 1775–1777.* Madison: Wisconsin Historical Society, 1908.

West, Martin. "Clark's 1780 Shawnee Expedition." In *The Life of George Rogers Clark, 1752–1818: Triumphs and Tragedies,* edited by Kenneth C. Carstens and Nancy Carstens, 176–97. Westport, Conn.: Praeger, 2004.

——. *Clark's Shawnee Campaign of 1780.* Springfield, Ohio: Clark County Historical Society, 1975.

"William Whitley Narrative." *Register of the Kentucky Historical Society* 36, no. 116 (July 1938).

Whitaker, Arthur Preston. *The Spanish-American Frontier, 1783–1795.* Lincoln: University of Nebraska Press, 1927.

White, Richard. *The Middle Ground: Indians, Empires, and Republics in the Great Lakes Region, 1650–1815.* New York: Cambridge University Press, 1991.

Young, Chester Raymond, ed. *Westward into Kentucky: The Narrative of Daniel Trabue.* Lexington: University Press of Kentucky, 2004.

Index

378   INDEX

Cornstalk (Shawnee), 25–26, 27, 39
Cornwallis, Charles, 181, 210, 214, 222,
 230–31, 232, 233
Corps of Discovery. *See* Lewis and Clark
 Expedition (Corps of Discovery)
Council Door (Delaware), 269
Cracraft, Charles, 227, 228
Craig, Isaac, 209, 215, 219, 222
Crane (Wyandot), 268
Crawford, William, 24, 237–38, 242
Creeks, 68
Cresap, Michael, 20–21, 22
Cresap, Thomas, 20
Cresswell, Nicholas, 28, 36
Crockett, Joseph, 209, 241
Croghan, George, 15, 220
Croghan, William, 220–21, 225, 237,
 261, 314, 316, 320, 322
Cruzat, Francois, 96
Cumberland Gap, 13, 32, 43
Cumberland River, 32, 42
Cuyahoga River, 265, 290

Dalton, Valentine, 205
Daniel, Walker, 257
Danville, Ky., 287
Dartmouth, William Legge (earl), 27, 54,
 55
Deane, Silas, 49, 204
Declaration of the Rights of Man and of
 the Citizen, 298
Dejean, Philip, 103, 152
Delawares, 14, 16, 20, 24, 25, 39, 55, 61,
 161, 168, 188, 194, 198, 221, 237–38,
 266, 269, 270
Detroit, 4, 5, 82, 84, 86, 100, 102–103,
 104, 107, 110, 113, 121, 146, 155–56,
 159, 167, 170, 173, 176, 182, 188, 189,
 190, 198, 199, 204, 208–209, 215,
 220, 222, 223, 224, 228, 229, 232–33,
 246
Dickson, Josiah, 48

Dodge, John, 207, 253
Door of the Wabash (Piankeshaw), 140,
 168
Downes, Randolph, 325
Dragging Canoe (Cherokee), 33
Draper, Lyman, 91, 295
Dunmore, John Murray (lord), 11, 14, 15,
 23, 26, 27, 30, 36, 37, 40
Dunmore's War, 19–28, 30, 32, 37, 47

East Florida, 249, 300
Edinburgh, 288
Egushawa (Ottawa), 114, 143
Elliot, Matthew, 158
Embarrass River (Little Wabash River),
 120–21
Espy, Josiah, 318
Estill's Station, 233
Europe, 12

Falls of the Ohio, 71, 72, 93–94, 110, 161,
 170, 180, 182, 190, 228, 229, 265, 266,
 268, 273, 285, 315, 317
Fauchet, Jean Antoine Joseph, 306, 307
Ferguson, Richard, 319, 321
Filson, John, 23
Finney, Walter, 267, 273
Fitzhugh, Dennis, 319, 323
Fleming, William, 26, 174–75, 252, 324
Floridablanca, Jose Monino y Redondo
 (count), 278–79
Floyd, George Rogers Clark, 319–20
Floyd, John, 24, 26, 40, 191, 194, 208,
 223, 224–25, 229, 232, 233, 242, 244
Forts: Crown Point, 35, 40; Detroit, 106,
 156–57; Dunmore, 15, 26; Falls of the
 Ohio/Nelson, 71, 216–17, 233,
 236–37, 239, 241, 244, 251–52;
 Fincastle, 24, 25, 29, 40, 70; Finney
 (Miami River), 267–68; Finney/
 Steuben (Falls of the Ohio), 271;
 Gage/Clark, 60, 77, 163, 170, 205;

Helm, Leonard, 69, 72, 95–96, 110–11,
    141, 146, 148–49, 150, 160, 161, 170,
    171, 201, 202–203
Henderson, Richard, 32, 33, 41–42, 46
Henry, Moses, 160
Henry, Patrick, 4, 45, 46, 49, 50, 60,
    65–67, 69, 89, 93, 97–98, 99, 117,
    155–56, 162, 164–65, 166, 178, 215,
    272–73, 276, 280
Hesse, Emanuel, 182, 183, 185, 187
Higgins, James, 17, 18
Higgins, Richard, 10
Higgins, William, 18
Hockhocking River, 25
Holston River, 44, 66, 69, 71
Homan, William, 193
Horsehead Bottom, 20
Hudson River, 210, 222
Hurons, 16, 55, 156, 188
Hutchins, Thomas, 71–72

Illinois, 59–60, 62, 67, 68, 70, 73–77,
    99–102, 104, 113, 165, 179–80,
    203–205, 253
Illinois River, 170, 182, 187
Illinois Tribe, 83
India, 12
Indian spirituality, 108–109, 158–59, 269
Innes, Harry, 294–95
Ireland, 288
Iroquois (Six Nations), 13–14, 16, 31, 54,
    166, 225, 226, 265
Irvine, William, 242–43, 246

James River, 210
Jaudenes, Josef de, 288, 303
Jay, John, 248, 278–79, 280, 282, 286, 324
Jefferson, Peter, 8
Jefferson, Thomas, 4, 8–9, 45, 47, 65,
    152–54, 162, 176–79, 188, 194, 199,
    202, 203, 208–209, 210–16, 217, 218,
    230, 233, 259–60, 264, 266, 289,

294–95, 302, 303, 311, 315, 316, 321,
    324, 329, 332–33
Johnson, Guy, 54, 250
Johnson, William, 54
Jones, David, 11, 15
Jones, John, 42–47, 48

Kanawha River, 14, 15, 23, 29, 31, 70
Kaskaskia, 59, 61, 62, 65, 66, 72, 74,
    78–82, 94, 99, 110, 112, 113, 114–15,
    118, 139, 160, 165, 167, 171, 177, 182,
    183, 203–205, 206, 325, 326
Kaskaskia River, 114
Kaskaskias, 83, 201
Kenton, Simon, 58, 244
Kentucky, 8, 13, 14, 23, 28, 30–31, 32,
    40, 42–47, 48, 52–53, 57, 61, 62, 64,
    90, 116, 139, 169, 170, 171, 173–74,
    182, 187, 188–89, 190, 199, 200, 216,
    223, 224, 227, 230, 231, 233, 238, 241,
    244, 246, 249, 252–53, 256–57, 264,
    287–88, 292, 293, 303, 326
Kentucky River, 30, 71, 228, 233, 234
Kickapoos, 61, 83, 109, 158, 183
Killbuck (Delaware), 20, 21, 39, 188
King, Martin Luther, Jr., 3
Knox, Henry, 282
Kyashuta (Mingo), 39

La Balme, Augustin Mottin de, 204–206
Laffront, Jean Baptiste, 95
Lake Champlain, 35
Lake Erie, 56, 106, 249
Lake Huron, 249
Lake Michigan, 182
Lake Ontario, 249
Lake Superior, 249
La Mothe, Guillaume, 106, 110, 121, 122,
    143–44, 150, 152, 153
Langlade, Charles, 182, 183
Lee, Arthur, 49, 266, 267
Lee, Francis Lightfoot, 266

Lee, Hancock, 28

Lee, Richard Henry, 45, 266

Legras, Jean, 271–72, 274

Lernoult, Richard, 104, 106, 156, 157

Lewis, Andrew, 25, 26, 38

Lewis, Charles, 23

Lewis, Meriwether, 5, 7, 314, 315–17, 330

Lewis and Clark Expedition (Corps of
 Discovery), 5, 7, 259–61, 315–17, 328

Lexington, Ky., 301, 302, 303

Leyba, Fernando de, 88–89, 90, 92, 113,
 183–87, 278, 330

Leyba family, 90–91, 92–93, 183

Licking River, 180, 189, 190, 193, 198,
 233, 234, 239, 273

Limestone Creek, 47–48, 180, 233, 234,
 239

Limestone (Maysville), Ky., 274

Lincoln, Abraham, 3

Lincoln, Benjamin, 258

Linctot, Godefroy de, 170, 198–99, 205

Lindsay, Joseph, 227, 254

Linn, Benjamin, 60–61, 67, 206

Linn, William, 51, 59, 61, 73, 94, 191,
 206

Linn Station, 229

Little Carpenter (Attacullallah), 32

Little Kanawha River, 19

Little Miami River, 192, 194, 239, 245

Little Scioto River, 20

Little Turtle (Miami), 205

Little Wabash River (Embarrass River),
 120–21

Livingston, Robert, 45

Lochry, Archibald, 223, 226–28, 267

Logan, Benjamin, 52, 192, 194, 196, 228,
 335, 238–40, 244, 246, 273, 274, 305,
 306

Logan, John, 40

Logan, John (Talgayeeta), 21, 23

Logan's Station (St. Asaph's Station), 40,
 48, 53, 57, 62

London, 104

Long Hunters, 13, 14

Lord, Hugh, 60

Lorimer, Louis, 246

Lorimer's Trading Post, 246

Louisiana, 5, 6, 50, 51, 74, 88, 96–97,
 165, 181, 240, 262, 279, 281, 306,
 311

Louis XVI, 50, 297, 298

Louisville, 9, 170, 171, 173, 236, 261,
 264, 273, 283, 310, 316, 318, 319,
 328

Lower Blue Licks, 48

Loyal Land Company, 8, 12

Luzerne, Anne-Cesar, chevalier de,
 204

Lynne, Edmund, 174, 194

Macutte Mong (Ottawa), 146

Madison, James, 10, 286, 293, 311

Mad River, 194, 276

Maisonville, François, 104, 122, 143–44,
 150, 153

Mangourit, Michel-Ange de, 300

Marietta, Ohio, 304

Marshall, John, 309

Marshall, Thomas, 252

Martin, Joseph, 199

Martin's Station, 44, 189, 190, 244

Maryland, 8, 40, 261–62

Mascoutens, 109

Mason, George, 65, 329, 331

Matchekewis (Ojibwa), 182

Maumee River, 104, 107, 205, 292

May, John, 174, 273, 274

Mayfield Creek, 180

Maysville (Limestone), Ky., 274

McAfee, William, 195

McAfee's Station, 233

McBeath, John, 142–43

McCarty, Richard, 59, 61, 62, 118, 121,
 140, 146, 170